The Lineaments of Wrath

Books by James W. Clarke

American Assassins:
The Darker Side of Politics

Last Rampage:
The Escape of Gary Tison

On Being Mad or Merely Angry:
John W. Hinckley, Jr., and Other Dangerous People

The Lineaments of Wrath:
Race, Violent Crime, and American Culture

James W. Clarke

Race, Violent Crime, and American Culture

The Lineaments of Wrath

Transaction Publishers
New Brunswick (U.S.A.) and London (U.K.)

This book is printed on acid-free paper that meets the American National Standard for Permanence of Paper for Printed Library Materials.

Library of Congress Catalog Number: 97-51699
ISBN: 1-56000-358-8
Printed in the United States of America

Library of Congress Cataloging-in-Publication Data

Clarke, James W., 1937–
    The lineaments of wrath : race, riolent crime, and American culture / James W. Clarke.
        p. cm.
    Includes bibliographical references and index.
    ISBN 1-56000-358-8 (alk. paper)
    1. Violence—United States—History. 2. United States—Race relations—History. 3. Violent crimes—United States—History. 4. Racism—United States—History. I. Title.
HN90.V5C56   1998
305.8'00973—dc21   97-51699
                                                                       CIP

For Courtney
and her generation

Contents

Acknowledgments

Writing about race and violence in America is like trying to thread one's way through a political minefield. I can appreciate now, in a way I never had before, why race remains this nation's most divisive and intractable problem. I am grateful to friends and strangers alike who have helped me. Three persons, in particular, deserve special mention.

My curiosity about the incendiary nature of American race relations was first stirred by the tumultuous events of the 1960s. During a sojourn in the South, a colleague and I wrote a piece based on the reactions of Southern white and black school children to the assassination of Martin Luther King, Jr. Irving Louis Horowitz, editor of what was then a new scholarly journal, *Transaction*, published that troubling article in the October 1968 issue. It was not only my first publication, it may have been the most important, for it changed the course of my interests and career as I ventured into the minefield.

Never one to draw back from important issues, no matter how controversial, Professor Horowitz proved it again in 1996 when he published a second article of mine on black-on-black violence. This appeared in the July/August issue of the by-then-retitled *Society*. Now to have as publisher of this book a man acquainted with this research from the beginning, and one who also is so widely respected in the social and behavioral sciences, is most gratifying.

I am also indebted to Professor Albert Weale, co-editor of the *British Journal of Political Science*, for guiding me, as it were, through a particularly treacherous area of the minefield. As a result of his good advice and refreshing display of editorial backbone, another article, also drawn from my current research, was published in the April 1998 issue of that journal. "Without Fear or Shame: Lynching, Capital Punishment, and the Subculture of Violence in the American South," challenges a dominant sociological paradigm, as well as the conventional interpretation of a critical period of American race relations.

Over the twenty-five or so years that I have been teaching in the area of race and public policy, I learned much from conversations with an old friend, Lucinda Harris. It was because of her that I began to question some of the standard, but very antiseptic, interpretations of American race relations I was assigning in my classes. A descendent of Mississippi slaves, born to Oklahoma sharecroppers early in this century, Lucinda had personally endured many of the hardships and tragedies described in this book. I asked her many questions: fear? crop liens? domestic violence? Is that really the way it was? Did you ever witness anything like that? Yes, was usually her answer, most black folks she knew during those times did, she would explain. At the same time, I was aware of the enormous current difficulties she faced as a consequence. She has survived a hard life, but not unscathed, for many of her loved ones have not.

A number of scholars provided assistance at various stages of this research: Richard Maxwell Brown (University of Oregon), Vine Deloria, Jr. (University of Colorado), David Garrow (Emory University), Ted Robert Gurr (University of Maryland), Desmond King (St. Johns College, Oxford University), Gary La Free (University of New Mexico), Stanley Lieberson (Harvard University), and John Monahan (University of Virginia). For the same reason, I am grateful to colleagues Joel Feinberg, Michael Gottfredson, Peter Goudinoff, Henry Kenski, Clifford Lytle, and Martha Moutray at the University of Arizona. Gloria Stern and editor Laurence Mintz also provided provided helpful suggestions and criticism throughout. I, of course, remain solely responsible for what I have written.

Over the years a number of graduate and undergraduate students and staff have helped in a variety of ways too numerous to recount in the detail they deserve, but each is greatly appreciated: Francis Neely, Gwen Torges, and Andrea Gerlak provided vital assistance, especially in the analyses of hundreds of slave interviews, thirteen volumes of evidence on Ku Klux Klan violence, and the lynching and capital punishment data; the analysis of the blurry, microfilmed Department of Justice *Peonage Files* would have been taken much longer without Jon Law's patience, stamina, and strong eyesight; Alisa Wabnik and Susan Knoppel brought important information on youth violence and gangs to my attention; and Clifford Brown helped assemble demographic and violent crime statistics. Likewise, the staff in the Political Science Department—Bill Lockwood, Denise Allyn, Trish Morris, Roxanne Payton, and Vicki Healey—always came through when I needed them. A fine Montana friend, Richard Hunt, was kind enough to loan me his Billie Holiday tapes a couple of summers ago.

An important part of this research was completed during a sabbatical leave granted by the University of Arizona, coupled with a research professorship awarded by the Social and Behavioral Sciences Research Institute. For both, I am most appreciative. I would also like to acknowledge the cooperation and help provided by the staff at the Univerity of Arizona Library, especially the folks in Government Documents, Interlibrary Loan, and Special Collections, most notably Atifa Rawan, Cynthia Bower, Robert Mitchell, and Carla Stoffle.

It is my good fortune to be married to a very talented woman, Jeanne Nienaber Clarke, who has read, reread, and discussed this manuscript with me more times than we both care to remember. Without her patient editorial assistance, unflagging encouragement, and keen familiarity with academic politics (that kept the minefield in perspective, most of the time), this difficult and consuming project surely would have ended differently.

As always, my children, Julie and Michael, remain a source of inspiration and great pride which I have expressed elsewhere on other occasions. So it is for Courtney, for whom her grandfather has so much affection and hope, that this book is dedicated.

.

Preface

This book joins two abiding interests of mine, race relations and violent crime. The two, unfortunately, are closely related in American history. In 1968, within days after the event, I conducted research on the reactions of black and white Southern children to the assassination of Martin Luther King, Jr. The racial differences were stark, with many whites blaming the victim and applauding his assassin; black children, at that time, were simply perplexed and overwhelmed with sadness. A few years after that, I wrote a second article drawn from conversations with black children in Washington, D.C. in the aftermath of the rioting that followed King's death. In that study, anger accompanied the shock and sadness. Later, I wrote about the motives of the white man who killed Dr. King. *The Lineaments of Wrath* addresses deeper, unanswered questions about the sources of racial hatred and violence that occurred to me in the course of that research.

The book has two major objectives: The first is to describe and explore, with careful documentation from an extensive array of primary[1] and multidisciplinary sources, the reasons for a shocking pattern of nearly four centuries of violence between whites and blacks in America. The second is to examine, as well, its consequences, which are most vividly observed in the peculiar self-destructive quality of black-on-black violence that has grown to crisis proportions in American inner cities. The title is taken from a phrase Thomas Jefferson used to describe what he called the "unhappy" effects of slavery that he observed in the faces of white and black children. Just how unhappy these experiences were will become evident in the troubling, often graphic, testimony of the victims that appears throughout this book.

Rates of violent crime in the United States increased sharply in the 1960s and, despite recent declines, have remained extraordinarily high among blacks. Since more than half of these crimes are committed by young black males, dark skin and violent crime are closely linked in the minds of Americans. In the last decade of the twentieth century, fear and hostility permeate the streets of America's inner cities and lap at the edges of gated white suburbs. The fact that the typical victim is also a young black male has done little to modulate the growing concern of whites that they may become the next victim of a black murderer, rapist, or mugger.

It was a very different situation just one hundred years ago. Lynching, like street crime today, reached epidemic proportions in the rural South of the 1890s. In that decade alone, more than 1,100 blacks were tortured and murdered in this ritualistic manner. As the nineteenth century drew to a close, it was black people who feared the chance encounter and the darkness of night.

Street crime and lynching, however, provide but a glimpse, for there is a much more enduring pattern of violence that has defined relations between whites and blacks since the first slaves were led off a ship in 1619. For most of that time, black Americans have lived with a continuing threat of arbitrary acts of white brutality for which there was virtually no recourse. The cultural consequences of generations of men and women living under these conditions have been either ignored, or treated very antiseptically in the literature on race relations.

Yet terror continued as a means of social control long after slavery ended. Indeed, slavery represented a relatively more benign, less random, period of violence than what followed emancipation. Moreover, the movement of the black population to cities and into industrial labor, which accelerated during the twentieth century, produced a different pattern of violence that has evolved since then into today's bloody struggle for control of inner-city streets. The cumulative effects of these experiences have resulted in two very different racially defined views on crime and punishment, and in the meaning of justice itself.

In recent years, opinions on crime and punishment unquestionably have hardened along racial lines. Among blacks, there is deepening distrust of law enforcement, which is still viewed as preying on black males. Among whites, there are growing fears that inner-city violence may spread into segregated white neighborhoods and communities. These different concerns were most vividly reflected in the Los Angeles riot of 1992. The worst race riot in American history brought together two televised events that symbolize the tragedy of American race relations.

The sense of outrage that black viewers felt as they watched a videotape showing four white police officers beating a defenseless black man senseless—as other officers stood by—is impossible to exaggerate. The scene recalls descriptions of lynch mobs in the last century;

yet these four officers were acquitted by an all white jury, and the rioting began. Disbelieving whites watched televised scenes as mobs burned and looted vast areas of the city. But one scene, in particular, will probably remain etched in white America's memory. As cameras rolled in a heliocopter hovering overhead, horrified viewers watched as black youths, shaking their fists skyward, danced about a terrified white man who had been dragged from his truck. Then one of his attackers suddenly moved in to smash his skull with a concrete block; another followed, stomping the unconscious body as the others cheered.

This book investigates the sources of such hostility in the darkest and most forbidding depths of American racial history. It is a search for the causes of what President Bill Clinton has called, in his Second Inaugural Address, the nation's "constant curse." Whenever possible, the actual words of victims, offenders, and eyewitnesses are used to trace the development of what has become the most threatening domestic crisis of the twentieth century, and probably the next as well.

It is important at this point, however, to emphasize what this book is *not*. It is not intended to be a conventional, descriptive history of the black experience in America. Thus, it is not "balanced," in the good times/ bad times sense of "heartwarming" triumphs offsetting "heartrending" defeats. More than thirty years ago in the foreword he wrote to Kenneth Clark's important book, *Dark Ghetto*, Gunnar Myrdal praised the author for rejecting the "false objectivity" and the attendant insistence on a "balanced view" that has clouded our understanding of America's enduring race problem.[2] To suggest balance where none exists is to *distort* historical reality and its consequences. As abundant documentation in a wide variety of cross-validating sources makes clear, the ongoing racial conflict described in these pages did not end in a draw: The black underclass lost. That is one of the great tragedies of the American experience which this book confronts and seeks to explain.

This is *not* a book about the black working-, middle-, and upper classes who surmounted tremendous obstacles to succeed; it seeks to explain why an underclass did not. Thus with each succeeding chapter the focus narrows to that segment of the black population. It follows a trail of carefully documented evidence concerning the consequences of custom and policy that brings into sharp relief the reasons for this tragedy. It is a bleak and, at times, a deeply troubling story of America's past. This longitudinal perspective enhances not only an understanding of the black underclass, but also the unyielding pattern of white violence and oppression that gave it life. Although cause and effect must remain problematic in retrospective research such as this, with violent crime, as with other deadly diseases, informed reflection about cause and effect is a vital first step in the search for solutions.

The current epidemic of black-on-black violence is part of a trend that began generations ago in slavery's vicious aftermath. In addition to the countless injuries and staggering loss of life, the frustration and anger that have swelled within the black community as a consequence, have eroded relationships between men and women, and now jeopardize the well-being of their children. As this century draws to a close, sexual competition, illegitimacy, drugs, modern weaponry, and gangs, which are replacing families, have fueled an unprecedented pattern of self-destructive behavior that threatens to destroy the black community itself from within.

Finding solutions will not be easy. The partial successes of the modern civil rights period have demonstrated that, in some circumstances, structural relationships between the races may change in response to programmatic reforms. Some noteworthy progress has been made, for example, in education and employment among members of the black middle class who embraced these reforms. But changing the self-destructive subculture of the black inner city, experience has shown, is much more difficult.

Black status and the violent subculture that gives it meaning are rooted in molds established in a sometimes forgotten, but defining, past. Once the origins and generational transmission of this scourge of violence are understood, it may be possible to formulate solutions. But it is unrealistic to believe, as some do, that this crisis can be resolved with simply more jobs, better schooling, and/or changes in the welfare system. The ravaging effects and emotional scars left by generations of cruelty and stress describe an inner-city subculture whose pathologies are resistent to the usual remedies. As black leaders such as Malcolm X, Jesse Jackson, Colin Powell, and Louis Farrakhan, have agreed, transforming that subculture will require something more than government programs alone to restore what was lost in the crucible of a brutalizing past.

For those who are offended by violence and blunt testimony of its effects, this book will be a deeply disturbing, perhaps prohibitive, experience. Graphic descriptions of racial atrocities are presented—some of them for the first time outside the original records—not only to document the horror, but to give the reader a visceral appreciation of it. My hope is that she or he might imagine what it was like for the victims and those who loved them. Their voices deserve to be heard, for only then can one understand both the terror that blacks have confronted throughout most of their history on American soil and the festering wounds those experiences left. For generations.

Notes

1. Among the many primary sources I have drawn upon are slave narratives, plantation documents, and the interviews of former slaves conducted by the Works Progress Administration, the records of the Bureau of Refugees, Freedmen, and Abandoned Lands (Freedmen's Bureau), the testimony of victims of Ku Klux Klan violence solicited by the *Joint Select Committee to Inquire into The Condition of Affairs in the Late Insurrectionary States* in 1872, the Tuskegee Institute/ NAACP files on lynching from 1882 to 1962, state and organizational documents on convict labor, the *Peonage Files* of the Department of Justice, Bureau of Census reports, and crime statistics from the Federal Bureau of Investigation and the Bureau of Justice Statistics.
2. New York: Harper & Row, 1965, x.

1

Violence Begets Violence

*"The most formidable evil threatening the future of the United
States is the presence of the blacks on their soil. From whatever
angle one sets out to inquire into the present embarrassments or
future dangers facing the United States, one is always brought up
against this basic fact...Hitherto, whenever the whites have been
the more powerful, they have kept the Negroes down in degradation
or in slavery. Everywhere where the Negroes have been stronger,
they have destroyed the whites; and that is the only reckoning there
has ever been between the two races."*

—Alexis de Tocqueville, 1839[1]

*"He was the craziest nigga alive. America's nightmare. Young,
black, and didn't give a fuck."*

—Narrator, "Menace II Society," 1993[2]

Homicide rates in the United States exceed by far those of any other
industrial nation. Moreover, despite recent declines, in 1995 homicide
rates were three times higher than they were thirty years ago. Even
though approximately 80 percent of the victims of violent crime were
attacked by someone of the same race, it is the black offender who
most white Americans fear.[3] As Figure 1.1 confirms, race is clearly a
factor in this nation's violent crime.

For as long as records have been kept, the homicide rates of blacks
have been four to ten times higher than those of whites.[4] The same
pattern is also reflected in arrest rates for violent crimes, where black
arrests for adult crimes range from six to more than ten times higher
than comparable rates for whites. Arrest rates for black juvenile violence reveal roughly the same differentials, ranging from five to eleven
times higher than whites.[5] Since 1965 national arrest rates reveal that
approximately half of the violent crime committed each year in America
is attributable to young black males who represent less than three per-

1

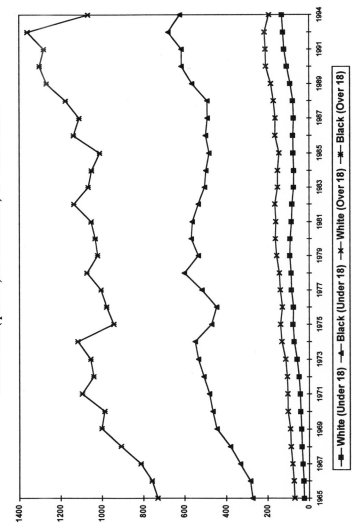

FIGURE 1.1

Arrest Rates (per 100,000 Inhabitants) for Violent Crimes

White (Under 18) ── Black (Under 18) ── White (Over 18) ── Black (Over 18)

Source: Graph derived from U.S. Department of Justice, Federal Bureau of Investigation, *Age-Specific Arrest Rates and Race-Specific Arrest Rates for Selected Offences, 1965–1992,* FBI Uniform Crime Reports (Washington, D.C.: USGPO, 1993), pp. 181, 193.

cent of the total population.[6] In 1986 the Department of Health and Human Services announced that black-on-black violence had reached such epidemic proportions that it would henceforth be treated as a problem in public health as well as crime.[7] In 1992 the violent crime rate for blacks was the highest ever recorded by National Crime Victimization Survey.[8] As the twentieth century draws to a close, there are more black men confined in jails and prisons than there are enrolled in colleges and universities; approximately 7 percent of all black males are incarcerated on any given day; approximately one in three black men in their twenties is under custody of some sort in the criminal justice system; nearly half of the nation's prison population is black, as are 40 percent of those awaiting execution.[9]

But perhaps the most troubling fact about the scourge of violence reflected in these statistics is that both the murderers and their victims are getting younger. Children are not only having babies they are unprepared to raise, they are killing one another with withering regularity. Teenage black males are, by far, the most likely victims of violent crime. Consider the following statistics from volumes of supporting evidence on black males age twelve to twenty-four.

Between 1973 and 1992, violent crime victimization among this group increased 25 percent. Black juveniles were four times more likely to be homicide victims than their white counterparts.[10] Between 1987 and 1991, there was an 85 percent increase in the number of juveniles arrested for murder and a 50 percent increase in those arrested for other forms of violent crime. Although representing only 1.3 percent of the population, in 1992 these youngsters accounted for 17.2 percent of the nation's homicides, an astonishing rate of 114.9 per 100,000. That is nearly ten times higher than the rate for white males of the same ages, fourteen times higher than the rate for the general population, and even higher than the homicide rate for older black males, which is eight times the national rate.[11]

The problem of violent crime has been attributed to a familiar list of causes: poverty, unemployment, broken homes, poor education, teenage pregnancy, gangs, and drugs. These difficulties, in turn, as many have suggested, merely reflect the effects of a hostile social structure that denies opportunity and creates frustration that leads to violence.[12] In 1994, for example, approximately 33 percent of the black population lived below the poverty line. But as subsequent chapters will reveal, these troubling statistics can be more completely understood as *symptoms of violence*, as well as causes, for the roots of

America's seemingly intractable racial problems run deep into a violent history and culture that some are reluctant to acknowledge.

The black experience in America is unique in that they, alone among immigrant groups, have endured an explicit and unrelenting legacy of violence directed against them. Other immigrant groups and, of course, Native Americans were subjected to persecution and even warfare on American soil. But nothing in those bitter experiences compares to the suffering and carnage that blacks endured for nearly four centuries.

In view of this, the resilience of the black community is extraordinary. After centuries of oppression and discrimation, some of which continues, most black Americans were able to overcome the many obstacles placed before them by a racist society; their record of achievement is remarkable. But these many generations of racial injustice have shaped and molded a violent subculture among the casualties of that struggle. Known variously as the black lower class or, more recently, the "underclass," they have been left, as sociologist William Julius Wilson concluded, "truly disadvantaged."[13]

Most blacks, regardless of social class, think about crime, punishment, and justice differently than do most whites. They share the belief that justice is uncertain in American courts; that color and money too often determine arrests, convictions, and the severity of punishment; and most agree that white policemen cannot be trusted.[14] Despite recent progress in American race relations, racial suspicion and hostility continue.

But the black victims who appear in crime reports and on autopsy tables are usually those who remain at the bottom of society, the truly disadvantaged who inhabit America's inner cities. It is they whose primary contact with white society is the police; and it is they who live and die prematurely in this subculture, either as a direct result of violence, or because of the daily stress caused by living with it.[15]

The roots of that subculture can be traced to the first generation of black males that came of age after emancipation. Honor and respect became uppermost for them: denied land, education, and livable incomes, that was all that was left to define their manhood. For similar reasons, that tradition continues among the black underclass in America's inner cities. Honor and respect still follow a primordial formula of physical courage and sexual prowess. On dangerous city streets, status among young black males gathers much of its meaning from the ability to harm, intimidate, and dominate others. Sexual exploits and an aggressive disdain for white authority, especially police officers, also convey a sense of empowerment in this otherwise powerless segment of the population.

Cultures are defined by persistent patterns of behavior and systems of beliefs and values that support and condone them. In the black underclass, those beliefs and values are most vividly expressed in the "gangsta" rap music of the 1990s. For centuries, black music, from early slave songs, through folk and gospel, blues to jazz, and soul has conveyed the soul of its people. Along with the joys of love and the sadness of hard times, unmistakeable themes of betrayal, anger, and vengeance run through this tradition. But at no time has the sense of betrayal and anger been more explicit than in gangsta rap. Violence and sadistic sexuality are joined in its lyrics as they have never been before in black music. Hatred of the police and contempt for women are recurring themes. Gangsta rappers claim their lyrics reflect the hostile reality of life in the inner city. The statistics presented in figure 1.1 support that claim.

Rap music is but a symptom, but its commercial success in the 1990s, and the heroic status accorded its performers, leaves little doubt that it expresses beliefs and values that resonate in the inner city. Such values frame and condone a subculture of violence based on male dominance, unrestrained aggression and sexuality. Domestic violence, murder, and illegitimate births measure its effects. The question is, why?

One of the most consistently confirmed findings in the behavioral sciences is that a violent past is the single best-known predictor of future violence.[16] A violent past not only predisposes one to violence, it is also likely that violence itself becomes a causal determinant of future violence. Moreover, there is a well-documented intergenerational continuity to this pattern within families as well as cultures.[17] The basis for such behavior—whether biological, social, or some combination of both—remains a subject of continuing research and debate.[18] I will argue, however, that one must look south to discover the origins of racial violence in American society. Throughout Southern history, there has always been near unanimity among whites, regardless of social class, on matters of race and the appropriateness of violence, in its many forms, to establish and maintain their dominance over blacks.

The South remains the most violent region of the United States. Brawls, duels, assassinations, and murder are familiar events in Southern history. And accompanying it all was slavery, a system whose primary means of discipline was the lash. Violence was an integral part of Southern culture; only its forms and weaponry hint of class distinctions in the way it was carried out. While yeoman farmers brawled with knives and gouged out one another's eyes, the landed gentry fought duels complete with matched pistols and attendants in waiting. But all had a place in a peculiar way of life that distinguishes the South from other regions of the country.[19]

What then accounts for not only the violence itself, but the extraordinary savagery that accompanied it?[20] Theories of class conflict cannot explain the highly emotional, often sexual, and almost invariably sadistic violence of the post-Civil War period. The lynching festivals of unspeakable brutality, for example, that closed the nineteenth century take the investigator well beyond interpretations based on class conflict.[21] Case evidence reveals that participants in these grisly events were drawn from all social classes and all walks of life. Moreover, there was no shame or fear of prosecution: spectators often included members of whole communities, husbands, wives, and children.

Rather than class consciousness, it was the belief of whites in their biological superiority that was *the* central tenet in a cluster of values and beliefs that framed and supported a *regional culture* of violence that targeted blacks. In such a subculture, legitimate class interests that could have divided whites were sacrificed for the racial privileges inherent in a white supremacist society. Max Weber's concept of "ethnic status" offers a more complete understanding than does class interest of the dynamics of southern race relations. Weber and, more recently, historian George M. Frederickson, have proposed that ethnic status was neither necessarily derived from economic or class hierarchies, nor from one's relationship to the means of production, as Marx argued. Instead, inequalities in ethnic status were based on "life styles and the distribution of *honor* and prestige in a society"— qualities that may or may not coincide with social class. Ethnic status, Weber wrote, "is specifically open to the mass of the population, since it can be claimed by anyone who shares in the *common ancestry* which is subjectively believed to exist."[22]

Both Weber and Frederickson agree, for example, that the racism of nonslaveholding whites was symptomatic of such status anxiety rather than class interest alone. Even though victimized themselves by slavery, Weber writes, "their social 'status' could only be preserved if the blacks remained relegated to the bottom of the class system."[23] So it is for this reason that the economic incentives of the "haves" were joined with the psychological incentives of the "have nots" to unify Southern whites on matters of race. Honor demanded as much.

At the same time, defiance and resistance were the requirements of honor among their black protagonists. Consequently, as those perspectives spread, each change in the status of blacks—from slave to free, nonvoter to voter, rural to urban, farm laborer to factory worker, South to North—triggered a renewed onslaught of interracial violence with only its forms and locale reflecting the changing circumstances of blacks.

Thus, out of the turmoil of Southern history two racially antagonistic conceptions of status emerged that distinguished white and black subcultures. Preserving and protecting that status became a matter of honor for males of both races; its most obvious manifestation was the contempt shown toward members of the opposite race. With roots in the Southern experience, branches of that antagonism would reach wherever the two cultures came in contact.

* * *

There is something elemental about skin color in human affairs that few can escape or ignore. The experiences of generations of violence based on color became ingrained in the values and behavior of those who practiced and endured it. Just as child abuse leaves permanent emotional scars, racial abuse leaves enduring cultural scars. For like personality, culture represents a collective reservoir of thoughts and emotions that channel behavior over time.

Criminologists Marvin E. Wolfgang and Franco Ferracuti have proposed a cultural theory of criminal violence based on that hypothesis. Consistent with Weber's and Frederickson's thoughts on Southern race relations, the theory also provides the means to assess the contemporary implications of that history. Building on Wolfgang's earlier work on violent criminals, their central concept was a "subculture of violence." This concept, they suggest, provides a framework through which to analyze patterns and differentials in violent crime over time and across generations.[24] Such subcultures, for example, have been identified in eleventh-century communities of assassins in the Middle East, criminal tribes in India, and the Sicilian Mafia. The existence of a subculture presupposes a complex pattern of norms, attitudes, and actions, the authors claim, that reflects

a potent theme of violence current in the cluster of values that make up the lifestyle, the socialization process, the interpersonal relationships of individuals living in similar conditions.[25]

Parents play a key role in the socialization process by what they do, or do not, teach through their own behavior. Children, we know, are predisposed to identify with and imitate their parents. Wolfgang and Ferracuti propose that even children who are estranged from, or who even dislike, their parents may still identify with them to the extent of adopting the same behavior patterns. Parental rejection, for example, is thought to be an important element in the etiology of aggression, since even rejection does not prevent imitation of the very qualities the child hates or fears. It is also true that the efficiency and success of the transfer of certain values varies with the personality of the child and its biological susceptibility to such influences. Thus children in the same family or social environment may differ in the effect either parent, or both, has on them.[26]

Outside the family, other members of the subculture also demand and enforce adherence to their values. The social isolation, concentration, and homogeneity of particular regions or neighborhoods, for example, magnify the "intensity, duration, repetition, and frequency" of the learning process and its successful inculcation of values.[27] Much like a war situation, those who resist that process, who do not endorse the principle of violence against the enemy, are penalized by those who do. Homicide, the authors suggest, resembles war in that a perspective of "it's either him or me" prevails when opponents are committed to violence as a means of resolving differences. Also, like war, the outcome is determined by prowess, resources, and chance.[28]

As later chapters reveal, these formulations describe the two different violent and uniquely American subcultures anticipated by Weber's and Frederickson's formulations. A regional culture of white supremacy was embedded within the South's agricultural economy and criminal justice systems. Features of that economy which evolved over centuries—slavery and the exploitive systems of sharecropping and credit manipulation that followed—were dependent upon, and sustained by, state systems of criminal justice. After emancipation, revised criminal codes designed to entrap the landless, uneducated, unemployed, and impoverished black male defined a new system of involuntary servitude that replaced plantation slavery. Its central mechanism was debt peonage. Convict labor, lynching, and mob violence awaited those who challenged it.

Blacks did not emerge from these experiences unscathed. The cumulative effect of generations of such injustice, and the relentless *white-on-black* violence that was its most ruinous manifestation, molded a second violent subculture among its victims. Subsequent chapters explain how that subculture evolved out of the rural South, and through the urban transformation in America's major cities, to define the self-destructive nature of the twentieth century's black underclass.[29]

The defining elements in both white and black subcultures are high and enduring rates of personal violence that are condoned and facilitated by a widely shared ethos.[30] It is the *self-destructiveness* of the black underclass, however, that draws the nation's attention as it approaches a new century.

* * *

In the strictest sense, the chapters that follow cannot offer a literal test of the theory, as one would expect in experimental research. The scope of a retrospective study that spans nearly four centuries, many generations, and a wide variety of sources, precludes that.[31] But these chapters will reveal an abundance of cross-validating evidence that is consistent with the Wolfgang and Ferracuti formulations, as well as the belief, now widely accepted among mental health experts, that violence begets violence.

Notes

1. A. de Tocqueville, *Democracy in America* (New York: Doubleday Anchor, 1969; orig., 1838), 340, 342.
2. Hughes Brothers, New Line Cinema, 1993.
3. Bureau of Justice Statistics, *Criminal Victimization in the United States, 1993* (Washington, DC: U.S. Department of Justice, forthcoming); Bureau of Justice Statistics, *Murder in Large Urban Counties* (May 1993); R. Chilton, "Homicide Arrest Trends and the Impact of Demographic Changes on a Set of U.S. Central Cities," in National Institute of Justice, C. Block and R. Block (eds.) *Trends, Risks, and Interventions in Lethal Violence: Proceedings of the Third Annual Spring Symposium of the Homicide Research Working Group* (Washington, DC: U.S. Department of Justice, July 1995), 99–113; Bureau of Justice Statistics, *Crime Data Brief: Young Black Male Victims* (Washington, DC: U.S. Department of Justice, December 1994). See, also, F.M. Sanborn, "Negro Crime," in W.E.B. Dubois (ed.), *Proceedings of the Ninth Atalanta Conference for the Study of Negro Problems* 9 (Atlanta, GA: Atlanta University Press, 1904; reprinted as *Some Notes on Negro Crime, Particularly in Georgia* (New York: Octagon, 1968); T. Sellin, "The Negro Criminal: A Statistical Note," *The Annals of the American Academy of Political Science* 140 (1928), 52–64; H.C. Brearly, *Homicide in the United States* (Chapel Hill: University of North Carolina, 1932); R. Farley, "Homicide Trends in the United States," *Demography* 17,2 (May 1980), 178, 186; Y. Shin, D. Jedlicka and E.S. Lee, "Homicide Among Blacks," *Phylon* 38 (December 1977), 398–407; L.A. Fingerhut and J.C. Kleinman, "International and Interstate Comparisons of Homicide Among Young Males," *Journal of the American Medical Association* 263, 4 (June 27, 1990), 3292–3295; Federal Bureau of

Investigation, *Crime in the United States: Uniform Crime Reports* (Washington, DC: U.S. Government Printing Office, 1940–1992); P.C. Holinger, *Violent Deaths in the US: An epidemiologic Study of Suicide, Homicide and Accidents* (New York: Guilford Press, 1987); R. Farley, "Homicide Trends in the United States," in D.F. Hawkins (ed.), *Homicide Among Black Americans* (New York: University Press of America, 1986), 13–28; M. Riedel, M.A. Zahn, and L.F. Mock, *The Nature and Patterns of American Homicide* (Washington, DC: National Institute of Justice, May 1985), 35, 38–39, 42–43; W. Wilbanks, "Criminal Homicide Offenders in the U.S.: Black vs. White," in Hawkins, *Homicide*, 43–55; *Report of the Secretary's Task Force on Black and Minority Health* (Washington, DC: Department of Health and Human Services, 1985), Executive Summary; E.E.H. Griffith and C.C. Bell, "Recent Trends in Suicide and Homicide Among Blacks," *Journal of the American Medical Association* 262, 16 (October 27, 1989), 2265; also, P.W. O'Carroll and J.A. Mercy, "Patterns and Recent Trends in Black Homicide," in Hawkins (ed.), *Homicide*, 31–36; M.W. Zawitz, P.A. Klaus, R. Bachman, L.D. Bastian, M.M, DeBerry, Jr., M.R. Rand, and B.M. Taylor, *Highlights from 20 Years of Surveying Crime Victims: The National Crime Victimization Survey, 1973–92* (Washington, DC: Bureau of Justice Statistics, 1993), 22–23; Bureau of Justice Statistics, "Violent Crime," (April 1994); D.K. Gilliard and A.J. Beck, "Prisoners in 1993," *Bureau of Justice Statistics Bulletin* (June 1994).

4. M.E. Wolfgang and F. Ferracuti, *The Subculture of Violence: Toward an Integrated Theory in Criminology* (London: Tavistock, 1967), 264, 298–299.

5. *FBI Uniform Crime Reports*, "Age-Specific Arrest Rates and Race-Specific Arrest Rates for Selected Offenses" (Washington, DC: U.S. Department of Justice, 1993), 181, 193; see, also, K. Maguire and A.L. Pastore, *Sourcebook of Criminal Justice Statistics 1994* (Washington, DC: U.S. Department of Justice, Bureau of Justice Statistics, 1995), 403.

6. *Uniform Crime Reports for the United States*, Federal Bureau of Investigation (Washington, DC: U.S. Department of Justice, 1964 to 1992).

7. It estimated, for example, that between 1979 and 1981 some 59,000 blacks died "excess deaths," meaning fatalities that would not have occurred if the mortality rates for blacks were the same as those for whites. A major cause of these deaths among blacks males up to the age of forty-four was homicide. See, *Human Surveillance: High Risk Racial and Ethnic Groups, 1970–1983* (Atlanta, GA: Centers for Disease Control, 1986); Bureau of Justice Statistics, *Crime Data Brief: Violent Crime* (April 1994) and *Crime Data Brief: Young Black Male Victims* (December 1994).

8. *National Crime Victimization Survey* (Washington, DC: U.S. Department of Justice, Bureau of Justice Statistics, 1973 to 1992).

9. M. Mauer, *Intended and Unintended Consequences: State Racial Disparities in Imprisonment* (Washington, DC: The Sentencing Project, January 1997), 15; M. Mauer, *Young Black Men and the Criminal Justice System: Five Years Later* (Washington, DC: The Sentencing Project, 1995); M. Mauer, *Americans Behind Bars: The International Use of Incarceration, 1992–1993* (Washington, DC: The Sentencing Project, 1994); Bureau of Justice Statistics, *Capital Punishment 1995* (Washington, DC: U.S. Department of Justice, December 1996).

10. Office of Juvenile Justice and Delinquency Prevention, *Juvenile Offenders and Victims: A Focus on Violence* (Washington, DC: U.S. Department of Justice, May 1995), 14–20.

11. Bureau of Justice Statistics, *Crime Data Brief: Violent Crime* (April 1994); Bureau of Justice Statistics, *Crime Data Brief: Young Black Male Victims* (Wash-

ington, DC: U.S. Department of Justice, December 1994); also, Office of Juvenile Justice and Delinquency Prevention, *Juvenile Offenders and Victims: A Focus on Violence* (Washington, DC: U.S. Department of Justice, May 1995); Centers for Disease Control, "Homicide Among Young Black Males—United States , 1978–1987." *Morbidity and Mortality Weekly Report* 39 (1990), 869–73; Bureau of Justice Statistics, *Violent Crime* (April 1994). See, also, Office of Juvenile Justice and Delinquency Prevention, *Juvenile Offenders and Victims: A Focus on Violence* (U.S. Department of Justice, May 1995); A. Blumstein, "Violence by Young People: Why the Deadly Nexus," *National Institute of Justice Journal* (August 1995), 2–9.

12. See, for example, D.L. Taylor, F.A. Biafora, Jr., and G.J. Warheit, "Racial Mistrust and Disposition to Deviance Among African American, Haitian, and Other Caribbean Island Adolescent Boys," *Law and Human Behavior* 18 (1994), 291–317; G. LaFree, K.A. Drass, and P. O'Day, "Race and Crime in Postwar America: Determinants of African-American and White Rates, 1957–1988," *Criminology* 30 (1992), 157–188; J. Balkwell, "Ethnic Inequality and the Rate of Homicide," *Social Forces* 69 (September 1990), 53–70; R. Sampson, "Urban Black Violence: The Effect of Male Joblessness and Family Disruption," *American Journal of Sociology* 93 (September 1987), 348–382; W.J. Wilson, *The Truly Disadvantaged: The Inner City, The Underclass, and Public Policy* (Chicago: University of Chicago Press, 1987), esp., 13, 61, 104; J.R. Blau and P.M. Blau, "The Cost of Inequality: Metropolitan Structure and Violent Crime," *American Sociological Review* 47 (1982), 114–129; J. Braithwaite, *Inequality, Crime, and Public Policy* (London: Routledge & Kegan Paul, 1979).

13. W.J. Wilson, *The Truly Disadvantaged: The Inner City, the Underclass, and Public Policy* (Chicago: University of Chicago Press, 1987). See, also, his *The Declining Significance of Race: Blacks and Changing American Institutions* (Chicago: University of Chicago Press, 1978).

14. W.A. Henry III, "Pride and Prejudice," *Time* (February 28, 1994), 22. See, also, for example, E. Cose, *The Rage of a Privileged Class* (New York: HarperCollins, 1994); W. Grier and P.M. Cobbs, *Black Rage* (New York: Basic Books, 1968); J.L. Hochschild, *Facing Up to the American Dream: Race, Class, and the Soul of the Nation* (Princeton, NJ: Princeton University Press, 1995).

15. A.T. Geronimus, J. Bound, T.A. Waidmann, M.M. Hillemeier, and P.B. Burns, "Excess Mortality Among Blacks and Whites in the United States," *New England Journal of Medicine* 335, 21 (November 21, 1996).

16. Wolfgang and Ferracutti, *The Subculture of Violence;* J. Monahan, *The Clinical Prediction of Violent Behavior* (Rockville, MD: National Institutes of Mental Health, 1981); and J.W. Clarke, *On Being Mad Or Merely Angry: John W. Hinckley Jr. and Other Dangerous People* (Princeton, NJ: Princeton University Press, 1990).

17. C.P. Widom, "The Intergenerational Transmission of Violence," in N.A. Weiner and M.E. Wolfgang (eds.) *Pathways to Criminal Violence* (Newbury Park, CA: Sage, 1989); and M. Daly and M. Wilson, "Homicide and Cultural Evolution," *Ethology and Sociobiology* 10 (1989), 102.

18. E.O. Wilson, *On Human Nature* (Cambridge, MA: Harvard University Press, 1978), esp. chapter 5; J.Q. Wilson and R.J. Herrnstein, *Crime and Human Nature* (New York: Simon and Schuster, 1985), esp. chapter 2; M. Daly and M. Wilson, *Homicide* (New York: Aldine de Gruyter, 1988; idem, "Homicide and Cultural Evolution," *Ethiology and Sociobiology* 10, (1989), 99–110; R. Wright, *The Moral Animal: Evolutionary Psychology and Everyday Life* (New York: Pantheon, 1994); D.T. Courtwright, *Violent Land* (Cambridge, MA: Harvard University Press, 1996).

19. H.P. Whitt, J. Corzine, L. Huff-Corzine, "Where is the South? A Preliminary Anallysis of the Southern Subculture of Violence," in National Institute of Justice, C. Block and R. Block (eds.) *Trends, Risks, and Interventions in Lethal Violence: Proceedings of the Third Annual Spring Symposium of the Homicide Research Working Group* (Washington, DC: U.S. Department of Justice, July 1995), 127–148; L. Bastian, "Criminal Victimization 1993," Bureau of Justice Statistics Bulletin (May 1995), 3. For earlier discussions of regional variations in violence, see, S. Hackney, "Southern Violence," *American Historical Review* 74 (1979), 906–925; R.D. Gastil, "Homicide and a Regional Culture of Violence," *American Sociological Review* 36 (June 1971), 412–427; J. Reed, "To Live-and-Die in Dixie: A Contribution to the Study of Southern Violence," *Political Science Quarterly* 86 (September 1971), 429–443; H.S. Erlanger, "The Empirical Status of the Subculture of Violence Thesis," *Social Problems* 22 (December 1974), 280–292; C. Loftin and R.H. Hill, "Regional Subculture and Homicide: An Examination of the Gastil-Hackney Thesis," *American Sociological Review* 39 (October 1974), 714–724; W.G. Doerner, "A Regional Analysis of Homicide Rates in the United States," *Criminology* 13 (May 1975), 90–101;

20. G.M. Frederickson, *Arrogance of Race: Historical Perspectives on Slavery, Racism, and Social Inequality* (Middletown, CT: Wesleyan University Press, 1988), 157.

21. Neither does Marx's notion of "false [class] consciousness" clarify matters. It seems highly improbable that the white lower class was skillfully deceived into believing that they shared the same class interests as the wealthy landholders and merchants who controlled the Southern economy. And, as others have argued, if such a perspective ever existed, it is unlikely that it could have been sustained through decades of major social and economic changes that occurred in the South in the latter third of the nineteenth century and the first half of the twentieth. There is abundant evidence that lower-class whites were always quite aware of their position near the bottom of the economic order. See, Frederickson, *Arrogance of Race*, 157–158.

22. Instead of the rigid, deterministic implications of class analysis, Weber's concept of "ethnic status" allows one to locate race relations in the evolving socioeconomic and political contexts that followed the Civil War and continue to the present. At the same time, however, Weber's explanation does not exclude class, but rather directs attention instead to its *interaction* with ethnic status instead of assigning *a priori*, or causal, importance to either. See, Frederickson, *The Arrogance of Race*, 159.

23. Runciman (ed.), *Max Weber*, 43–57, 359–369; Frederickson, *Arrogance of Race*, 158–160.

24. Inferential support for the theory has been found in Whitt, Corzine, and Huff-Corzine, "Where is the South?, 127–148; L. Huff-Corzine, J. Corzine, and D.C. Moore, "Southern Exposure: Deciphering the South's Influence on Homicide Rates," *Social Forces* 64: 906–24; and R.N. Parker, "Poverty, Subculture of Violence, and Type of Homicide," *Social Forces* 67 (June 1989), 983–1007. See, also, G.A. Fine and S. Kleinman, "Rethinking Subculture: An Interactionist Analysis," *American Journal of Sociology* 85 (July 1979), 1–20.

25. M.E. Wolfgang, *Patterns of Criminal Homicide* (Philadelphia: University of Pennsylvania Press, 1958); Wolfgang and Ferracuti, *The Subculture of Violence*, 140–141, 272–284.

26. Wolfgang and Ferracuti, *Subculture of Violence*, 147–149.

27. Wolfgang and Ferracuti, *Subculture of Violence*, 155.

28. Wolfgang and Ferracuti, *Subculture of Violence*, 156.

29. Critics of the theory have identified certain limitations in its usefulness in explaining the well-documented differentials in black and white violent crime in America that do not apply to the present study. Among them are Wolfgang's and Ferracuti's emphasis on psychometric methods and scaling techniques to isolate the "social values" that establish the "ecological areas and boundaries" of the subculture. Such attitudinal measures are limited to the degree they leave out important historical processes and experiences that are associated with the formation of the values observed. For example, the probable consequences of patterns of interaction between members of the violent subculture and groups reflecting the parent culture would be left out in their methodology. Thus in the American context significant situational, structural, and institutional factors that distinguish the black historical experience from that of whites would be ignored. Most notably, for example, the functioning of the criminal justice system would not be taken into account as an important determinant of values and standards of conduct. In the present study, the criminal justice system is a central concern. See, D.F. Hawkins, "Black and White Homicide Differentials: Alternatives to an Inadequate Theory," in D.F. Hawkins (ed.), *Homicide Among Black Americans* (New York: University Press of America, 1986), 109–127; see, also, T.J. Bernard, "Angry Aggression Among the 'Truly Disadvantaged'," *Criminology* 28 (November 1990), 73–96; G.A. Fine and S. Kleinman, "Rethinking Subculture: An Interactionist Analysis," *American Journal of Sociology* 85 (July 1979), 1–20.

30. Wolfgang and Ferracuti have described the essential attributes of violent subcultures in seven principal propositions that have informed this research:
    1. No subculture can be totally different from or totally in conflict with the society of which it is a part.
    2. To establish the existence of a subculture of violence does not require that the actors sharing this basic value element express violence in all situations.
    3. The potential resort or willingness to resort to violence in a variety of situations emphasizes the penetrating and diffusive nature of this culture theme.
    4. The subcultural ethos of violence may be shared by all ages in a subsociety, but this ethos is most prominent in a limited age group ranging from late adolescence to middle age.
    5. The counter-norm is nonviolence.
    6. The development of favorable attitudes toward, and the use of, violence in this subculture involve learned behavior and a process of differential learning, association, or identification.
    7. The use of violence in a subculture is not necessarily viewed as illicit conduct, and the users therefore do not have to deal with feelings of guilt about their aggression. See, Wolfgang and Ferracuti, *Subculture of Violence*, 158–161.

31. As others have noted, the fact that this subculture of violence is reflected in only a relatively small segment of the black population, the difficulties of discovering evidence of it by means of standard opinion surveys and aggregate demographic approaches are apparent. Commenting on the inappropriateness of such standard methods, one scholar concluded that "methodological and statistical approaches other than those typically utilized will have to be employed." That is the purpose and the reason for the design of this study. See, R.N. Parker, "Poverty, Subculture of Violence, and Type of Homicide," *Social Forces* 67 (June 1989), 1002–1003. See, also, S.J. Ball-Rokeach, "Values and Violence: A Test of the Subculture of Violence Theory," *American Sociological Review* 38 (December 1973), 736–749; H. Erlanger, "The Empirical Status of the Subculture of Violence Thesis," *Social Problems* 22 (December 1974), 280–292.

Part I

Slavery

2

The Lineaments of Wrath

*"There must, doubtless be an unhappy influence on the manners of
our people, produced by the existence of slavery among us. The
whole commerce between master and slave is a perpetual exercise
of the most boisterous passions—the most unremitting despotism on
one part, and degrading submission on the other. Our children see
this, and learn to imitate it, for man is an imitative animal. This
quality is the germ of all education in him. From his cradle to his
grave he is learning to do what he sees others do.... The parent
storms; the child looks on, catches the* lineaments of wrath, *puts on
the same airs in the circle of smaller slaves; and thus nursed,
educated, and daily exercised in tyranny, cannot but be stamped
with its odious peculiarities. The man must be a prodigy who can
retain his manners and morals under such circumstances."*
— Thomas Jefferson, 1787[1]

*"Generally speaking, it requires great and constant efforts for men
to create lasting ills; but there is one evil which has percolated
furtively into the world: at first it was hardly noticed among the
usual abuses of power; it began with an individual whose name
history does not record; it was cast like an accursed seed somewhere on the ground; it then nurtured itself, grew without effort,
and spread with the society that accepted it; that evil was slavery."*
— Alexis de Tocqueville, 1835[2]

The first African slaves shipped to America in 1619 were captured,
probably by members of another African tribe, and sold to Dutch traders on the West African coast. Twenty out of an unknown number survived the crossing and were brought ashore in Jamestown, Virginia on
August 20 of that same year. The following year the Pilgrims first set
foot on Cape Cod. An international slave trade grew and flourished in
this manner until 1808 when it ended on terms agreed upon in 1787 at
the Constitutional Convention in Philadelphia.

At the time of the Revolution of 1776, the contradiction between the glittering principles enunciated in the Declaration of Independence and the flourishing slave economy was resolved by redefining the humanity of slaves. In the white imagination, black Africans were consigned to a position on an evolutionary ladder a rung or two below their white masters. Slaves were considered chattel, beasts of burden who did not possess the natural rights of life, liberty, and equality, nor were they permitted to pursue the happiness that white Americans claimed as a birthright. And so in this manner, except for the most reflective persons like Thomas Jefferson himself, the dilemma between human rights and slavery was resolved.

The exact number of slaves brought to the American colonies before 1788 is unknown since records reflect numbers brought to the Caribbean area as well as the colonies. With the Declaration of Independence in 1776, states in the North one by one abolished slavery. Most did so gradually with *post-nati* abolition laws that stipulated that the children born to slave parents were free. Vermont, with only fifty slaves, led the way in 1777; New Jersey, the last Northern state to do so, followed in 1804. Estimates suggest that by 1780, the slave population had grown through trade and natural increase to approximately 562,000. In 1864, the Freedmen's Inquiry Commission estimated that some 128,000 slaves had been imported during the last twenty years of the international slave trade between 1776 and 1808 when it formally ended. In the eight years between 1800 to 1808, trading was especially heavy as the slave population grew by nearly 40 percent, the largest increase of the slave period. Human cargo filled ships on one leg of a triangular trade route that carried manufactured goods from Europe to Africa, slaves to America, and raw materials on the return to European ports. These were profitable trade routes that contributed to the significant English, Dutch, and American family fortunes that were amassed during its existence.[3]

A domestic slave trade continued to flourish after that with slaves being sold like livestock for prices ranging as high as two thousand dollars for a well-disciplined, muscular, young adult male. The number of slaves had grown to 1,771,656 by 1820. Forty years later 4,441,830 blacks were counted in the United States census; only 11 percent of them were free; over 90 percent of the total was concentrated in what were to become the Confederate states. Slaves accounted for approximately one-third of the total population in that region. In some states like South Carolina, Georgia, Florida, Alabama, Mississippi, and Louisiana, slaves accounted for nearly half or more of the population.[4]

What was slavery like? W.E.B. DuBois probably explained as well as anyone the meaning of slavery. "It is difficult to imagine," he wrote in 1935:

> We think of oppression beyond all conception: cruelty, degradation, whipping and starvation, the absolute negation of human rights; or on the contrary, we may think of the ordinary worker the world over today, slaving ten, twelve, or fourteen hours a day, with not enough to eat, compelled by his physical necessities to do this and not to do that, curtailed in his movements and his possibilities...
>
> [T]here was in 1863 a real meaning to slavery...It was in part psychological, the enforced personal feeling of inferiority, the calling of another Master; the standing with hat in hand. It was the helplessness. It was the defenselessness of family life. It was the submergence below the arbitrary will of any sort of [white] individual.... Gradually the whole white South became an armed and commissioned camp to keep Negroes in slavery and to kill the black rebel.[5]

For others who had actually endured the humiliation and felt the pain of the lash, slavery had more immediacy. Scholars estimate, for example, that between one-quarter and one-third of slave families were broken by slave sales.[6] Mollie Kinsey remembered the horrors of slave auctions and the fate of an older sister in these words:

> Dey had slaves in pens, brung in droves and put in dem pens jes' lak dy wus cows. Dey sold 'dem by auctionin' off to the highest bidder. I wus only a chile and nevah went 'round much. Dey put girls on the block and auctioned dem off. "What will you give fer dis nigger wench?" Lot of girls wus being sold by their master who wus their father, taken rat out of the yards with their white chilluns and sold lak herds of cattle.
>
> My sister was given away when she wus a girl. She tole me and ma that they'd make her go out and lay on a table and two or three white men would have in'ercourse with her befo' they'd let her git up. She wus jes' a small girl...She died when she wus still in her young days, still a girl. Oh! You is blessed to live in this day and don't know the tortures the slaves went through.[7]

As a child, Hannah Murphy never forgot the sight of seeing men and women like her parents trying to escape:

> I seen many mens runnin' away frum de bloodhoun's. Sometimes we chilluns be in de quarter playin', and a man would come runnin' along fast, breathin' hard, so skeared! De houns be behind him. Den I kin 'member how they' d whip 'em when dey ketch him. Dey would make de men drop down dey pants and lay down across big logs and dey'd whip 'um. De womans dey'd drop dey bodies and dey'd whip 'em across de back and 'round de waises till de blood come.[8]

A former slave, Solomon Bradley, remembered how the sight of a helpless woman being whipped made him "wild" with rage.[9] Another, Andy Marion, recalled a whipping he received, saying

I's jus' 'bout half died. I lays in de bunk two days, gittin' over dat whippin,' gittin' over it in de body but not in de heart. No, suh, I has dat in de heart till dis day.[10]

Mary Reynolds said simply that "Slavery was the worst days that was ever seed in the world."[11]

Was there a common experience reflected in the words of Mollie Kinsey, Hannah Murphy, Solomon Bradley, and Mary Reynolds? Or were their experiences unusual, carefully culled from a reservoir of memories of good treatment and times that were only occasionally unpleasant when slaves misbehaved? Overwhelming evidence from a wide variety of sources reveals that such experiences were *not* unusual. Solomon Northup, a man who had escaped slavery, wrote in 1853 that *all* slaves recognized the evils of the system and wondered how anyone could believe otherwise:

> They do not fail to observe the difference between their own condition and the meanest white man's, and to realize the injustice of laws which place it within his power not only to appropriate the profits of their industry, but to subject them to unmerited and unprovoked punishment, without remedy, or the right to resist, or to remonstrate.[12]

* * *

All human rights, of course, are eradicated by slavery. Indeed the purpose of American slavery was to employ strict, unyielding, and degrading discipline to create feelings of fear, vulnerability, and inferiority in the slave population. Total control, slaveholders recognized, was necessary to produce the complete compliance they insisted upon. With that purpose in mind, the law as a means to protect life, liberty, and property did not apply to slaves. This meant that slaves were legally powerless to protect themselves, their families, and those things they valued from their masters or, for that matter, any other white person inclined to prey upon them. From the time of the first European settlement through the Civil War, colonial and later state slave codes and laws evolved and changed in their severity and restrictiveness, but certain themes remained.

All were written to ensure the complete subordination of slaves to the white population; and, second, all protected the institution of slavery itself from anyone, including slaveholders themselves, who might threaten to weaken it through humanitarian acts or gestures. To this end, slaves could not own property or marry legally; they could not legally learn to read and write; they could not defend themselves legally through word or deed, or contradict the word of a white person;

promises made to them had no force or validity; and there were no practical limits on corporal punishments administered to them for wrongdoing. Slaves were not often incarcerated, however, for it made little sense for a slaveholder to deny himself their labor.[13]

Following the same logic, during the seventeenth century, killing a slave was considered a crime only if the slave was owned by someone else—a crime against the owner, not the actual victim. Murdering one's own slave was considered different only in degree from slaughtering a pig or a steer. The difference being that, unlike the slaughter of ordinary livestock, there would be no economic purpose in killing a slave whose flesh could not be consumed. Historian Eugene Genovese explains the logic this way: "[A] master could not murder a slave. He might cause his death, but he could not, legally, murder him. Would a man willingly destroy his property? Certainly not. Therefore, no such crime as the murder of one's own slave could present itself to a court of reasonable men."[14]

In nineteenth-century Mississippi, slaves had dual status as property and persons, meaning that slaves could be tried as persons for wrongdoing, but considered as the property of another if sentenced to death. In the latter instance, the state was required to compensate for the property loss by reimbursing the slaveholder. In 1846, for example, the Mississippi legislature drafted legislation to provide that "one-half of the value of the slave or slaves condemned to die, by the sentence of any court of competent jurisdiction within this State, and who shall suffer death accordingly, shall be paid to the owner out of the State Treasury."[15]

Frederick Law Olmsted, who toured the South observing its culture in 1854, wrote,

> I do not think that I have ever seen the sudden death of a negro noticed in a southern newspaper, or heard it referred to in conversation, that the loss of *property*, rather than the extinction of *life*, was not the occasion of interest.

For example, the *Lynchburg Virginian* described how a white youth whimsically shot a young slave this way: "The load took effect in the head, and caused death in a few hours. The negro was a valuable one. Mr. Mays had refused $1,200 for *him*." In similar fashion, the *New Orleans Daily Crescent* reported that "Mr. Tilghman Cobb's barn at Bedford, Va. was set fire to by lightning on Friday, the 11th and consumed. Two negroes and three horses perished in the flames."[16]

Although by the 1850s most Southern states had gradually changed their laws to acknowledge that killing a slave was, in fact, murder and, therefore, a criminal act, there were generous loopholes to avoid punishment. If a slave died, for example, as a result of "moderate correction," it was considered an accidental death, not murder. And killing a rebellious slave was also justifiable under state law as self-defense.[17] But regardless of the law and circumstances, convictions were exceedingly rare because slaves were not permitted to testify against whites, nor sit on juries, in any of the Southern states. As late as 1858 the Code of Tennessee, for example, contained this provision:

> A negro, mulatto, Indian, or person of mixed blood, descended from negro or Indian ancestors, to the third generation inclusive, though one ancestor of each generation may have been a white person, whether bond or free, is incapable of being a witness in any case, civil or criminal, except for or against each other.[18]

In other words, a white person could assault, rape, or murder a non-white, and, unless another white was willing to testify to that fact, the guilty person could not be punished. In Natchez, Mississippi, for example, a prominent free black man, William Johnson, was killed by a white man in the presence of slave and free black witnesses. Because they were not eligible witnesses, the assailant went free.[19] "The slave, who is but 'a chattel' on all other occasions," abolitionist Charles Goodell wrote,

> with not one solitary attribute of personality accorded to him, becomes 'a person' whenever he is to be punished. He is the only being in the universe to whom is denied self-direction and free agency, but who is, nevertheless, held responsible for his conduct, and amenable to law.... He is under the control of law, though unprotected by law, and can know law only as an enemy, and not as a friend.[20]

As another observer commented in 1857, "Of all the evils to which the slave is exposed...the most pestilent in its effects, is the practical outlawry to which he is subjected by the refusal of his evidence in the courts of justice.... For him the court of law is no sanctuary."[21] Courts offered no sanctuary for slaves in South Carolina where Olmsted observed,

> The precariousness of the much-vaunted happiness of the slaves can need but one further reflection to be appreciated. No white man can be condemned for any cruelty or neglect, no matter how fiendish, on slave testimony. The rice plantations are in a region very sparsely occupied by whites: the plantations are nearly all very large—often miles across: many a one of them occupying the whole of an island—and rarely is there more than one white man upon a plantation at a time during the summer. Upon this *one* man each slave is dependent, even for the necessities of life.[22]

In those rare instances when whites were tried and convicted for violent crimes against slaves, the guilty were usually fined rather than imprisoned, and then for paltry amounts. "The only curb upon the power of the master," W.E.B. Du Bois wrote, "was his sense of humanity and decency, on the one hand, and the conserving of his investment on the other." Although there is no way to know exactly how many slaves were executed as a result of criminal convictions, such economic concerns kept the numbers far below what was to follow after emancipation.[23]

The formal court system in the slave colonies and, later, states, functioned primarily to handle capital cases that threatened to disrupt the important solidarity that slaveholders sought to maintain amongst themselves. Disputes that developed regarding one another's slaves, for example, such as a slave accused of stealing from another plantation or harming another owner's slave would have a much higher probability of going to court than a slave accused of some infraction on his own plantation. Even then, however, punishments for black-on-black crime were much less severe than slave crimes against whites. In Alabama, for example, if a slave killed another slave or a free black, the punishment was up to one hundred lashes and a brand burnt into one hand. In contrast, slaves who committed a violent offense of any kind against whites almost always forfeited their lives.[24]

Slave crimes that did not involve persons or property beyond plantation boundaries would always be handled by the owner himself. As Chief Justice Thomas Ruffin of the North Carolina Supreme Court wrote in 1829:

> We cannot allow the right of the master to be brought into discussion in the courts of justice. The slave, to remain a slave, must be sensible that there is no appeal from his master.[25]

What protections slaves did enjoy under law or custom almost always derived from their value as the property of their owners. Again, the analogy to livestock is accurate. Slaveholders protected their own slaves from the arbitrary actions of others—whites as well as other slaves—that could jeopardize their investment.

* * *

Along with the codified system of slave treatment, an informal system of plantation justice evolved in the South which was much more important in the daily lives of slaves. On the plantation slave owners ruled, dealing directly and independently with slave misbehavior in virtually any way they saw fit. Any behavior that deviated from an unyielding standard of conduct requiring hard work and complete obedience was considered a challenge to an owner's authority and was universally punished. To ignore such behavior, slaveholders understood, was to jeopardize not only their own status, but also the viability of the system itself. The form and degree of punishment, however, varied from plantation to plantation and with circumstances, depending also upon the personality, moods, and, often, the amount of alcohol consumed by masters and overseers. In every instance, however, slaves remained completely vulnerable to the whims of their masters and overseers. One of the inherent tragedies of slavery is that the paramount need to exert absolute control over other human beings circumscribed the morality of even the most humane slaveholders.[26]

The most common penalty for slave misbehavior, whether it was malingering, stealing, or running away, was whipping. Whipping was a frequent and ritualistic event on most plantations, the preferred means to ensure discipline and the status of slaveholders. "[N]o other penalty carried the same meaning or so embodied the social relations of the peculiar institution," writes historian R.C. Wade, "The lash in the white hand on the black back was a symbol of bondage recognized by both races."[27] Such experiences define a recurring theme in the memories of the overwhelming number of the 3,581 former slaves interviewed in the 1920s and 1930s.[28] Countless slaves were whipped and virtually all those who weren't either saw it happen, or observed the scars on victims that remained for life. Even though most of those interviewed were children, or in their youth, at the time they witnessed or endured these events, the searing memories remained vivid even in the twilight of their lives. As subsequent chapters reveal, recent research confirms that abused children do not easily forget the experience. There is no reason to believe that the victims of slavery were any different. My own analysis, for example, of 1776 slave interviews contained in the 1977 and 1979 editions reveals that at least 55 percent of those interviewed witnessed one or more whippings, and 17.5 percent reported being whipped themselves at least once. Evidence of this practice is also abundant in a wide variety of cross-validating sources: plantation records, the diaries of slaveholders, slave sale notices, and reports of travelers such as Olmsted, as well as in the testimony of former slaves.[29]

Slaves were most often whipped for what were overwhelmingly nonviolent offenses. The most common were malingering, stealing, and running away. It is little wonder that people forced to work from dawn to dusk six days a week would seize any opportunity to rest by slowing the pace of that work; it is little wonder that people whose diets were always monotonous, and frequently insufficient, would steal to feed themselves and their loved ones; nor is it surprising that people living under these circumstances would seek relief by running away. The system itself virtually ordained such "misbehavior"; emotional and physical survival demanded it.

Whipping was a swift, direct, and inexpensive means of discipline that did not involve the loss of the victim's labor. It was a ritual of discipline, repeated often for all to see. As historian Charles Joyner explained,

> When a master supervised—or administered—punishment, no less than when he dispensed gifts and favors, he did so in rituals that contrasted the dependent position of the slave with his own status of dominance.... Thus formalized public punishment dramatized in a particularly acute way, free of etiquette, euphemism, and illusion, the enforcement of rules of deference and social behavior.[30]

Whipping usually served to inflict pain and humiliation rather than to maim or kill. It made more sense to sell poorly disciplined, or recalcitrant, slaves, and that was commonly done. Moreover, scars on the flesh of slaves could reduce their value to prospective buyers by suggesting a troublesome investment. Ella Johnson described how slave traders lost money when they tried to sell her aunt:

> she was sold to the 'Nigger Traders', a group of white men who bought and sold slaves. Annice was forced to leave her husband and mother but was allowed to take her little girl, Mariah, with her. The 'Nigger Traders' took her from Greenville, South Carolina, to New Orleans, and on the way one of the traders saw Annice crying, and whipped her terribly. So when they got to New Orleans and Annice was put on the slave block at auction, nobody wanted to buy her because she had been whipped. You see her back was just raw, and the white folks said a slave was bad if they had to be whipped.[31]

In 1853, the *New York Tribune* reported that whipping scars could reduce the value of an adult male slave by more than half.[32] But when so many slaves bore scars, the effect was diminished. Such rational economic calculations were often obliterated by rage when whipping provided a convenient outlet for a white man's frustrations and sadistic impulses. Slaves were often punished, Mary Chestnut wrote, "when their masters and mistresses are brutes, not when they do wrong."[33]

Former slave Maltilda Mumford never forgot one such brute on a Georgia plantation, nor some white women who, like Mary Chestnut, were sickened by his brutality:

De las' overseer come down befo' de war start, he like to kilt us. He'd strip us down to de wais'—tie men to trees and drink and beat 'em jus' to be whipping. I 'member dere wuz two old women, dey couldn't work much. De overseer so mean, he tie 'em to a buggy, stark mother nekked, put a belly band on 'em, and driv' 'em down de road like dey wuz mules, whippin' 'em till dey drop down in de road. Dere wuz some white ladies what see it, and dey reported him and prosecuted him, and he got run out of de county.[34]

But he probably had little trouble indulging his sadism elsewhere. That some slaveholders derived perverse enjoyment from the practice, as these accounts suggest, is evident in the remarks of a sugar planter who reflected wryly, after emancipation, on the lost pleasures of the whip:

Eaton [the overseer] must find it very hard to lay aside the old strap—As for myself, I would give a good deal to amuse myself with it, a little while. I have come to the conclusion that the great secret of our success was the great motive power contained in that little instrument.[35]

Fugitive slave bulletins and posters, as well as sheriffs' committal notices during the period suggest that whippings were frequently excessive. Descriptions of slaves often mentioned wounds such as, "large raised scars or whelks in the small of his back and on his abdomen nearly as large as a person's finger," or "a large scar immediately on her chest from the cut of a whip," or "many scars on his back,"and "the appearance of frequent and severe flogging."[36]

* * *

Even Robert Fogel and Stanley Engerman, whose controversial view of slavery, in 1974, stirred such rancor among historians, agreed that whipping was "an integral part of the system of punishment and rewards," insisting only that "it was not the totality of the system."[37] Subsequent scholarship revealed, however, that Fogel's and Engerman's controversial estimate that each slave was probably whipped less than once a year badly misrepresented the actual incidence and severity of whipping even on the one plantation used as a basis for their estimate. Rather, as the late historian, Herbert G. Gutman, pointed out in his critique of their work, a closer examination of the plantation diary of Bennet H. Barrow, upon which their estimate is based, reveals a consistent pattern of physical abuse that extended over the ten years he kept an unusually complete record of the whippings he administered.[38]

Not only did Barrow whip individuals regularly, including children, he usually did it ritualistically, staging what he described as "whipping frolick[s]" during which he would whip, in succession, large numbers of slaves who watched the flesh of others being laid open as they awaited their own punishment. In laconic phrases like, "half to day," or "all grown cotton pickers," he meticulously recorded such events in his diary. One is struck by the casual, almost incidental, way the whippings he administered, as well as the maulings of runaways by tracking dogs, are interspersed with his observations on the weather, the price of cotton, horse racing, and various aches and pains. There is no evidence of guilt and only one brief hint of remorse for having whipped a sick woman. It is the banality of his entries which reveal that whipping was as much a part of the rhythms of life on Barrow's Louisiana plantation as planting and picking cotton.

What kind of man was Bennet H. Barrow? According to his biographer, writing in 1943, "Barrow treated his slaves *better* and took more time in the organization of his labor system than did many of the neighboring planters."[39] The following decade historian Kenneth Stampp concluded that Barrow was "a substantial and respected man in his community...in no sense a crude parvenu," whose treatment of his slaves "illustrates the difficulty of distinguishing between cruelty and reasonable 'correction.'"[40] By the 1970s the judgment on Barrow was split between historians Eugene Genovese who considered him "harsh"[41] and Fogel and Engerman, who insisted that, by their standards, the Louisiana planter whipped infrequently and usually with restraint.

Since Barrow's conscientious record keeping was so unusual among slaveholders, there is no way to be sure how this reflective planter compared to others. He saw himself as a fair and reasonable taskmaster who expected nothing more than a complete day's work and total obedience from his slaves. In return, he would provide for them, as he wrote in his "Rules of Highland Plantation" in 1838, "evry necessary of life, without the least care on [their] part." If we can believe the sentiments and concerns expressed in a diary he had every reason to believe would remain private, Barrow certainly did *not* see himself as being cruel to his slaves; he even condemned those slaveholders who were.[42]

Yet Barrow whipped regularly and, in his words, often "severely." The appendix to his diary, for example contains a list of "Misconduct and Punishments: 1840–1841."[43] During this two-year period, slaves were disciplined 331 times for misconduct; of that number, 156, or nearly half, included whipping. Since Barrow often conducted mass whippings, his monthly average over this two-year period of 6.5 whippings is not very meaningful, except to say that all of Barrow's slaves must have lived in fear. The most frequent specific reasons for whipping that Barrow listed were "not trashing cotton well," "not picking cotton," "up after 10 o'clock," and "up too late." By his own admission, perhaps his most severe beating was given to "Bet," a woman who was, he wrote, "Careless in dropping seed, disowning it, etc."[44] His most frequent victim appears to have been a male slave, "Ginney Jerry" whose name and misdeeds appear more regularly than any other. Consider a sampling of entries from Barrow's diary:

[October 20, 1838] Cloudy cool—picking Cotten appearance of rain—gathered 12 Loads corn yesterday—turns out poorley—Son James went out Fox hunting with me this morning—bids fair to be a first rate Horseman—beautiful chase of 1/2 hour & caught it—G. Jerry did not weigh Cotten at 12 I think he has run off—Whiped about half to day. highest picked 115. wet at that—heavy rain till night.

[January 4, 1839] Cloudy cold—Finished gathering corn yesterday—hauling to day—3 cribs Full—2 smaller ones & one Large one. one Large one two 3ds full—Whiped evry hand in the field this evening commencing with the driver.

[October 20, 1839] Cool wind from the North quit strong during the night—verry smokey for some days past—most wintry looking day this Fall—Yellow Fever still in Town—Gave my negros about my lot the worst Whipping they ever had. Big Lucy the D_____t villan ever lived.

Nor was whipping the sole source of sadistic punishment Barrow's slaves endured. Barrow regularly "ducked" slaves when he was angry with them. Ducking was a terrifying practice of repeatedly plunging a slave's head underwater until they were on the verge of hysteria and loss of consciousness:

[November 29, 1844] Dark Foggy morning, war caught Dennis Last night at the scaffold yard, fooled then by Bets Nat. give the worst Whipping he ever had—& ducking—Finished picking cotten.

[June 4, 1845] Cloudy warm—Finished Ploughing all cotten Above by…ok second time & part the 3d time, Finished hoeing bottom field & planted 5 acres more by 11 ok Had Quite a Frolic Among the negros Last Sunday missed several of my young Hogs. found 8 or 10 Guilty, ducked & gave them a good thrashing, Mr. *Ginney* Jerry next morning Felt insulted at his treatment & put out, would give "freely" $100 to get a shot at him. [Ginny Jerry subsequently ran away and remained on the loose.]

Barrow also turned loose packs of vicious dogs to track down, maul, and tear the flesh from the limbs of runaways before they were whipped:

[September 6, 1845] Cloudy Very warm—The negro hunters came this morning, Were not out Long before we struck the trail of Ginny Jerry, ran and trailed about a mile treed him, made the dogs pull him out of the tree, Bit him very badly, think he will stay home a while, never saw such trailing as one of his sluts did, raining evry day since Jerry Left his camp Monday, & they trailed him by Bushes, to his new one & caught him, Very hard rain at 2 0.

[October 15, 1845] Clear cold morning, Hunting Ruffins Boy Henry [a runaway], Came across Williams runaway Caught him Dogs nearly et his legs off—near killing him—stand at Uncle Bats

[November 11, 1845] Raining at day light, Cleared off at 11 ok Mrs. Haile & Mrs Flower left for Woodville, Dr K & sister here last night, the negro dogs to Mrs Wades Quarter, went through Ruffins beyond & Back. gave up, Et dinner, concluded he [a runaway] had returned to Wades, Went in his pasture & 5 minutes had him up & a going, And never in my life did I ever see as excited beings as R & myself, ran 1/2 miles and caught him dogs soon tore him naked, took him Home Before the other negro at dark & made the dogs give him another over hauling, has been drawing a knife & Pistol on persons about Town.[45]

* * *

Was Barrow's self-reported cruelty unusual among slaveholders? In 1839, the third year of Barrow's diary, a book by Theodore Dwight Weld entitled *American Slavery As It Is: Testimony of a Thousand Witnesses* was published.[46] Drawing upon public records and newspaper accounts in the South, Weld presented a carefully documented pattern of brutality that has yet to be successfully challenged. Writing as he traveled through the South in 1854, fifteen years after Weld, Frederick Law Olmsted observed that little had changed:

> The whip was evidently in constant use…There were no rules on the subject, that I learned; the overseers and drivers punished the negroes whenever they deemed it necessary, and in such manner, and with such severity, as they thought fit.

Finding the practice so disturbing, Olmsted once asked an overseer, "It must be very disagreeable to have to punish them as much as you do?" "Yes," the man replied, "it would be to those who are not *used* to it—but it's my *business*, and I think nothing of it."[47]

And it was business, a practice equivalent to tallying up one's expenses or taking inventory. Levi Ashley, for example, described the practice of the Mississippi slaveholder who owned him:

> Marse John kep' a li'l book, an' whenever a nigger didn' do right to please him, he put dey name in dis book. Den when Friday night come, he would call up all de ones whose name was in de book an' tell 'em to strip, an' dey had to pull off ever'thing, just' lak dey come into this worl', women an' men. Den he would tell de driver to lay on de lash, an' would tell him jus' how many lashes to put on each of 'em. He laid de lash on heavy.[48]

As a rule, however, most slaveholders did not record their cruelty so conscientiously as Barrow. Plantation records are typically much less complete on the subject of whipping; many plantations kept no records at all. Besides it was so common as to require little notice. "Quite frequently," historian John Blassingame writes, "even the most cultured of planters were so inured to brutality that they thought little about the punishment meted out to slaves."[49] Cruelty was endemic in all slave holding communities, according to Kenneth Stampp, and even more so in newly settled areas.[50] Thus one is left with the conclusion that Bennet Barrow was unusual only in that he described his in a diary.

Conscience was obviously no problem for Barrow. Nor was excess short of murder. One can only imagine what he meant when he wrote that he gave someone "a good thrashing," or the "worst whipping I ever gave a young negro." What was "a severe whipping" or "a good thrashing"? Barrow doesn't explain. But Olmsted's description of a whipping he witnessed provides some idea of the cruelty as well as the degree to which those who administered them were inured to the pain and suffering they inflicted. He describes how when touring a plantation with an overseer they discovered a young slave girl hiding among the bushes in a gully away from the work party. After questioning her and finding her explanation unsatisfactory, the overseer replied, "That won't do, get down on your knees." Olmsted described what happened next:

> The girl knelt on the ground; he got off his horse, and holding him with his left hand, struck her thirty or forty blows across the shoulders with his tough flexible, "raw-hide" whip. They were well laid on, as a boatswain would thrash a skulking sailor, or as some people flog a baulking horse, but with *no appearance of angry excitement* on the part of the overseer. At every stroke the girl winced, and exclaimed, "Yes, sir!" or "Ah, sir!" or "Please, sir!" not groaning or screaming. At length he stopped and said, "Now tell me the truth." The girl repeated the same story. "You have not got enough yet," said he, "pull up your clothes—lie down." The girl without any hesitation, without a word or look of remonstrance or entreaty, drew closely all her garments under her shoulders, and lay down upon the ground with her face toward the overseer, who continued to flog her with the rawhide, across her naked loins and thigh, with as much strength as before. She now shrunk away from him, not rising, but writhing, groveling, and screaming, "Oh, don't, sir! oh, please stop, master! please, sir! please, sir! oh, that's enough, master! oh, Lord! oh, master, master! oh, God, master, do stop! oh, God master! oh, God, master!"

Olmsted could watch no more. Later, the overseer explained to him with a "laugh" that, "She meant to cheat me out of a day's work—and she has done it, too."

> "Did you succeed in getting another story from her?" Olmsted asked.
> "No; she stuck to it."
> "Was it necessary to punish her so severely?"

"Oh yes, sir, (laughing again.) If I hadn't punished her so hard she would have done the same thing again to-morrow, and half the people on the plantation would have followed her example. Oh, you've no idea how lazy these niggers are; you northern people don't know anything about it. They'd never do any work at all if they were not afraid of being whipped."[51]

* * *

The cruelist of the many ironies evident in American democracy during the slave period was that white men were free to whip and abuse black men and women for challenging rules that held them in bondage. It is difficult to imagine the pain, humiliation, and outrage of being whipped "raw," as slaves described it, for often capricious reasons. It may have been more difficult, however, to witness loved ones being tortured in this manner as one remained helpless to do anything to stop it.

What is known for sure is that the insensate violence of slavery left permanent scars on minds as well as flesh, etching the "lineaments of wrath," as Jefferson feared, on two different, racially distinct cultures. For, as later chapters will demonstrate, whites would be as unable to break their habit of authority as blacks were to accept it, and so the violence continued, changing only in form in response to modifications in the status of black victims.

Abolitionist Charles Goodell was probably right. Perhaps the most enduring legacy of slavery is that when human beings are controlled, but unprotected, by law they come to "know law only as an enemy, and not as a friend."[52] Any other response is difficult to imagine.

Notes

1. Thomas Jefferson, *Notes on the State of Virginia* (Boston: Printed by David Carlisle for Thomas & Andrews et al., 1801), 240–241.
2. A. de Tocqueville, *Democracy in America* (New York: Doubleday Anchor, 1969; orig., 1835), 340.
3. H. Gannett, *Statistics of the Negroes in the United States* Occasional Papers, No. 4 (Baltimore, MD: Trustees of the John F. Slater Fund, 1894), 5–6; *Final Report of the American Freedmen's Inquiry Commission to the Secretary of War*, U.S. Senate, 38th Congress, 1st sess. June 22, 1864), 56.
4. *Freedmen's Inquiry Commission*, 56; Gannett, *Statistics of the Negroes*, 9–15, 21.
5. W.E.B. Du Bois, *Black Reconstruction in America: 1860–1880* (New York: Atheneum, 1962; orig., 1935), 8–9, 12.
6. J.A. Manfra and R.R. Dykstra, "Serial Marriage and the Origins of the Black Stepfamily: The Rowanty Evidence," *Journal of American History* 72 (1985), 18–44; J. Oakes, *The Ruling Race: A History of American Slaveholders* (New York: Vintage, 1983), 176–179; and J. Blassingame, *The Slave Community* (New York: Oxford University Press, 1979), 173–177.

7. G.P. Rawick (ed.) *The American Slave: A Composite Autobiography* (Westport, CT: Greenwood Press, 1977), (Georgia), Supp. Series 1, v.4, p. 2, 373; see also Harry Bridges interview, *The American Slave* (Mississippi), Supp. Series 1, v.6, p.1, 207–208.

8. Rawick, *The American Slave*, (Georgia), Supp. Series 1, v.4, 7, 466–467.

9. *Freedmen's Inquiry Commission*, 67.

10. Rawick, *The American Slave* (Texas), Series 1, v.4, 15.

11. Rawick, *The American Slave* (Texas), Supp. Series 2, v.8, p.7, 3287.

12. S. Northup, *Twelve Years a Slave* (London, 1853), 260; see, also, Blassingame, *The Slave Community*, 194–195.

13. A. L. Higginbotham, *In the Matter of Color: Race and the American Legal Process* (New York: Oxford University Press, 1978), 170–171.

14. E. D. Genovese, *Roll Jordan Roll: The World the Slaves Made* (New York: Vintage, 1976), 37–39.

15. *Mississippi Laws* (1846), ch. 31; quoted in J.T. Currie, "From Slavery to Freedom in Mississippi's Legal System," *Journal of Negro History* 65 (Spring 1980), 114–115.

16. F.L. Olmsted, *A Journey in the Back Country* (New York: Schocken, 1970; orig., 1860), 63.

17. M.R. Belknap, *Federal Law and Southern Order* (Athens: University of Georgia Press, 1987), 2–3.

18. Code of Tennessee, 1858, sec. 3808, p. 687; quoted in the *Freedmen's Inquiry Commission*, 65.

19. E.A. Davis and W.R. Hogan, *The Barber of Natchez* (Baton Rouge: Louisiana State University Press, 1954), 262–271; see, also, Currie, "From Slavery to Freedom," 114.

20. Quoted in D.J. Flanigan, *The Criminal Law of Slavery and Freedom, 1800–1868* (New York: Garland, 1987), 73.

21. J. Stirling, *Letters from the Slave States* (London, 1875), 291–292; see, also, M.S. Hindus, *Prison and Plantation: Crime, Justice, and Authority in Massachusetts and South Carolina, 1767–1878* (Chapel Hill: University of North Carolina Press, 1980), 129.

22. F.L. Olmsted, *A Journey in the Seaboard Slave States* (New York: Negro Universities Press, 1968; orig., 1856), 487.

23. Du Bois, *Black Reconstruction*, 10–11; Currie, "From Slavery to Freedom," 115–16.

24. Flanigan, *The Criminal Law of Slavery*, 25.

25. *State v. Mann*, 13 N.C. (2 Dev.), 263, 267 (1829); quoted in Belknap, *Federal Law and Southern Order*, 2.

26. Oakes, *The Ruling Race*, 1983), 159–160, 163, 167; K. M. Stampp, *The Peculiar Institution* (New York: Vintage, 1956), 162–163.

27. R.C. Wade, *Slavery in the Cities* (New York: Oxford University Press, 1964), 186.

28. Scholars owe an important debt to George P. Rawick who undertook the enormous task of compiling these interviews. While the original twelve volumes were in preparation, still more WPA interviews were brought to Rawick's attention, most of them from Texas, that had never made their way into the Library of Congress collection. These he published in ten additional volumes in 1979. Taken together, the twenty-two supplemental editions published in 1977 and 1979 consist of 1,776 interviews. See, G.P. Rawick (ed.), *The American Slave: A Composite Autobiography* (Westport, CT: Greenwood Press, 1972, 1977, 1979).

29. See, for example, Stampp, *The Peculiar Institution*, 174–179, 209–210; Genovese, *Roll Jordan Roll*, 64–67; and Oakes, *The Ruling Race*, 159–160, 163,

167; S.C. Crawford, *Quantified Memory: A Study of the WPA and Fisk University Slave Narrative Collections* (unpublished Ph.D. dissertation, University of Chicago, 1980). For the argument that whipping has been exaggerated by historians, see, R.W. Fogel and S.L. Engerman, *Time on the Cross: The Economics of American Negro Slavery* (Boston: Little, Brown, 1974), 144–157. Persuasive critiques of Fogel and Engerman's position may be found in the following: P.A. David, et al., *Reckoning With Slavery: A Critical Study in the Quantitative History of American Negro Slavery* (New York: Oxford University Press, 1976); H.G. Gutman, *Slavery and the Numbers Game* (Urbana: University of Illinois Press, 1975); and T.L. Haskell, "The True and Tragical History of *Time on the Cross*," *New York Review of Books*, 2 (October 1975), 33–39.

30. C. Joyner, *Down by the Riverside: A South Carolina Slave Community* (Urbana: University of Illinois Press, 1984), 57.

31. Rawick, *The American Slave* (Georgia), Supp. Series 1, v.4, p.2, 347–348.

32. *New York Tribune*, March 10, 1850; quoted in H.G. Gutman, "Slave Work Habits and the Protestant Ethic," in A. Weinstein, F.O. Gatell, and D. Sarasohn (eds.) *American Negro Slavery* (New York: Oxford University Press, 1979), 109, fn.17.

33. C.V. Woodward and E. Muhlenfeld (eds.) *The Private Mary Chesnut: The Unpublished Civil War Diaries* (New York: Oxford University Press, 1984), May 18, 1861, 42.

34. Rawick, *The American Slave* (Georgia), Supp. Series 1, v.4, p.2, 464.

35. Quoted in J.C. Sitterson, *Sugar Country: The Cane Sugar Industry in the South, 1753–1950* (Lexington: University of Kentucky Press, 1953), 235.

36. Quoted in Stampp, *The Peculiar Institution*, 186–187.

37. Fogel and Engerman, *Time on the Cross*, 147.

38. Fogel and Engerman, *Time on the Cross*, 145; Gutman, "Slave Work Habits," 94–109; and E.A. Davis (ed.) *Plantation Life in the Florida Parishes of Louisiana, 1836–1846 as Reflected in the Diary of Bennet H. Barrow* (New York: AMS Press, 1967); hereafter cited as *Plantation Life* or *Barrow Diary*.

39. Davis, *Plantation Life*, 37 (emphasis added).

40. Stampp, *The Peculiar Institution*, 186.

41. Genovese, *Roll Jordan Roll*, 64.

42. *Barrow Diary*, 407.

43. *Barrow Diary*, 431–440.

44. Davis, *Barrow Diary*, 431–440.

45. *Barrow Diary*, 431–440.

46. T.D. Weld, *American Slavery As It Is: Testimony of A Thousand Witnesses* (New York: American Anti-Slavery Society, 1839).

47. Olmsted, *A Journey in the Back Country*, 82 (emphasis added).

48. Rawick, *The American Slave* (Mississippi), Supp. Series 1, v.6, p.1, 77–78.

49. Blassingame, *The Slave Community*, 262.

50. Stampp, *The Peculiar Institution*, 185 (emphasis added).

51. Olmsted, *A Journey in the Back Country*, 85–87 (emphasis added).

52. Quoted in Flanigan, *The Criminal Law*, 73.

3

Scarred in the Flame of Withering Injustice[1]

When white folks go to meetin'
They never crack a smile,
But when colored folks in church
You'll here um laugh er mile...
—Slave poem[2]

"Of course [we would] steal. Had to steal. That the best way to git
what [we] wanted.... Those white folks made us lie. We had to lie
to live."
—A former slave[3]

It is little wonder, as Mary Chestnut observed so often in her diaries, that slavery eroded the moral basis of white society.[4] That erosion, as Jefferson feared, was reflected in the "lineaments of wrath" that marked the countenances of slaveholders and defined the "odious peculiarities" of their early American culture. Is there any reason to doubt that such a system would not have a similarly profound effect on the manners and morals of black slaves as well? At least one Georgia planter, like Jefferson, recognized the probable enduring consequences for the black victims of such systematic mistreatment and injustice. Nathan Bass warned his fellow planters during the 1850s that indiscriminate physical abuse was ultimately unwise. "The slave knows," he explained, "when he intentionally violates orders, and when he deserves correction; and if inflicted capriciously or cruelly, it has a tendency to make him reckless and harden him in crime."[5]

Like Solomon Bradley, a slave who earlier in these pages described a beating he witnessed, the brutalizing experiences of of slavery must have also made other slaves "wild" with loathing and rage, deepening their contempt for a system of state laws and plantation rules that condoned, even required, such behavior. It is little wonder that such expe-

35

riences molded conceptions of right and wrong among slaves that were different from the standards of morality and justice shared by the ruling white majority.

Slave religious faith and worship had always been different from whites, reflecting the persistence across generations of African beliefs and practices combined with the influences of Luther, Calvin, and American revivalists of the slave period. Even after slaveholders permitted slave conversions to Christianity, sorcery, voodooism, and conjurism—the remnants of African culture—were blended in by slaves and became an important part of their religious faith. The conjurer, W.E.B. DuBois explained, appeared early on the plantation and remained long after emancipation:

> He...found his function as the healer of the sick, the interpreter of the unknown, the comforter of the sorrowing, the supernatural avenger of wrong and the one who rudely, but picturesquely, expressed the longing, disappointment and resentment of a stolen and oppressed people.[6]

In contrast, white slaveholding Christians believed they found justification for slavery and their own racism in Old Testament authoritarianism. White ministers who sought to convert slaves, emphasized the omnipotence of the white masters and taught that obedience was the key to salvation. As Charlie Bell, once enslaved in Mississippi, recalled:

> Mr. Mo' built a log church for his labor on de plantation. A white preacher come twice a month ter speak ter us. His text would always be 'Obey yo' marster an' mistress that yo' days may be lingerin' upon God's green earth what he give you. We didn't have no nigger preachin' ter us when I was little.[7]

When armed patrols of white men on horseback roamed the countryside looking for runaway slaves and slaves traveling without "passes" to other plantations, they also sought out clandestine black religious services. Lizzie Brown, who had been a slave in Mississippi, described what happened when such meetings were discovered:

> One time niggers from the different plantations sneak off and had preaching in a big ditch. Uncle Pat made him a pulpit out of a log and the niggers stand up at the other end and listen to him...all a-sudden.... They turned around and patarollers wus all around 'em. They wus surrounded. Some of 'em got away but the patarollers got a lot of 'em. And did they whip 'em...the patarollers sho wus a 'noyance to the niggers in them days.[8]

When slave preaching was permitted, it was monitored carefully to ensure that the white perspective on subservience was not challenged.

A former slave, Cora Shepherd, for example, described the policy on her Georgia plantation:

> My old marster let us have prayer meetin' Saturday night regular…colored man preach. Better not 'sturb his niggers when old carriage driver John Jefferson preach! I 'member his text:
>
> Love yo' marster, Love yo' Miss. Obey! Be subdued to yo' marster and yo' missess.
>
> Den he would preach: Marvel not—ye must be born again![9]

A *Catechism* prepared for slaves in 1844 illustrates why so many slaves rejected this peculiar white version of Christianity:

> Q. What command has God given to Servants, concerning obedience to their Masters?
>
> A. Servants obey in all things your Masters…fearing God.
>
> Q. How are they to try to please their Masters?
>
> A. With good will, doing service unto the Lord and not unto men…
>
> Q. But suppose the Master is hard to please, and threatens and punishes more than he ought, what is the Slave to do?
>
> A. Do his best to please him.
>
> Q. When the Slave suffers *wrongfully*, at the hands of his Master, and to please God, takes it patiently, will God reward him for it?
>
> A. Yes.
>
> Q. Is it right for the Slave to *run away*, or is it right to harbour a runaway?
>
> A. No.
>
> Q. Will Servants have to account to God for the manner in which they serve their Masters on earth?
>
> A. Yes.[10]

At the same time attempts like this were made to convince slaves of the morality of submission, white clergymen sought to reassure their patrons that Christianity provided no bar to paternalistic slavery since it was "permitted by the Deity himself."[11] While variations in tolerance, forgiveness, and the severity of punishment for wrongdoing could be observed in the brand of Christianity slaveholders approved for their charges, complete obedience remained, of necessity, an unyielding principle. For Calvinists it was preordained.[12] Accordingly, slave disobedience was *always* wrong in the eyes of the slaveholder, but it might also be a considered sin in the eyes of the slaveholder's God. In either case, economic necessity and spiritual convenience were merged in this perverse theological hierarchy.

But when a conflict arose between spiritual and economic considerations, it was the latter that commonly took precedence. "It was much
more than malice that drove so many Southern masters to whip slaves
for praying to God for this or that," historian Eugene Genovese writes,
"and to demand that they address all grievances and wishes to their
earthly masters."[13] To such persons, it was the principle of human lord-
ship that was uppermost.

* * *

Slave religion, in contrast, reflected a different perspective and culture. It was adapted to different needs, addressed different themes in
the gospels, focused on different scripture, and emphasized different
issues than white Christianity. Slaves, for example, emphatically rejected the notion that their enslavement fulfilled the biblical curse on
Ham. They were not easily persuaded by this and other white religious
beliefs such as the belief in original sin. Instead they acted independently as agents of change to humanize the stern, judgmental, joyless
religion of their masters.[14] They imagined a compassionate, forgiving
God, a heavenly father who could overlook human foibles and even
had a sense of humor. Surely, they believed, so many of life's simple
pleasures, like sex and avoiding work, could not be as sinful as white
ministers insisted. So slave religious services provided escape, an opportunity to shout and clap and sing and laugh, as the congregation
might have when a slave preacher offered these words in prayer:

> O mah God an' mah father, ain't you see how dis groun' do tremble same like
> judgement day? Come down hyuh, Lawd, an' help po' people in dere trial and
> tribbilation, but o, do Mass Gawd, be sho an' come yo'self an' doan sen Yo' Son,
> 'cause dis ain' no time for chillun...[15]

But above all, slave prayers revealed a longing for deliverance, and
the hope of divine retribution for those who had enslaved them. Slave
preachers condemned oppression, likening themselves to the Israelites
in their search for the "promised land." Slaves loved to sing spirituals
embellishing themes they knew were forbidden:

> O, gracious Lord! When shall it be,
> That we poor souls shall all be free;
> Lord, break them slavery powers—
> Will you go along with me?
> Lord break them slavery powers,
> Go sound the jubilee!
> Dear Lord, dear Lord, when slavery'll cease,

Then we poor souls will have our peace;
There's a better day a coming.
Will you go along with me?
There's a better day a coming,
Go sound the jubilee![16]

Slave religion, however, included more than a patient, long-suffering wait for deliverance and eternal life in the hereafter. Slaves also embraced a different philosophy of life guided by different standards of daily conduct. Work, for example, had no value as it did for white Protestants influenced by the doctrines of Calvin and Luther. Slaves loafed, feigned illness, met their cotton quotas with rocks in their baskets, broke tools, mistreated farm animals, and basically did anything they could get away with to get back at their masters. There was no guilt, no sense of wrongdoing. Instead there was only contempt for the white man's hypocritical religious beliefs. That contempt is conveyed humorously in this slave folktale about a conversation between "Old Massa" and his slave about dreams they had had. "It was like this," the slaveholder began,

I dreamed I went to Nigger Heaven last night, and saw there a lot of garbage, some old torn-down houses, a few old broken down rotten fences, the muddiest, sloppiest streets I ever saw, and a big bunch of ragged, dirty niggers walkin' around.

"Umph, umph, Massa," the slave replied,

You sho' musta et de same thing I did las' night, 'case I dreamed I went up to de white man's paradise, an' de streets was all of gol' an' silver, and dey was lots o' milk an' honey dere, an' putty pearly gats, but dey wasn't a soul in de whole place.[17]

It was not necessary to assume, as Du Bois did, that slaves had brought with them from tribal Africa this different cultural perspective on the value and purpose of work. Forced labor was simply recognized by slaves for what it was: a form of daily injustice to be avoided or subverted whenever possible. Some slaveholders, like William Wells Brown, understood this. His slaves, he acknowledged, "were always glad to shirk labor and thought that to deceive whites was a *religious* duty."[18]

Brown was right. There were few slave preachers willing to condemn such behavior. Instead, it was either ignored or, most likely, justified. They and those who listened to them understood that lying and cheating were necessary for survival.

"They didn't half feed us," one North Carolina slave recalled. "They fed the animals better. They gives the mules the roughage and such, to chaw on all night. But they didn't give us nothing to chaw on. Learned us to steal that's what they done. Why, we could take anything we could lay our hands on, when we was hungry. Then they'd whip us for lying when we say we don't know nothing about it. But it was easier to stand when the stomach was full."[19]

As this statement reveals, slaves did not consider stealing from the master or, for that matter, from whites in general, morally wrong: it was merely "taking," as Frederick Douglass and many other former slaves explained it.[20] Stealing was closely associated with the sufficiency of diets slaves were provided. An occasional stolen chicken, a few eggs, or a sack of cornmeal could mean the difference between sickness and health for people who often lived on protein-deficient diets. If slaves were fed adequately, they were less likely to steal; if they were hungry, stealing became an important way to fill empty stomachs.[21] Moreover, it was completely justified in the minds of slaves like Josephine Howard:

[The master and the overseers] all de time tellin de black folks it wrong to lie an' steal, but de white folks do plenty lyin' an' stealin', and' dat's de truth. Why did white folks steal my mamma an' gran'ma? I's heard mamma tell 'bout it lots of times,"…De white folks had lied 'bout givin' 'em presents so dey could get 'em on de boat an 'bring 'em here an' sell 'em an' dat's de sinfullest stealin' dey is…Lord have mercy, it sure was awful de way black folks was done. Dey wasn't nothin' de whites don't do to 'em—work em like dey was mules an' treat 'em jes' like dey don't have no fellin'…I hear dat call in de mornin' *like it was jes' yestiddy*— all right, everybody out, an' you better get out too iffen you don't want to feel dat old bullwhip 'cross your back.[22]

"My mother said she had a hard time getting through. Had to steal half the time," Rachel Fairley told a WPA interviewer in Arkansas,

They had to work all the time. When they went to church on Sunday, they would tell them not to steal their master's things. How could they help but steal when you didn't have nothin'? You didn't eat if you didn't steal…Master was mean and hard. Whipped them [her parents] lots…. You had to eat what you could get then.[23]

Thievery and deception also provided a sense of excitement, camaraderie and accomplishment in a world where such feelings and ordinary opportunities to experience them were rare. One former slave recalled the pleasure of roasting a stolen chicken with some "black fair one." It made him feel "good, moral, [even] heroic," he said, for such actions were, "all the chivalry of which my circumstances and condition of life admitted."[24]

Stealing was also a satisfying form of revenge, a former slave explained because, *we felt we were living under a system of cheating and lying and deceit* and...*did not see the wrong of it*, so long as we were not acting against one another. I am sure that, as a rule, any one of us who would have thought nothing of stealing a hog, or a sack of corn, from our master, would have allowed himself to be cut to pieces rather than betray the confidence of his fellow slave.[25]

When slaves steal from their master, another former slave explained, "The only question is, 'Can we keep it from master?' If they can keep their backs safe, conscience is quiet enough on this point. But a slave that will steal from a slave, is called mean as master."[26]

Since they were afraid to express their true feelings to slaveholders, dissimulation became a way of life for slaves. Smiles and nods concealed loathing as responses to humiliation; tears and wails frequently concealed relief and joy at a master's funeral. The artistry of deception became a source of personal satisfaction as well as status with one's peers, and slaves boasted about their triumphs in song and verse:

> O some tell me that a nigger won't steal,
> But I've seen a nigger in my corn-field;
> O run, nigger, run, for the patrol will catch you,
> O run, nigger, run, for 'tis almost day.
> I fooled Old Master seven years,
> Fooled the overseer three.
> Hand me down my banjo,
> And I'll tickle your bel-lee.[27]

And so the "trickster" tradition of black folklore grew out of such experiences. Cheating a white person was not wrong, it was smart and enormously satisfying if you could get away with it. Black children loved to hear these songs about clever slaves outwitting loutish masters, and sang along with their elders. The lessons taught, the values conveyed, as one white Aid Society schoolteacher discovered in 1866, were not lost on these young minds:

"Now children," the teacher said to the black children before him, "you don't think white people are any better than you because they have straight hair and white faces?

"No, sir."

"No, they are not better," he agreed, "but they are different, they possess great power, they formed this great government, they control this vast country...Now what makes them different from you?"

"*Money*," the children shouted in unison.

"Yes, but what enabled them to obtain it?" he asked.

"Got it off us, stole off we all," they replied.[28]

* * *

Thomas Jefferson once observed that one hour of slavery was "fraught with more misery" than the century and a half of the tyranny cast off in the Revolution of 1776.[29] While not all slaves responded in the same way spiritually to the circumstances of enslavement, there is considerable evidence that two related, but separate and antagonistic, cultures began to evolve in the moral vacuum of slavery, one white and one black, but both uniquely American. For American slaves, historian Kenneth Stampp concluded, "success, respectability, and morality were measured by *other* standards, and prestige was won in *other* ways."[30]

Christianity is based on the premise that conscience must develop at an early age to modulate the inborn destructiveness of human beings. Freud agreed, suggesting that civilization could not have evolved, nor would it survive, in the absence of human empathy. Conscience defines humanity, but the South forfeited its conscience when it embraced chattel slavery and the "savage ideal" of human bondage, for human bondage is human sacrifice. Lacking the moral legitimacy many of their black victims refused to grant, slaveholders had to rely on fear and brute force to control them.[31]

As a consequence, the primary moral value among slaves seemed to be the protection—by whatever means—of one another from the depravity and brutality of their masters. Abundant evidence from the words of slaves themselves indicates that wrongdoing had been redefined as a result of the suffering and injustices of slavery. It was in this manner that a slave culture based on different moral premises, evolved.[32]

Long after slavery had ended, Freud wrote that "the primitive, the savage and evil impulses of mankind have not vanished in any individual, but continue their existence.... They merely wait for opportunities to display their activity."[33] The culture of white supremacy provided those opportunities; the black culture molded by it provided more. Whippings, rape, and other forms of physical and psychological intimidation became for Southern whites what lying, stealing, and sabotage had become for slaves—acceptable forms of behavior required for survival. And so cultures are formed.

Notes

1. The title is taken from a phrase in Martin Luther King used to describe slavery in his "I Have a Dream" speech, August 28, 1963. Referring to the Emancipation Proclamation, King said, "This momentous decree came as a great beacon of hope to millions of Negro slaves who had been *scarred in the flame of withering injustice.*"

2. Quoted in A. Lomax, *The Folksongs of North America* (Garden City, NY: Doubleday, 1960), 463.
3. Quoted in L.W. Levine, *Black Culture and Black Consciousness* (New York: Oxford University Press, 1977), 123.
4. M. Chestnut, *The Private Mary Chestnut: The Unpublished Civil War Diaries*, edited by C.V. Woodward and E. Muhlenfeld (New York: Oxford University Press, 1984).
5. N. Bass, "Essay on the Treatment and Management of Slaves," Southern Central Agricultural Society, *Transactions, 1851–1856*, 198; quoted in E. Genovese, *Roll Jordan Roll: The World the Slaves Made* (New York: Vintage, 1972), 66 (emphasis added).
6. W.E.B. DuBois, "The Religion of the American Negro," *New World* IX (December 1900), 618 (emphasis added); see, also, J.W. Blassingame, *The Slave Community* (New York: Oxford University Press, 1979), 39–41, 130–148.
7. G.P. Rawick, *The American Slave: A Composite Autobiography* (Westport, CT: Greenwood Press, 1972; 1976); (Mississippi) Supp. Series 1, v.6, p.1, 123–124.
8. Rawick, *The American Slave* (Mississippi) Supp. Series 1, v.6, p.1, 265–266.
9. Rawick, *The American Slave* (Georgia) Supp. Series 1, v.4, p.2, 555.
10. C.C. Jones, *The Religious Instruction of the Negroes in the United States* (New York: Negro Universities Press, 1969; orig., 1842), 266.
11. F.T. Schmidt and B.R. Wilhelm, "Early Pro-Slavery Petitions in Virginia," *William and Mary Quarterly* 30 (January 1973), 133–146; see, also, J. Butler, *Awash in a Sea of Faith: Christianizing the American People* (Cambridge, MA: Harvard University Press, 1990), 129–151.
12. Genovese, *Roll Jordan Roll*, 244.
13. Genovese, *Roll Jordan Roll*, 165.
14. Genovese, *Roll Jordan Roll*, 244–247.
15. Quoted in Lomax, *The Folk Songs of North America*, 463.
16. Quoted in Blassingame, *The Slave Community*, 144; see, also, 133–148.
17. J. M. Brewer, "Juneteenth," in F. Dobie (ed.) *Tone the Bell Easy* (Texas Folklore Society, 1932); and Lomax, *The Folk Songs of North America*, 464.
18. K.A. Stampp, *The Peculiar Institution: Slavery in the AnteBellum South* (New York: Vintage, 1956), 97–124; Genovese, *Roll Jordan Roll*, 285–324; W.E.B. Du Bois, *The Gift of Black Folk* (Boston: Stratford, 1924), 14, 29; W. W. Brown, *My Southern Home*, 52, quoted in A.J. Raboteau, *Slave Religion* (New York: Oxford University Press, 1978), 296.
19. N.R. Yetman (ed.), *Life Under the "Peculiar Institution": Selections from the Slave Narrative Collection* (New York: Holt, Rinehart and Winston, 1970), 116.
20. F. Douglass, *My Bondage and My Freedom* (New York and Auburn: Miller, Orton, Mulligan, 1855), 189–191; J. Henson, *Truth Stranger Than Fiction: Father Henson's Story of His Own Life* (Boston: J.P. Jewett, 1858), 21–23; see, also, J. Stroyer, *Sketches of My Life in the South* (1879), 9–10, 27, 42–45; and H.G. Gutman, *The Black Family in Slavery and Freedom, 1750–1925* (New York: Vintage, 1977), 279–281.
21. S.C. Crawford, *Quantified Memory: A Study of the WPA and Fisk University Slave Narrative Collections* (unpublished Ph.D. dissertation, University of Chicago, 1980), 15–20.
22. Rawick, *The American Slave* (Texas) Supp. Series 2, v.4, p.4, 1806–1807.
23. Rawick, *The American Slave* (Arkansas) Series 2, V.8, Parts 1–2, 258–260.
24. Henson, *Truth Stranger Than Fiction*, 21–23; see, also, Stampp, *The Peculiar Institution*, 334–335.

25. J. Brown, *Slave Life in Georgia* F.N. Boney (ed.) (Savannah, Ga.: Beehive Press, 1972; orig. 1855), 71–72; quoted in Raboteau, *Slave Religion*, 296–297 (emphasis added).

26. L. Clarke, "Questions and Answers," in *Interesting Memoirs and Documents Relating to American Slavery* (London, 1846), 92; quoted in Levine, *Black Culture*, 125.

27. W.F. Allen, C.P. Ware, and L. M. Garrison, *Slave Songs of the United States* (New York, 1951; orig., 1867), 89; quoted in Levine, *Black Culture*, 125.

28. H.L. Swint, *The Northern Teacher in the South, 1862–1870* (Nashville, TN, 1941), 89; quoted in Levine, *Black Culture*, 124.

29. Quoted in G.S. Wood, "Jefferson at Home," *New York Review of Books* XL, 9 (May 13, 1993), 9.

30. Stampp, *The Peculiar Institution*, 334 (emphasis added).

31. S. Freud, *Civilization and Its Discontents* (New York: W.W. Norton, 1962).

32. T. Turpin, *Christian Advocate and Journal, 8 (January 31, 1834)* and C. Stearns, *The Black Man of the South and the Rebels* (New York, 1872), 355, 373–374, 381; cited in Raboteau, *Slave Religion*, 298–299.

33. Freud quoted in H.S. Hughes, *Consciousness and Society: The Reorientation of Social Thought, 1890–1930* (New York: Vintage, 1958), 143–44; see, also, B. Wyatt-Brown, *Southern Honor: Ethics and Behavior in the Old South* (New York: Oxford University Press, 1982), 460–461.

Part II

Reconstruction

4

No More Auction Block

If I had my way,
O Lordy, Lordy,
If I had my way;
If I had my way:
I would tear this building down.
                                        —Slave song[1]

No more auction block for me, No more, no more,
No more auction block for me, No more, no more,
Many thousands gone.
No more driver's lash for me, No more, no more,
No more driver's lash for me, No more, no more,
Many thousands gone.
                                        —Slave song[2]

In view of the assault on mind, body, and spirit that was the bitter reality of slavery, the desire among slaves to be free was surely consuming. Yet, until the publication of Herbert Aptheker's *American Negro Slave Revolts* in 1943, scholars had been inclined to discount the significance of the many attempts slaves made to free themselves.[3] Perhaps it is because none was successful against the overwhelming odds that they faced—outnumbered, unarmed, and unable to communicate—in a totalitarian system. Since then scholars have acknowledged the many instances of slave resistance, recognizing that, despite the odds against their success, the attempts continued. More recent detailed accounts of these previously obscure events leave little doubt that over the course of American history untold numbers of determined men and women preferred to risk almost certain death rather than remain enslaved.[4]

Historians Michael and Judy Newton have documented more than one hundred slave insurrections involving three or more slaves, that resulted in loss of life or property. That works out, on average, to about

one every three years from 1619 to 1865.[5] Some of these were spontaneous reactions to specific instances of cruelty and deprivation. Others
were part of what might be considered guerrilla campaigns. For example, scores of skirmishes occurred between whites and bands of fugitive slaves, called "maroons." These bands, sometimes with Indian
allies, made sporadic raids on plantations and white settlements seeking plunder and, also, to expand their numbers with liberated slaves.
Still others were revolts intended as opening salvos in a war to overthrow the system itself.[6]

Taken together, such events happened regularly enough that they
had a profound and enduring effect on Southern white culture. Fear of
insurrection grew as the slave population steadily increased with an
expanding cotton economy in the nineteenth century. During some periods, most notably in the thirty years preceeding the Civil War, the
South was preoccupied with that fear. It is impossible to calculate the
number of innocent slaves who were flogged or killed, along with the
actual perpetrators, during the various insurrection panics that periodi-
cally seized the South.

Similar apprehensions were evident in the North as well, where there
was great uncertainty about the wisdom of freeing some four million
African slaves who might then migrate North. Most white Americans,
even those who favored emancipation, were convinced that blacks represented a biological and cultural threat. Nowhere was the ambivalence
about emancipation more clearly illustrated than in the words and actions of the man who eventually liberated them, Abraham Lincoln.

Among slaves, the desire for freedom was universal and enduring. It
is documented not only in the revolts discussed in this chapter, but also
in the countless, and overwhelmingly nonviolent, acts of personal
resistence described earlier. But the point is made, perhaps most forcefully, in the tens of thousands of blacks who eagerly joined the fight for
freedom during the Civil War.

* * *

The first recorded instance of organized slave resistance occured on
September 13, 1663 in Virginia. A rumored plot by slaves and inden-
tured servants resulted in the preemptive beheadings of several of the
alleged plotters. In what was to become a widely practiced custom,
their severed heads were displayed on chimney tops as a warning to
others. The first actual insurrection took place forty-nine years later in
1712. At that time some thirty slaves set fire to a building in New York

City and then killed nine and wounded six of the whites who responded. The rebels were quickly captured and twenty-four were subsequently tried and convicted. Thirteen were hanged, three were burned at the stake, and one was broken on the wheel. Six others committed suicide and one reportedly died of starvation.[7] That same same year another slave conspiracy was discovered and crushed in Goose Creek, South Carolina. Similar incidents with the same results continued throughout the eighteenth century, many of them in South Carolina.[8]

The most serious of these occurred on September 9, 1739 in Stono, where some twenty slaves attacked a local arsenal, killing two guards. Seizing arms, their ranks grew to an estimated eighty persons as they burned and killed their way south toward Spanish Florida. Twenty-three whites died before they were stopped by the militia. Thirty-four of the rebels were killed and forty more were captured and quickly executed. By the end of the eighteenth century, more than forty actual or anticipated insurrections had been recorded.[9]

A truly massive slave insurrection would have taken place in 1800 had the plot not been discovered. At that time an elaborate plan was devised by Gabriel Prosser and others to seize the armory in Richmond, Virginia. On August 30, an estimated one thousand slaves "armed with clubs, scythes, home-made bayonets, and a few guns" moved to the attack. Heavy rains, flooding, and an impassable bridge, however, prevented them from reaching the city. This delay and the ultimate betrayal of Prosser by two of his confederates enabled the militia to respond. Forty-one blacks said to be ringleaders in the conspiracy were captured and hanged, including Prosser.[10] Perhaps because Prosser refused to reveal the details of the elaborate plot to Governor James Monroe, his death marked the beginning of a panic that held white Virginians in its grip for the next several years. Some seventeen real or imagined plots were reported during that time in Virginia alone, with still more alleged in neighboring North Carolina. The hysteria was reflected in the severity of the penalties given to the alleged conspirators. Based on the flimsiest evidence, the accused were either flogged or hanged in public specatacles. In an especially grisly ceremony, two women were burned at the stake in Wayne County, North Carolina.[11]

A decade later, more than five hundred slaves turned against whites in Saint John the Baptist Parish, Louisiana. On January 8, 1811, these inadequately armed slaves battled desperately with the militia before being subdued. Sixty-eight slaves died during the initial clash; the remainder were hunted down and either killed or captured over the next two days. The severed heads of sixteen leaders of the rebellion were displayed on poles.[12]

Some seventeen conspiracies and actual revolts involving fewer numbers of slaves were recorded over the next ten years. Then in June, 1822, authorities learned of plans for a major insurrection in Charleston, South Carolina. The plot was inspired by Denmark Vesey, a native-born African artisan and preacher who had purchased his freedom. Hundreds, probably thousands, of blacks were involved. In preparation, they stealthfully made and accumulated weapons to use in what was to be a five-pronged attack on the city. The focus of the initial assault was to be a raid on armories and stores to obtain firearms and provisions to continue the attack. Ultimately the rebels hoped to flee to the black republic of Haiti. But the plan was betrayed before it could be implemented. Of those arrested, forty-eight were flogged and thirty-seven, including Vesey, were executed.[13]

It was not only news of massive conspiracies like Vesey's that stoked white anxiety; those fears were also regularly reinforced by rumors of smaller uprisings. Southerners understood that they were living on a racial powder keg. Each incident was viewed as the potential spark that would set off the apocalypse. One never knew when or where it might happen. Something like a report from Kentucky, in September 1825, that seventy-seven slaves escaped after killing the crew of an Ohio River boat carrying them south, could have been the spark. Or it might have been the series of mysterious fires set in Mobile and Huntsville, Alabama during January and February 1829, or more fires in Augusta, Georgia later that year. The threat was *always* there.[14]

That threat, and the South's worst fears, were confirmed on the warm Sunday evening of August 21, 1831, when Nat Turner led a handful of slaves on what began as an assault on his owners and grew into a gory rampage across Southhampton County, Virginia. Three days and twenty miles later the mutilated bodies of at least fifty-seven white men, women, and children marked Turner's bloody trail. More than one hundred slaves were killed in the ensuing counterattack, a number of them innocent people; fifty-three of Turner's suspected followers were captured and, of that number, twenty-three were hanged; and Turner, after eluding authorities for another two months, was captured, tried, and convicted in one day, and executed six days later.[15]

Fears of slave rebellions that had lapped at the edges of Southern consciousness for generations swelled into an incoming tide of anxiety after the Turner uprising. Reason was compromised by fear and an obsession with surveillance and control. Nat Turner would live on in the mind of the South; he had become every white Southerner's nightmare.

The ferocity of the rampage and its spritual and philosophical underpinnings revealed in the confession of its remorseless leader assured that. It was unsettling. Compared to most slaves, Turner had been a docile, compliant house servant, admittedly treated well by the owners he had savagely murdered. He was also a religious man, a Christian who had turned his religious faith against his oppressors, claiming his violent acts reflected a divinely inspired prophecy of Old Testament retribution and deliverance. What more, fearful whites must have wondered, could they expect of those hundreds of thousands of slaves whose rage, unlike the relatively privileged Turner's, flowed from unrelenting hardships, backbreaking field labor, and the lash? Turner's raid gave them a glimpse into the depths of racial hatred that countless slaves harbored against them. After that, Southern whites recognized that eternal vigilance was not only the price of liberty, it was also the price of protecting their own lives and property.

This horrifying spectre of mass insurrection marked an important change in the institution of slavery itself. For the first time responsibility for controlling the slave population shifted beyond the slaveholders themselves to *all* whites. Every Southerner, Nat Turner had demonstrated, was a potential victim of black rage. Now, not only slaveholders, but every white man, woman, and child had a vital stake in a potential race war, and the threat grew in direct proportion to the expanding cotton economy and slave population. Long before the formation of the Ku Klux Klan, armed patrols of white men roamed country roads at night, stopping any unsupervised black, checking vacant buildings for clandestine meetings of black conspirators, scouting the timber and river bottoms for runaways. So great was the perceived threat, that these "patrollers" were invested with the authority to apprehend, try, and punish any suspect as they saw fit. For the first time, the property rights of slaveholders were subordinated to the greater apprehension about public safety in the South.

As fear spread, white determination to keep the black population unarmed and immobile grew into an obsession which was sedulously fed and nourished by rumors of countless revolts faithfully reported in newspapers. The fact that armories had been a primary target in every major slave conspiracy had not escaped attention. Without weapons and horses, whites understood, slaves remained at a decided disadvantage in any incident that might arise. The culmination of such anxieties was the emergence of a seige mentality, as the South became fixated on surveillance and control of its slave population. What amounted to a state of martial law was imposed that prevailed throughout the South and continued until the end of the Civil War.[16]

And it was effective. There was a noticeable decline in the number of slave insurrections reported after 1831 in the South. The reason, however, was not slave apathy, contentment, or loyalty to kindly, paternalistic masters, as some have imagined, but increased surveillance. In spite of the rapid growth of the slave population, slaves in the South still remained outnumbered by whites by a ratio of two to one. Outnumbered, unarmed, and now under constant and intensified surveillance, the growing restiveness of the slave population was tightly constrained precisely during the time that emotions and tensions over the issue of slavery began to build in Congress and the nation. It was not until the Civil War, when the attention of Southerners focused on invading Union armies, that reports of slave insurrections began to appear once again.

* * *

In view of the fears of slave violence that plagued Southerners, it is surprising that so many of them were surprised, nevertheless, to discover that they could not count on the loyalty of their own slaves when the Civil War began. The reason for this is that what most slaveholders feared were the slaves owned by others, not their own. This self-satisfied, often religious, aristocracy had deceived itself into believing that the nodding daily compliance of each slaveholder's own slaves indicated contentment and approval. The fact that it did not, came as a shock. Mary Chestnut acknowledged as much in a diary entry during the first year of the Civil War when she wrote,

> Gen. Wool says this war on our part is to extend slavery. They are beginning to find out they cannot trust the black man—not, as they expected, every one an enemy of their master's—but nearly all spies.[17]

There could be no doubt that slaves welcomed the advance of Union armies. Despite warnings and threats, many willingly provided Yankee officers and soldiers with information about the location of bridges, particular sites, distances, and the movements of Confederate forces. Others were more direct, showing soldiers where their masters had hidden food and valuables. As General Sherman's army burned and pillaged its way across Georgia near the end of the war, slaves welcomed him as a savior, an answer to their prayers. There was also little doubt in Sherman's mind, or in the minds of his officers, that many slaves wanted not only freedom, but revenge. It was as if they had waited and prayed for someone like Sherman, an avenger, who would not only free them, but would also exact hard punishment on their white oppressors. "We work on, 'til Sherman come and burn and slash his way through de state in de spring of 1865," an old slave told a WPA interviewer years later. "I just reckon I 'member dat freedom to de end of my life."[18]

As did so many others. Near Herndon, Georgia, a slave woman suggested to an officer that the ornate home of her master should be burned. When he asked why, she replied that, "'Cause there has been so much devilment here, whipping niggers 'most to death to make 'em work to pay for it."[19] Slaves told Sherman's men of the awful cruelties they had endured, then laughed and cheered, a reporter noted, when soldiers torched factories and tore up railroad tracks. "Many a dark population has worked on dat [railroad]" an old slave explained, looking at the now twisted rails, "contractor for dis section whipped some of 'em to death—buried one in dose woods."[20]

* * *

But the Civil War was fought to preserve the Union, not to free the slaves, although it is true that the South did fight hard and bravely to preserve slavery—and with it, state's rights, and a totalitarian way of life based on both. But Union armies responded to the first shots fired at Fort Sumter, South Carolina only to assert the authority of the federal government to prevent the secession of the states that had aligned themselves against the Union in a new Confederacy. What the government of the United States did about the issue of slavery was incidental to its primary objective of reunifying the country.

No one believed this more fervently than Abraham Lincoln. Despite his reputation as the "Great Emancipator," President Lincoln's goal, some would say his obsession, throughout his administration, was to preserve the Union; it was not to liberate black men and women enslaved by an institution he personally abhorred. As far as Lincoln was concerned, the issue of slavery was on the bargaining table, a matter he was willing to negotiate. Regardless of his personal feelings and opposition to slavery, Lincoln's public position on the issue was pragmatic, political, and negotiable. He made this abundantly clear in many public statements, among them a letter in August 1862 to Horace Greeley, perhaps the most influential newspaper publisher in the country:

My paramount object in this struggle is to save the Union.... If I could save the Union without freeing any slave I would do it, and if I could save it by freeing all the slaves, I would do it; and if I could save it by freeing some and leaving others alone, I would also do that. What I do about slavery and the colored race, I do because it helps save the Union.[21]

A majority in Congress agreed, seeing themselves and those they represented as being very different culturally and biologically from African slaves. Most believed that slavery was a matter for the states to decide individually, despite the wide publicity the tiny abolitionist movement gave to its horrors. Congress had no Constitutional authority, most of its members insisted, to intrude into the internal affairs of the states. But that changed when the war began. Then Congress reacted decisively on the issue of secession; but it was not clear during the first two years of the war whether any slaves would be freed, whatever the outcome.

Ultimately, it was military necessity and not morality that finally forced Congress and President Lincoln to confront the issue of slavery, but their ambivalence, even on those grounds was apparent. Both Congress and the president understood that most white Americans, not simply Southerners, were opposed to emancipation, or cared little about it one way or another. Lincoln himself was genuinely worried about the consequences of abruptly freeing some four million slaves and was hesistant to do so.

The Emancipation Proclamation, issued on January 1, 1863, was Lincoln's most controversial and unpopular act during an administration characterized by unusual criticism and controversy. It was roundly condemned by whites North and South.

* * *

Although the Proclamation had little immediate practical effect in physically freeing slaves (it also excluded slaveholding Unionists in the border states from its provisions), it did liberate their spirits. After years of abortive attempts to free themselves, or believing that freedom would be theirs only in the next world, it now seemed within reach. For emancipation was for the first time linked to the president's unyielding desire to preserve the Union. As word spread across the South, slave labor became less predictable. Slowdowns and shortages made supply lines uncertain for hard-pressed Confederate armies. As sullen slaves moved slowly about their tasks, others fled to Union-controlled territory, tens of thousands volunteering for military service to hasten an end now, it seemed, in sight. Quick to seize the advantage of this potential new source of manpower, Lincoln's secretary of war, Edwin M. Stanton, authorized the recruitment and formation of black regiments in the Union army.

Next to emancipation itself, Stanton's action was the most momentous of the war for blacks, for it joined the issue of freedom with equality. After generations of unarmed and futile slave resistance, blacks, at last, were given the opportunity to lash back at their oppressors as armed soldiers, man against man. It offered a new and exhilarating experience. Exact figures vary, but by the spring of 1865, approximately 179,000 black men were wearing the blue, with 80 percent of that number coming from the slave and border states. Countless others simply disappeared across Union lines.[22]

As casualty lists grew and their situation became more desperate in the bloody campaigns that followed Gettysburg, Confederate leaders, in similar fashion, also considered impressing slaves into combat. But even that desperation was not sufficient to overcome the ghost of Nat Turner and the South's recognition of the risks, and perhaps the irony, in arming black men to fight to remain enslaved. It was difficult even for a Southerner, steeped for generations in the arts of denial and self-deception on racial matters, to imagine that black men could be counted upon to fight *for* Confederate officers who had possibly sold their parents, raped their sisters, and laid open their own backs with the lash. Instead, slaves were often taken from their masters and pressed into the most arduous labor under the command of hard-pressed Confederate officers who, unlike slaveowners, had not even a remote economic interest in their welfare. Maltreatment and suffering were commonplace. Impressed slaves were customarily assigned to work that involved great hardship and the risk of disease in locations considered too difficult or dangerous for whites. Men toiling in malarial swamps, salt mines, smallpox hospitals, and burying gangrenous bodies were likely to be black. With many rebel soldiers hungry, in rags, and fighting shoeless by the end of the war, it is not surprising that slaves fared so badly.[23]

Conditions in the Union army were better for blacks, but racism and discrimination were rampant. Black soldiers were assigned disproportionately to fatigue duty until the last year of the war, shouldering shovels and axes instead of muskets, pushing wheelbarrows instead of canons, performing work that otherwise would be done by prisoners manacled to balls and chains. Living conditions were also much worse for black soldiers than they were for whites. In Missouri, for example, more than a third of three black regiments died from diseases associated with the inadequate shelter and poor sanitation that distinguished their units from whites.[24] But perhaps the most galling form of discrimination was unequal pay. Black soldiers, regardless of rank, were paid ten dollars a month compared to a base pay for whites that started at thirteen dollars and increased with rank. Many black regiments demanded equality and refused to accept discriminatory pay. Shamed by the glaring injustice, Congress finally responded in June 1864 with an appropriations bill authorizing equal pay for black soldiers retroactive to January 1, 1864.[25]

The South's fears about the loyalty of its slaves led to even harsher discipline and the imposition of more stringent controls. And those black men who abandoned slavery for a blue uniform in the fight against it knew that severe punishment and hardship were almost certain for the families they left behind. As the following affidavit from a black soldier's wife in Kentucky illustrates, those who remained behind found themselves at the mercy of cruel and frustrated men:

> I am a married woman and have four children.... When my husband enlisted my master beat me over the head with an axe handle saying he did so that he beat me for letting [my husband] go off. He bruised my head so that I could not lay it against a pillow without the greatest pain. Last week my niece who lived with me [fled to the Union lines]. This made my master very angry and last monday March 20 1865 he asked me where the girl had gone. I could not tell him. He then whipped me over the head and said he would give me two hundred lashes if I did not get the girl back before the next day.... [On Wednesday] He then tied my hands and threw the rope over a joist stripped me entirely naked and gave me about three hundred lashes. I cried out. He then caught me by the throat and almost choked me then continued to lash me with switches until my back was all cut up...when I ran away I had to leave my children...[26]

Another slave woman described how she was sought out and brutally beaten because of her son's enlistment:

> [My son's former master] brought a gun and threatened to shoot me if I offered to resist or run.... [He] then came up with a large whip & accosted me saying he would have to die before seeing me as he wanted to live to give me one good thrashing.... [He] then took me off from the house about 1/2 mile into the woods. He then took the bridal rein from his buggy & hung me up by the neck for some time & then took me down & compelled me by force to strip naked & then tied my hands to a limb of the tree so that my feet but just touched the ground. then cut limbs from the trees with which he scourged me for a long time whipping from my head to my feet cutting some severe gashes & among some of the injuries inflicted he broke one of my fingures with the but end of his heavy whip...[27]

Black combat soldiers who were captured by Confederate forces had much to fear, for they were considered traitors rather than prisoners of war and treated accordingly. A Union officer described a massacre of over three hundred soldiers that followed when his unit, two-thirds of whom were black, was overwhelmed at Fort Pillow, Tennessee in April 1864:

> [Recognizing] that it would be useless to offer further resistence, our men threw down their arms and surrendered. For a moment the fire seemed to slacken. The scene which followed, however, beggars all description. The enemy carried our works at about four o'clock P.M., and from that time until dark and at intervals throughout the night, our men were shot down without mercy and almost without regard to color. This horrid work of butchery did not cease even with the night of murder, but was renewed again the next morning, when numbers of our wounded were basely murdered, after a long night of pain and suffering on the field where they had fought so bravely. Of this display of Southern Chivalry, of this whole sale butchery of brave men—white as well as black—after they had surrendered; and of the innumerable barbarities committed by the rebels on our sick in Hospital and the bodies of our dead...[were] horrid in the extreme and fully confirming even the most seemingly exagerated Statements.[28]

Later the same year a black soldier, Sam Johnson, described a similar slaughter he narrowly escaped in Plymouth, North Carolina:

> Upon the capture of Plymouth by the Rebel forces, all the negros found in blue uniform or with any outward marks of a Union soldier upon him was killed...I saw some taken into the woods and hung.... Others I saw stripped of all their clothing, and they stood upon the bank of the river with their faces riverwards and then they were shot.... Still others were killed by having their brains beaten out by the butt end of the muskets in the hands of the Rebels...
>
> All were not killed the day of the capture.... Those that were not, were placed in a room with their officers, they (the Officers) having previously been dragged through the town with ropes around their necks, where they were kept confined until the following morning when the remainder of the black soldiers were killed.[29]

Black soldiers fighting in the Civil War were actually engaged in two important conflicts: one a savage battle with the Confederacy for their freedom; the other a tenacious struggle to obtain something approaching equal treatment from the Union officers and men who were fighting, at least in theory, in the same cause. But neither Confederate atrocities nor discrimination within the ranks of the army they served slackened the flow of blacks into Union service.[30] Along with freedom, military service provided an important first step in a black soldier's quest for equality. Enlistment assured a black soldier's freedom, but the act of putting his own life on the line in combat also provided feelings of purpose, accomplishment, pride, and with them, an insistence from that moment onward that he be treated as a man like any other. Those rare emotions, all but denied under slavery, are reflected in the words of Corporal Thomas Long, a black soldier who spoke to his regiment at a Sunday morning service in March 1864:

> If we hadn't become sojers, all might have gone back as it was before; our freedom might have slipped through de two houses of Congress & President Linkum's four years might have passed by & notin been done for we. But now tings can never go back, because we have showed our energy & our courage & our naturally manhood.
>
> Anoder ting is, suppose you had kept your freedom widout enlisting in dis army; your chilen might have grown up free, & been well cultivated so as to be equal to any business; but it would have been always flung in dere faces—"Your fader never fought for he own freedom"—and what could dey answer? *Neber can say that to dis African race any more*, (bringing down his hand with the greatest emphasis on the table). Tanks to dis regiment, never can say dat any more, because we first showed dem we could fight by dere side.[31]

* * *

Black soldiers fighting in the cause of their own freedom also meant that the government's inaction on the slavery issue could no longer continue as the war drew to a close. Corporal Long was right, things could never go back; slavery had to be abolished; compromise was no longer an option. But by the time the Thirteenth Amendment was ratified on December 18, 1865, Lincoln had been assassinated and a Southerner, Andrew Johnson, was president and schemes were already in the works to subvert it.

Years after the assassination, one of his generals, Benjamin F. Butler, claimed that Lincoln had confided to him shortly before he was assassinated that he feared the outbreak of a race war in the South after the armistice. According to Butler, Lincoln restated his belief that colonization was probably the only way to avoid it. "I can hardly believe that the South and North can live in peace, unless we can get rid of the negroes," Butler recalled him saying. Another source close to Lincoln, Gideon Welles, the secretary of the navy, said that Lincoln feared that "the disbanded [Confederate] armies would turn into robber bands and guerillas" who would use force to supplant slavery.

Some historians have disputed the accuracy of Lincoln's reported views on colonization but, as following chapters will reveal, there can be little doubt about the foresight of his prediction that a defeated South would wage an undeclared war against its former slaves, if need be, to regain control over them. It must have been just as evident to a man of Lincoln's insight that black men who had fought and won their freedom would not easily give it up.[32]

Notes

1. R.M. Kennedy, *Mellows: A Chronicle of Unknown Singers* (New York, 1925); quoted in L.W. Levine, *Black Culture and Black Consciousness* (New York: Oxford University Press, 1977), 159.
2. "Many Thousands Gone," in W.F. Allen, C.P. Ware and L.Mck. Garrison, *Slave Songs of the U.S.* (New York: A. Simpson & Co., 1867); see, also, A. Lomax, *The Folk Songs of North America* (New York: Doubleday, 1960), 455–456. In more recent times, the song has been recorded as "No More Auction Block" by Odetta, Pete Seeger, and Bob Dylan.
3. H. Aptheker, *American Negro Slave Revolts* (New York: International Publishers, 1987; orig., 1943).
4. See, for example, E.D. Genovese, *From Rebellion to Revolution: Afro-American Slave Revolts in the Making of the Modern World* (Baton Rouge: Louisiana State University Press, 1979); G.W. Mullin, *Flight and Rebellion: Slave Resistance in Eighteenth-Century Virginia* (New York: Oxford University Press, 1972); F.M. Szasz, "The New York State Slave Revolt of 1841: A Re-Examination," *New York History* XXVIII (July 1967), 215–230; J.D.L. Holmes, "The Abortive Slave Revolt at Point Coupee, Louisiana, 1795," *Louisiana History* XI (Fall 1970), 341–362; J.H. Dorman, "The Persistent Spectre: Slave Rebellion in Territorial Louisiana," *Louisiana History* XVIII (Fall 1977), 389–404; and T.P. Slaughter, *Bloody Dawn: The Christiana Riot and Racial Violence in the Antebellum North* (New York: Oxford University Press, 1991).
5. M. Newton and J.A. Newton, *Racial & Religious Violence in America: A Chronology* (New York: Garland, 1991), 9–187;
6. For the most complete general accounts, see, Genovese, *From Rebellion to Revolution*; and Aptheker, *American Negro Slave Revolts*.
7. R.M. Brown, *Strain of Violence* (New York: Oxford University Press, 1975), 190–191.
8. Newton and Newton, *Racial and Religious Violence*, 31–65.
9. Newton and Newton, *Racial & Religious Violence*, 38–65.
10. Aptheker, *American Negro Slave Revolts*, 219–222.
11. Newton and Newton, *Racial & Religious Violence*, 66–69.
12. Newton and Newton, *Racial & Religious Violence*, 70.
13. Aptheker, *American Negro Slave Revolts*, 264–273; Newton and Newton, *Racial & Religious Violence*, 80.
14. Newton and Newton, *Racial & Religious Violence*, 82–84.
15. Aptheker, *American Negro Slave Revolts*, 293–302; Newton and Newton, *Racial & Religious Violence*, 86.
16. J. Williamson, *A Rage for Order* (New York: Oxford University Press, 1986), 7–12.
17. C.V. Woodward and E. Muhlenfeld (eds.) *The Private Diary of Mary Chestnut: The Unpublished Civil War Diaries* (New York: Oxford University Press, 1984), March 20, 1861, 132.
18. G.P. Rawick (ed.) *The American Slave: A Composite Autobiography* Series I, V.III, South Carolina Narratives, P. 4, (Westport, CT: Greenwood Press, 1972), 92–93.
19. Henry Hitchcock Diary, December 1, 1864, Henry Hitchcock Papers, Library of Congress; quoted in C. Royster, *The Destructive War* (New York: Alfred A. Knopf, 1991), 344.
20. Henry Hitchcock Diary, November 17, 1864, Henry Hitchcock Papers, Library of Congress; quoted in Royster, *The Destructive War*, 344.

21. R.P. Basler (ed.), *Abraham Lincoln: His Speeches and Writings* (Cleveland, OH: World Publishing, 1946), 652.

22. Berlin et al., *The Black Military Experience*, Series II, 12, 13–15.

23. I. Berlin et al., *Freedom: A Documentary History of Emancipation, 1861–1867, The Destruction of Slavery* Series I, Vol. I (New York: Cambridge University Press, 1985), 672–673.

24. Berlin et al., *The Black Military Experience*, Series II, 483–487.

25. Berlin et al., *The Black Military Experience*, Series II, 362–368.

26. Affidavit of Clarissa Burdett, 27 Mar. 1865, filed with H-8 1865, Registered Letters Received, ser. 3379, TN Asst. Comr., RG 105 [A 6148], National Archives; reproduced in Berlin et al., *The Destruction of Slavery*, Series I, Vol. I, Doc. 237, 615–616.

27. Affidavit of Minerva Banks, 19 Sept. 1865, enclosed in Buck & McMullen to Brig. Gen. C. B. Fisk, 19 Sept. 1865, B-128 1865, Registered Letters Received, ser. 3379, TN Asst. Comr., RG 105 [A-6084] National Archives; reproduced in Berlin et al., *The Destruction of Slavery*, Series I, Vol. I, Doc. 253, 654.

28. Lt. Mack J. Leaming to Hon. Edwin M. Stanton, 17 Jan. 1865, v. 32, Union Battle Reports, ser. 729, War Records Office, RG 94 [HH-4] National Archives; reproduced in Berlin et al., *The Black Military Experience*, Series II, Doc. 214c, 546–547; see, also, U.S. Congress, Joint Committee on the Conduct and Expenditures of the War, "Fort Pillow Massacre," *House Reports*, 38th Cong., 1st sess., no. 65.

29. Maj. Gen. Benj. F. Butler to Lieut. Gen. U. S. Grant, 12 July 1864, enclosing affidavit of Samuel Johnson, 11 July 1864, V-92 1864, Letters Received by General Grant, ser. 105, Headquarters in the Field, RG 108 [S-30], National Archives; reproduced in Berlin et al., *The Black Military Experience*, Series II, Doc. 236, 589.

30. See, for example, Berlin et al., *The Destruction of Slavery*, Series I, Vol. I, 48, 54, 265, 338, 411, 481–482, 513, 517, 608, 610, 613, 615–618, 623–624, 654–655.

31. Thomas Wentworth Higginson, March 24, 1864, Higginson Papers, Houghton Library, Harvard University; quoted in J. M. McPherson, *The Negro's Civil War* (New York: Ballantine, 1991; orig., 1965), 217.

32. B.F. Butler, *Autobiography and Personal Remembrances: Butler's Book* (Boston, 1892), 903; H.K. Beale (ed.), *Diary of Gideon Welles, Secretary of the Navy Under Lincoln and Johnson* (New York, 1960), II, 279; quoted in M.E. Neely, Jr., "Abraham Lincoln and Black Colonization: Benjamin Butler's Spurious Testimony," *Civil War History* 25, 1, (March 1979), 77–83; and G.M. Frederickson, "A Man but Not a Brother: Abraham Lincoln and Racial Equality," *Journal of Southern History* XLI (February 1975), 57.

5

The Paradox of Emancipation

"Wherever I go—the street, the shop, the house, the hotel, or the steamboat—I hear the people talk in such a way as to indicate that they are yet unable to conceive of the negro as possessing any rights at all. Men who are honorable in their dealings with their white neighbors will cheat a negro without feeling a single twinge of their honor. To kill a negro they do not deem murder; to debauch a negro woman they do not think fornication; to take the property away from a negro they do not consider robbery. The people boast that when they get freedmen affairs in their own hands, to use their own classic expression, 'the niggers will catch hell'...whenever opportunity serves they treat the colored people just as their profit, caprice or passion may dictate."

—A federal official in Louisiana, September 28, 1865[1]

The South's defeat and the end of slavery meant the nation then had to decide how to rebuild Southern society, both socially and economically, in its absence. The attempt to address those issues after the war marked the beginning of what historians call "Presidential Reconstruction." In light of President Lincoln's views on racial equality and his successor's agreement with them, it is not surprising that the terms of surrender were more lenient than one might have expected during the last two destructive years of the war. But Lincoln had made his intentions regarding the postwar South clear as early as December 1863 when he issued his Proclamation of Amnesty and Reconstruction. It was the terms set out in that earlier proclamation that Andrew Johnson followed when he became president. Johnson's goal, like Lincoln's, was to restore self-government as quickly as possible in the South. Neither had any intention of transforming the South, or its institutions, except to prohibit slavery. Lincoln did allow that he favored state legislation to provide education for former slaves that was "consistent as a temporary arrangement with their present condition as a laboring, landless, and homeless class."[2]

Perhaps the most immediate symbolic threat to white supremacy was the presence in the South of some eighty thousand black soldiers still in uniform after the war ended. Regardless of how they behaved, armed black soldiers were something Southern whites, obsessed for generations with the fear of black insurgency, refused to tolerate. Nothing was viewed as being more disruptive of a return to "normal" race relations. Nor did anything else so anger a region that had sacrificed approximately one-quarter of its able-bodied young men in a lost cause. Accused and suspected of every conceivable crime and impropriety, black soldiers found it difficult to defend themselves. The punishments inflicted on them by their own Union officers, for example, exceeded those meted out to white soldiers for the same infractions, and often compared with treatment they had endured as slaves.

"A report of any white citizen against one of our men, whether it be credible or not, is sufficient to punish the accused," a black soldier complained. "Men have been bucked and gagged in their company streets, exposed to the scorching rays of the sun and the derision of the majority of officers, who seem to take delight in witnessing their misery."[3]

There was overwhelming evidence when the war ended that white soldiers, whether in Union blue or Confederate gray, were closing ranks against their black counterparts. A traveler, spending the night with a South Carolina plantation owner a few months after the war ended recorded this dinner table conversation:

> "I met Dr. M____," said one of the ladies, "as I come down, and he said they begun to form a company to protect us against the niggers. He was goin' to be the commissary, he said, and they'd chosen the commander, too. I told him that's what ruined us before; there was too many wanting to be officers, and not enough of soldiers.
> "I hadn't heard anything of that," said her uncle, "but it's going to be necessary. I'm told that the nigger soldiers in Georgetown have been getting very independent latterly; but the Yankee officers, they say, make short work of it with 'em. I hear that one or two of 'em were shot down last week, and tumbled into the river, man and gun.
> "Who did it?
> "Their own officers, the Yankees. That's a case of nigger shooting that won't be trumpeted all over Lincolndom, I expect.
> "I wish they'd shoot 'em all," said his wife; "I'm glad when I hear o' one of 'em got out o' the way. If I could get up tomorrow morning and hear that every nigger in the country was dead, I'd just jump up and down."[4]

"I candidly confess" volunteered a wealthy planter whose South Carolina estate spread back from the banks of the Great Pedee river, "that I look forward to the extermination of the freedmen."[5]

With President Johnson anxious to appease Southerners like these, it was predictable that black soldiers would be mustered out of the service, or transferred to posts on the western frontier, as quickly as possible.[6]

At the same time black soldiers were disappearing, the Johnson administration was issuing pardons to all but the highest-ranking Confederate civil and military leaders, and persons owning property valued at more than twenty thousand dollars. Persons eligible for pardons were required only to swear an oath of allegiance to the United States, its Constitution, and its laws. With that done, state legislatures and local officials could be elected, conventions convened, new state constitutions drafted, congressional representatives selected, and all property restored except slaves. The only change for newly freed blacks was that their fate would now be in the hands of Southern politicians rather than slaveholders.

Southerners, quick to take advantage of the unexpected presidential leniency, had a foremost objective in mind: that was to restore control over the black population as quickly as possible, putting them back to work rebuilding an economy wrecked by war and debt. Within the limits circumscribed by the Thirteenth Amendment, Southern whites intended to reconstruct a society as close as possible to the one they had fought unsuccessfully to defend.

* * *

Land reform was the most critical racial issue confronted when the war ended. Former slaves understood that without land and the opportunity it provided to become self-sufficient, freedom would remain an empty concept. Owning land and working it, without white supervision and harassment, was every slave's dream. From the beginning, whites were determined to deny that dream. They knew that landless blacks were dependent blacks, with no alternative except to work on terms dictated by them.

It was the actions of General William Tecumseh Sherman that appeared briefly to make that dream a coming reality. As Sherman's men cut a devastating swath across Georgia and South Carolina, a growing multitude of slaves followed in his path, often cheering as flames licked up the sides of buildings and across countless of acres of cotton. Confronted with the obligation to provide somehow for their welfare, and unable to do it with what remained of army rations, Sherman, in desperation, issued Special Field Orders No. 15. The orders granted to slave families "possessory titles" to as much as forty acres of confiscated and abandoned lands along the coastal areas of South Carolina, Georgia, and Florida. There, Sherman instructed, they could build shelters, grow crops and feed themselves without the need of his army's assistance. Sherman's intent was to provide only a temporary reservation for slaves, a battlefield solution to a pressing refugee problem. But by the end of the war some 20,000 former slaves had settled on 100,000 acres of confiscated land.[7]

Sherman's act had the unintended effect of raising hope among slaves that the federal government intended to provide them with "forty acres and a mule" when the war ended. The hope it inspired, the "mania for owning a small piece of land," as one diarist described it, spread quickly.[8]

In 1865, Congress created the Bureau of Refugees, Freedmen and Abandoned Lands over the president's veto. The Freedmen's Bureau, as it was called, was to serve as a relief organization to assist blacks in the transition from slavery to freedom. Among other things, the bureau was to administer the redistribution of some eight hundred thousand acres of abandoned land that were to be returned to production. It was also to establish a race-blind system of justice to administer all new labor arrangements involving former slaves.

Had land been redistributed to former slaves, it would have enhanced their fortunes as nothing else could have; it would have, as well, radically altered the racial status quo in South, and probably the future of American race relations. President Johnson opposed it and even the Radical Republicans in Congress, who were sympathetic to blacks, were ambivalent about giving them land.

The opportunity to own land, it seemed to former slaves, was virtually a birthright in nineteenth-century America. Earlier in the midst of the Civil War, in 1862, Congress had passed the Homestead Act. This momentous act made vast tracts of land in the West available for settlement to white Americans free of charge. It provided tens of thousands of Americans, many of them European immigrants, with an unprecedented opportunity for self-advancement. So enormous were its implications that when the Civil War ended, military commands were moved West to provide protection for the thousands of "homesteaders" who were by then invading the ancestral lands of American Indian tribes.

But the situation was different in the South. There, the confiscated land had been *owned* by white men, not merely *occupied* by Indians. That these same white men had just engaged the United States in the bloodiest war in its history did trouble some members of Congress. Still, that body could not find it within itself to condemn the property of even traitorous white men. The sanctity of private property, it seemed to them, was inviolable; that there was something about condemning a white man's property that struck at the very core of what the nation stood for. So with few exceptions, Southern land remained within white ownership and control.

Without money, very few blacks were able to purchase land, even at depressed postwar prices. Even blacks with money found land purchases difficult, as white landowners, confronted with strong community pressure and threats of violence, refused to sell to them. Even when they were willing, banks refused to loan money to black purchasers. Only a small number of blacks were able to surmount these difficulties to acquire land. Some black Civil War veterans, for example, were able to purchase small plots with their mustering-out pay; other blacks, such as those in the Sea Islands of South Carolina, pooled their meager resources to acquire dispossessed lands; still others acquired "squatters rights" to poor land that no one else wanted; but the vast majority of blacks were denied even the opportunity to acquire land. Many of those who did were subsequently evicted after civil government was restored in the South.[9]

Blacks understood completely the stakes in this new racial power struggle. "Gib us our own land and we take care of ourselves," a black man told a newspaper reporter in Charleston when the war ended, "but widout land, de ole masses can hire us or starve us, as dey please."[10] There was no question about that, for Southerners also understood that landless dependency was essential to their control and exploitation of black labor.

For blacks, the denial of land was not only a devastating disappointment, it was also, in their view, an outrageous injustice. As workers of the land for generations, they felt they had claim to a share of it, especially when the original owners had forfeited their rights in a costly rebellion.

But President Johnson did not see it that way. With hasty pardons he restored property rights to many former Confederates. He then followed with an executive order forbidding federal attorneys to seek confiscation of any additional land. In July 1865, the chief commissioner of the newly established Freedmen's Bureau, General Otis Oliver Howard, issued Circular 13. Following Sherman's lead, this order instructed agents to "set aside" forty-acre tracts for freedmen. But the president ordered him to to rescind the order immediately. Freedmen's Bureau Circular 15 replaced it. Drafted in the White House, and issued by the bureau in September, the new order restored all but a tiny portion of the land to the pardoned former owners.[11] Thus, land ownership was a dream never realized by blacks, a promise never kept. Nothing could have been further from President Johnson's mind as he pressed forward a policy of reconstruction that refused even to consider the notion of land redistribution to former slaves. Black disappointment was profound:

"Why, General Howard, do you take away our lands?" a committee of freedmen in South Carolina wrote, "we want Homesteads,"

> we were promised Homesteads by the government. If it does not carry out the promises its agents made to us, if the government haveing concluded to befriend its late enemies and to neglect to observe the principles of common faith between its self and us its allies in the war you said was over, now takes away from them all right to the soil they stand upon save such as they can get by working for *your* late and their *all time* enemies...we are left in a more unpleasant condition than former.... You will see this is not the condition of really freemen.
>
> You ask us to forgive the land owners of our island. *You* only lost your right arm in war and might forgive them. The man who tied me to a tree and gave me 39 lashes and who stripped and flogged my mother and my sister and who will not let me stay in his empty hut except I will do his planting and be satisfied with his price and who combines with others to keep away land from me well knowing I would not have anything to do with him if I had land of my own—that man, *I cannot well forgive*. Does it look as if he has forgiven me, seeing how he tries to keep me in a condition of helplessness?[12]

As troops were evicting freedman Bayley Wyat from land he had claimed in Virginia, he cried out in frustration and anger:

> We has a right to the land where we are located. For why? I tell you. Our wives, our children, our husbands, has been sold over and over again to purchase the lands we now locates upon; for that reason we have a divine right to the land.... And den didn't we clear the land, and raise de crops ob corn, ob cotton, ob tobacco, ob rice, ob sugar, ob everything. And den didn't dem large cities in de North grow up on de cotton and de sugars and de rise dat we made?...I say dy has grown rich, and my people is poor.[13]

When people who are victimized cry out in anger, as Bayley Wyat and many others like him did, refusing to accept their fate as mere misfortune, we hear the unequivocal voice of injustice.[14] Wyat understood that poor is the way Southern whites wanted black people to remain. Free, perhaps, but without land, poor. Rationalizations were offered by some for the refusal to redistribute land. Among them was the argument that the undeniable black preference for food crops and subsistence agriculture would result in the land not being used productively to grow cotton, a crop that many former slaves, understandably, detested as the "slave crop." Cotton was associated in their minds, one textile manufacturer observed after the war, "with memories of the overseer, the driver, and the lash, in fact with the whole system of slavery."[15]

But political power and economic advantage were the real reasons land was not redistributed to blacks in the South. In an agricultural economy those who control the land, control society. Both races understood that if blacks remained landless, emancipation would change little about the way both races had lived for centuries. The policy ensured, as one Union officer observed, "a practical return to slavery."[16]

* * *

With or without land, however, in the absence of a system of equal justice, freedom would remain but an empty dream.[17] Nothing illustrates the failure of Reconstruction more clearly than the Freedmen's Bureau's inability, despite good intentions and sometimes sincere efforts, to establish a system of justice worthy of the name in the South.

Within months of Appomattox, the charitable terms of the Johnson Administration's policy had been met and legislatures convened across the South to draft new constitutions. As these new legislatures met, one observer predicted accurately, "Their whole thought and time will be given to plans for getting things back as near to slavery as possible."[18] He was right. Included within the new legislation passed with great haste were laws that specifically defined the new terms of existence for the former slaves. These "Black Codes," as they were called, denied or restricted the civil rights of blacks to a degree that amounted to virtual reenslavement. For even though slavery had been abolished, white supremacy continued, and the assumptions, values and actions that had nurtured it for generations remained essentially unchanged. It is not surprising, therefore, that in addition to denying them land, that blacks did, as Southerners put it, "catch hell."

Under the pretense of providing certain new rights for blacks—for example, to marry one another, make contracts, sue and be sued, and the largely illusory right to own and acquire property—the real purpose of the Black Codes was to control and maintain the subservient position of black agricultural labor. With that objective in mind, these codes, often supplemented with local ordinances, contained provisions that were intended "to keep niggers in their place."

Codes varied from state to state, but most contained certain essential elements. Restrictions were placed on whether and where a black could own, lease, or rent property. In some states, like South Carolina, restrictions were placed on when and where blacks were permitted to sell farm produce. Ownership of firearms was either tightly restricted or denied. Hunting, fishing and grazing rights were also restricted, all with the purpose of ensuring black dependency on whites for food. In addition, curfews and travel restrictions limited their evening activities and mobility in and out of white-only zones. There was no more than a twilight to dusk distinction between slavery and what followed under the Black Codes. One of the "revised" statutes passed by the Mississippi legislature in 1865, for example, stated that

> all penal and criminal laws *now in force* in this State, defining offences and pre-scribing the mode of punishment for crimes and misdemeanors committed by slaves, free negroes or mulattoes...are hereby *reenacted*, and declared to be in full force and effect, against freedmen, free negroes and mulattoes, except so far as the mode and manner of trial and punishment have been changed or altered by law.[19]

Under these new laws, blacks were prohibited from earning a living in any job other than plantation labor and on terms agreeable to white employers. State enforced labor contracts ensured long hours, low wages, and extended commitments that had to be met before wages were paid. Quitting a contract job was considered a criminal offense for blacks, punishable by whipping, being placed in stocks, or up to a year of uncompensated labor. The same offense for whites was resolved as a civil matter. Such restrictions, which bound an employee to low wages and possibly intolerable working conditions, were then buttressed with "anti-enticement" laws which made it a crime for an employer to hire workers away from another by offering higher wages or other in-centives.[20] The labor regulations and criminal laws included in the Black Codes left blacks virtually powerless to defend themselves, for they were not permitted to sit on juries or to testify in court against whites. The state systems of criminal justice were rigged to deny them any voice whatsoever.[21]

* * *

Perhaps the most outrageous of these new state laws were those con-cerned with vagrancy. Vagrancy convictions became a primary means to ensure that involuntary labor would be available, when needed, to public or private employers. Criminal codes were rewritten, defining this victimless offense so broadly that virtually any black man without a hoe in his hand and a white person to speak on his behalf, could be arrested and required to prove his employment. If he could not, to the satisfaction of his accuser and a justice of the peace, the vagrant could be fined or jailed. Since few unemployed blacks had money to pay fines, jail was the usual outcome.

In Mississippi, for example, blacks had to have written evidence of a lawful home as well as pay a one dollar per year capitation tax or be subject to arrest for vagrancy.[22] This net of entrapment snared more than the unemployed. Almost anyone could be arrested under broadly cast vagrancy statutes: transients, prostitutes, persons selling or entertaining without a license, gamblers and persons who "misspend what they earn," fortune tellers, disobedient persons, beggars, and drunkards. "The vagrant contemplated," an Alabama legislator admitted, "was the plantation negro."[23]

In the same fashion, the police and courts preyed upon the hungry who stole food to feed themselves and their families. Stealing a few ears of corn or a melon from a white man's fields often meant a sentence of weeks or months of hard labor. "Three days for stealing, and eighty-seven for being colored," a black newspaper editor in New Orleans complained of the sentencing practices.[24]

Whatever the crime, however, few blacks remained in jail, for that would have defeated the purpose of the new system. Instead, local magistrates were authorized to "hire out" arrestees. A black male arrested for vagrancy or petty theft soon found himself working on convict labor gangs. Or he might have his fine paid by an employer, who would then work the vagrant without compensation until he had repaid the debt to the employer's satisfaction.

* * *

In similar fashion, apprenticeship laws were drafted by state legislatures which turned over custody of black children to white guardians/employers if a judge ruled that doing so was "better for the habits and comfort" of the child. Orphans and children from large families whose parents were deemed unable to support them were the most likely victims. Too often the "guardian" was a former slaveholder who sought to exploit the labor of his impoverished former slaves' children. Moreover, children entrapped by apprenticeship laws were subject to corporal punishment for disobedience. Just as the slaves they once again were, they could be whipped or worse by their so-called guardians/masters, and often were.

In Alabama, for example, John Childers, a former slave, wept as he told congressional investigators of the fate of his ten-year-old daughter:

"I found my little daughter at home. She had run away from this place where she was abused; But I saw the rest of the children playing in the yard, and she was in the door sitting there, and I thought that was strange because she was a mighty playful child, and I asked, 'What are you sitting here for?' And she says, 'Pappa, I am so sore I can't play…Mr. Jones has beat me nearly to death.' I says, 'He did?' She says, 'Yes.'

"She was hired out as a nurse to see to [the Jones'] baby; she had taken the baby out in the front yard among a parcel of arbor vitae; and being out there, the baby and she together, she was neglectful, so as to leave the baby's cap out where it was not in the place when the mother of the child called for the cap, and it could not be found. That is what she told me when I came home that she was whipped for…

"'[She said] Look here, Papa, where he cut me,' and there were great gashes on her thighs, as long as my finger…I charged on her mother then for hiring her to Mr. Jones…She says, "…Mr. Jones told me he would treat my children well if I would let him have them.'"

A witness who saw the incident described what the Joneses had done to the little girl:

"Mrs. Jones slapped her down in the house and stamped her, [the child tried to run away. Whereupon], Mr. Jones got on his mare and run and overtook her…she was scared and told him she [did not intend to] run away. He took her in the peach orchard and whipped her under a peach-tree and stamped her, and took her to the fence by the coattail and throwed her over and struck her on the fence twice, and he knocked the blood out of her, and then turned her loose and told her to go," [saying], "he would take her from under her mammy's coattail and kill her, God damn her."

Eight days later Amanda Childers died of her injuries.[25]

In Alabama, Mississippi, and Kentucky, former slaveowners, such as Mr. and Mrs. Jones, were given preference in apprenticeship assignments. Using the ruses of guardianship and apprenticeship, the courts were able to keep employers supplied with the cheap labor of orphans or any children whose desperate parents were unable to feed and clothe them; still other parents were deemed unsuitable by white judges. In Maryland and North Carolina, for example, thousands of children were turned over to white guardians without the consent, and sometimes without the knowledge, of their parents. In this manner, the tradition of *disrupting black families for economic gain* that began with slave sales was given legal sanction by Southern courts after emancipation. Appalling levels of child abuse and neglect occurred under these circumstances, but were rarely investigated by state authorities.[26]

* * *

The Freedmen's Bureau failed almost completely to address crimes such as these. It also failed in its mission to ensure fair labor contracts and standards for black adults. Bureau courts were the first disappointing experience blacks had with the federal justice system, despite the fact that these courts were specifically established to provide a just alternative to the notoriously unfair state judicial proceedings. Bureau courts were authorized, for example, to intervene in state civil proceedings if blacks were denied fair treatment. But bureau agents rarely did so successfully. In every Southern state but Louisiana, the testimony of blacks was excluded from state civil courts. Southern whites were adamant in their refusal to accept equal justice, but especially so with respect to black testimony against them in court.

"Well, don't it seem kind o' hard to hev a nigger come an' make oath agin ye—a right coal-black nigger?" a white woman in Lumberton, North Carolina asked, expressing the concerns of Southerners everywhere. "How is that? Is it right or ain't it?"

"Well...I'll tell you what I think," a man in Fayetteville insisted, "a white man can't live in this country if a nigger can get to testify. I want to wait till they have more of an idea of the nature of an oath before I let one of them give evidence against me. Why, our lives wouldn't be safe."[27]

Another offered the more valid point that it was useless to have blacks testify because all-white juries would not believe them. "[Blacks have] the right to testify for and against each other in cases where no white man is concerned," he said,

> they have always had, and of course it will be continued to them; but I don't think the Southern people are prepared to admit nigger testimony against a white man. What would be the good of putting niggers in the witness-box? You must have niggers in the jury-box, too, or nigger evidence will not be believed. I don't think you could find twelve men in the whole state who would attach any weight to the testimony of ninety-nine niggers in a hundred."[28]

These folks from North Carolina echoed the views of most white Southerners. Black complaints against white employers who cheated them were inadmissable in state and local courts. Thus bureau courts were overwhelmed with such complaints, but failed to respond effectively to most of them. Blacks also learned that although they could offer testimony in bureau courts, there was little to be gained and much to be lost. Violent retaliation that the bureau was powerless to prevent, and unlikely to prosecute, was a certain response.[29]

Nor was the bureau anxious to move into this area. Its agents—carpetbaggers and scalawags in the eyes of Southern whites—quickly learned that ensuring racial justice for black men and women in the South entailed placing one's own fortunes and life at risk. Within six months of the South's surrender, Freedmen's Bureau schools, churches, meeting halls, and, for that matter, any place blacks assembled had become targets of white wrath throughout the South. Records of the bureau reveal that atrocities were so common that the risk of the race war Lincoln reportedly feared before his death could not be discounted and, indeed, was viewed as a distinct possibility.[30]

The assaults on bureau agents and blacks were wanton, perverse, often without immediate provocation. It was as though the frustrations of a cause lost in war were now redirected toward the innocent and those who sought to assist them. To whites long accustomed to absolute control, even the most innocent black person's deviation from a rigid standard of servility was likely to trigger a violent response.

"I have heard planters complain very earnestly of the insubordinate spirit of their colored laborers," Carl Schurz reported after the war, "because they remonstrated against the practice of corporal punishment. This was looked upon as a symptom of an impending insurrection."[31]

"I know the nigger," a Virginia planter explained only three months after Appomattox,

> The employer must have some sort of *punishment*. I don't care what it is. If you'll let me tie him up by the thumbs or keep him on bread and water, that will do. Over here in Rockbridge County, as I came along I saw a nigger tied up by the wrists. His hands were away up above his head. I went along to him, and says I, 'Boy, which would you like best now, to stay there where you are, or to have me take you down, give you forty good cuts, and let you go?' 'Rather have the forty lash,' says he. So he would, too. You folks used to make a good deal of talk because we gave our niggers a flogging when they deserved it. I won't ask leave to flog, if you'll let me use some of your Northern punishments. All I want is just to have it so that when I get the niggers on to my place, and the work is begun, they can't sit down and look me square in the face and do nothing.[32]

Southern women were no different. "It is hard to have to lay our loved ones in the grave," a white woman in Georgia explained as the war was drawing to a close, "to have them fall by thousands on the battle-field, to be stripped of everything. But the hardest of all is nigger equality, and I won't submit to it."[33]

* * *

And the South did not submit. The old phobias remained. Southern whites believed that neither military defeat nor emancipation had given blacks the right to be treated as equals, or to treat *them* as equals. It was an attitude, indeed it was the *culture* of white supremacy, that the Freedmen's Bureau could not change. Limited by insufficient funds, too few personnel, and the unyielding hostility of white Southerners, the bureau efforts to bring racial justice to the South were doomed to failure from the very beginning. By October 1866, barely a year after the its courts were established, state civil authorites had regained control of the courts and the system established by the Bureau was coming unraveled. Racial justice in the South was already a mockery.[34]

Blacks could be, and were, vulnerable to attack for virtually any action that could be construed by whites as a departure from the demeanor of slaves. In the eyes of whites, that made them "bad niggers." "Of the countless cases of postwar violence," historian Leon Litwak has written,

> ...the largest portion related in some way to that broad and vaguely defined charge of conduct unbecoming black people—that is, "putting on airs," "sassiness," "impudence," "insolence," "disrespect," "insubordination," contradicting whites, and violating racial customs.[35]

More than seventy years after emancipation, Thomas Hall, who had been a slave in North Carolina, recalled the paradox of the experience:

> Conditions and rules were bad and the punishments were severe and barbarous [under slavery]. Some marsters acted like savages.... Mothers were sold from their children. Children was sold from their mothers, and the father was not considered in anyway as a family part. These conditions were here before the Civil War and the conditions in a changed sense have been here ever since. The whites have always held the slaves in part slavery and are still practicing the same things on them in a different manner...
> Lincoln got the praise for freeing us, but did he do it? He give us freedom *without giving us any chance to live to ourselves* and we still had to depend on the Southern white man for work, food and clothing, and he held us through our necessity and want in a state of servitude but little better than slavery. Lincoln done but little for the negro race and from living standpoint nothing. White folks are not going to do nothing for negroes except keep them down...The Yankees helped free us, so they say, but they let us be put back in slavery again. When I think of slavery it makes me mad...the white folks have been and are now and always will be against the negro.[36]

The paradox of the Thirteenth Amendment was that in freeing slaves from their masters, it made them vulnerable, as never before, to the violent whims of *all* white men. To newly freed slaves expecting more, there was little difference between Southern laws and lawlessness. They were victimized in either case. Still blacks remained overwhelmingly nonviolent as the hopes and dreams of Thomas Hall and countless numbers of others like him sank deeper and finally disappeared in the quagmire of southern injustice.

Notes

1. Col. Samuel Thomas, Asst. Commissioner, Bureau of Refugees, Freedmen, and Abandoned Lands for Mississippi and N.E. Louisiana, to Gen. Carl Schurz, Sept. 28, 1865, in 39 Cong., 1 Sess., Senate Exec. Doc. 2, "Report of Carl Schurz on the States of South Carolina, Georgia, Alabama, Mississippi, and Louisiana," in *Message of the President of the United States*, 81; quoted in L. F. Litwak, *Been in the Storm So Long: The Aftermath of Slavery* (New York: Vintage, 1980), 364.

2. *Statutes at Large*, vol. 13, 737–739; quoted in I. Berlin et al. (eds.), *Freedom: The Wartime Genesis of Free Labor: The Lower South*, Series I, Vol. III (New York: Cambridge University Press, 1990), 57–58.

3. J.R. Dennett, *The South As It Is: 1865–1866* (New York: Viking, 1965; orig. 1865–66), 193–94.

4. Quoted in Dennett, *The South As It Is*, 193–194.

5. J.R. Dennett, *The South As It Is*, 191.

6. *Christian Recorder*, September 9, 1865; quoted in Litwak, *Been in the Storm*, 171; see also, 267–270.

7. Special Field Orders, No. 15, Headquarters Military Divisions of the Mississippi, 16 Jan. 1865, Orders & Circulars, wer. 44, RG 94 [DD-38] National Archives; reproduced in Berlin et al. (eds.), *Freedom, The Wartime Genesis of Free Labor*, Series I, Vol. III, Doc. 59, 338–340.

8. A.R. Childs (ed.), *The Private Journal of Henry William Ravenel 1859–1887* (Columbia, SC, 1947), 272; quoted in E. Foner, *Reconstruction, 1863–1877* (New York: Harper & Row, 1988), 104.

9. Foner, *Reconstruction*, 105–106; Berlin et al. (eds.) *Freedom, The Wartime Genesis of Free Labor*, Series I, Vol. III, 57–61.

10. W. Reid, *After the War: A Southern Tour* (Cincinnati, OH, 1866), 59; quoted in Foner, *Reconstruction*, 104.

11. Foner, *Reconstruction*, 159.

12. O.O. Howard, *Autobiography of Oliver Otis Howard*, 2 vols. (New York: Baker & Taylor, 1907), 2: 237–239 (last emphasis added); see, also, Foner, *Reconstruction*, 160.

13. *A Freedman's Speech* (Philadelphia, PA, 1867); quoted in Foner, *Reconstruction*, 105.

14. J.N. Shklar, *The Faces of Injustice* (New Haven, CT: Yale University Press, 1990), 83.

15. A. Warren Kelsey to Edward Atkinson, September 2, 1865, Edward Atkinson Papers, Massachusetts Historical Society; quoted in Foner, *Reconstruction*, 108.

16. H.E. Tremain, *Two Days of War: A Gettysburg Narrative and Other Excursions* (New York, 1905), 276; quoted in Foner, *Reconstruction*, 161.

17. See, for example, J. Oakes, "A Failure of Vision: The Collapse of the Freedmen's Bureau Courts," *Civil War History* 25 (1979), 66–76.

18. B.F. Flanders to H.C. Warmoth, November 23, 1865: quoted in Foner, *Reconstruction*, 199.

19. See, for example, 1865 Mississippi Laws, Ch. IV, V, VI, XXIII, and XLVIII; quoted in J.T. Currie, "From Slavery to Freedom in Mississippi's Legal System," *Journal of Negro History* (Spring 1980), 118–119; see, also, W.E.B. Du Bois, *Black Reconstruction in America: 1860–1880* (New York: Atheneum, 1969; orig., 1935), 167–180; Foner, *Reconstruction*, 199–201, 208–209, 215, 225, 244, 257, 372, 519, 593; and Litwak, *Been in the Storm*, 366–371, 375, 408, 369–370.

20. Foner, *Reconstruction*, 200.
21. C.L. Flynn, *White Land, Black Labor: Caste and Class in Late Nineteenth Century Georgia* (Baton Rouge: Louisiana State University Press, 1983), 123–125; Foner, *Reconstruction*, 202–203.
22. J.W. DuBose, *Alabama's Tragic Decade, 1861–1874*, J.K. Greer (ed.) (Birmingham, AL: Webb, 1940), 55; see, also, Foner, *Reconstruction*, 200–201.
23. Du Bois, *Black Reconstruction*, 173–175; and Litwak, *Been in the Storm*, 319–321, 367–370; Currie, "From Slavery to Freedom, 118; DuBose, *Alabama's Tragic Decade*, 55, quoted in Foner, *Reconstruction*, 201, see, also, 199–200.
24. New Orleans *Tribune*, November 29, 1865; quoted in Litwack, *Been in the Storm*, 286.
25. Testimony of John Childers, November 1, 1871; testimony of Jane Killens, November 1, 1871, *Joint Select Committee to Inquire into the Condition of Affairs in the Late Insurrectionary States*, 13 vols. (Washington, DC, 1872), *House Reports*, 42d Congress, 2d sess., Alabama, 1719–1724, 1733–1734.
26. Du Bois, *Black Reconstruction*, 175–176; Litwak, *Been in the Storm*, 237–238, 365–366; and Foner, *Reconstruction*, 201.
27. Dennett, *The South As It Is*, 168.
28. Dennett, *The South As It Is*, 132.
29. See, for example, V.B. Howard, "The Black Testimony Controversy in Kentucky, 1866–1872," *Journal of Negro History* 58, 2 (1973), 140–165; and B.A. Crouch, "A Spirit of Lawlessness: White Violence; Texas Blacks, 1865–1868," *Journal of Social History* 18 (Winter 1984), 217–232.
30. J.A. Carpenter, "Atrocities in the Reconstruction Period," *Journal of Negro History* 47 (October 1962), 234–247; B.A. Crouch and L.J. Schultz, "Crisis in Color: Racial Separation in Texas During Reconstruction," *Civil War History* 16 (1970), 37–49.
31. U.S. Senate, *Executive Documents*, 39th Congress, 1st sess., no. 2, 31–32; see, also, A.W. Trealease, *White Terror: The Ku Klux Klan Conspiracy and Southern Reconstruction* (New York: Harper & Row, 1971), xxi–xxii.
32. Dennett, *The South As It Is*, 53 (emphasis added).
33. "Carleton" to *Boston Journal*, February 13, 1865, reprinted in *National Freedman*, I (April 1, 1865); quoted in Litwak, *Been in the Storm*, 255.
34. Oakes, "A Failure of Vision," 70.
35. Litwak, *Been in the Storm So Long*, 278.
36. G.P. Rawick (ed.), *The American Slave*, Series 1, V. 14, North Carolina Narratives, 360–362 (emphasis added).

6

The Failure of Reform

"the barbarism of the rebellion [is] in its renaissance."
——A federal official, New Orleans, August 1, 1866[1]

*"My mind ain't sprightly like it used to be, and heaps of
things what went on when I was young, I forgets, and heaps
of them what I want to forget I can't. Them was terrible
days...Our trouble would have all been over, if it hadn't been
for that Ku Klux. Lord have mercy! How they did scare us."*
——Calline Brown, a former slave in Mississippi[2]

Within a year after the Thirteenth Amendment was ratified, freedmen realized that little had changed in their lives. Politicians now made the rules they lived by, instead of slaveholders, while sheriff's deputies and bureaucrats had filled the shoes of overseers. The exploitation and injustice that characterized slavery continued in only slightly altered form.

Freedmen's Bureau reports and newspaper accounts of these conditions called attention to the need for further federal legislation to shield the black population from the hostile state governments that by then were once again ruling their lives. The entire system of criminal justice had been redesigned to entrap, intimidate, and coerce them. White-on-black violence was rampant.[3]

In South Carolina a frustrated Freedmen's Bureau agent reported in November 1865 that, "In the interior of the State, where military force cannot readily reach.... It is difficult to reach the murderers of colored people, as they hide themselves and are screened by their neighbors."

In the Edgefield district of the same state, the report continued,

Several affidavits have been received of cruelties practised here. One freedman with two males and one female children were stripped naked, tied up, and whipped severely, threats of murder being made if complaint was made to the military. Another man was whipped severely with a stick and cut over the eye with a knife,

and, as he ran away to escape from their cruelty, was shot at. A woman was severely whipped and carried off to jail, and, as she has disappeared, fears are enter-
tained that she has been murdered. Two children were severely whipped and their
mother driven off the plantation without any pay for work done.

"One man was shot and killed in the presence of his wife, who begged
for his life," a bureau agent reported from another South Carolina district. "Two other men were tied up, cruelly flogged, then shot (and, it is
believed, killed, as the men have disappeared), while the wife of one of
the men received fifty lashes."[4]

From Georgia, also, in early 1866, with the sights and sounds of the
Civil War still fresh, a Freedmen's Bureau commissioner wrote to report a terrifying state of lawlessness toward blacks. When asked to
investigate certain "outrages" committed against blacks, he described
a local sheriff's reply that "it would be unpopular to punish white men
for anything done to a negro—it might be unsafe—that he was not
going to obey the orders of any 'damned Yankee'—and that the rebellion was not over yet in Henry County." Assistant commissioners from
across the South sent similar reports to the commissioner of the
Freedmen's Bureau, Major General Oliver Otis Howard, describing the
system of justice under the Johnson state governments as a travesty.
"Worse than a farce," one observed; "a condition differing little from…
slavery—save in name," wrote another.[5]

Indeed, little had changed about the South after the Civil War, and
the evidence was everywhere. Some of the flimsy motives behind the
white atrocities on blacks are described in Freedmen's Bureau reports
in words such as, "shot him as he was passing in the street to 'see him
kick';" and "Killed him because he did not take off his hat to Murphy."[6]
Another account described an incident in Louisiana where a black man
answered a white boy "too quickly" and nearly lost his life. The man
was knocked down and beaten by a group of whites, a bureau report
noted, before being "taken thro' town and across the Levee, and there
stripped and terribly beaten [again], with raw-hides by Kingsley, and
some 6 or 8 other men, who put a rope around his neck, nearly choked
him, jumped upon him etc." Local authorities, the report noted, "took
no notice of the affair." In Pine Bluff, Arkansas, whites rounded up
blacks in a small settlement and set fire to their houses. The next morning, a man who discovered the scene reported that the mob had done
more. "[It was] a sight that apald me 24 Negro men woman and children were hanging to trees all round the Cabbins."[7]

The appalling violence and contempt the South demonstrated toward
Washington produced a major political reaction in 1866. That year the

Republican radicals in Congress seized the initiative, intent on restoring civil order in the South. To their dismay, Southern Democrats found themselves, after nearly a year of having things their own way, confronting Republicans committed to serious reform. And reform came quickly in the form of a new civil rights bill that was introduced in January 1866. Only a month later the Civil Rights Act of 1866 became law over President Johnson's veto. The act marked the first attempt by Congress to give meaning to, and to implement, the Thirteenth Amendment.

The act spelled out for the first time what "freedom" was to mean for blacks. It expanded black civil rights and federal authority to protect those rights by making native-born blacks citizens of the United States, "without regard to any previous condition of slavery or involuntary servitude." It also provided them with all rights of citizenship, including "full and equal benefit of all laws and proceedings for the security of person and property, as is enjoyed by white citizens." Having no confidence in the willingness of state and local authorities to abide by the law, Congress authorized the president to use federal troops, if necessary, to enforce it, albeit an unlikely event as long as Andrew Johnson remained in the White House.[8]

Republican concerns about the constitutionality of the act, as well as the threat of repeal when contentious Southern Democrats returned to Congress, were the motives behind the decision to incorporate its provisions into a new constitutional amendment. The Fourteenth Amendment was drafted to include the essential provisions of the Civil Rights Act, specifically those guaranteeing citizenship, due process, and equality under law. Proposed on June 13, 1866, the amendment was intended to remove the temptation to Democrats who might have challenged the act's constitutionality. The Fourteenth Amendment represented a direct congressional assault on discriminatory state legislation, most notably the notorious Black Codes. State officials who compromised the civil rights of blacks would now face the threat of federal prosecution. Those provisions alone make it, perhaps, the most significant amendment in the Constitution.

Meanwhile, atrocities against blacks continued. After emancipation, race rioting, which had until then been a Northern phenomenon, flared in the South as many blacks left plantations to seek new lives in towns and cities. The first broke out on May 1, 1866 in Memphis. The rioting continued for three days leaving forty-eight persons dead, all but two of them black. The precipitant, which was to become a metaphor for American race relations for the next century, was a collision between two horse-drawn wagons, one driven by a white, the other by a black.

When police arrested only the black, a group of black Civil War veterans protested. They, in turn, were attacked by a contingent of whites, composed largely of policemen and firemen. As outnumbered and terrified blacks pleaded with Freedmen's Bureau representatives for protection they were unable to provide, the violence spread to black neighborhoods in South Memphis where even women and children were attacked. At least five black women were raped as white mobs burned and pillaged recently constructed black shanties, schools, and churches.[9]

On July 30, another riot flared in New Orleans when a delegation of twenty-five whites met to draft a proposal to enfranchise blacks under the terms of the Fourteenth Amendment. Fighting started when a white mob attacked a celebratory procession of several hundred blacks marching to fife and drum toward the Mechanics Institute where their white sponsors had assembled. General Philip H. Sheridan later described "an absolute massacre," as the mob charged and overwhelmed the marchers. In what was to become a familiar response, the mob was quickly assisted by large numbers of police and firemen as attention shifted from the marchers to those trapped inside the Institute. Refusing to acknowledge pleas for mercy and white flags of surrender, the mob slaughtered thirty-seven victims, all but three of them black. Only one of the white attackers was killed when he was shot accidentally by a policeman. "Poor marksmanship of the negroes," was the official explanation offered for the disparity in casualties. Four whites and 261 blacks were arrested.[10]

Later, Cyrus Hamlin, the son of Vice President Hannibal Hamlin and also, like Sheridan, a Civil War veteran, wrote that he saw nothing in the war to compare with "the wholesale slaughter and little regard paid to human life" he saw that day in the streets of New Orleans. As newspaper reports of the carnage spread across the country, it seemed obvious to many Northerners that the lenient Reconstruction policies of Andrew Johnson had created an intolerably dangerous situation for blacks.[11] In Georgia, for example, a frustrated black leader urged the Freedmen's Bureau to assume a greater role in settling disputes between blacks and whites, explaining that "we have no chance of justice before the [state] courts." A bureau official agreed. "Blacks," he wrote to the commissioner on October 14, 1866, "would be just as well off with no law at all or no Government."[12] It was a prophetic conclusion that blacks shared.

Such reports and the insensate violence of the Memphis and New Orleans race riots of 1866 removed any lingering doubts among Republicans about just how desperate the situation had become for blacks in the South. It was as though the ferocity with which Southerners had battled Yankees for four frustrating years was simply redirected toward unarmed and defenseless blacks after the surrender. With no hope of action from a hostile and now politically isolated president, and the South's recalcitrance reflected in recurring violence as well as its legislatures' refusal to ratify the Fourteenth Amendment, Congress was forced to act once again. Early in 1867, Republicans decided that, despite serious reservations, one possible solution was to give blacks the right to vote while, at the same time, imposing further restrictions on former Confederates. That way, they reasoned, blacks could influence the election of politicians who were more responsive to their needs. In January 1867, Congress overrode another presidential veto to enact a law enfranchising blacks in the District of Columbia.

Congress followed that action quickly with the passage of the Reconstruction Acts of 1867. Recognizing that civil rule in the South was a travesty, Congress ignored the president it had failed to impeach by one vote and declared a state of martial law in the former Confederate states. These three acts essentially overturned the Johnson reconstuction policies, abolishing the recently elected state governments, and dividing the South, except Tennessee, into five districts which it placed under military command. Other provisions laid out new procedures for the states to reassemble civil governments, among them drafting new constitutions without discriminatory racial codes, and requiring more restrictive terms for amnesty. Although the Fourteenth Amendment did not give blacks the vote, it penalized states that withheld it by reducing their representation in Congress. Congressional representation, for example, could be reduced in the same proportion that eligible black voters bore to the total number of eligible voters. The threat provided a powerful incentive to enfranchise blacks. But undoubtedly, the bitterest sanction of all for the South was the requirement that the Fourteenth Amendment be ratified in order to restore civil government and congressional representation.

It seemed as though the Republican Congress had, once more, run out of patience with civil government in the South. It must also be said that perhaps at least as important as their concerns about the rights and safety of blacks, congressional Republicans wanted to protect themselves from an electoral resurgence of Southern Democrats. Forcing the enfranchisement of blacks and restricting the vote of former Confederates was an obvious way to ensure continued Republican control in Congress.

But any congressional action seemed only to intensify Southern bitterness and resistance. Blacks continued to be the scapegoats for such frustrations. A Freedmen's Bureau agent from New Orleans reported in 1867 that "whenever [state officials] can grind a poor Black man down, they do it to gain popularity, '[since] it is nothing but a cursed nigger.'" Later the same year, General Nelson A. Miles wrote from North Carolina that black men and women were "almost as much within the grasp of their former owners as in the days of slavery." Moreover, Miles and others on the scene knew that it would not be relinguished easily.[13]

In the midst of this chaos, the nomination and election of General Ulysses S. Grant as president in 1868 seemed, at first, to offer blacks hope for change. His predecessor had resisted every effort to deal fairly with the racial crisis. Certainly, blacks had reason to believe that Grant, the man who had commanded the armies that won their freedom, would be more sympathetic than Andrew Johnson. Grant was, but only to a degree, and then, only for a while. Neither the fact that some 700,000 newly registered blacks had voted for him in 1868, nor that 291 of them had been lynched the same year by former Confederates, seemed to stir his interest in racial justice.

But congressional Republicans were concerned. They were aware that in some Southern states like Georgia and Louisiana eligible blacks were prevented from voting in the election that lifted Grant into the White House. The prospect of such continued interference, and the threat that black suffrage laws could well be eventually repealed by Southern Democrats, heightened their concerns about the future of Republican strength in the South. Such worries were the reasons behind their decision to draft yet another constitutional amendment—the third in four years.

The Fifteenth Amendment was proposed on February 16, 1869 and sought to protect the voting rights of black males by prohibiting abridgement or denial of that right "on account of race, color, or previous condition of servitude." As Southern states one by one had reluctantly ratified the Fourteenth Amendment, congressional Republicans understood that there would be a resurgence of Democratic strength at the national level as civil government was restored in the South. The Fifteenth Amendment, they reasoned, would counter that resurgence to some extent with black Republican votes and put repeal beyond reach. Blacks, it was assumed correctly, feeling a debt to Lincoln and the Republican Party for emancipation, civil rights and the ballot, would vote Republican if given the chance. Without that partisan incentive, it is unlikely that Radical Republicans would have been able to attract the necessary votes for passage. For the conservative wing of the party, giving black males the vote seemed the best way avoid civil rights issues that divided and bedeviled party members. The vote, Congressman James A. Garfield said, "confers upon the African race the care of its own destiny. It places their fortunes in their own hands."[14] And *not* in the Republican Party's, he could have added.

That same lack of enthusiasm for civil rights was even more evident in the White House where President Grant—the former conquering general whose name, like Sherman's and Lincoln's, was accompanied by curses throughout the South—continued nonetheless to make conciliatory gestures toward those in that region who despised him. Such concessions were also intended to appease national business interests weary of race issues and seeing little to be gained in a struggle to ensure black civil rights. Grant turned his back on those his military victories had freed and who now cast their votes overwhelmingly for him in gratitude. He sought instead to advance the interests of an emerging industrial elite anxious to build railroads and exploit new investment opportunities in the undeveloped South and West.

It was not a difficult decision. Many of Grant's conservative supporters had never been enthused about drawing black voters into the Republican Party. Before the end of the president's first term, they believed black votes were expendable in view of growing Republican strength in the Midwest. With such considerations in mind, Grant launched a series of policy initiatives to restore self-government and states' rights in the South, while at the same time cutting back the federal commitment to racial justice. Funds for the Freedmen's Bureau, for example, were steadily reduced during his administration, further limiting its mission and effectiveness. Grant later confided to his cabinet what his actions had already confirmed. "[The Fifteenth Amendment] had done the Negro no good," he said, "and been a hindrance to the South, and by no means a political advantage to the North."[15]

* * *

While Radical Republicans were drafting constitutional amendments and moving to restore order in the South, other forces were at work in that troubled region to ensure that such actions failed. Although the exact time and place of its founding remains imprecise, it appears that the Ku Klux Klan was born in the hills of Tennessee. In early June 1866, six Confederate veterans met in Pulaski to discuss what might be done to save the cause of white supremacy that appeared to have been lost at Appomattox. Determined to resist federal rule and efforts to force racial equality on the South, these young men came from good families, were well-educated by the standards of the day, quite religious, and considered throughout their lives as "useful and public-spirited" citizens of their communities. They all also believed that white supremacy had to be maintained at any cost. Klan members, often fathers and sons, were drawn from all walks of Southern life, but its leaders came, like these young founders, from the "best" families and backgrounds. The organization quickly flourished in numbers and respectability. In 1867, the Klan chose as its first Grand Wizard a Confederate war hero, General Nathan Bedford Forrest, the commander in charge of the Fort Pillow massacre just three years before.[16]

The Klan represented a uniformed, paramilitary extension of the earlier practice of slave patrols that had roamed the countryside looking for runaways or slaves away from their plantations without passes. The "pattarollers" as they were called by slaves, often whipped, but rarely killed slaves for they were too valuable. The Klan was different. The violence and mayhem it inflicted on blacks was shocking even by Southern standards. In the fall of 1868, for example, the Klan proclaimed a "nigger hunt" in Louisiana's Bossier Parish that claimed one hundred and sixty-two lives.[17]

By the time the Fifteenth Amendment was declared in force on March 30, 1870, Klan violence had escalated into what can only be described as a reign of terror. Although there is no way to know for sure, estimates place formal Klan membership at some 550,000 at that time, with countless sympathizers on the periphery of the organization.[18] Between 1868 and 1870 hundreds of blacks had been lynched by the Klan; many others had been whipped or simply disappeared. Unable to ignore a deluge of reports of the unspeakable atrocities being committed across the South, often to intimidate black voters, congressional Republicans passed the Enforcement Act of 1870. The act made it a criminal offense, punishable in *federal* courts with heavy fines and stiff jail sentences, for a state official to discriminate against black voters; a second related act strengthened federal enforcement powers in cities. In each instance the new federal regulations were intended to protect the voting rights of blacks and, in so doing, expand the electoral base of the Republican Party. They were also intended to restrict the electoral influence of Democrats in the South (as well as in big cities) where that party was strongest.

Partisan politics and electoral advantage continued to consume more space than civil rights in the minds of Republican politicians anxious to establish the Grand Old Party as a permanent and dominant national force. Divisions widened, for example, within party ranks over whether it should persist in pressing this divisive issue in the South. Some Republicans thought the cause was hopeless, requiring probably a permanent military presence to ensure black safety. But that in itself was an unpalatable solution to men now growing hesitant about further extensions of federal authority into matters that fell within the constitutional purview of the states. President Grant, as well as other Republican leaders, for example, believed that it was inappropriate for the federal government to invoke its authority to implement the Enforcement Act of 1870 until the states had first exhausted their own resources, or had proven unwilling to do so. As a consequence, federal authorities made almost no effort to force compliance anywhere except in Kentucky. Elsewhere the effects of the law were negligible. In the two years following its passage, the whippings and murders continued and at least eighty-seven more blacks were lynched by the Klan. The Klan had, in every sense of the word, become the terrorist arm of the Democratic Party in the South.[19]

The continuing carnage, not to mention human decency, demanded some response. Even Grant, inclined toward inaction, was forced to act. With no other alternative, the president at last proposed legislation to curb it. In response, Congress appointed a committee in March, 1871 to investigate Klan violence. The following month, it also passed the Ku Klux Klan Act, or Force Bill, as it was sometimes called. The act was intended "to enforce the Provisions of the Fourteenth Amendment to the Constitution of the United States and for other Purposes." The Civil Rights Act of 1866, and the constitutional amendments that followed it, had sought to protect blacks from the hostile actions of *state governments*, but left crimes committed by *individuals* within the domain of local law enforcement. By this time, however, it was evident that local law enforcement would not protect blacks anywhere in the South. Whites broke the law with impunity if their victims were black. Police would not arrest; juries would not convict.

The Ku Klux Klan Act of 1871 sought to change that with federal enforcement. It gave federal judges the authority to exclude from juries any persons they considered to be in sympathy with the accused. It also authorized the president to suspend the writ of *habeas corpus* and use federal troops to force compliance. The act represented another significant example of the willingness of congressional Republicans to use federal authority to punish criminal acts of individuals that were ignored or condoned by the states. The act was aimed at "any person" seeking to deprive another of "any rights, privileges, or immunities secured by the Constitution."[20] For a brief period, it looked like a serious federal effort would be made to guarantee the safety and recently granted civil rights of blacks.

But there was no follow through. With the new conservative mood and agenda in Washington, the incentives for heroic effort had disappeared. By the end of President Grant's first term, only Attorney General Amos T. Ackerman remained committed to a policy of protecting the lives and civil rights of blacks. Other cabinet members were either disinterested or disdainful. Grant's own concerns about the civil liberties of his former Confederate enemies clearly took precedence over whatever interest he might have had in the welfare of the slaves his armies had liberated.

The indifference toward civil rights evident in Grant's cabinet was reflected in the words of his secretary of state, Hamilton Fish, who was, by then, impatient with the attorney general's worries about the safety of blacks. Ackerman had atrocities "on the brain," Fish wrote, complaining that he was tired of hearing Ackerman's accounts of racial violence at cabinet meetings. "It has got to be a bore to listen twice a week to this thing," he griped to a friend.[21]

High on the Republican agenda now were matters of concern to the nation's industrial leaders who were taking over, not only the party, but an emerging industrial economy as well. As the passions of the war subsided with time, there was little to distinguish this group's racial views from their counterparts in the South. It was discouraging to some who felt the party was betraying its principles. "I feel greatly saddened by this business," Attorney General Ackerman wrote in 1871:

> The contempt for the law in the South has revealed a perversion of moral sentiment among southern whites, which bodes ill to that part of the country for this generation. Without a thorough moral renovation, society there for many years will be...certainly far from christian."[22]

An attorney on the scene that same year in Mississippi agreed. The lives of blacks, he said, had been reduced "to something like the condition of a stray dog."[23]

But by then that was a condition a changing Republican party could live with. Despite the extraordinary record of continuing violence and intimidation in every southern state, President Grant used his executive power to declare a "condition of lawlessness" only in South Carolina, and then only briefly in 1871 at the insistence of Attorney General Ackerman. In that instance, the writ of *habeas corpus* was suspended and troops were sent in to occupy nine upcountry counties in October, 1871. But out of the thousands of atrocities committed by the Ku Klux Klan during this period, only a few hundred of those arrested ever went to trial; fewer still were convicted; and, for those, the punishments were usually trivial. White-on-white violence, which was a foremost concern, did subside, however, in large part because carpetbagger and scalawag Republicans simply withdrew from the struggle, leaving blacks to fend for themselves. The personal risks, they realized by then, were unacceptably high and the situation was hopeless. This episode in South Carolina marked the high point of federal efforts to protect black lives and property for nearly nine decades to come. But the prosecution ended in failure, its momentum drained in legal wrangles ultimately lost over the questionable constitutionality of the federal prosecution.[24]

In December 1871, after only a few months of perhaps too vigorous prosecution of Klan terrorists, Amos Ackerman was dismissed as Attorney General. The dismissal provided a gauge of the influence railroad tycoons Collis P. Huntington and Jay Gould wielded in the Republican Party and over the president. Ackerman's departure, as Huntington and Gould understood, left no one in the Grant administration who would any longer squander time and energy on what they considered to be an ill-conceived commitment to racial justice.[25] With Ackerman gone, the party hastened to recaste its priorities and image to advance the programs of industrial capitalism and financial extravagance that characterized the last quarter of the nineteenth century.

In step with his party's new agenda, President Grant signed another Amnesty Act in 1872 which restored political rights to all but a few of the South's remaining political and economic elite. By the end of that year, federal prosecutions for racial violence had declined sharply at the same time pardons had mounted. The violence itself continued. Even congressional interest in the safety and welfare of blacks was fading into the White House's indifference. In 1872, for example, and despite the ongoing violence, it failed to renew the *habeas corpus* provision of the KKK Act. Without it enforcement was impossible.[26]

By April, 1873, Amos Ackerman's replacement as Attorney General, George H. Williams, had ordered his district attorneys to suspend further prosecutions; by the end of that year earlier charges that had been brought against violent offenders were being formally dropped. By that time, also, presidential pardons had become commonplace.

Except for a tiny group accused of particularly heinous offenses, persons who had fled to avoid prosecution were informed that they could return to their homes without fear of arrest. For those somehow unable to avoid punishment, a stiff federal sentence for murdering a black person was no more than five years in prison and a thousand dollar fine.[27]

At the same time Attorney General Williams was offering forgiveness to whites, they continued to prey upon blacks. In 1873, for example, racial violence flared in Colfax, Louisiana. A dispute had arisen during the gubernatorial election of 1872. When armed, but outnumbered, black Republicans tried to barricade themselves in the county courthouse, they were attacked with canon and rifle fire by white Democrats. "The result," a black legislator testified, "was that on Easter Sunday of 1873, when the sun went down that night, it went down on the corpses of two hundred and eighty negroes." Among the casualties were fifty blacks who were wantonly executed after they had surrendered. Only two whites died in what amounted to purely and simply a massacre, the bloodiest of the Reconstruction period.[28]

The Civil Rights Act of 1875 was the last attempt by Congress to impede the advance of this virulent new strain of racial oppression that had replaced slavery. The act was intended to invoke federal authority to provide "full and equal enjoyment" of public accomodations such as "inns, public conveyances on land or water, theaters, and other places of public amusement." It also sought to prevent the disqualification of jurors based on "race, color, or previous condition of servitude." Southern whites correctly viewed the act as an invitation to mayhem, for without federal protection blacks who acted on its promise would pay a heavy price. Even outside the South, the law had many opponents and few defenders. It was never enforced.[29]

That it would not be was evident in Mississippi the year it was enacted. White Mississippians showed their contempt for Washington by forcing state Republicans from office under threat of assassination. Vigilante groups roamed the countryside enforcing plantation-style discipline on blacks. The "Mississippi Plan," as this exercise in state's rights was called, effectively nullified the Fourteenth and Fifteenth Amendments. Mississippi set the course in 1875 that the rest of the South would follow for the remainder of the century. Meanwhile the federal government stood by and watched indifferently.

President Grant's refusal to send troops to quell the violence in Mississippi added momentum to the cause of white supremacy everywhere. It was a clear signal that the federal government's commitment to racial justice had run its course. Despite the continuing scourge of violence, federal troops were steadily withdrawn from the South during Grant's first and second terms, leaving blacks, once more, at the mercy of their former masters. When Grant entered the White House in 1869, there were no more than twenty thousand Union soldiers remaining in the South. By the time he left office in 1876, there were fewer than six thousand, with nearly half of those scattered thinly across the Texas frontier to protect white settlers from Indians.[30]

Additionally, Supreme Court decisions cleared the way by limiting federal authority to protect black lives and property. U.S. Supreme Court decisions had already begun to pare much of the meaning from the Fourteenth Amendment. The court had so narrowly construed and limited federal authority in the *Slaughterhouse Cases* of 1873, for example, that it became virtually useless as a means to protect individual rights.[31] Any remaining fears of federal prosecution for racial crimes of violence were dispelled in 1876 when the court fatally weakened the Enforcement Acts by ruling in two cases that only states—and *not* individuals—were subject to federal prosecution under the Fourteenth Amendment.

In one of those cases, *U.S. v. Cruikshank*, the court overturned the only three convictions obtained in the government's prosecution of the hundreds involved in the bloody Colfax massacre in Louisiana. The *Cruikshank* decision registered a landmark victory for states' rights, setting a precedent that fundamentally removed the federal government's authority to protect individual rights. It was as though the court had issued a license to kill. In fact, it had. For by this time no one could believe that whites would ever be held accountable in southern state courts for harming blacks.[32]

The Compromise of 1877 marked the end of whatever faint hopes might have remained for positive racial change in the South. The compromise, which resolved the disputed presidential election of 1876 between Republican Rutherford B. Hayes and Democrat Samuel Tilden, set the course of race relations in the United States for the next eighty years. In return for the presidency, Hayes and the Republican leadership agreed to withdraw the few remaining federal troops stationed in the South, and to abandon the last two teetering Republican governments in Louisiana and South Carolina. Thus political power in the South was restored to the Democratic Party. Southern Democrats praised the compromise as a major victory for states' rights and white supremacy, as well they should have. The South had lost the Civil War, but it had won the battle for states' rights and white supremacy. In agreeing to the Compromise, the Republican party had made a choice that would define its future from that time forward. With that decision, historian C. Vann Woodward writes, "The party of abolitionist radicalism had now become the party of vested interests and big business...and its leader was Rutherford B. Hayes."[33]

* * *

As every major scholar of the period has concluded, Reconstruction was a failure for blacks.[34] Without an unyielding federal commitment to enforce the law in the South, the positive effects of the well-intentioned reforms enacted during this brief period changed almost nothing, even in the short run. Substantial evidence indicates, for example, that the gains made through black voting and office holding were fleeting and without lasting impact; similarly, efforts of the biracial Union League Clubs formed to advance social and economic equality were shortlived, falling victim to Klan violence and racial disputes within them. The primary consequence of these efforts was to set in motion a vicious white backlash of unprecedented violence that left blacks in circumstances that were, in important respects, *worse* than they had been during slavery.

Reconstruction failed for many reasons, but the single most important reason was because blacks were denied, as no other Americans ever have been, the opportunity to own land. For without land of their own to establish self-sufficiency, uneducated and impoverished blacks were left without resources, and utterly vulnerable to racial oppression that the newly restored state governments would quickly institutionalize.

Notes

1. Joseph Holt to Henry C. Warmoth, August 1, 1866, Henry C. Warmoth Papers, University of North Carolina; quoted in E. Foner, *Reconstruction, 1863–1877* (New York: Harper & Row, 1988), 263.
2. Quoted in G.P. Rawick (ed.), *The American Slave: A Composite Autobiography* (Westport, CT: Greenwood Press, 1972, 1976), Mississippi, Supp. Series 1, v.6, p.1, 235, 237.
3. C.L. Flynn, *White Land, Black Labor: Caste and Class in Late Nineteenth Georgia* (Baton Rouge: Louisiana State University Press, 1983), 123–125; Foner, *Reconstruction*, 202–203.
4. Quoted in J.R. Dennett, *The South As It Is: 1865–1866* (New York: Viking, 1965; orig. 1865–66), 221–22.
5. D. Tillson to E. Foster and A.M. Campbell, October 16, 1866 (Georgia); J.B. Kiddoo to O.O. Howard, June 26, 1866 (Texas); R.K. Scott to O.O. Howard, December

18, 1866 (South Carolina); quoted in J.A. Carpenter, "Atrocities in the Reconstruction Period," *Journal of Negro History* 47 (October 1962), 238–239.

6. J.B. Kiddoo to O.O. Howard, October 25, 1866, Freedmen's Bureau Records, National Archives; quoted in J.A. Carpenter, "Atrocities...," 243.

7. J.A. Mowrer to Brig. Gen. S. Thomas, March 9, 1867, Freedmen's Bureau Records, National Archives; quoted in J.A. Carpenter, "Atrocities...," 243–244; W.L. Mallet to T. Stevens, May 28, 1866, Stevens Papers; quoted in Foner, *Reconstruction*, 119.

8. 42 U.S.C, 1981, 1982 (1964 ed.), 14 Stat. 27.

9. J.G. Ryan, "The Memphis Riot of 1866: Terror in a Black Community During Reconstruction," *Journal of Negro History* 62 (July 1977), 243–257.

10. D.E. Reynolds, "The New Orleans Riot of 1866, Reconsidered," *Louisiana History* 5,1 (Winter 1964), 5–27.

11. Cyrus Hamlin to Hannibal Hamlin, August 19, 1866, Hannibal Hamlin Papers, University of Maine, Orono; quoted in Foner, *Reconstruction*, 263.

12. A. Colby et al. to D. Tillson, (August 1866), Unregistered Letters Received, Ser. 632, Ga. Asst. Comr. RG 105, National Archives (Freedmen and Southern Society Project, University of Maryland, A-5349); N.G. Gill to O.O. Howard, October 14, 1866, Letters Received, Ser. 15, Washington Headquarters, RG 105, National Archives (Freedmen and Southern Society Project, University of Maryland, A-9528); quoted in Foner, *Reconstruction*, 205.

13. N.A. Miles to O.O. Howard, December 4, 1867, National Archives; cited in Carpenter, "Atrocities in the Reconstruction Period," 240.

14. Letter of April 16, 1870, J.A. Garfield to R. Folger; quoted in Foner, *Reconstruction*, 449.

15. Quoted in A. Nevins, *Hamilton Fish: The Inner History of the Grant Administration* (New York: Dodd, Mead, 1936), 853–854; see, also, Foner, *Reconstruction*, 577.

16. A.W. Trelease, *White Terror: The Ku Klux Klan Conspiracy and Southern Reconstruction* (New York: Harper & Row, 1971), 3, 14, 51–52, 296, 340–41, 354, 363.

17. Report of Lt. J.C. De Gress, June 24, 1867; N.A. Miles to O.O. Howard, December 4, 1867 (North Carolina), Freedmen's Bureau Records, National Archives; quoted in J.A. Carpenter, "Atrocities...," 240–241; A.W. Trelease, *White Terror: The Ku Klux Klan Conspriracy and Southern Reconstruction* (New York: Harper & Row, 1971), 130.

18. *The Ku Klux Klan: A History of Racism and Violence* (Montgomery, AL: Southern Poverty Law Center, 1991), 47.

19. Trelease, *White Terror*, 215, 385–387; see, also, R.M. Brown, *Strain of Violence: Historical Studies of American Violence and Vigilantism* (New York: Oxford University Press, 1975), 323.

20. 42 U.S.C., 1983, 17 Stat. 18.

21. A.T. Ackerman to L.W. Merrill, November 9, 1871; Ackerman to A.H. Terry, November 18, 1871, Ackerman Papers, University of Virginia; quoted in Foner, *Reconstruction*, 458; K.L. Hall, "Political Power and Constitutional Legitimacy: The South Carolina Ku Klux Klan Trials, 1871–1872," *Emory Law Journal* 33 (Fall 1984), 921–951.

22. Letter from A. Ackerman to General A. Terry, November 18, 1871, Akerman Letterbooks, University of Virginia; quoted in Hall, "Political Power and Constitutional Legitimacy," 949.

23. Testimony of Joshua S. Morris, *Joint Select Committee to Inquire into the Condition of Affairs in the Late Insurrectionary States*, 13 vols. (Washington, 1872), *House Reports*, 42d Congress, 2d sess., Mississippi, 305.

24. Trelease, *White Terror*, 401–403.
25. Huntington subsequently evolved into what could be considered a benevolent white supremacist. While making millions developing mines and railroads in the West, he became an advocate of black education in the South and urged their employment in his shipping and drydock company in Newport News, Virginia. See, D. Lavender, *The Great Persuader* (Garden City, NY: Doubleday, 1970), 350–51.
26. A decade later, the Supreme Court would declare the Act itself an unconstitutional extension of federal authority.
27. Trelease, *White Terror*, 416–418; Foner, *Reconstruction*, 458; Hall, "Political Power and Constitutional Legitimacy," fn. 82, 941.
28. J.G. Taylor, *Louisiana Reconstructed, 1863–1877* (Baton Rouge: Louisiana State University Press, 1974), 268–270; T. Tunnell, *Crucible of Reconstruction: War, Radicalism, and Race in Louisiana* (Baton Rouge: Louisiana State University Press, 1984), 189–193.
29. *The Civil Rights Cases*, 109 U.S. 3 (1883); *The Nation* 24 (April 5, 1877), 202; quoted in J.H. Franklin, "The Enforcement of the Civil Rights Act of 1875," *Prologue* 6 (Winter 1974), 225–235.
30. J.E. Sefton, *The United States Army and Reconstruction, 1865–1877* (Baton Rouge: Louisiana State University Press, 1967), 261–262.
31. *The Slaughterhouse Cases*, 16 Wallace 36 (1873).
32. *United States v. Cruikshank*, 92 U.S. 542 (1876); see, also, *United States v. Reese* 92 U.S. 214 (1876).
33. C.V. Woodward, *Origins of the New South, 1877–1913* (Baton Rouge: Louisiana State University Press, 1971; orig. 1951), 28; see, also, C.V. Woodward, *Reunion and Reaction: The Compromise of 1877 and the End of Reconstruction* (New York: Oxford University Press, 1991; orig. 1951); V.P. DeSantis, *Republicans Face the Southern Question: The New Departure Years, 1877–1897* (Baltimore, MD: Johns Hopkins University Press, 1959), 73–74, 132; J.M. Kousser, *The Shaping of Southern Politics: Suffrage Restrictions and the Establishment of the One-Party South* (New Haven, CT: Yale University Press, 1974), 24.
34. See, for example, W.E.B. Du Bois, *Black Reconstruction in America, 1860–1880* (New York: Atheneum, 1969, orig. 1935; K. Stampp, *The Era of Reconstruction, 1865–1877* (New York: Knopf, 1965); and E. Foner, *Reconstuction, 1863–1877* (New York: Harper & Row, 1988).

7

KKK: The Assault on Black Families

*"The Reconstruction period has been hell on the Negro
race, but we suffered through, somehow. If we had another
time like that to go through, I believes I would hang myself,
so es I would not suffer again."*
                                        —Polly Shine, a former slave.[1]

*"In those days it was 'Kill a mule, buy another. Kill a nigger,
hire another.' They had to have a license to kill anything but
a nigger. We was always in season."*
    —A black recalling life in Mississippi after the Civil War.[2]

The reign of terror that former slaves endured during the immediate
post-Civil War period was often the work of the Ku Klux Klan. Some
of the Klan violence in the late 1860s and early 1870s was politically
motivated—an attempt to keep blacks from voting Republican, or to
prevent them from voting at all.[3] Abundant evidence of its effectiveness is revealed in an eleven-month Congressional investigation that
began on March 23, 1871. Thirteen volumes of evidence recount a period of extraordinary brutality that continued long after the investigation ended.[4]

It would be a mistake, however, to believe that all the savagery described in these thousands of pages of testimony might have been
avoided if Congress had not passed the Fifteenth Amendment, if black
males had not been given the vote. Terror was also the means violent,
embittered men used to indulge other more primitive passions; inflicting pain on black victims often seemed to serve as an end in itself, an
exercise of power that the perpetrators savored as much as the sexual
perversity that so often accompanied it.

What was it like to be black and live in the South during this
period of "reform"? In the words of Polly Shine, a former slave, it

was "hell." This chapter explores what that hell was like in the words of some of the countless black men, women, and children who, like Polly Shine, suffered through it. Three hundred and ninety three whites and 225 blacks testified to Klan atrocities in Alabama, Florida, Georgia, Mississippi, North Carolina, and South Carolina during the four-year period preceeding the investigation. Blacks were also hard hit by terrorist violence in Louisiana, Tennessee, Texas, and Virginia, but hearings were not held in those states. In Louisiana, for example, over two thousand people died in mob violence in 1868 alone. Texas recorded 1,035 lynchings in the three years following the war, and most of the victims were black. By comparison Tennessee seemed relatively tranquil with only 168 lynchings during a twelve-month period ending in July 1868. Blacks, especially, but also white Republicans, were exposed to a reign of terror unprecedented in American history. The figures cited are conservative, for no one can be sure exactly how many more people were whipped, beaten, raped, mutilated, or murdered in uninvestigated crimes. But by any count, the numbers were staggering, well into the thousands. It was during this period that, in the words of W.J. Cash, the South embraced "the savage ideal as it had not been established in any Western people since the decay of medieval feudalism."[5]

Skin color determined the nature of the violence, for white victims fared better than blacks. Although Northern white carpetbaggers and Southern Union sympathizers were whipped, murdered, and had their houses burned to the ground, it was rare that they were sexually mutilated, or their bodies desecrated; nor were their wives and children physically harmed.

The same can not be said for blacks. Black males were the most frequent victims of these whippings, castrations, and murders. The custom of giving them a choice between emasculation or death, for example, began during this period. Slaves were too valuable to castrate. But the Klan also wreaked havoc on black *families*. Wives, mothers, and children, as well, were often victimized, and almost always forced to witness the atrocities committed on their parents. The mothers of small children provide some of the most poignant testimony found in these volumes.

What follows is a tiny, but representative, sampling of the thousands of vicious attacks on black families that were documented by Congressional investigators from roughly 1868 to 1872. The stories that follow are ugly and disturbing, but they are necessary to convey a visceral understanding of the trauma blacks endured during this period, as well as to provide some insight into why its consequences would endure.

* * *

In 1870, Henry Lowther, a black man from Wilkinson County, Georgia was abducted by Klansmen and carried into a swamp. There he was given a choice between death or emasculation.[6] "They said I had taken too great a stand against them [Democrats]," he explained later. They also claimed that he was having a sexual relationship with a white woman whose land he tended, a charge Lowther denied. But Lowther had also angered his attackers when he attempted to use the court to collect debts owed him by white men.

> I worked for my money and carried on a shop. They all got broke and did not pay me, and I sued them. They have been working at me ever since I have been free. I had too much money.

"They went on then into the swamp," he said, describing the attack,

> and came to a halt again, and stood there and talked awhile. There were eight men walking with me—one hold of each arm, three in front of me with guns, and three right behind me. After some conversation, just before they were ordered to march, something was said, every man cocked his gun and looked right at me. I thought they were going to shoot me, and leave me right there. The moon was shining bright, and I could see them. I was satisfied they were going to kill me, and I did not care much then.

But then they gave their victim, a sneering choice: "They asked me whether I preferred to be altered or killed. I said I preferred to be altered."

It was quickly accomplished, carried out by men familiar with such procedures.

> After laying me down and getting through they said: "Now as soon as you can get to a doctor go to one; you know the doctors in this county, and as soon as you are to leave do it, or we will kill you next time."

Bleeding badly, Lowther crawled over a mile before he came to a darkened house. It was about three in the morning, he guessed, when he called at the door for help. A white man opened the door, looked at him and, without a word, shut the door in his face. When he finally reached the house of a doctor known to treat impoverished blacks, he learned the doctor had fled, fearing Klan retaliation.

"Blood was all over town," Lowther said, "at the doctor's gate, and everywhere else. It was running a stream all the time I was trying to find the doctor, and I thought I would bleed to death."

Eventually, some black women heard his cries and saw the trail of blood. Lowther's young son managed to get the bleeding stopped and saved his father's life. It was seventeen days before Henry Lowther could take a step, but he knew it could have been worse.

"They [castrated] Bill Brigan," he said. "The way they did him was, they tied him down on a log and took a buggy-trace to him and whipped one of his seed entirely out and the other very nearly out."

There were no arrests in either crime, despite the fact that Lowther identified Bob and Henry Hyman and Andrew Porter as three of his attackers.[7]

* * *

The slightest suspicion of sexual indiscretion could cost a black man his life. America Tramblies was a black preacher in Lee County, Alabama in 1870. Reverend Tramblies supported the Republican Party, but that appeared to be his only fault. Even Democrats "spoke well of him," according to another black man who knew him, because they knew that "he was an honest, kind-hearted man, a minister of the Gospel."

But that was not enough to spare this black preacher's life. It all started when a white woman moved into the county to teach black children. When whites refused to provide lodging for her, Reverend Tramblies and his wife invited her to board with them. They were anxious to have their daughters attend her classes. It did not matter to the Klan that the teacher was an "old woman" who slept in a separate room with the children. America Tramblies was shot and killed in the glow of a Klan lantern as his wife lay beside him in bed.[8]

* * *

But it was the depraved nature of the assaults on innocent women and small children that provide, perhaps, the most vivid exposure of the perverse sexual obsessions that so often drove these men in disguise. During a typical Klan attack *all* family members were customarily forced to strip naked. This *never* occurred with white victims. Rachel Arnold described, for example, how her sister was whipped while she, her mother, and female children were humiliated in White County, Georgia:

> they tore her [sister's] clothes off and made her lie down in the yard. Two men stood on her, one on her head, and the other on her feet; and then they whipped

her while they were standing on her. [Then] they made us all lay down, children and all, and show ourselves.[9]

Mrs. Arnold had no idea why they were treated this way, but she did know that forcing black men and women to strip naked before being whipped and degraded was to be expected of white men.

* * *

Joe Brown told a similar story of how a group of some sixty Georgia Klansmen assaulted his family in an orgy of sadistic cruelty. Brown's wife, Mary, had witnessed a Klan murder and could have possibly identified the killers. The Klan intended to silence both of them. After forcing him and his wife to strip naked, they were whipped as their small children screamed in terror. When the whipping stopped, a "trace-chain" was attached to both their necks and looped over a beam. Saying they were going to hang the couple in front of their children, they hoisted them off the ground as the children sobbed and begged for their parents' lives. Minutes later, when Mrs. Brown lost consciousness, they changed their minds, apparently deciding that a little entertainment would be more satisfying. Instead of hanging them, Brown said,

> "They made all the women show their nakedness; they made them lie down, and they jabbed them with sticks, and made them show their nakedness; and they made the little children show their nakedness."
>
> "How many children have you?" he was asked.
>
> "Two boys and one little girl. There were two [other] little boys, but they did not get up—the littlest ones. They made my mother-in-law, and my sister-in-law, and my wife, and two little girls lie down and show their nakedness."
>
> "Did they do any mischief to the children?"
>
> "They jabbed them with a stick, and went to playing with their backsides with a piece of fishing-pole."

"They had a show of us all there; they had us all lying in the road, Mary Brown, Mary Neal, and my next youngest daughter," the grandmother said, recalling the horror. "They had us all stripped there, and laughed and made great sport. Some of them just squealed the same as if they were stable horses and just brought out."[10]

* * *

Samuel and Hannah Tutson were attacked by nine Klansmen in Clay County, Florida in May 1871. One of the attackers, Cabell

Winn had earlier tried to force the Tutson's off the small farm they had purchased for one hundred and fifty dollars. When the Tutsons refused to leave, the disappointed land speculator recruited George and Barney McCrea, Dave Donley, Jim Phillips, Henry Baxter, Bob Lane, and two other friends, to help kick down their door in the middle of the night.

"George McCrea ran right to me and gathered me by the arm," Mrs. Tutson explained. "As I saw him coming, I took up the child—the baby—and held to him. [My husband] threw his arms round my neck and held on to me. Cabell Winn catched hold of my foot, and then there were so many hold of me I cannot tell who they were...I started to scream and and George McCrea catched me by the throat and choked me. I worried around and around, and he catched the little child by the foot and slinged out of my arms. I screamed...then there were so many around they got me out of doors."

At the same time, Samuel Tutson said, he tried to reach his wife, but

someone standing by the door caught me by my right arm, and I could not get to her...then they dragged my feet from under me and flung me down across a cellar door and near broke my back...then they dragged me over the fence and took me away down the hill...and tied me to a pine and whipped me...Dave Donley struck me over the eye before...they tied me, and they stamped on me and kicked me...Cabell Winn stuck me with a pistol and choked me, and ran my head up against the tree, and told that if it was not for *sin*, he would blow my "God-damned brains out."

Meanwhile, four of the Klansmen had dragged Mrs. Tutson to the edge of a field and tied her to a tree where, she said, Winn gave her one more chance to give up their land.

"He coaxed me and begged me to give it up before they whipped me...[When she refused] They pulled off all my linen, tore it up so that I did not have a piece of rag on me as big as my hand...'What are you going to do to me?'" she cried. "'God damn you, we will show you,'" was the reply. "They whipped me [with saddle girths] from the crown of my head to the soles of my feet," until someone said, 'Stop, and let her get her breath.' I was just raw."

When three of her attackers "went off to the horses [to get] liquor," George McCrea tried to rape her:

[He would] treat me shamefully. He would make me squat down by the pine and say, 'What are you trembling for?' I would say that I was cold, and was afraid that I would freeze. He would get his knees between my legs and say, 'God damn you, open your legs.... Old lady, if you don't let me have to do with you, I will kill you.

When she refused, instead of killing her, McCrea resumed the whipping. When the others returned with the liquor, she said "they poured it on my head, and I smelled it for three weeks, so that it made me sick."

The Tutsons had three children aged nine, five, and a baby ten months old who witnessed the attack.

"That was the one [the baby] you had in your arms when they jerked it away?" she was asked.

"Yes, sir."

"Did the baby get hurt?"

"Yes, sir; in one of its hips. When it began to walk one of its hips was very bad, and every time you would stand it up it would scream."

Samuel and Hannah Tutson were whipped so savagely that Mr. Tutson "could not sit up" afterward. "The blood oozed out through my frock all around my waist," Mrs. Tutson told investigators, "clean through, when I got to [a neighbor's place].

A month after the attack, the nine attackers were arrested, but all were subsequently released by the Clay County sheriff. Samuel Tutson was not surprised. He was aware of how things were done in Clay County, Florida. When he asked the sheriff about their release, the sheriff replied that "he had been around and shook hands with them all, and that's the way he got up with them." Fear of retaliation forced the Tutson's to abandon their farm and leave the county.[11]

* * *

Similar crimes involving mothers and small children were reported in South Carolina where, for example, Jackson Surratt and his wife, Jane, were awakened on a warm Saturday night near Spartanburg, dragged from their beds, blindfolded, and led with two of their children from their cabin. Mr. Surratt's mistake was refusing to vote the way he was told, but his whole family would pay for it. Klansmen made Mrs. Surratt leave her screaming seven-month-old baby behind. Then the whole family was required to strip naked and lie on the ground. Savage beatings followed. Later when Mrs. Surratt stumbled back to her baby, she recalled that, "I couldn't hold my child on my lap to suckle it; I had to lay it on the bed and [kneel] by it."

"What did they do to your son and daughter?" she was asked.

"They whipped them. They whipped my son miserably bad," she replied. "They whipped my daughter very bad; she has not been able to do much since; I don't believe she will ever get over it."[12]

* * *

Even when children were not directly attacked, they were forced to watch the suffering and humiliation of their parents. Klansmen believed that it was a good way to teach them a "lesson." In Walton County, Georgia, for example, Augustus and Lettie Mills were badly whipped and "run out" of their home because Augustus had testified against a white man, William Felker, who ran an illegal still and had whipped many blacks.

"William Felker [and others] bulged through the door with his pistol in his hand, and ordered me to lie still until the light was kindled," Augustus testified:

> When the light was kindled up, he said, "Now get up." I told him that I had been sick, that I had been chilling. He said, "Get up; we will cure you of chills; you never will have any more." I got up and went out into the room. He went back then and ordered my wife to get up [from bed]. He made us all get down and pull off our clothes; and then he whipped us. He gave me between twenty-five and thirty licks, as near as I can recollect; I did not count them. He gave my wife pretty near that much, and he gave Tobe [a sixteen year old hired hand] about the same. And he struck us over the head with a pistol. My little girl cried, and he drew his pistol over her, and told her if she did not hush he would smash her.

> "How many children had you?" Mills was asked.

> "Four."

> "Were they all there?"

> "Yes, sir."

> "How old were they?"

> "One was six years, and one was four years old, and one was two years old; and then the other is a little better than a year old now; it was not a year old then, though."

> "Was your wife suckling it at the time?"

> "Yes, sir."

> "At the time she was whipped?"

> "Yes, sir."

> "Have you seen Mr. Felker since?"

> "I saw him here the other day."

> "Have they done anything with him, or have they let him go?"

> "I understand that they let him go."[13]

* * *

Klan terrorists sometimes encountered stiff resistance as black husbands and fathers tried to defend themselves and their families despite the dismal odds they faced of surviving such acts. George Houston was one of a small number of such courageous men to live to tell about it. Klansmen in Sumter County, Alabama were angry in 1869 because Houston had joined the Union League and opposed Democrats. "I was opposed," Houston explained later, "[Because] colored men were being shot down like dogs, when I knew that the that the [Democrat] officers of the county could stop it. I told the sheriff that to his face...I tried to hold up the [at least eight or nine] men that had been shot down by violence; some at night, some by daylight; some were found in the stock-pools with their guts cut out."

That was no way for a black man to talk to a sheriff in Sumter County and his family, too, would suffer for it. Not long afterward, Houston was attacked in his house by Klansmen. Bullets tore through the walls, one striking him in the thigh, another hitting his young son in the leg as he dove out a window. When a figure moved out of the shadows for a better shot at the helpless boy, his hooded head snapped backward as a single blast from Houston's shotgun struck him in the face. Houston escaped and hid in the Sucarnoochee swamp as Klansmen scoured the area looking for him. Denied any hope of justice as a white man's killer, he and his family were forced to flee the county, leaving behind a farm and all that they owned.[14]

* * *

Abe Lyon was not so lucky as George Houston. In nearby Choctaw County, Alabama, Eliza Lyon described how she and their three children watched as Klansmen killed him then mutilated his body on June 6, 1871:

> It was about 11 o'clock at night. They knocked on the door and asked in a loud voice was Abe Lyon in. I said, 'Don't go out, Abe: it sounds like more voices than one...[Then] the men burst the door open and threw a rope over his head and drew his arms down to him, and picked him up and toted him out. I hallooed and screamed for help, but no one came near...four men—white men—came up to me, and [held guns] on each side of my head, and one in my face and one right here in my chest, and they told me if I didn't hush holloing they'd blow a hole through me.
>
> They shot him with a double-barreled gun.... At the next [shot] someone hallooed to them all to fire, and all fired, I reckon...for the holes was counted they shot in him; and Dr. McCall counted thirty-three holes...
>
> I picked up [her three children] and run for about a quarter of a mile, and stopped in a thicket of woods to see what they were going to do.... They came back to the house and tore up everything.... They shot off all the pistols and shot my dog...and it sounded like a hundred shots at once.
>
> [After they shot her husband], They were going to let him alone, but some gentleman in the crowd says, 'Don't; let's cut his head off,' and they all went back and cut his head loose around to there, to the middle of the side of the neck,

cutting around from in front. I have got the penknife that they used; they broke it in his throat...

According to his wife, the Klan was angry because Abe Lyon had "voted the radical ticket, and stood to it in any crowd." The Klan had also learned that the Lyon family had saved six hundred dollars that they had placed in a box hidden in the house. That's why the house was ransacked.

"Was anyone ever prosecuted for this?" she was asked.

"Not a thing was done," she answered. "Nobody put themselves to any trouble about it." Eliza Lyon lost her husband, the money, the farm, and everything else she owned. "I just left it there," she said. "I suppose I will never get it; I am afraid to go back."[15]

* * *

A similar story was told by Betsey Westbrook, whose husband, Robin, was murdered by Klansmen on July 18, 1871 in the town of Jefferson, Alabama. After smashing their way into the house, the beating began. Westbrook's vigorous attempt to defend himself infuriated his attackers. His wife described the scene:

> The man struck him with his gun. The man had a gun and run at him and struck him on the head, and his hat fell off of his head. Then my husband took the dog-iron up and he struck three or four of them, and the first man he struck he knocked down. They got him jammed up in the corner, and one man went around behind him and put two loads out of a double barreled gun in his shoulders...and then he dropped the dog-iron; and another man says, "Kill him, God damn him," and he took a pistol and shot him right down here in the neck, over the left shoulder. Then he fell right down and hollered...then they just all got up and run out. He didn't live more than half an hour after they shot him.
>
> My boy was in there while they were killing my husband, and he says, "Mammy, what must I do?" and I says, "Jump outdoors and run." He went to the door and a white man took him by the arm and says, "God damn you, I will fix you too," but he snatched himself loose and got out of the door, and another one whacked him on the back of the head...They shot two loads after him, but he got clear away. If I hadn't made him run they would have killed him too..."

Robin Westbrook was murdered because, his wife explained, "He would hold up his head and say he was a strong radical; he would hang on to that..."

"What was done with any of those men who killed your husband?" Mrs. Westbrook was asked.

"They didn't do anything with them," she answered.

Despite the fact that both she and her son could identify the killers, she explained,

They never made no botheration; they didn't seek after them. If they had sought after them they would have found some of them lying up with the licks my husband had struck with his dog-iron...for they bled more than he did...They didn't bother about anything else that I could see.[16]

* * *

The sociopathic patterns of violence described in this chapter converge in the murder of young Billy Blair. In December 1868, Augustus Blair's only son, Billy, made the mistake of defending himself when he was assaulted at a "hog-killing," by three white Alabamans, Bunk and Pony Hinds and their buddy, Jim Henry Cox. A couple of other blacks joined in to make it an even fight, so the Hinds and Cox backed off, saying, "You fight now, but you will not fight when the Ku Klux come."

A few nights later, the Ku Klux did come, eleven of them, including Bunk, Pony, and Jim Henry. They broke down the door to Blair's house in Limestone County, dragging the eighteen-year-old boy out into the darkness where they stripped him. These Klansmen announced that they would butcher him just like they had the hog. And they did, slowly and methodically.[17]

"Oh Lord! Lord! here's Billy cut to pieces," a sister sobbed to her mother and sisters when she saw her dying brother's unspeakable wounds.

All but three of Billy Blair's killers escaped punishment by fleeing to Arkansas. The three who were arrested were released on bond and never prosecuted.[18] Billy Blair's parents, sisters, and probably any one who ever knew him were forever marked by the horror of that night.

* * *

Family names—the Blairs, the Westbrooks, the Houstons and Arnolds and Surratts and Browns and Mills, to name just a few of the thousands of victims—stand like tombstones in a journey through the tragedy of Klan violence that followed emancipation. Endorsed by the communities they "defended," the Ku Klux Klan targeted not only men, but also their wives and children. Black families came under attack as they never had under slavery; and many, as these accounts reveal, were destroyed by it, not only physically but economically, as well, as fathers perished leaving families destitute without them. The emotional toll is incalculable. There seemed to be no limit to the Klan's depravity and viciousness. As a black man, John Johnson described it, "they killed people just like snakes."[19]

Atrocities occur, history has shown, in the absence of fear and guilt. Fear of punishment sets boundaries on human behavior; conscience and the compassion it reflects define our humanity. Without them, the human potential for savagery is unrestrained. Operating with the approval of their communities, and beyond the reach of federal authorities, Klan terrorists had little to fear; they killed and maimed with impunity. Moreover, within a culture that devalued and trivialized the lives of black men and women, there was a remarkable absence of guilt among whites for the atrocities they committed against them. Shame and remorse were unfamiliar emotions to the perpetrators of such crimes.

Violence is a disease of human relationships. In clinical terms, individuals who repeatedly commit brutal and remorseless crimes may be described as sociopaths. When their crimes are condoned and facilitated by their communities, as they were in the American South, the foundations of civilization itself are sacrificed. Appeals by black victims to the moral sensibilities of their oppressors were fruitless because, for the perpetrators of this violence—and those who condoned it—conscience had been forfeited in a subculture of violence.

Notes

1. Quoted in J. Mellon (ed.), *Bullwhip Days: The Slaves Remember* (New York: Weidenfeld & Nicolson, 1988), 406.
2. Quoted in W.R. Ferris, "Black Folklore from the Mississippi Delta" (Ph.D. diss., University of Pennsylvania, 1969), 68; see, also, N.R. McMillen, *Dark Journey: Black Mississippians in the Age of Jim Crow* (Chicago: University of Illinois Press, 1989), 224.
3. T. Tunnell, *Crucible of Reconstruction: War Radicalism and Race in Louisiana, 1862–1877* (Baton Rouge: Louisiana State University Press, 1984), 153; A.W. Trelease, *White Terror: The Ku Klux Klan Conspiracy and Southern Reconstruction* (New York: Harper & Row, 1971), 83, 92–94, 127–28.
4. *Report of the Joint Select Committee to Inquire into The Condition of Affairs in The Late Insurrectionary States*, 42d Cong. 2d Sess., 13 vols., February 19, 1872, ; hereafter cited as *KKK Investigation*.
5. W.J. Cash, *The Mind of the South* (New York: Vintage, 1969; orig., 1941), 134–135.
6. Klansmen in Wilkinson County seemed to have an agenda of sex-related atrocities. A few weeks before Lowther was emasculated, the county sheriff had been murdered by the Klan for living with a black woman and their five children. The couple was tied together to an iron bar and drowned in a creek as their terrified children watched.
7. Testimony of Henry Lowther, October 20, 1871, *KKK Investigation*, Georgia, 356–363.
8. Testimony of Oscar Judkins, October 18, 1871, *KKK Investigation*, Alabama, 1042–1048.

9. Testimony of Rachel Arnold, October 21, 1871, *KKK Investigation*, Georgia, 389.

10. Testimony of Mary Brown, Mary Neal, and Caroline Benson, October 21, 1871; Joe Brown, October 24, 1871, *KKK Investigation*, Georgia, 375, 386–387, 501–502.

11. Testimonies of Samuel and Hannah Tutson, November 10, 1871, *KKK Investigation*, Florida, 54–64.

12. Testimony of Jackson and Jane Surratt, July 8, 1871, *KKK Investigation*, South Carolina, 520–526.

13. Testimonies of Letty and Augustus Mills, October 23, 1871, *KKK Investigation*, Georgia, 465–470; see, also, Testimony of Charles Smith, October 26, 1871, and Ruben Sheets, October 27, 1871, Georgia, 597–601, 651–653.

14. Testimony of George W. Houston, October 17, 1871, *KKK Investigation*, Alabama, 997–1002.

15. Testimony of Eliza Lyon, October 24, 1871, *KKK Investigation*, Alabama, 1262–1267.

16. Testimony of Betsey Westbrook, October 24, 1871, *KKK Investigation*, Alabama, 1242–1247.

17. This graphic testimony may be too disturbing for some readers:

> They are "stabbing me with a knife...I feel the blood...," the elder Blair heard his son scream, as the Klansmen began their grisly work: "The calves of his leg were split up and cut across, and his thighs were split open and cut across," Blair recalled, and "they tried to take the cap off of his knee, and all his hands and arms were cut and slit up..."
>
> "Go on, God damn you; you will have no use for no blood no how mighty soon," one attacker shouted at the boy as his father crept toward the scene, following his son's bloody trail "all the way up the hill."
>
> "They were punching and cutting him," Blair said and then "they took him down and beat on his head.... He never hollered once, but I could hear [a wheezing, rattling sound in his throat] as they were choking him, and others were cutting him with a knife as they held him there."
>
> "You feel here and see how you like these gashes," Blair heard someone taunt the dying boy, "Do you reckon they will do you?" Then Blair described how, "This man hauled off and struck [the boy] and then jumped on to him and stamped him, and they shot off their pistols then and got on their horses and went away."

18. Testimony of Augustus Blair, October 9, 1871, *KKK Investigation*, Alabama, 674–679.

19. Testimony of John Johnson, October 27, 1871, *KKK Investigation*, Georgia, 664.

Part III

The Restoration

8

Convict Labor

"Before the war we owned the negroes.... But these convicts: we don't own 'em. One dies, get another."
—A Southern white businessman, 1883[1]

"We cannot see why we should be watched more vigilantly by the police, apprehended for smaller offenses, and condemned with less hesitation than are the whites; why we are excluded almost invariably from serving on juries; why we are subjected to the awful lynch law, a visitation so seldom happening to a white man."
—Nashville Daily American, August 17, 1885[2]

"Then Jesus told his angel to 'git two wings ter cover your head, two ter cover your feet, go down ter Jerusalem and shake jail, and buckle loose the jail and let my chillen free.'"
—A Southern black preacher, c. 1930s[3]

With the restoration of civil government after the Compromise of 1877, Klan terrorism of the sort described in the last chapter became less essential to maintaining white supremacy. The brief and largely illusory political gains blacks had made during Reconstruction were relentlessly wiped out through violence and intimidation; moreover, for most, social and economic circumstances had worsened as their personal safety became more problematic. Without even the pretense of federal prosecution for crimes against blacks, there was no longer any need for disguises and nighttime raids. Thus, in the last quarter of the nineteenth century, Klan terror was supplanted by state systems of criminal justice as the dominant forces in controlling a landless and impoverished black population. Instead of men in hoods and robes, they now wore uniforms and badges. Often they were the same men.

* * *

The end of the Civil War brought about the most significant change in the history of Southern penology. Emancipation changed the status of one-third of the South's population, shifting responsibility for black misconduct from the slaveowner to the state, and flooding the criminal justice system with a whole new population of potential offenders. With the Southern economy in a shambles and government still in disarray, the former Confederate states were unprepared to handle this new responsibility. Many Southern jails and prisons had been destroyed or badly damaged in the war. The penitentiaries in Georgia, South Carolina and Virginia had been burned; those in Alabama, Arkansas, Louisiana, Mississippi, Tennessee, and Texas were partially destroyed; and Florida had no state prison at all until after the war when it converted a federal arsenal at Chattahoochee. North Carolina, like the rest of the South, simply lacked the revenues to repair even its existing facilities let alone build and maintain new ones that would be able to accomodate both whites and blacks in segregated areas. Prisons, in this sense, provided one the first clues as to how the South would eventually deal with the "equal protection" provision of the Fourteenth Amendment.[4]

Whites realized that it made no sense to confine black criminals in penitentiaries and jails, for the same reason that it made more sense to whip a slave and put him back to work than it did to lock him unproductively in stocks or a sweat box. An idle black was an abomination to the typical Southerner, especially when the South needed cheap labor to rebuild itself. Thus, an intricate system of state laws and local ordinances rapidly evolved to entrap and prey upon impoverished black males to commandeer their labor. Except for their "race blind" language, these laws were virtually identical to the infamous "Black Codes" of early Reconstruction. Their purpose, of course, was the same. The key element in their success was the landless vulnerability of freedmen; the target was the young, black male.

The system owed much to the wording of the Thirteenth Amendment. That amendment had abolished slavery and involuntary servitude, Southern lawmakers acknowledged, *except as punishment for crime.* That important exception meant that all enterprising Southern legislators had to do was to expand the definition and seriousness of certain crimes that impoverished blacks were likely to commit. "If a State can make a crime within the meaning of this amendment, whatever it chooses to call a crime," a federal official observed, "it can nullify the amendment and establish all the involuntary servitude it may see fit."[5] And that's what happened.

State criminal codes were revised to cast the widest possible net for the unwary and unlucky. Petty theft was elevated to grand larceny in some states and certain misdemeanors were reclassified as felonies. An accident like breaking a piece of machinery, or the accidental death of a farm animal, could be blamed on "negligence," and require repayment or jail. A conviction for an unlucky escapade like gambling, or fornicating, or getting drunk could mean months on a county labor gang, especially if the offender was a healthy, black male without money to pay a fine. An investigator in Bibb County, Georgia discovered that 149 people, almost all of whom were black, had been given combined sentences totaling nineteen years for offenses like spitting and walking on the grass surrounding public buildings. Almost as absurd were the infamous "pig laws." Stealing a pig in Mississippi, for example, carried a five-year sentence; a burglary conviction in South Carolina could mean life imprisonment. A black convict in a Georgia prison camp had been given a twenty-year sentence for "hog-stealing." Another in Louisiana was given a one-year sentence for stealing "five dollars' worth of gunny sacks."[6]

In some states, Alabama for instance, it was also customary to cover "court costs" by adding "hard labor" to sentences. Often the time added to cover costs exceeded the original sentence. For example, Abe McDowell, a black man from Wilcox County, was given a two-year sentence for stealing a pig valued at one dollar. But then three years, nine months, and eleven days were added to his sentence to cover court costs. James Jackson suffered a similar fate in Greene County. Originally sentenced to seventy days at hard labor for misdemeanors, a judge estimated costs then added four years, two months, and twenty days to his sentence. In Florida, a prison official admitted that "it was possible to send a negro to prison on almost any pretext, but difficult to get a white man there unless he committed some very heinous crime."[7]

How diligently such laws were enforced depended on the demand for labor. When demand was high during planting or harvest, for example, even doing nothing at all offered no guarantee of safety. Strict enforcement of broadly written vagrancy laws provided ample opportunity for police to prey upon unemployed blacks when labor was in short supply.[8] A visitor to Atlanta in 1878 was told that, "blacks are sent to the chain-gang very readily; when men are wanted for the chain-gang they are always got."[9] In Alabama, Georgia, Mississippi, Arkansas, and Texas, for example, it eventually became the duty of police officers to supply names of "suspected" vagrants to facilitate "vagrancy roundups" whenever labor was in short supply. In 1877, the *Vicksburg Daily Commercial* reported that "the majority of the loafing 'cullerd populations' have gone to the country to pick cotton." A few days later it advised that "Cotton pickers will soon be wanted in the country. Bring up the idlers and those who are without employment."[10]

The system shamelessly exploited the fact that few blacks had the money to pay the exorbitant fines levied on them. When the city of Savannah, for example, needed swamps drained and roads repaired in 1884, it looked to its "idle negroes, principally boys from 12 years and upwards."[11] Convictions for petty offenses carried typical penalties of a fine "not exceeding two hundred and fifty dollars, or by imprisonment not more than six months."[12]

Some states even went further by limiting hunting and grazing on public lands to enhance black economic vulnerability and dependence on white employers. Without land and money, blacks who refused to sign labor contracts could be charged with vagrancy; those who breached their contracts faced criminal rather than civil charges; others were often forced to steal to feed themselves and their families. Accordingly, landless black males were confronted with essentially two unattractive choices: they could either agree to such exploitative labor contracts, or risk arbitrary arrest for vagrancy or a variety of other petty offenses, and face months or even years of convict labor when they were convicted.

Criminal surety laws provided a major link between the criminal justice system and the agricultural economy.[13] These laws gave white employers the opportunity to pay the fines of blacks caught in this web of entrapment; in return, they could claim the arrestee's labor until the bond was repaid. The catch was that such persons were then at the mercy of their employers until they could "work off" their debts to the employer's satisfaction. On Monday mornings it was customary for prospective employers to appear at county jails, offering to pay the fines of blacks arrested over the weekend. Blacks too poor to pay their fines for such flimsy convictions as "gambling" or "drunk and disorderly" conduct, as well as vagrancy and breech of contract, contributed to a cheap and accessible pool of bonded labor that could be drawn upon at the convenience of white planters and businessmen.

On the surface, surety laws seemed reasonable enough, but their purpose was white control of black labor. Like most public officials, the mayor of Shreveport, Louisiana rationalized the exploitive nature of the practice as a good way to handle petty crime:

[A negro] is brought before the police court, and tried, and convicted.... The judge almost invariably binds him over in some very small amount; whereupon some planter, anxious for labor, will come in and go on his bond, take him out, pay the thing in full.... This is I might say, the *universal* system.[14]

But the time required to work off fines had a familiar way of extending far beyond the original sentences, providing weeks and months of cheap labor for dishonest employers. Some would pay a man's fine, then turn a profit by subleasing him to someone else for a few dollars more.

In addition, a notoriously abused fee system under which counties paid sheriffs personally to maintain their prisoners provided another incentive to arrest blacks and extend their sentences as long as possible. Under this system, a sheriff might be paid, say thirty cents per diem per prisoner for food. It was common, however, to spend less and pocket the money. In Jefferson County, Alabama, for example, one sheriff received food fees of $37,689 and kept $25,126 for himself. In the same manner, "fee constables" literally made their living arresting blacks on a fee per arrest basis, usually on trivial charges. Thus the worst, most incompetent, employers could always rely upon a widening pool of free black labor provided by constables, justices of the peace, and sheriff's deputies, who profited themselves in the process.[15]

Black newspapers complained about the double standard of justice and the way the system preyed shamelessly upon poor black men. Indeed many questioned the meaning of crime in a system so flawed. "All of the hog, sheep, cow and chicken stealing by the dishonest members of [our] race since the world began," the *Richmond Planet* wrote, "will not begin to equal one hundredth part of the amount of money which has been stolen by members of the white race, who lay claim to all of the intelligence, religion, and learning."[16]

Gabe Butler, a former Mississippi slave described the situation this way:

You kno' you niver heard tell uf a slave bein' ter de pen[itentiary], en now de niggers goes ter de pen ebber time de courts meet. Dey had better wish dey wus slaves.[17]

For those entrapped by the system, it was worse than slavery. The often remarked upon rise in black "criminality" after emancipation, as Gabe Butler observed, can be largely explained by these policies. Selective law enforcement and the demand for free labor accounted for much of the growth in the black prison population, not a biological susceptibility to crime, as so many commentators of the period claimed.[18]

* * *

As demand for free labor continued to grow, convict leasing became a widespread practice among the states and large private companies. Strong backs and heavy lifting were needed for major projects vital to the overall recovery and development of the post-war regional economy. There were roads, railroads and levees to be built and maintained, timber and turpentine to be harvested, coal and phosphate to be mined. Convict labor offered the most economical way to accomplish those objectives, becoming the functional equivalent of chattel slavery.

Putting black convicts to work for large private businesses had great psychological appeal in the former slave states. "The negro has a constitutional propensity to steal and in short to violate most of the ten commandments," a South Carolina politician explained, "The State should farm out such convicts."[19]

"Farming out" prison labor to private companies was not a new idea. Convict leasing had been in use before the Civil War in Kentucky and Louisiana, but its popularity increased dramatically with the war's end because of the prison shortage.

Under the lease system a state would relinquish a portion, or all, of its prison population to the highest bidder. In addition to paying the lease, the lessee would also agree to feed, clothe, house and provide security for the prisoners at facilities owned by the lessee.[20] But political corruption was endemic and the cost of leases varied widely from year to year and from state to state, depending upon the kind of deal that had been struck. In 1868 Georgia leased one hundred black prisoners for a year to the Georgia and Alabama Railroad for $2,500. Eight years later it leased all its prisoners to three bidders for $25,000 per year. In 1877 Florida leased eighty-two prisoners to a construction company for only $100 a year; in 1884 the entire prison population of Tennessee was leased to the Tennessee Coal and Iron Railroad for $100,000 a year. In Alabama, short-term leases with rates at $2.50 to $5.00 per convict per month were negotiated with railroads and planters as well as coal and steel companies. The profit motive and the absence of government regulation ensured that food, shelter, and clothing provided by the lessees were usually inadequate; so bad, in fact, that one observer described the leasing system as, "[I]n every way a disgrace to civilization."[21]

But even reform-minded Republican state governments had recognized earlier during Reconstruction that leasing offered a profitable solution to the problem of inadequate prisons. It was a solution quickly seized upon by Southern Democrats when they regained control in 1877. Democrats quickly expanded the lease system, granting long-term leases to companies to rebuild and expand Southern industries. Requiring prisoners "to pay for their own keep" not only would save state revenues, it was just good politics. To Southern Democrats, convict leasing seemed to be a consummate solution to a variety of problems.[22]

The cultural links between the leasing system and slavery could not be missed. In 1880, for example, an Alabama prison warden advertised three grades of prisoners for lease: "Full hands" were leased at $5.00 a month; "medium hands" for $2.50; and "dead hands" were leased without charge except for their keep. But the convict lease system proved to be worse than slavery because lessees had no pecuniary interest in their convicts as slaveholders had had in their slaves.[23] "Before the war we owned the negroes," a Southern lessee explained in 1883,

> If a man had a good negro, he could afford to take care of him: if he was sick, get a doctor. He might even get gold plugs in his teeth. But these convicts: we don't own 'em. One dies, get another.[24]

By 1880 all the former Confederate states and Kentucky were leasing most of their prisoners to private companies who cared little whether their charges lived or died. In Mississippi county supervisors were required by law to lease the entire county jail population to the highest bidder, regardless of other considerations.

As the South continued to rebuild itself in the late nineteenth and early twentieth centuries, the pool of black convict labor grew rapidly to keep pace with demand. Throughout this period, nearly 90 percent of the inmates in Southern prisons were black, despite the extraordinary levels of white violent crime against blacks. In 1870, the black prison population in the Southern states was 6,031; in 1880, it was 12,973; in 1890, the number had climbed to 19,244; by 1910, it had grown to 28,620. Even these numbers underestimate the total impact of the penal system on the black male population, for only "live" prisoners were counted, and county jail populations were excluded.[25]

* * *

As the inmate population grew in response to labor demand, so did the numbers of those who died during their captivity. The mortality among leased convicts, especially blacks, was extraordinary. In 1890, F.H. Wines, an ardent prison reformer of the period, told the Annual Congress of The National Prison Association that

> The convicts in [lease camps] were virtually slaves; and, so far as they were affected by existing legislation, slavery, which had been abolished by the proclama-

tion of Abraham Lincoln, was reestablished, not only for negroes, but for whites, and without any of the alleviations of patriarchal slavery. The new master had no pecuniary or personal interest in the men whom he had purchased for a limited period, to restrain him from overworking or otherwise abusing them. They were placed in the immediate custody of men who, for the most part, belonged to the overseer class.... The mortality, under this system, was something frightful to contemplate.[26]

Nowhere were private companies in tighter control of the prison system than in Arkansas, Louisiana, and Mississippi. In Louisiana Major Samuel Lawrence James built a business empire with convict labor in the 1870s that endured for the remainder of the century. James was described by admirers and critics alike as "the largest slaveholder in post-bellum Louisiana." There is no record of any Louisiana slaveholder owning as many slaves and treating them so poorly as James did the convicts he leased.[27]

Approximately 84 percent of James's convicts were black. In addition to cane cutting and cotton picking, he used blacks to build and maintain the levees along the Mississippi. Levee work was very lucrative because the state was willing to pay well to protect its rich Delta lowlands from the devastating floods that could destroy its vital agricultural economy. Blacks were used almost exclusively for this work because it was extremely arduous and dangerous. Many convicts died accidental deaths in drownings and cave-ins as tons of mud and sand had to be continually moved by men with shovels and wheelbarrows working on crumbling banks above swirling floodwaters. Between 1870 and 1901, some three thousand convicts, almost all of them black died working for James. In 1883, an investigator wrote that, "the year's death-rate at the convict camps of Louisiana must exceed that of any pestilence that ever fell upon Europe in the Middle Ages." A report in 1901 indicated that "it is manifest that out of the total number of prisoners more than half were not physically able to perform this work" and died of illness and exhaustion.[28]

Alabama labor camps were no better. The *Mobile Register* reported in 1875 that Alabama convicts "died like cattle in slaughter pens...laboring with manacled limbs in swamps and sleeping in [an] unwholesome atmosphere." Prison officials claimed that the more than 20 percent death rate among the twelve hundred black inmates at the infamous Pratt Mines north of Birmingham was exaggerated by the press. The convicts were "better housed, better fed, better clothed, and receive better medical care," a company spokesman insisted, than "a majority of the same class" who are "free." The deaths that did occur could not be helped, he continued, because "the negro is physically and mentally inferior" in his ability to adapt. A Pratt convict was required to mine as much as four tons of coal a day to avoid punishment.[29]

In Alabama, like most Southern states, prison inspectors had no authority to act beyond making reports to indifferent legislators. In the 1880s the average rate of death in prisons outside the South was 14.9 per thousand predominantly white prisoners, while the average in the South was 41.3 per thousand, the overwhelming number of whom were black.[30]

Georgia camps, also, were deplorable. The National Prison Reform Congress reported that 40 percent of the convicts at a work camp in Richmond County died over a four-month period in 1878. In response to this shocking revelation, a Georgia official, like his Alabama counterparts, blamed the victims. Complaining that the Prison Reform Congress was being misled, he wrote that

> the mortality is not so great as one would infer...and it is really caused, not by cruelty but [by]...defective hygiene [and] the habits of negro convicts.... On the contrary, the trouble in most cases is too great lenity [sic] and too much freedom,—in fact, lack of punishment.[31]

The same year, 1878, an estimated twenty percent of the convicts in Florida and South Carolina also died.

Death was a familiar visitor at every prison camp in Georgia. At the Dade Coal Mine camp, for example, an investigator wrote of the scenes he observed as "an experience never to be forgotten":

> [The convicts] are worked in the mines where the temperature averages about sixty degrees, and where the cold water drips down constantly upon the workers. They are then compelled, on leaving the mine, to go to their quarters and sleep in these saturated clothes.... In many instances we found the men working in such places as rendered it necessary for them to lie on their stomachs while at work, often in mud and water with bad ventilation, in order to get out the daily amount of coal that would save them from the punishment to be inflicted by the whipping boss.[32]

In the "quarters," food was described as

> meagre, unwholesome, and unfit to build up the wasted energies of the human frame.... The water supply was insufficient for bathing and the men complained that they did not get enough water to drink. The roof of the sleeping quarters leaked and the prisoners often had to sleep in wet beds. The men were chained nightly, by short chains, to a long chain running the entire length of the building.

For such reasons, an investigator wrote in 1885, "ten years, as the rolls show, is the utmost time that a convict can be expected to remain alive in a Georgia penitentiary." Blacks, it was noted, were being given sentences of ten to twenty years—or what amounted to death sentences—for "simple stealing, without breaking in or violence."[33]

Mortality in North Carolina's company-owned camps was also staggering. Of the 776 North Carolina prisoners leased to railroads during 1879 and 1880, 178, or 23 percent, died. Explanations were given for only eleven of the fatalities—those killed trying to escape. Many others were simply worked to death. When asked about such cases, the warden agreed, giving this answer:

> [Many had] taken their regular shifts for several years in the Swannanoa and other tunnels on the Western North Carolina Railroad, and were finally returned to prison with shattered constitutions, and their physical strength entirely gone, so that [even] with the most skillful medical treatment and the best nursing, it was impossible for them to recuperate.[34]

The death rates among leased prisoners in Texas may have been worse than any state. "On railroad construction," the reformer, George W. Cable wrote,

> the average annual rate of mortality for 1879 and 1880, was 47 to the thousand, three times the usual death-rate for properly managed American prisons; at plantation labor it was 49 [per thousand]; at the iron-works it was 54 [per thousand]; and at the woodcutting camps more than half the entire average population died within two years.

Moreover, only 23 percent of these Texas fatalities died in prison hospitals, the rest died without treatment in the camps. Nor were they victims of a single deadly epidemic. Death came in a variety of guises: Scurvy, malaria, dysentery, pneumonia, "general debility," and "gunshot wounds" were the most familiar.[35]

Conditions in prison camps managed by the states and counties were not much better. In Mississippi convicts were chained together in swamps where they were forced to drink and relieve themselves in the same water. Food was scarce and not fit for consumption. In Alabama, the state allotment for feeding prisoners was only "from thirty to forty cents a day," which was often misappropriated by jailers who purchased the cheapest food and pocketed the difference. The Alabama Board of Inspectors of Convicts issued this assessment in 1902:

> The condition of many of the [public] jails in Alabama beggars description; prisoners are herded in them like sheep, with no ventilation, no sanitation, no bathing facilities, and no change of clothing (although they may be confined for months), reeking with filth and vermin; this with food of the roughest and poorest character not only invites but produces disease. This is a mild picture of existing conditions in many of the jails of the State.[36]

Although racial discrimination was indisputable, Southern prisons did not discriminate on the basis of age. Teenage offenders were confined with, and treated like, adults. In 1874, Tennessee leased 123 convicts who were under eighteen years of age; of these three were twelve and one was ten. And the practice continued. In 1883, Georgia leased out 137 boys between the ages of eleven and seventeen; in 1895, 105 of Arkansas's 981 leased convicts were boys between ages twelve and fifteen. Texas, however, may have the record for the youngest. In 1882, its records show that one of its 509 underage convicts was only seven years old. The old and the young were usually the first to die.[37] The overwhelming number of deaths at any age, of course, were black.

At the threshold of the twentieth century black convicts in the South lived and worked under much worse conditions—with lower life expectancies by far—than their slave forebears had on plantations a half-century before.

* * *

Astonishing brutality added to the casualties produced by deplorable living conditions and debilitating labor. Many convicts were murdered outright by guards, still others died lingering deaths from injuries sustained in beatings and other forms of torture. In Florida, for example, the disciplinary measures of "sweating," "watering," and "hanging by the thumbs," continued until 1877 when all but whipping were outlawed. Sweating was a familiar experience for blacks old enough to remember slavery. It consisted of enclosing the victim in a coffin-like box without ventilation or light until suffocation seemed certain and hysteria ensued. Watering was even worse, according to John C. Powell, a former prison camp warden. "The prisoner was strapped down," he wrote,

a funnel forced into his mouth and water poured in. The effect was to enormously distend the stomach, producing not only great agony but a sense of impending death, due to pressure on the heart, that unnerved the stoutest.

As during slavery, formal prison punishment, in contrast to spontaneous beatings, was usually carried out in a public spectacle calculated to instill terror in the hearts of all who witnessed it. Powell described one such event where,

A negro convict was strung up for some infraction of the rules. Whipcords were fastened around his thumbs, the loose ends flung over a convenient limb and made taut until his toes swung clear of the ground. The scared convicts huddled about the camp-fire and watched their comrade as he writhed and yelled, expecting every moment that the cords would be unfastened and his agony ended. But the captain had determined to make a salutary example, and let the negro hang...the poor wretch's anguish was a hideous thing to see...his muscles knotted in cramps under the strain, his eyes started from his head, and sweat ran from his body in streams. An hour passed—then two. His shrieks had ceased and his struggles grown feeble, so they let him down and he fell to the ground like a log—dead.

Powell acknowledged the brutality, but believed it was necessary. "There are many things about [convict labor] which may seem harsh, stringent and cruel, and would be, in a northern penitentiary, but are stern necessities here," because, he explained, "the bulk of our convicts are negroes." He took pride, however, in the fact that he had been one of those who convinced the state to discard these more severe methods of punishment. Whipping, he believed, was probably as effective and more humane.[38]

Powell's peculiar brand of humanitarianism, however, failed to persuade an investigating committee that visited a number of Florida prison camps in 1902. It reported that it had "found a system of cruelty and inhumanity that would be hard to realise, unless it could be seen and heard."[39]

Still, the evils of convict labor were no secret. As early as 1886, the *Second Annual Report of the United States Commissioner of Labor* had used words like "barbarous" and "atrocious" to condemn the leasing system. But because most prisoners were black, support for reforms was slow coming in the South. Even reform groups outside the South believed blacks were incorrigible and unfit for anything but hard labor. Reform and rehabilitation were considered a waste of money because their "vices and defects," as one reformer put it, were beyond the reach of "the advanced systems of treatment in use in some other wealthier states, where only white men are dealt with."[40]

"[The black convict] is not fitted for indoor work," a speaker told a meeting of the National Prison Association in 1906:

He is not wanted as an industrial rival to the white man, and there is no possibility (and perhaps it is not desirable) of introducing into southern prisons those forms of carrying on industries by machinery [as] in [Northern] prisons.[41]

In an attempt to placate Louisiana prison officials stung by criticism, the same reformer in 1905 tried to acknowledge, with unintentional irony, recent improvements in the Louisiana prison system,

[The life of a black convict] on the State farms is almost identical with that he would lead if working for wages. It is indeed more moral, more regular and more sanitary. He is well housed, well fed and well cared for in sickness and in health. He is not overworked.... He is easily controlled, but is liable to punishment by strapping for insubordination or persistent laziness. He will not often run from an armed overseer, and if he does...he runs but a short distance before he is treed by the dogs.[42]

Some commentators on penal systems in the South, like the person just quoted, tried to put a positive glow on the incremental reforms that did occur in the late nineteenth and early twentieth century. But, in fact, prison reform followed the same pattern as the reform legislation of the Reconstruction period: Laws and regulations were passed, but few were implemented. The reforms in sanitation, nutrition, and medical care that were made only underscored the antediluvian thinking of the period. In the 1880s, for example, the state of Georgia drafted these guidelines for humane treatment in a "General Notice to Lessees":

In all cases of severe illness the shackles must be removed. The convicts shall be turned off of the chain on the Sabbath and allowed to recreate in and about the stockade. When a convict is sick, the chains are to be taken off of him.[43]

* * *

Southern justice was designed after the Civil War as an intricate system of entrapment that made a mockery of both the Thirteenth and Fourteenth Amendments. Its purpose was obvious, simple, and perverse: It was not to control crime; it was, instead, to reestablish and sustain white control over black labor. "It was not then a question of crime," W.E.B. DuBois wrote of the situation in 1903, "but rather one of color, that settled a man's conviction on almost any charge." Few of the blacks entrapped in the system had committed serious or violent offenses, for blacks who were even suspected of such crimes against whites were customarily lynched during this period.[44]

The "fiendish cruelty," as one report described it, of convict leasing continued in various parts of the South until 1933. The policy ended, not because of concerns about the injustice and the welfare of prisoners, but outrage over the political corruption involving politicians and lessees, and the protests of free labor over unfair competition. Compassion had little to do with it in a region long desensitized to the suffering of its "niggers."[45]

Even as, one by one, Southern states eventually got rid of convict leasing, the value of a black inmate's life improved little. Substantial elements of the leasing system were preserved in the infamous state prisons and county chain gangs that took over its functions. Though facilities, food and medical care in the state and county managed systems were usually better than that provided by private lessees, the brutal and inhumane treatment of black prisoners continued.[46] The consequences of this corrupt and vicious system of human exploitation extended beyond the convicts themselves, taking a heavy toll on countless black families broken in the process.

Notes

1. Quoted in J. Zimmerman, "Penal Systems and Penal Reform in the South since the Civil War" (Ph.D. dissertation, University of North Carolina, 1947), 93.
2. Quoted in H.N. Rabinowitz, *Race Relations in the Urban South, 1865–1890* (Chicago: University of Illinois Press, 1980), 59.
3. Quoted in C.S. Johnson, *Shadow of the Plantation* (Chicago: University of Chicago Press, 1941), 159.
4. E.C. Wines, *State of Prisons and Child Saving Institutions* (New York: Cambridge University Press and J. Wilson & Sons, 1880), 111–112; B. McKelvey, "A Half Century of Southern Penal Exploitation," *Social Forces* 13 (1934–35), 112–123; Green, "Some Aspects of the Convict Lease System," 115.
5. C.W. Russell, *Report on Peonage*, (Washington, D.C.: Department of Justice, 1908), 31.
6. G.W. Cable, *The Silent South* (New York: Charles Scribner's Sons, 1885), 151–52; V.L. Wharton, *The Negro in Mississippi, 1865–1890* (Chapel Hill: University of North Carolina Press, 1947), 237–238; C.O. Keeler, *The Crime of Crimes; or, the Convict System Unmasked* (Washington, DC: Pentecostal Era, 1907), 7–12; and F.M. Green, "Some Aspects of the Convict Lease System in the Southern States," in F.M. Green (ed.) *Essays in Southern History* (Westport, CT: Greenwood, 1949), 120.
7. G.S. Sisk, "Crime and Justice in the Alabama Black Belt, 1875–1917," *MidAmerica* 40 (1958), 106–107; and J.C. Powell, *The American Siberia; or Fourteen Years' Experience in a Southern Convict Camp* (Gainesville: University of Florida Press, 1976; orig., 1891), 332. See, also, W.E.B. DuBois, *Black Reconstruction in America, 1860–1880* (Atheneum, 1962; orig., 1935), 506, 698–699.
8. A rambling and redundant Florida law was typical:

   Rogues and vagabonds, idle or dissolute persons who go about begging, common gamblers, persons who use juggling or unlawful games or plays, common pipers and fiddlers, common drunkards, common night walkers, thieves, pilferers, traders in stolen property, lewd, wanton, and lascivious persons in speech or behavior, keepers of gambling houses, common railers and brawlers, person who neglect their calling or employment and misspend what they earn and do not provide for themselves or for the support of their families, persons wandering from place to place able to work and who are without means and who neglect to earn their support and live by pilfering and begging, idle or disorderly persons, including therein those who neglect all lawful business and habitually misspend their time by frequenting houses of ill fame, gaming houses, or tippling shops, persons able to work but who are habitually idle and live upon the earnings of their wives or minor children, and all able-bodied male persons over eighteen years of age who aare without means of support, and whose parents or guardians are unable to support them, and who are not usually in attendance upon some school or educational establishment, but who live in habitual idleness *are declared to be vagrants.* (See, Florida Laws, secs. 3570–3571; quoted in Russell, *Report on Peonage*, 30.)

9. Russell, *Report on Peonage*, 17; chain gang remarks quoted in Rabinowitz, *Race Relations in the Urban South*, 49.

10. *Vicksburg Daily Commerical*, August 17, 1877, quoted in W. Cohen, *At Freedom's Edge: Black Mobility and the Southern White Quest for Racial Control* (Baton Rouge: Louisiana State University Press, 1991), 242.

11. *Savannah Morning News*, September 11, 1884, quoted in Cohen, *At Freedom's Edge*, 243.

12. Russell, *Report on Peonage*, 30.

13. Cohen, *At Freedom's Edge*, 244–45.

14. *U.S. Senate Report 693*, "The Removal of the Negroes from the Southern States to the Northern States," 46th Cong., 2d sess. (1880), Testimony of Andrew Currie, 79 (emphasis added).

15. *Annual Report of the Prison Inspector of Alabama, 1914*; *Report of the Sheriff of Jefferson County, Alabama, 1917*; see, also, E.J. Scott, *Negro Migration During the War* (New York: Oxford University Press, 1920), 20–21.

16. *Richmond Planet*, January 5, 1895; quoted in E.L. Ayers, *Vengeance and Justice in the 19th Century American South* (New York: Oxford University Press, 1984), 228.

17. Quoted in G.P. Rawick (ed.), *The American Slave: A Composite Biography* (Westport, CT: Greenwood Press, 1972), Supp. Series 1, v.6, p.1 (Mississippi), 317.

18. W.E.B. DuBois, *The Souls of Black Folk* (New York: New American Library, 1982; orig., 1903), 199–202; B. McKelvey, *American Prisons: A History of Good Intentions* (Montclair, NJ: Patterson Smith, 1977), 198; and Green, "Some Aspects of the Convict Lease System," 120; see, also, G.D. Jaynes, *Branches Without Roots: Genesis of the Black Working Class in the American South, 1862–1882* (New York: Oxford University Press, 1986), esp., 301–316. On biological theories of the period, see, for example, W.F. Quinby, *Mongrelism* (Wilmington, NC: James & Webb, 1876); and P.B. Barringer, *The American Negro: His Past and Future* (Raleigh, NC: Edwards & Broughton, 1900).

19. Quoted in G.B. Tindall, *South Carolina Negroes, 1877–1900* (New York: Columbia University Press, 1952), 267.

20. The lease system is not to be confused with the contract system which permitted private companies to contract with the state for products which are produced by prison labor in state penal institutions.

21. "Convict Labor," *Second Annual Report of the Commissioner of Labor, 1886*, 381–383; *Twentieth Annual Report of the Commissioner of Labor, 1905*, 15; A.E. Taylor, "The Origin and Development of the Convict Lease System in Georgia," *Georgia Historical Quarterly* (June 1942), 114; McKelvey, *American Prisons*, 199–202; Green, "Some Aspects of the Convict Lease System," 116–117; and Cable, *The Silent South*, 172.

22. Green, "Some Aspects of the Convict Lease System," 112–123; McKelvey, *American Prisons*, 197–207.

23. Before emancipation, for example, a Virginia planter complained to Frederick Law Olmsted about the poor quality of Irish laborers he had hired to drain a swamp. When Olmstead asked why he didn't use slaves instead, the planter replied that, "It's dangerous work (unhealthy?), and a negro's life is *too valu-*

able to be risked at it. If a negro dies, it's a considerable loss, you know." See, F.L. Olmsted, *A Journey in the Seaboard Slave States in the Years 1853–1854* (New York: Negro Universities Press, 1968; orig., 1856), 91.

24. McKelvey, *American Prisons*, 201–203, 207; lessee quoted in Zimmerman, "Penal Systems and Penal Reform," 93; see, also, M.T. Carleton, *Politics and Punishment: The History of the Louisiana State Penal System* (Baton Rouge: Louisiana State University Press, 1971), 45.

25. *Negro Year Book: An Annual Encyclopedia of the Negro, 1925–1926* (Tuskegee, AL: Tuskegee Institute), 396; see, also, F.H. Wines, "Twenty Years' Growth of the American Prison System," *Proceedings of the Annual Congress of the National Prison Association*, September 25–30, 1890 (Pittsburgh, PA: Shaw Brothers, 1891), 89; *Report of the Inspectors of Convicts, 1890*, (Montgomery, AL, 1890), 3–4; cited in Sisk, "Crime and Justice," 112; Wharton, *The Negro in Mississippi*, 237; and Green, "Some Aspects of the Convict Lease System," 282. See, *Second Annual Report of the Commissioner of Labor, 1886* (Washington, DC: 1887), 72–79; and *Twentieth Annual Report of the Commissioner of Labor, 1905* (Washington, DC: 1906), 600–609.

26. Wines, "Twenty Years' Growth of the American Prison System," *Proceedings*, 87.

27. Quoted in W.H. Hair, *Bourbonism and Agrarian Protest: Louisiana Politics, 1877–1900* (Baton Rouge: Louisiana State University Press, 1969), 109; see, also, Cable, *The Silent South*, 169–171; and Carleton, *Politics and Punishment*, 19–20, 29–30, 40–45.

28. State of Louisiana, *Board of Control, State Penitentiary, Annual Report—Calendar Year 1901* (New Orleans, LA, 1902), 28; *Journal of Proceedings of the House of Representatives of the General Assembly, 1902* (Baton Rouge, LA, 1902), 24; quoted in Carleton, *Politics and Punishment*, 88–89; Cable, *The Silent South*, 171.

29. Carleton, *Politics and Punishment*, 46; *Mobile Register*, February 15, 1875; quoted in Green, "Some Aspects of the Convict Lease System," 121, 122; *Proceedings of the Annual Congress of the National Prison Association*, November 16–20, 1889 (Chicago: Knight & Leonard, Printers, 1890), 138–139; W.D. Lee, "The Lease System of Alabama," *Proceedings of the Annual Congress of the National Prison Association*, September 25–30, 1890 (Pittsburgh, PA: Shaw Brothers, 1891), 104–118.

30. Cable, *The Silent South*, 142, 151; McKelvey, *American Prisons*, 209–210.

31. Quoted in Wines, *State of Prisons*, 193, 195–96.

32. *Journal of the Senate of the State of Georgia, 1881*, 593–594; *Senate Journal*, 1890, 722; quoted in Taylor, "Origin and Development," 122, 126.

33. *Senate Journal*, 1881, 595–96; quoted in Taylor, "Origin and Development," 122 (emphasis added).

34. Cable, *The Silent South*, 141.

35. Cable, *The Silent South*, 160.

36. *Raymond Gazette*, March 8, 1885; quoted in P.B. Foreman and J.R. Tatum, "A Short History of Mississippi's State Penal System," *Mississippi Law Journal* (April 1938), 263; *First Annual Report of the Department for the Inspection of Jails and Alms-Houses, 1909* (Montgomery, AL, 1910), 21–23; *Report of the Board of Inspectors of Convicts, 1902* (Montgomery, AL, 1902), 32–33; quoted in Sisk, "Crime and Justice," 110.

37. J.B. Lindsley, *Our Prison Discipline and Penal Legislation, with Special Reference to the State of Tennessee* (Nashville, TN, 1874), 38; Cable, *The Silent South*, 176; quoted in Green, "Some Aspects of the Convict Lease System," 120; see, also, *Second Annual Report of the Commissioner of Labor, 1886*, 507–601.

38. Powell, *The American Siberia*, 5–6, 8–9, 13, 21.

39. "Continuing Cruelties in the Convict Chain Gangs and Camps of the Southern United States," (London: The Howard Association, Bishopsgate Without, 1902); quoted in U.S. Department of Justice, *Peonage Files, 1900–1945*, (microfilm) reel no.1, 544.

40. *Biennial Report, Board of Control, State Penitentiary* (New Orleans, LA, 1914), 17–18; quoted in Carleton, *Politics and Punishment*, 95.

41. F.H. Wines, "The Prisons of Louisiana," *Proceedings of the Annual Congress of the National Prison Association* (Indianapolis, 1906), 156; see, also, Carleton, *Politics and Punishment*, 89–90.

42. F.H. Wines, *Detailed Report upon the Penal and other State Institutions Upon Thirty-Nine Parish Jails, for the Prison Reform Association of Louisiana* (New Orleans, LA, 1906), 7–8; quoted in Carleton, *Politics and Punishment*, 108.

43. Cable, *The Silent South*, 153.

44. DuBois, *The Souls of Black Folk*, 200–201.

45. Mississippi was the first to stop leasing in 1894. Tennessee followed the next year after years of conflict with coal miners who blamed their low wages and poor working conditions on the unfair competition of convict labor. Continuing revelations of corruption and brutality led more Southern states to abolish leasing. By 1908, leasing continued only in Florida, Alabama, and North Carolina.

   The death of a white inmate in 1921 finally forced the state of Florida to abolish its system. News of this death generated more national concern than the thousands of nameless blacks who had died before him in the same way. Concern about the adverse consequences of such exposure on the state's burgeoning tourist industry forced the legislature to abolish the system in 1924. Four years later, similar considerations forced Alabama to end leasing; the last, North Carolina, followed in 1933.

46. P. Daniel, "The Tennessee Convict War," *Tennessee Historical Quarterly* (1975), 273–292; A.C. Hutson, Jr. "The Overthrow of the Convict Lease System in Tennessee," *Publications*, East Tennessee Historical Society, 8 (1936); Green, "Some Aspects of the Convict Lease System," 121–123; and Sisk, "Crime and Justice," 113. On Florida's system, see, W.W. Rogers, "Introduction," to Powell, *The American Siberia*, xxi–xxii.

9

A Lawless Loyalty to Color

I asked that boss-man for to gimme my time;
Sez he, "Ole Nigger, you're a day behin'."
I asked him once, I asked him twaist;
Ef I ask him again, I'll take his life.
—Black folk song (Texas)[1]

I feel my hell a-risin' every day;
I feel my hell a-risin' every day;
Someday it'll bust this levee
and wash the whole wide world away.
—Black folk song (Tennessee)[2]

"There is nothing more disheartening to the true
friends of the negroes than the utter disregard of
law manifested in [their] lawless loyalty to color."
—*Atlanta Constitution*, July 19, 1883

In view of the flagrantly discriminatory system of criminal justice that filled the South's convict labor camps, it is little wonder that the crime rate for Southern blacks was three-and-a-half times greater than the rate for whites at the close of the nineteenth century,[3] especially when white-on-black crimes like lynching were accepted customs not reflected in arrest records. Economically motivated and predatory, law enforcement boosted arrest rates for what were overwhelmingly nonviolent, and often petty, crimes. But growing numbers of black males began to lash back. This chapter describes the origins of a new epidemic of interrracial violence that began a generation after emancipation.

* * *

A new generation of black males had come of age in the 1880s, the age when most boys are inclined toward risk-taking and testing the limits of authority whether in the home or in society at-large. A child born in 1865, for example, would have been eighteen in 1883. The first generation to be born "free," but these young men had been weaned on fear as children and schooled in the mayhem of Klan violence. Now as they approached manhood they were treated as potential predators, dangerous beasts no white man needed a license to hunt. Lost in their struggle for survival was the patience of slave elders, leaving behind only the residue of bitter memories and smoldering resentments. Disillusioned with a system of justice that jailed them for petty offenses while whites guilty of raping and murdering their loved ones went free, they understood better than anyone that the unfair sentences of judges were in reality simply the means used to claim their labor. The failed promises of emancipation added depth to their alienation. To these young men, badges and uniforms meant trouble—as surely as white hoods and robes had when they were children. As the symbols and enforcers of white supremacy, their distrust and hatred of law enforcement officers came as naturally to them as their parents' and grandparents' had for Klansmen and overseers.

"Are we going to be murdered like dogs right here in this community, and not open our mouths?" the editor of a black newspaper in Atlanta asked in 1883 after recounting a long list of charges of police brutality and discrimination. Respect and a man's honor demanded some response, he insisted to his readers.[4]

A growing contempt for all whites was also evident, especially among younger males. An article written in 1890 by a black student for the Fisk University newspaper, attributed this new militance to "younger Negroes [who] are ignorant of the so-called instinctive fear of their fathers...[who are] prone to brood in bitterness and suppressed rage over their wrongs, [and who are] more sensitive to injustice and quick to resent." Sharing that spirit, the same writer described blacks who tolerated the insults of whites as being "cur-like; licking the hand that smites us..." Such groveling, the article continued, invites contempt. "We must first respect ourselves if we [w]ould have people respect us."[5]

Without "instinctive fear" and denied "respect," a response other than rage is difficult to imagine. That some would act on that emotion is predictable; that more did not is remarkable. Like the abused children so many of them had been, most blacks attempted to seclude themselves as much as possible from their oppressors; a much smaller number, however, turned mean, and that meanness changed the nature of black crime and race relations in the South. It was this small but significant segment of the black male population that wanted to give these despised offspring of slaveholders and Klansmen—these proponents of the chain gang and "surgery below the belt"—a taste of the fear black men and women had endured for centuries.

The alternatives to violence were scarce in a society that had emasculated black men economically, socially, and politically. Denied ordinary status and the white man's respect, they would command his fear through the only means left to them, the primal masculine forces of strength and sexuality. Less inclined than their elders to ignore wrongs, growing numbers of this generation wanted revenge. In view of the Ku Klux Klan's sexual depredations many of them must have witnessed, and some certainly experienced, against black women and children, they understood that next to subduing the despised white male himself, no revenge was sweeter than taking his women. Honor, with its unyielding demand for respect, and the visceral satisfactions of raw physical force were all that remained.[6]

* * *

An outlaw tradition grew out of those feelings. Challenging the rules, to be sure, was a time-honored tradition among a people schooled in bondage. One can only imagine, for example, the satisfaction that Bennet Barrow's nemesis, Ginney Jerry, must have given the other slaves who labored and suffered with him on that Louisiana plantation. Men and women like him were surely admired, for no amount of whipping, it seemed, could break their defiant spirits. It was their names and deeds that were recounted in slave rhymes and song, not those of faithful servants who did their master's bidding.

The authoritarian nature of slavery ensured that coercion, defiance, and raw physical force remained entwined in the lives and culture of blacks even after emancipation. Free black men with a steady gaze, unwilling to retreat from angry employers, and increasingly scornful of police, became the scourge of white supremacists, a threat to a cherished way of life.[7]

It was a rare black person who had not witnessed white atrocities directly. Men who had come of age living with the daily threat of harassment from any white who felt like it, and even whimsical murder at the hands of Klansmen, were no longer inclined to turn the other cheek when their lives, families, or livelihoods were threatened. A lawless felon to whites, the new black outlaw soon became a symbol of courage and resistance to blacks, taking his place in black folklore along with countless recalcitrant slaves like Ginney Jerry and Fannie Moore's mother who struck back at the whites who tyrannized their lives.

Fear is the mother of hatred. Although the black outlaws who appeared after emancipation were relatively few in number, almost all blacks understood what motivated them and applauded their courage and drew satisfaction from the distress they caused whites. Defiant expressions like "I didn't come here to be nobody's dog", "Ain't let nobody treat me dis way", "Ain't gonna be bossed aroun' no mo'", and "I ain't gonna let nobody, Nobody make a fool out o'me", made blacks feel good about themselves and were celebrated in black folklore.[8] For many blacks, these tough statements were a welcome relief to slave laments about the sweet by-and-by. For them, the words conveyed a refreshing—and compelling —mix of courage and masculinity in a society that had done everything possible to deny those qualities in black males.

Although the law-abiding, vast majority of blacks sometimes condemned the outlaw's violence, all could empathize with its dynamics. Few black men and women had not felt deep within the outlaw's sense of outrage. And fewer still could deny the thrill they must have felt when his actions stirred fear in the eyes and bellies of white men. In an unjust society, things were turned over, inverted; "right" and "wrong" had become ambiguous concepts defined only by force and a white man's word. And there could be no question about the color-coded injustice. An assessment of criminal justice in the South during the last quarter of the nineteenth century led to this conclusion:

> Of the thousands of cases of murder of blacks by whites since emancipation there has been scarcely a legal execution, and comparatively few prison sentences. The offender usually escapes with the sterotyped verdict, "Justifiable homicide," or at the best with a nominal fine. If the relations were reversed, whatever the provocative circumstances, the Negro would almost certainly be sentenced to death or to life imprisonment, if indeed the mob allowed the case to reach a judicial hearing. To say that these flagrant discrepancies have not had their influence upon the black man's attitude toward the law, would be to deny that he is controlled by ordinary human motives.[9]

Black misgivings about Southern justice were, by that time, profound: A "bad nigger" who defied the system was a man to be admired; a "good nigger" was a white man's toady. "Negroes came to look upon courts as instruments of injustice and oppression," W.E.B. DuBois wrote in 1903,

> and upon those convicted in them as martyrs and victims. When the real Negro criminal appeared, and instead of petty stealing and vagrancy we began to have

highway robbery, burglary, murder, and rape, there was a curious effect on both sides of the color-line: the Negroes refused to believe the evidence of white witnesses or the fairness of white juries, so that the greatest deterrent to crime, the public opinion of one's own social caste, was lost, and the criminal was looked upon as crucified rather than hanged.

On the other hand," DuBois continued,

the whites, used to being careless as to the guilt or innocence of accused Negroes, were swept in moments of passion beyond law, reason, and decency. Such a situation is bound to increase crime, and has increased it. To natural viciousness and vagrancy are being daily added motives of revolt and revenge which stir up all the latent savagery of both races.[10]

The moods DuBois described were evident everywhere. The "morbid and exaggerated solidarity" of blacks against the criminal justice system, another writer of the period observed, amounted to nothing less than a "blind moving of the instinct of self-protection."[11]

In a region of pervasive injustice, becoming an "outlaw" could take many forms. The definition of the term itself depended solely on the color of one's skin. For example, labor disputes between black workers and white employers had become, with this new generation, the most common source of violence. The white penchant for cheating blacks out of their wages now involved a calculated risk. In 1891, for example, black laborers in the Arkansas delta near Memphis formed a "Cotton Pickers League" to protest their fifty cents per day wages in the fields. Led by Ben Patterson, a black man thirty-one years of age, the group went on strike, refusing to leave the plantation. The strike had significant economic implications, for it symbolized the threat the new black militancy posed to a Southern economy based on debt peonage and low-wage, unorganized labor. In the conflict that followed, an overseer and two workers were killed. Patterson and a band of fourteen strikers were hunted down by a large posse and murdered in "mass lynchings." Their message, however, was not lost on whites: growing numbers of young black men like Ben Patterson were willing to strike back, even if it meant losing their lives. To whites, he was an outlaw who got what he deserved; to blacks he was a courageous man, a hero who had died defending his rights.[12]

Even as the tiny, emergent black middle class continued to place value on "good behavior" and never having been "in trouble with the law," black-on-white crime was losing whatever stigma it might have had with the black lower-class. Indeed, one observer described the new mood among lower-class blacks as an "idealization" of violence that increasingly knew no racial boundaries.[13] With growing frequency, they took the law into their own hands to settle disputes among themselves as well as with whites. Harming or murdering whites (predominantly males), for example, were the stated reasons for lynching blacks in 45 percent of the cases; and the overwhelming number of blacks executed in Southern prisons had allegedly killed or harmed white victims.[14] Virtually all the perpetrators were young males.

But it was in Southern cities that racial clashes became most frequent and threatening to whites because the black population was more concentrated, its numbers and solidarity more intimidating. Removed, also, from the disciplinary influence of landowners who controlled their paychecks and, to a considerable extent, their lives, urban blacks were less inhibited, less constrained by plantation etiquette, and more risk-oriented than they had ever been. In the squalor and crowding of Southern cities and towns, unpleasant contacts between lower-class blacks and whites became more frequent as blacks tested the limits of de facto exclusion and segregation in public transportation and facilities. The experience of an Atlanta policeman in 1888 illustrates the sense of apprehension this new mood created. The officer had failed to arrest a black man who had assaulted a white, an almost unheard of event. He did so, he explained, because "it might have provoked a riot as the negro that did the cutting was inclined to be boisterous and his colored brothers were rather decided in their expressions of sympathy."[15]

By this time, also, blacks understood that white law enforcement was notably indifferent to crime *within* the black community. When police officers appeared, they knew it was most likely to make an arrest for a crime committed elsewhere; law enforcement had little to do with protecting the safety and welfare of black communities. Dead "niggers" were like dead dogs to policemen—of little concern. Disputes between blacks were commonly ignored, or else trivialized, by police and left to be settled by the aggrieved parties themselves. Such disputes often turned violent. A police officer explained the official attitude this way:

> If a nigger kills a white man, that's murder. If a white man kills a nigger, that's justifiable homicide. If a nigger kills another nigger, that's one less nigger.[16]

But it was the new brashness and solidarity among blacks that became a troubling consideration for police officers when they entered black neighborhoods. City policemen were among the first to understand that they no longer were dealing with "plantation niggers."[17] "In the mind of the quick-trigger policeman," one observer wrote, "is the fear of the 'bad nigger.'...Sensing the danger of scared policemen, Negroes in turn frequently depend upon the first shot."[18]

Getting "the first shot" was a new perspective for blacks whose violence toward whites had heretofore been primarily reactive. For the first time, police became the targets of black revenge. Always eager, as DuBois noted, to arrest a black man for petty and imaginary offenses, white lawmen now had to consider the consequences more carefully. That was confirmed in 1900, for example, when a young black man in New Orleans became a hero in the black community because he did what countless blacks must have fantasized about doing for as long as they could remember. Robert Charles gunned down a policeman after he had been harassed and struck with a nightstick for resisting a purely arbitrary arrest. Charles was wounded in the exchange of gunfire and over the next four days fought a one-man battle against the police who pursued him. Fleeing from house to house with the obvious sympathy and assistance of the black community, Charles killed three more policemen and wounded several others before he was finally killed. The New Orleans newspapers called him "a ravisher and a fiend," sexually laden terms that had nothing to do with Charles' actions. But to the New Orleans' black community and to writer, Ida Wells-Barnett, Robert Charles was a hero, an innocent man who had died defending himself from ruthless white policemen.[19]

* * *

Confronted with the growing threat of angry, defiant blacks like Ben Patterson and Robert Charles, white suspicion and a sense of danger were evident wherever and whenever black males congregated. A new generation of white males had also come of age during the same period. Their "one less nigger" perspective on racial violence added another element to what was to become a formula for mayhem. The Fisk University newspaper, mentioned earlier, described them as, "younger [and] even more hostile and bitter than the older ones."[20] Removed from the paternalistic concerns and tolerances of slaveholding, but imbued with the same sexual obsessions and peculiar sense of honor as their forebears, these young men let no racial challenge go unanswered, no indiscretion could be ignored.

Mob assaults on black men became more brazen and wanton. Virtually any indiscretion by a black man—no matter how unintentional, or devoid of sexual content—seemed to be perceived as a precursor to a dark hand about to reach beneath a white woman's skirts. And for that, political leaders and newspaper editors continually reminded their audiences, Southern honor and virtue demanded the offender's life. Indeed, the survival of the white race, they insisted, required as much. The lethal entanglement of race, sex, male honor, and female virtue defined Southern culture as surely as hominy grits and azalea blossoms.[21]

"To swallow an insult from a negro would be perpetual infamy," a white South Carolinian explained, "whites do not think it wrong to shoot, stab, or knock down negroes on slight provocation." Newspaper editors warned that whites were determined to teach blacks who challenged the racial status quo "a lesson they would never forget."[22]

Blacks, of course, had already learned many lessons that they would never forget. Southern leaders were shocked and appalled, for example, at the now open contempt growing numbers of blacks displayed toward police officers and the criminal justice system. So it was, perhaps, with no awareness of the irony of his words, that the editor of the *Atlanta Constitution* wrote in 1883:

> [T]here is nothing more disheartening to the true friends of the negroes than the utter disregard of law manifested in [their] *lawless loyalty to color*. The meaning of the whole business is that negro thieves, negro murderers, negro lawbreakers of all kinds, are to be protected at all hazards.[23]

Not comprehending that blacks were at long last responding in kind to the state of Georgia's own historic "lawless loyalty to color," a month later the same newspaper picked up the theme:

> When a white criminal is pursued and arrested, we never hear of the white people surrounding the officers of the law and attempting a rescue. But the conditions are all changed when the criminal is a negro. The moment that a negro steals, or robs, or commits some other crime, his person seems to become sacred in the eyes of his race, and he is harbored, protected and deified. If he is captured, resists an officer and is shot, as he should be, and as a white criminal would be, immediately the leading negroes drum up a mass meeting and proceed to pass a string of senseless but sympathetic resolutions, after a series of harangues that would be a discredit to the Zulus.[24]

The *Constitution* was correct on one point. There was no shame or remorse for the kind of wrongdoing that landed most blacks in jail. Owing to the economic motives that drove the criminal justice system, arrest and incarceration were by this time so common among the black lower class that it carried no stigma, and no more social significance than an illness or accident. It was during this period that an arrest record first became a symbol of status, especially if "cutting or shooting" were involved. "Colored men," a white Tennessee newspaper editor wrote in 1877, "who have been in the Penitentiary come back and live among their fellows without receiving contumely or social disgrace." In fact, said another, they were "rather lionized."[25]

Another writer complained in 1889 that blacks no longer condemned "one of their own color who is guilty of a violation of the law, however gross, from which white people alone suffer." Instead, he continued, they were united

> in a conspiracy to protect the criminal, by throwing his pursuers off the scent. No political felon in a conquered country, whose boldness has endeared him to the hearts of his people, but exposed him to imprisonment at the hands of alien authorities, was ever silently and surreptitiously befriended with more ardor than such a burglar or incendiary thus out of the pale of the law, who throws himself upon the good offices of his race.[26]

This writer's reference to "a conquered country" and "alien authorities" should have provided a clue to the explanation that he sought, for by the 1880s blacks were well aware that they were living in a violent society where capricious white hostilities toward them had grown steadily worse after emancipation. What he and the *Constitution's* editors failed to understand is that if the law is not imposed on all offenders alike, it will breed contempt, not respect, in those it punishes. For generations, blacks had stood helpless before the law, pleading for justice, as whites raped and murdered, robbed and cheated their loved ones with complete impunity. Blinded by their own racism, Southerners were unable, or unwilling, to see that there was little reason for black people to respect either the law, or those who enforced it.

But not all white Southerners were so oblivious to the unanticipated consequences of their own "lawless loyalty to color" as the editors of the *Atlanta Constitution*. "I think there can be no doubt that a considerable amount of crime on the part of colored men against white men and women is due to a spirit of *getting even*," a white Kentuckian explained. "Not getting even with any particular individual, but just an indefinite getting even with the white race."[27]

* * *

Getting even. For black males confronted with daily injustices for which there was no legal recourse, there must have been little else on their minds. It is no wonder that defiant men like Ben Patterson and Robert Charles increased in number and were accorded the honor of heroes. To black people, Patterson and Charles were moral men who had stood up for their rights, and like so many before them, it had cost them their lives.

But other outlaws emerged during this period who were, unlike Patterson and Charles, simply predators, preying upon anyone unlucky enough to arouse their interest, or careless enough to present them with an opportunity to strike. Before this time the so-called "trickster" of black folklore was the model for rebellion. Deception and guile marked the escapades of this childlike nuisance to white authority. But he was essentially harmless, befuddling foolish whites and making black people smile.[28] The disappointments of emancipation and atrocities of the Ku Klux Klan changed that.

The outlaw was different. After generations of injustice, some black males had become mad-dog mean. Motivated, it seemed, by an unfocused, nihilistic rage, their only purpose was to assert raw force and create fear in those they despised. They attacked the weak as well as the strong, members of their own race as well as whites. The violence that had shaped their lives and twisted their minds was too complex, too overwhelming to be rechannelled into something constructive. And, of course, the South allowed little that was constructive for its black males, virtually nothing in which they could take ordinary pride, because a proud black man was an abomination to a Southern white. Sometimes the crimes of these outlaws were wanton, unnecessarily vicious acts with seemingly no motive beyond the pain they wanted to inflict, for inflicting pain seemed to provide an exhilarating sense of power that was denied in every other way. Like Nat Turner, it was as though their consciences had been lost somewhere in the depths of the racist society they had been born into and now wanted to destroy just as it had destroyed them. They now formed a small, but troubling, substratum of black society.[29]

Once fate is set in motion, it cannot be undone. Generational change set the stage for an unprecedented scourge of racial violence in the last quarter of the nineteenth century. Young black men, who had defied law and racial custom, would be tortured and killed by the thousands in ceremonial fashion by white lynch mobs. Honor, it seemed, demanded as much of both races.

Notes

1. (n.i.) Thomas, *Publications of the Texas Folklore Society* 5 (1926), 168; quoted in L.W. Levine, *Black Culture and Black Consciousness* (New York: Oxford University Press, 1977), 252.

2. A. Lomax, *Common Ground*, 8 (1948), 50; quoted in Levine, *Black Culture*, 418.

3. M.N. Work, "Negro Criminality in the South," *Annals of the American Academy of Political and Social Science* 49 (September 1913), 76; R.S. Baker, *Following the Color Line* (Williamstown, MA: Corner House, 1973; orig. 1908), 49.

4. *Atlanta Weekly Defiance*, October 29, 1881; quoted H.N. Rabinowitz, *Race Relations in the Urban South, 1865–1890* (Urbana: University of Illinois Press, 1980), 337.

5. *Nashville Tribune* editorial, reprinted in the *Fisk Herald* VIII (July 1890), 15; *Fisk Herald* VII (October 1889), 11–12; quoted in Rabinowitz, *Race Relations in the Urban South*, 335.

6. The emphasis on honor and respect can be traced to the "code of honor" that characterized the behavior of so many Southern white males of that era. It was a code of the frontier expressed succinctly in the often-quoted advice that Andrew Jackson's mother gave to her son. Advising him to be honest always, she also reminded him to remain equally true to his manhood. "[Never] sue anybody for slander or assault and battery," he recalled her telling him. "Always settle them cases *yourself.*" And, of course, Jackson was well known for heeding that advice. For blacks, of course, there was little choice: Honor was *all* a black person had to defend, and it had to be defended personally. See, for example, W.H. Sparks, *The Memories of Fifty Years* (Philadelphia, PA, 1870), 148; C.S. Sydnor, "The Southerner and the Laws," *Journal of Southern History* v.1 (February 1940), 12; B. Wyatt-Brown, *Southern Honor: Ethics and Behavior in the Old South* (New York: Oxford University Press, 1982); E.L. Ayers, *Vengeance and Justice: Crime and Punishment in the 19th-Century American South* (New York: Oxford University Press, 1984); and B. Wyatt Brown, *Honor and Violence in the Old South* (New York: Oxford University Press, 1986).

7. See, for example, Rabinowitz, *Race Relations in the Urban South*, 44–45.

8. Quoted in Levine, *Black Culture*, 252.

9. K. Miller, *Race Adjustment* (New York: Arno Press, 1969; orig., 1908), 80; see, also, G. Myrdal, *An American Dilemma: The Negro Problem and Modern Democracy* (New York: Harper & Row, 1944), 550–553.

10. W.E.B. DuBois, *The Souls of Black Folk* (New York: New American Library, 1969; orig. 1903), 201 (emphasis added). On the breakdown in community deterrence to crime, see, also, W.D. Weatherford and C.S. Johnson, *Race Relations* (New York: Negro Universities Press, 1969; orig., 1934), 430.

11. Quoted in E.G. Murphy, *Problems of the Present South* (New York: Negro Universities Press, 1969; orig., 1904), 174; see, also, E. Foner, *Reconstruction: America's Unfinished Revolution, 1863–1877* (New York: Harper & Row, 1988), 601.

12. W. Holmes, "The Arkansas Cotton Pickers Strike of 1891 and the Demise of the Colored Farmers Alliance," *Arkansas Historical Quarterly* XXXII (Summer 1973), 107–119; L. Goodwyn, *Democratic Promise: The Populist Movement in America* (New York: Oxford University Press, 1976), 292–294.

13. J. Dollard, *Caste and Class in a Southern Town* (Madison: University of Wisconsin Press, 1988, orig., 1937), 272–276.

14. Department of Records and Research, Tuskegee Institute, Tuskeegee, Alabama.

15. *Atlanta Constitution*, August 7, 1888; quoted in Rabinowitz, *Race Relations in the Urban South*, 338.

16. Quoted in R. Fosdick, *American Police Systems* (Montclair, NJ: Patterson Smith, 1972; orig., 1920), 45; see, also, Ayers, *Vengeance and Justice,* 231.

17. H.N. Rabinowitz, "The Conflict Between Blacks and the Police in the Urban South, 1865–1900," *The Historian* XXXIX (November 1976), 70–71; and E.J.

Watts, "The Police in Atlanta, 1890–1905," *Journal of Southern History* XXXIX (May 1973), 176.

18. A. Raper, "Race and Class Pressures," (unpublished manuscript, 1940), 53; quoted in Myrdal, *An American Dilemma*, 542.

19. I.B. Wells-Barnett, "Mob Rule in New Orleans: Robert Charles and His Fight to the Death," Chicago, 1900; reprinted in I.B. Wells-Barnett, *On Lynching* (Salem, NH: Ayer, 1991).

20. *Fisk Herald* VII (October 1889), 11–12; quoted in Rabinowitz, *Race Relations in the Urban South*, 335.

21. See, for example, J. Williamson, *The Crucible of Race: Black-White Relations in the American South Since Emancipation* (New York: Oxford University Press, 1984), 111–139; and G.C. Wright, *Racial Violence in Kentucky, 1865–1940* (Baton Rouge: Louisiana State University Press, 1990), 80; and B. Wyatt-Brown, *Southern Honor: Ethics and Behavior in the Old South* (New York: Oxford University Press, 1982), 453–54. For earlier treatments of the Southern obsession with interracial sex, see, for example, E.G. Murphy, *The Basis of Ascendancy* (1909); W. Archer, *Through Afro-America* (1910); H.H. Johnston, *The Negro in the New World* (1910); T.P. Bailey, *Race Orthodoxy in the South* (1914); F. Tannenbaum, *Darker Phases of the South* (1924); and, of course, J. Dollard's, *Caste and Class in a Southern Town* (1937) and W.J. Cash's *The Mind of the South* (1941).

22. "South Carolina Morals," *Atlantic Monthly* 33 (April 1877), 470; quoted in Ayers, *Vengeance and Justice*, 235; see, also, DuBois, *Souls of Black Folk*, 201.

23. *Atlanta Constitution*, July 19, 1883; quoted in Rabinowitz, *Race Relations in the Urban South*, 60 (emphasis added).

24. *Atlanta Constitution*, August 26, 1883; quoted in Rabinowitz, *Race Relations in the Urban South*, 337–338.

25. Quoted in Foner, *Reconstruction*, 601.

26. P.A. Bruce, *The Plantation Negro as a Freeman: Observations on His Character, Condition, and Prospects in Virginia* (New York: G.P. Putnam's Sons, 1889); quoted in Ayers, *Vengeance and Justice*, 230.

27. W.D. Weatherford, "Lynching: Removing Its Causes," address delivered before the Southern Sociological Congress, New Orleans, April 14, 1916; quoted in Wright, *Racial Violence in Kentucky*, 78 (emphasis added).

28. R.D. Abrahams, *Deep Down in the Jungle...Negro Narrative Folklore from the Streets of Philadelphia* (Chicago: Aldine, rev. ed. 1970), 62–65; B. Jackson, *"Get Your Ass in the Water and Swim Like Me": Narrative Poetry from Black Oral Tradition* (Cambridge, MA: Harvard University Press, 1974), 30–35.

29. Abraham, *Deep Down in the Jungle*, 65–66, 74–79; Jackson, *"Get Your Ass in the Water,"* 30–35. For a discussion of these sociopathic characteristics, see, for example, E. Hobsbawm, *Bandits* (London: Weidenfeld & Nicolson, 1969), ch. 4; L.W. Levine, *Black Culture*, 417–420.

10

The Scourge of Lynching

"We stuffed ballot boxes. We shot them. We are not ashamed of it.... We will not submit to negro domination under any conditions you may prescribe. Now you have got it. The sooner you understand it fully and thoroughly, the better off this country will be."

—Senator "Pitchfork Ben" Tillman, 1900[1]

"[The black man] makes no distinction between political and social equality...he lies in wait...and assaults the fair young girlhood of the South."

—*Atlanta Journal*, August 1, 1906[2]

Southern trees bear strange fruit,
Blood on the leaves and blood at the root,
Black body swinging in the southern breeze,
Strange fruit hanging from the poplar trees.
Pastoral scene of the gallant South,
The bulging eyes and the twisted mouth.
Scent of magnolia, sweet and fresh,
And the sudden smell of burning flesh.
Here is a fruit for the crows to pluck,
For the rain to gather, for the wind to suck,
For the sun to rot, for a tree to drop,
Here is a strange and bitter crop.

—Billie Holiday, "Strange Fruit," 1939.[3]

On Sunday afternoon, April 23, 1899, Sam Hose was lynched after church services in Palmetto, Georgia. Hose had admitted killing his employer in self-defense when the latter tried to shoot him during a dispute over wages. To that undisputed fact was added the totally fictitious rumor that Hose had also sexually assaulted the slain man's wife. The *Atlanta Constitution* offered a five-hundred dollar reward for Hose's capture, announcing that he would be burned alive. Bulletins were subsequently tacked up everywhere people gathered, announcing the place and date of the scheduled burning. Public interest was so aroused that special excursion trains were scheduled to carry curious spectators from Atlanta. Ladies clothed in their Sunday finery watched from carriages, gazing excitedly over the heads of men carrying small children on their shoulders as the ritual began.

Hose was led to a stake placed in the middle of a dirt road. There he was bound with chains. Yelps and cheers rose from the throng of some two thousand people as Hose's ears were sliced off and thrown to anxious onlookers. As he writhed in agony, fingers and toes were amputated before the screaming man's tongue was removed with a pair of pliers. Only then was the coal oil poured ceremoniously over his prostrate body. There was a loud cheer as he was set aflame. When the flames receded, the charred corpse was eviscerated, an enterprising Georgian removing internal organs to sell as souvenirs. Bones went for a quarter; slices of his heart and liver were cheaper at ten cents each. And there were buyers. All this was described in local newspapers. There were no arrests.[4]

On Christmas Day 1920, Henry Lowry, a black farm worker from Nodena, Arkansas asked his employer for wages owed to him. An argument followed, blows were exchanged, and Lowry was shot and wounded by the employer's son. Lowry, who was also armed, returned the fire, killing the employer and a daughter who was standing next to him. Lowry fled to Texas where he was eventually arrested. Fearing for his life in Texas, he believed the governor of Arkansas when he was promised protection and a fair hearing if he would waive his rights and return to that state for trial. At Sardis, Mississippi a whiskey-soaked mob intercepted the train carrying Lowry and the two police officers sent to bring him back. The terrified man was pulled from the train as the two policemen watched helplessly or, perhaps, indifferently. With Lowry in hand, word was sent to concerned parties, in Arkansas and Tennessee, including newspapers, announcing the time and place of a forthcoming public burning. A reporter for the Memphis *Press* attended the event and described what he saw:

> More than 500 persons stood by and looked on while the Negro was slowly burned to a crisp. A few women were scattered among the crowd of Arkansas planters, who directed the grewsome (sic) work of avenging the death of O.T. Craig and his daughter, Mrs. C.P. Williamson.
>
> Not once did the slayer beg for mercy despite the fact that he suffered one of the most horrible deaths imaginable. With the Negro chained to a log, members of

the mob placed a small pile of leaves around his feet. Gasoline was then poured on the leaves, and the carrying out of the death sentence was under way.

Inch by inch the Negro was fairly cooked to death. Every few minutes fresh leaves were tossed on the funeral pyre until the blaze had passed the Negro's waist.... Even after the flesh had dropped away from his legs and the flames were leaping toward his face, Lowry retained consciousness. Not once did he whimper or beg for mercy. Once or twice he attempted to pick up the hot ashes in his hands and thrust them in his mouth in order to hasten death. Each time the ashes were kicked out of his reach by a member of the mob.

As the flames were eating away his abdomen, a member of the mob stepped forward and saturated the body with gasoline. It was then only a few minutes until the Negro had been reduced to ashes...

The only time Lowry spoke was when the mob dragged his wife and young daughter forward and forced them to watch him burning.

The Arkansas sheriff in whose jurisdiction the atrocity occurred was asked why nothing had been done to stop it. "Nearly every man, woman and child in our county wanted the Negro lynched," he replied. "When public sentiment is that way, there isn't much chance left for officers [to do anything about it]."[5]

"When public sentiment is that way," as the sheriff said, (and remains that way over time and across space as it did in the South), one may reasonably conclude that such actions and values are embedded in a regional culture of violence.[6] The case evidence is overwhelming that white supremacists used lynching as the most terrifying and visible means to demonstrate their absolute power over blacks. Lynching supplanted whipping after emancipation as *the* public exhibition of raw primordial power of white over black. Both were part of Southern culture.

Grisly scenes like those described above in Southern newspapers were repeated thousands of times from the end of the Civil War though the 1930s. According to the Tuskegee Institute records, more than three thousand blacks were lynched between 1882 through the 1950s in the United States. Nearly 96 percent of that number died in the South, 87 percent in the eleven former slave states of the Old Confederacy.[7] This peculiarly racial dimension of Southern lynching is revealed in table 10.1. And these numbers are conservative, for they represent only the documented cases where bodies and supporting evidence were located. There is no way to be sure, for example, what happened to many blacks who simply disappeared. Did they just forsake their families and vanish? Or were their bodies weighted and thrown into rivers, or left to decay in remote swamps and shallow graves?[8] As lynching became more controversial in the 1920s and 1930s it became more surrepti-

TABLE 10.1
Lynching by Race in the Former Slave States, 1882–1962

State	Average Percent Black Pop.	Non-Black Victims	Black Victims	Total	Percent Black Victims
Alabama	39%	49	299	348	86%
Arkansas	26%	58	226	284	80%
Florida	34%	25	257	282	91%
Georgia	40%	39	491	530	93%
Kentucky	11%	63	142	205	69%
Louisiana	41%	56	335	391	86%
Maryland	18%	2	27	29	93%
Mississippi	52%	40	538	578	93%
Missouri	6%	53	69	122	57%
N. Carolina	30%	15	85	100	85%
S. Carolina	50%	4	156	160	98%
Tennessee	20%	47	204	251	81%
Texas	17%	191	352	493	71%
Virginia	30%	17	83	100	83%
Total	**29%**	**609**	**3,264**	**3,873**	**84%**

Source: Department of Records and Research, Tuskeegee Institute, Alabama

tious. In 1939, for example, a Southern white informer told Congressional investigators that,

> [My] acquaintance with lynchers and the lynched extends over a lifetime. It is
> [my] judgment that countless Negroes are lynched yearly, but their disappear-
> ance is shrouded in mystery, for they are dispatched quietly and without general
> knowledge...[9]

* * *

The lynching epidemic, that began after the Civil War and accelerated during the last quarter of the nineteenth century and continued
well into the twentieth, was a direct result of the generational conflict
described in the last chapter. Lynching reflected a new era of violence,
another way of expressing the same old hatreds and fears that had fueled

racial animosities throughout Southern history. During this era, lynchings became a public spectacle, much as flogging had been under slavery. Lynching was nothing if not a pagan ritual of human sacrifice.

Before the end of the Civil War, lynching was primarily a frontier practice and its victims were usually white. It was most common in places where the distance between law and a demand for swift and certain justice had not yet been bridged. Until 1868, a majority of lynching victims were white men accused of crimes like murder and rape, and stealing livestock. That same year, 1868, the Ku Klux Klan began to expand its campaign of terror in the South, and lynching began to take on its deepening racial tones.

Lynch mobs behaved differently, depending on the race of their victims. Lynchings of whites were characterized by the swiftness with which victims were dispatched. Justice in the frontier West allowed little time for reflection. The white villains of the region were rarely tortured and almost always hanged rather than killed by other means. In contrast, when blacks were lynched in the South it was the ceremony and ritual, rather than swiftness, that usually defined the event. Ritualized torture and mutilation were customary and, as often as not, the cause of death; dismemberment frequently followed. Only Indians were treated as brutally in the West, and for the same reason: they were not white.

Racial lynchings began in the South shortly after emancipation and reflected the new vulnerability of free blacks. During the peak years of Klan terror from 1868 to 1871, for example, at least 409 blacks were lynched, 291 of them in 1868 alone. Racial lynching continued throughout the 1870s, but no records were kept of the number or the race of the victims. Some estimates indicate, for example, that as many as 2,000 people were killed Louisiana in 1868 alone; between 1865 and 1868, more than 1,000 victims were lynched in Texas. There can be little doubt that many of those killed in Louisiana and Texas were black.[10] The Tuskegee Institute records indicate that as frontier settlements advanced and territorial governments were established in the West, fewer whites were lynched (see figure 10.1). The number of white lynching victims declined steadily after peaking at 270 lynchings between 1884 and 1885. In 1886, the number of blacks lynched (seventy-four) first exceeded the number of whites (sixty-four) who met the same fate. From that year forward lynchings claimed more black than white victims. The numbers document the emerging generational clash described in the last chapter. Except for brief episodes in 1903, 1909, and 1915 when a total of forty-one whites were lynched, the number of

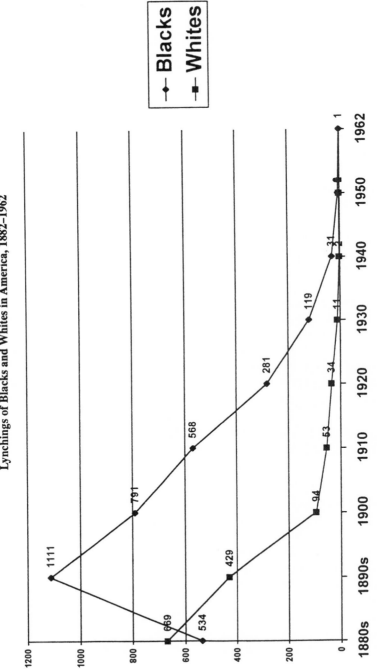

FIGURE 10.1
Lynchings of Blacks and Whites in America, 1882–1962

Blacks
Whites

Source: Department of Records and Research, Tuskegee Institute, Alabama

whites lynched annually never exceeded single digits after the turn of the century.[11]

The sharpest initial yearly increase in lynching occurred in 1889 when ninety-four black victims were recorded. That increase coincides with the race-baiting political and newspaper campaigns that were launched to curb the spread of populism. Southern Democrats were concerned about the appeals white populists were making to the down-trodden of both races. Attempting to undercut such appeals, the fever-ish rhetoric and print of the period played on white fears of black sexuality, the same familiar thoughts that had fueled the fantasies and plagued the imaginations of their slaveholding ancestors. The black man's desire for political equality, these sweating, red-faced orators proclaimed, would lead to a progression of social demands that would lead ultimately to the bedchambers of white women. The message got through; the alarm was sounded and heeded. During the period of populism's greatest strength in the 1890s, 1,111 blacks were lynched, an average of 111 per year, or at least two per week, almost all them in the South.[12]

The presidential election year of 1892 was the worst with 161 lynch-ings. But while lynchings seemed to accompany political instability, they did not follow elections per se. For example, when populists and Demo-crats united behind candidate Williams Jennings Bryan in 1896 in a hotly contested bid for the presidency, lynchings dropped to seventy-eight from the previous year's high of 110. Then the next year, after Bryan's defeat, the figure rose sharply to 124.[13] Nor were chronological patterns similar among the states. Bad years varied from state to state.[14]

Sociologists have attempted to discover the causes of lynching by statistically analyzing such data as demographic characteristics, elec-tion returns and economic cycles. But the inconclusive results of these studies suggest that lynching was not closely associated with census figures, voter preferences, or fluctuations in the business cycle.[15] Con-trary to some reports, the price of cotton, for example, had little to do with lynching. When cotton prices dropped some growers may have taken out their frustrations by lynching blacks, but the evidence over time points to other factors. Demography explains lynching only in the limited, and intuitively obvious, sense that blacks were lynched with greater frequency *only* in the South where over 90 percent of the black population lived.

Jurisdictional distinctions are evident but difficult to interpret. Lynch-ings occurred regularly and throughout the South, but the pathology was more virulent in some states than others. Why is not clear. The most deadly states were Georgia and Mississippi, where for nearly half a century between 1882 and the 1930s their white citizenry lynched an average of more than eight black victims a year. Even at the low end of these atrocities, Virginia and North Carolina, with an average of more than one lynching per year during the same period, still far exceeded any state outside the South.[16]

Certain regional patterns of lynching have also been identified. Historian Edward Ayers found that lynchings were most frequent in the Gulf Plain that extends along the coast from Texas to Florida. The cotton uplands of Mississippi, Louisiana, Arkansas and Texas were also very treacherous areas for blacks. What these especially dangerous regions shared, Ayers explains, were the rural frontier qualities of social isolation, transience, and ineffective law enforcement. But such generalizations are easily over-interpreted, for the differences between regions are slight, especially, one imagines, to the blacks who lived in them. The difference, for example, between ninety-five lynchings over a five year period in the Gulf Plain and eighty-three lynchings during the same period in the Central Plateau probably provided little comfort for those blacks living in the "safer" region. It was the unpredictability and recurrence of lynchings that terrified blacks. Lynchings could occur anywhere in the rural South, and at virtually anytime.[17]

The violent clash of new generations of black and white males described in the previous chapter is reflected in the reported motives of lynch mobs. Seventy percent of the blacks lynched between 1882 through the 1950s were accused of violent crimes against whites. Most were young men. Murder and felonious assault (45 percent), usually in disputes over wages and debts, were the most common reasons given, followed by rape and attempted rape (25 percent). The remaining 30 percent of those lynched were accused of nonviolent offenses. Idiosyncratic reasons such as insulting language or behavior, expressing sympathy for a lynching victim, disputing a white man's word on even trivial matters, insisting on one's constitutional rights, threatening to sue, defending oneself against assault, or simply having the misfortune of straying into the path of mean, drunken, white men account for 25 percent; another 5 percent were lynched for stealing. There is *no* evidence to support the contention that blacks were lynched, as so many Southerners claimed, because courts were too lenient.[18] As earlier chapters have revealed, this was clearly not the pattern when black defendants were involved.

* * *

If one were to believe the words of Southern politicians and newspaper editors, rape—which accounts for just one quarter of the lynchings—was the reason for almost all of them. Although it is true that rape involving black men and white women did increase after emancipation, the danger was greatly exaggerated, probably because white men, like blacks, understood this was one important way blacks could get even. In view of the documented history of sexual assaults by Klansmen on black women and children, it was perhaps logical for such men to fear retaliation of the same sort. Within such troubled minds, something as natural as returning a woman's glance, or smile, or a careless compliment, provided ample reasons to take a man's life. For black men, any but the most obsequious behavior around white women was treated as an intolerable breech of racial and sexual etiquette. In February, 1897, for example, Robert Morton was lynched in Rockford, Kentucky for writing a letter to a white woman. The mere fact that Morton had written such a letter was considered "insulting and insinuating" to the the mob that killed him. The local newspaper reported the lynching indifferently, allowing that Morton "did not bear a good reputation." Another black male was lynched in the same state because he had allegedly "contemplated" sex with his white employer's wife.[19]

Southerners had always been fascinated with the sexuality of their slaves.[20] Moreover, earlier chapters have described the unmistakeable sexual theme in many of the atrocities Klansmen committed against black families. But the fear of black-on-white rape during slavery was largely a reflection of fantasies and lively imaginations, for few white women were ever raped by slaves. Records show that a Georgia slave was hanged for rape in 1812; two more were hanged in Mississippi for rape and murder in 1843. Between 1850 and 1860, forty-three slaves were executed for murder, but only three for rape.[21] Although no one knows how many unrecorded slave murders may have been for that reason.

Clouding the issue of rape both during slavery and after emancipation is the unknown number of alleged black rapists who were lynched for having consensual sex with white women. When such relationships were discovered, a frightened and dishonest woman's surest defense was to claim rape. Some probably did to avoid disgrace and ostracism, but how many is impossible to determine.

The white wife of an Ohio minister, however, did make one such rare confession, eventually admitting that she had been having an affair with a black lover when her anxieties about pregnancy and curious neighbors led to the false accusation that she had been raped. Had she done this in the South, her lover would have surely been lynched. In

Ohio, he received a long prison sentence. Four years into that sentence, the guilt-ridden woman finally made this confession:

> I met Offett at the post office. It was raining. He was polite to me, and as I had several bundles in my arms he offered to carry them home for me, which he did. He had a strange fascination for me, and I invited him to call on me. He called, bringing chestnuts and candy for the children. By this means we got them to leave us alone in the room. Then I sat on his lap. He made a proposal to me and I readily consented. Why I did so I do not know, but that I did is true. He visited me several times after that and each time I was indiscreet. I did not care after the first time. In fact, I could not have resisted, and had no desire to resist.[22]

Countless female slaves, of course, were raped by white men or had consensual sex with them. As Mary Chestnut noted in her diary, the lighter skin, eyes, and hair alone of many slaves left little doubt of their mixed-racial ancestry.[23] But black fathers of mulatto children were less common. That changed, however, a generation after emancipation when social and sexual contact between black men and white women became more frequent.

The race of the victim determined the punishment, if any, of the rapist. Neither whites nor blacks were ever lynched for raping black women. Even arrest was unlikely in these instances, because it was assumed that black women welcomed sexual aggression. If the victim was white, however, the assumption and consequences were different, especially if the offender was black. In 1887, for example, two whites and a black were being held in the Flemingsburg, Kentucky jail on separate charges of attempted rape. In each case, the victims were white women. A mob broke into the jail and lynched the black, leaving the two whites behind unharmed to face trial.[24] That was the pattern throughout the South.

* * *

In addition to the clash of new postemancipation generations of black and white males, "race-baiting" political campaigns contributed to the lynching epidemic by playing on the fear and passions inspired by interracial sex. Explicitly racist Democratic election campaigns grew at first in proportion to the threat posed by the Populist Party's challenge to Democratic rule in the late 1880s and early 1890s. But such campaigns continued to characterize primary election contests long after populism had faded from the scene. Without partisan issues to distinguish candidates, primary elections were commonly fought over which candidate, as grinning politicians themselves admitted privately, could "out-nigger" the other. As a campaign strategy, race-baiting worked. The South's best-known and most influential politicians employed it regularly. Their names stand as markers in a tour of Southern history and racial demogoguery: Ben Tillman and Cole Blease in South Carolina; James K. Vardaman and Theodore Bilbo in Mississippi; Tom Watson and Hoke Smith in Georgia; Jeff Davis in Arkansas; A.J. Montague in Virginia; Murphy J. Foster in Louisiana; Charles B. Aycock in North Carolina; Jim Ferguson in Texas; Tom Heflin in Alabama, to name only a few. These were the most prominent, but countless other candidates for every office from governor to the lowliest county and municipal offices stirred the coals of racial hatred to gain political advantage. Race baiting was part of Southern political culture.[25]

Campaign rhetoric was employed not only to rationalize past violence and injustice, but also to justify what was yet to come for those who challenged the racial status quo. The racial invective that characterized these contests had the effect of kerosene on the smoldering coals of Southern racism.[26] The black male's relentless pursuit of the white female's virtue became a standard theme of campaign oratory. In this manner, both the political and sexual implications of "negro domination" became fused in the minds of white voters. Like a poisonous tide, the racist rhetoric never stopped; it simply ebbed and flowed with the electoral calendar, but the climate of of fear and hostility remained unchanged.

"Pitchfork Ben" Tillman of South Carolina was a master of such rhetoric. Throughout a long and successful political career that began in 1890, Tillman stirred white audiences with lurid tales of the sexual depravity of blacks. His vivid imagination and florid language attracted large crowds wherever he spoke. This corpulent, unmannered man had once publicly thanked God that his daughters had married and now lived in "civilized" white regions beyond the reach of black "sex fiends." The black rapist, he fumed, was "innoculated with the virus of equality...a fiend, a wild beast, seeking who he may devour." Audiences may have caught their breath, for example, when he described diabolic black men with "breasts pulsating with the desire to sate their passions upon white maidens and wives." These heavily muscled monsters, he insisted, were ravishing up to one hundred innocent white women each year. The South, Tillman warned audiences prepared to believe his every word, was teetering "on the edge of a volcano" of racial and sexual mayhem.[27]

Some politicians, fearing the carnage of uncontrolled mobs and anarchy, were more hesitant than Tillman about endorsing racial vigilantism. But an image of weakness and the "nigger lover" label were of even greater concern. James K. Vardaman of Mississippi, for example, claimed he opposed lynching, but sympathized with its objectives. When blacks rape white women, Vardaman explained in a local newspaper interview, "there is nothing left to do with these human brutes but to kill them and at least get rid of them. That is all there is in it." Vardaman did sometimes condemn the macabre rituals and "brutal spirit" of the mob, admonishing his readers to dispatch their victims as quickly as possible.[28]

But, Vardaman notwithstanding, virtually any means to eradicate the perceived black peril was endorsed, including torture and mutilation. Trials were a waste of time when guilt was assumed, and there was a virtual consensus of approval for the severe and certain punishment lynching assured. There was no guilt or shame associated with these spectacles, nor did one need to fear prosecution, for violence in defense of white supremacy was no crime in the South. Among that region's political leadership, few were able to resist the temptation to win votes by pandering to racial fears that they, themselves, shared. When some politicians, like South Carolina's Ben Tillman and Georgia's Tom Watson, began their political careers, they opposed lynching. When they discovered that there were more votes to be gained by endorsing it, they joined the mob and, in effect, gave it legitimacy.[29]

* * *

Newspaper editors joined Democratic politicians in the race-baiting hysteria to such a degree that their partisanship and racism became one. Populists, for example, were called "the most dangerous and insidious foe of white supremacy" in the *Baton Rouge Daily Advocate*. Of the Republican Party, the same newspaper wrote that "the Africanization of the state was its cardinal doctrine." Democrats were "the party of the white man," those who favored political equality were "advocates of Negro domination," and any compromise on white supremacy was "a grave menace to our civilization." Echoing the same message in Arkansas, the *Pine Bluff Commercial* warned its readers that "the most dangerous foe to democracy is the Negro."[30]

Newspapers also played on the fears of whites in stories that linked political equality with black criminality and vigilantism. On the eve of a plebiscite on disfranchisement in North Carolina, for example, these lurid omens of the menace to come if the amendment failed, appeared in the *Raleigh News and Observer*:

THREATENED WITH ARSON AND MURDER
Horrible Menace Against Whites at Whitsett
NEGROES THREATEN TO APPLY THE TORCH
They Will Burn Franklintown
A SHAMEFUL SCENE
Negro Cursed and Abused an Old Man[31]

It was common for newspapers to report black crimes as though each was part of a grand conspiracy to destroy white society itself. "Bad niggers" had to be controlled, editors warned. Why, they wondered in editorials, were even law-abiding blacks foolishly pushing the limits of Southern patience with demands for political equality. It could only end badly, they insisted, for whites would never concede. "[N]egroes are becoming overbearing and need toning down," a St. Landry, Louisiana editor wrote in 1896. "We warn them to be careful, or they will be taught a lesson they will never forget."[32]

Even moderate papers, like the *Atlanta Journal*, followed the pattern in this editorial:

> [The black man] makes no distinction between political and social equality. He grows more bumptious on the street. More impudent in his dealings with white men; and then when he cannot achieve social equality as he wishes, with the instinct of the barbarian to destroy what he cannot attain to, he lies in wait, as that dastardly brute did yesterday near this city, and assaults the fair young girlhood of the South...It is time for those who know the perils of the negro problem to stand together with deep resolve that the political power shall never give the negro encouragement in his foul dreams of a mixture of races.[33]

Such editorials reflected and shaped the mood of the South, and soothed what might have remained of its conscience. Reporters typically described lynching victims in terms like "brute," "fiend," "beast," that assumed their guilt and thus rationalized the atrocity. A Winona, Mississippi newspaper editor's angry defense of a lynching in 1903 was typical: "The parties thus summarily dealt with in 49 cases out of 50 are negro brutes reeking with the guilt of a nameless crime."[34]

Even blacks who tried to defend themselves against unprovoked violence were condemned editorially. For example, after a black man was lynched in Wahalak, Mississippi in 1906, the remaining members of the small black community, who had nothing to do with the alleged crime, resisted a second attack by the same mob. The *Weekly Clarion Ledger* condemned the community, defended the marauders, and advocated further retaliation. Whites would not be safe, the editor stormed, until "the last of the obnoxious negroes have been done away with."[35]

Accounts of lynchings were frequently reported in an offhand, jocular style, in the same manner that black-on-black crime was reported, as if to amuse and entertain readers. As long as the victim was black, lynching was something Southerners could joke and chuckle about. In 1882, for example, the *Louisville Courier-Journal* described a lynching with this wry humor:

> His captors took him to a railroad trestle, about a half a mile from town, strung him up for safekeeping and left him. The lifeless body was cut down by the coroner this morning and planted. The general impression is that Judge Lynch did a very good job, considering the brief time the court had in which to make up his mind.[36]

"Blackbird on a Cherry Tree" was the headline for a lynching ten years later when the same paper quoted approvingly a member of yet another lynch mob:

> Oh but that nigger did plead for mercy and go on like a baby. He didn't have no nerve at all. They pulled him out, though, threw him into a wagon and started down the pike with him to the woods, he a hollerin' and all the gang a yelling and firing their guns.... Scales begged awful hard to get off and said he wasn't guilty, but it was no go.[37]

Further south the humor was less subtle. A Louisiana newspaper, for example, refered to a series of public burnings in 1901 as "negro barbeques."[38]

Sometimes lynching accounts were distributed in pamphlet form, often with religious overtones. One such pamphlet was printed in 1897 by an anonymous publisher in Tyler, Texas:

> Hilliard's power of endurance was the most wonderful thing on record. His lower limbs burned off before he became unconscious and his body looked to be burned to the hollow. Was it decreed by an avenging God as well as an avenging people that his sufferings should be prolonged beyond the ordinary endurance of mortals?[39]

Perspectives like these were deeply ingrained in Southern culture and endured. For example, in 1930 a Houston newspaper complimented a lynch mob for its restraint in these words:

> The crowd that gathered during the afternoon, and which burned the body of the Negro following his death, was perhaps the most orderly one ever congregated, and at no time during the afternoon or night were they rowdy, noisy or uncontrollable.[40]

The local black newspaper described the same scene differently:

> With all the savagery of cannibals and other uncivilized members of the human family, the maniacal white men, women, and children writhed, twisted, and leaped

The Scourge of Lynching

about the suspended burning body, shrieking, singing, and howling in ghoulish glee, shouting defiance to the law, as the body burned in the very shadow of the temple of God.... Little or no investigation is expected here, as no public buildings were destroyed by the mob, just another Negro out of the way.[41]

* * *

Thousands of lynchings could not have been carried out openly for decades without widespread public acceptance. If crowd attendance and enthusiasm are indications, lynchings seemed not only to expiate demons but, also, to provide entertainment and thrills. The number of whites who participated directly in these crimes during this period number in the thousands. Those who actually witnessed lynchings number easily in the tens of thousands.

But millions of Southerners simply said and did nothing, pretending, perhaps, that their silence absolved them of responsibility for what they knew was happening. But there was no way not to be aware of a reign of terror of this magnitude. This conclusion is based on a wide variety of indisputable facts: the support and outright advocacy of the practice expressed by Southern political leaders; the wide publicity associated with many of these events even *before* they occurred; the large crowds of spectators that sometimes attended; the tepid response of the clergy to such outrages; and the way so many newspapers responded indifferently or approvingly.

The absence of moral outrage and acceptance of the practice in the general population was evident in 1897, for example, in Hawesville, Kentucky when an accused black rapist was hanged by a lynch mob in front of an enthusiastic crowd of some eight hundred people. It was a Sunday afternoon and most of the spectators had gathered earlier for a religious revival meeting. The lynching was scheduled during a break in the services which were to resume afterward. Among those present were "not less than 200 women [who] were on the hill overlooking the public square," a newspaper reported, "and when the negro's dangling form went up their cheers rent the air." Within minutes of the hanging, the county coroner, with a resigned look on his face, pushed through the crowd of familiar faces to claim the body. His report, disclaiming knowledge of the perpetrators, was as predictable as the smiles of those who had greeted him at the scene.[42]

Attempts were sometimes made to rationalize the depravity, suggesting that lynchings were the result of frustrations caused by "the slowness and uncertainty of a trial by law. Until this is remedied," the *Troy Democrat* (Alabama) predicted, "we may expect more lynching bees."[43] Echoing the same note, an 1897 editorial in the *Dallas Morning News* insisted that, "If criminals were tried and punished for their offenses with a satisfactory degree of fairness and uncertainty, the lyncher would soon find himself without a job and without encouragement." Southern jurists, such as the chief justice of North Carolina and the Georgia Bar Association concurred.[44]

But there is no evidence to support this argument. The steady growth in black convict labor, alone, during this period denies it. Moreover, trials for blacks accused of violent crimes against whites were considered nothing more than an aggravating waste of taxpayer money. Guilt was assumed in such cases. Even those who were opposed to lynching still insisted that it was a problem for the states themselves to resolve. The thought of federal intervention, it seems, was more reprehensible than lynching.

Political rhetoric, crowd attendance, newspaper humor, and editorial approval were not the only indications that lynching enjoyed wide and enthusiastic community support; the most compelling evidence supporting the subculture of violence hypthesis is the de facto legal immunity from prosecution enjoyed by lynch mobs. Although at least 95 percent of all the thousands of blacks lynched in American history were lynched in the South, fewer than 1 percent of those responsible were ever arrested and convicted.[45]

There was also money to be made by preserving these grisly events in photographs and, later, sound recordings. Body parts, of course, remained popular with those seeking more tangible memories. It was during this period that the great electronics genius, Thomas A. Edison, was striving to create markets for his many inventions. In at least one instance, a sound recording was made of a lynching. The pleas for mercy and screams of agony, the listener heard, were used not only to entertain crowds at carnival sideshows but, also, to advertise the wonders of his "talking machine" at county fairs and other community gatherings. So it was at a town picnic in Pitman's Mill, Georgia in 1896 in the midst of the lynching epidemic. Thanks to the miracle of Edison's invention, a lynching could now be relived and shared with those unable to attend in person. Curious people stood in long lines before paying a nickel to have the tubes placed against their ears. It seemed like magic as men, women, and children waited excitedly to hear the sounds of an event that had occurred weeks, months, or perhaps, years before. One of them, a young boy, described years later what he heard that day:

"All Right Men. Bring Them Out," a voice shouted over a boisterous and jeering crowd. "Let's Hear What They Have to Say." Sounds of chains rattling and cursing men could be heard as the two victims are led to a crude platform built atop a large pile of timber and brush. In halting language the two black men confess to a rape and beg for mercy. "Who will apply the torch?" someone finally shouts. "I will," is the shrill reply. Then a cheer as the crackling flames can be heard licking their way upward. Piercing screams and hysterical pleas follow and continue as seconds stretch into minutes. Then only the sounds of the inferno as the crowd grows silent.

"That's all gentlemen," the vendor says. "Who's next?"[47]

* * *

Who's next? That was a question that must have been on the minds of probably every Southern black man, woman, and child as America entered the twentieth century.

The horrors of lynching and the sense of vulnerability it created left a permanent mark on black culture. "During and shortly after a lynching the Negro community lives in *terror*," Charles Johnson wrote in 1941,

Negroes remain at home and out of sight. When the white community quiets down, the Negroes go back to their usual occupations. The incident is not forgotten, but the routine of the plantation goes on. The lynching, in fact, *is part of the routine*.... The effect on children is *profound and permanent*. After a time the Negro community returns to "normal." Life goes on, but Negro youth "let white folks tend to their business." Contacts with whites are avoided as far as possible. The youth may work for white people but intimacy is avoided. The Negro servant or laborer continues friendly to his employers. The employers may even be liked and regarded as "good white folks," but ultimate trust is held in abeyance.[47]

"You don't understand how we feel down here," a white Mississippian explained in 1908. "When there is a row, we feel like killing a nigger whether he has done anything or not."[48] Blacks knew that was true. It was part of Southern culture.

Notes

1. Quoted in F.E. Simkins, *Pitchfork Ben Tillman* (Baton Rouge: Louisiana State University Press, 1967), 400.
2. Quoted in C.V. Woodward, *Tom Watson: Agrarian Rebel* (New York: Oxford University Press, 1970; orig., 1938), 379.
3. Lyrics by Lewis Allan, Edward B. Marks Music Co., Commodore Records, 1939.
4. *New York Tribune*, April 24, 1899; National Association of Colored People, *Thirty Years of Lynching in the United States, 1889–1918* (New York: Negro Universities Press, 1969; orig. 1919), 12–13.
5. R. Roddy, "Kill Negro By Inches," *Memphis Press*, January 27, 1921; W. White, *Rope and Faggot* (New York: Arno Press and the New York Times, 1969; orig. 1929), 23–25.

6. See, also, W.F. Brundage, *Lynching in the New South: Georgia and Virginia, 1880–1930* (Champaign: University of Illinois, 1993), 19.

7. H.A. Ploski and J. Williams (eds.), *The Negro Almanac: A Reference Work on the Afro-American* (New York: John Wiley & Sons, 1983), 347–48.

8. Figures sometimes vary slightly in other sources, often depending not on whether a death occurred, but whether a death was classified as a lynching or a simple homicide, or whether it occurred in one town or county or another. In view of the circumstances under which this information was obtained and reported, it is not surprising that some errors were made. The most extensive reexamination of these data is by E.M. Beck, S.E. Tolnay, and J.L. Massey, "Lynching in the American South Project," Department of Sociology, University of Georgia, Athens, Georgia. My own analysis of the Beck et al. data set reveals that overall trends, such as those reported in this research, remain unchanged. Moreover, few disagree that the documented cases understate the reality of what occurred.

9. *Lynching Goes Underground*, an unpublished report prepared for "Senators Wagner and Capper and Representatives Gavagan and Fish," (January 1940), 7–9; quoted in G. Myrdal, *An American Dilmemma: The Negro Problem and American Democracy* (New York: Harper & Row, 1944), 1350, fn. 40.

10. R.M. Brown, *Strain of Violence: Historical Studies of American Violence and Vigilantism* (New York: Oxford University Press, 1975), appendix 4, 323; *Report of the Joint Select Committee to Inquire into The Condition of Affairs in The Late Insurrectionary States*, 42d Cong. 2d Sess., 13 vols., February 19, 1872.

11. Department of Records and Research, *Lynching Files* (Tuskegee, AL: Tuskegee Institute); National Association of Colored People, *Thirty Years of Lynching in the United States, 1889–1918* (New York: Negro Universities Press, 1969; orig., 1919), 30, 38; J.E. Cutler, *Lynch-Law: An Investigation into the History of Lynching in the United States* (New York: Longmans, Green, 1905); Brown, *Strain of Violence*, 21–22, 214–218.

12. *Negro Yearbook, 1931–1932*, 293; *Negro Yearbook, 1952*, 278.

13. *Thirty Years of Lynching*, 29; Appendix II, 43–105.

14. For example, of the leading lynching states, Mississippi's worst years were 1891 and 1900 with 20 lynchings in each of those years; in Georgia it was 1899 with 27; Texas set its record in 1897 with 23; in Louisiana it was 1896 with 24. Only Alabama (19), Arkansas (18), and Tennessee (17) set lynching records in 1892, the record year overall. Worst years elsewhere were: Florida (14), 1900; North Carolina (4) and Virginia (12), 1893; South Carolina (14), 1898. A border state, Kentucky had its worst year (12) in 1894.

15. For various sociological theories of lynching and statistical attempts to test them, see, E.M. Beck and S.E. Tolnay, "The Killing Fields of the Deep South: The Market for Cotton and the Lynching of Blacks, 1882–1930, *American Sociological Review* 55 (August 1990), 526–539; S. Olzak, "The Political Context of Competition: Lynching and Urban Racial Violence, 1882–1914," *Social Forces* 69 (December 1990), 395–421; J.L. Massey and M.A. Myers, "Patterns of Repressive Social Control in Post-Reconstruction Georgia, 1882–1935," *Social Forces* 68 (December 1989), 458–488; S.E. Tolnay, E.M. Beck, and J.L. Massey," Black Lynchings: The Power Threat Hypothesis Revisited," *Social Forces* 67 (March 1989), 605–622; C.C. Phillips, "Exploring Relations Among Forms of Social Control: The Lynching and Execution of Blacks in North Carolina, 1889–1918," *Law & Society Review* 21, 3 (1987), 361–374; J.S. Reed, G.E. Doss, and J.S. Hurlbert, "Too Good to be False: An Essay in the Folklore of Social Science," *Social Inquiry* 57 (Winter 1987), 1–11; J. Corzine, J. Creech, and L.

Corzine, "Black Concentration and Lynchings in the South: Testing Blalock's Power-Threat Hypothesis," *Social Inquiry* 61 (March 1983), 774–796; J.M. Inverarity, "Populism and Lynching in Louisiana, 1889–1896: A Test of Erikson's Theory of the Relationship Between Boundary Crises and Repressive Justice," *American Sociological Review* 41 (April 1976), 262–280; and I.M. Wasserman, "Southern Violence and the Political Process;" W. Pope and C. Ragin, "Mechanical Solidarity, Repressive Justice, and Lynchings in Louisiana" (comments on Inverarity), *American Sociological Review* 42 (April 1977), 359–369.

16. Calculations based on the Beck, Tolnay, and Massey data set.

17. E.L. Ayers, *The Promise of the New South* (New York: Oxford University Press, 1992), 156–158, 495–497. A study of lynchings in Virginia and Georgia reveals that these events were somewhat more likely to occur in the southern regions of both states. The interpretive difficulties remain, however. See, W.F. Brundage, *Lynching in the New South: Georgia and Virginia, 1880–1930* (Urbana: University of Illinois Press, 1993), 107, 144.

18. *Negro Year Book, 1952*, 278; see, also, *Thirty Years of Lynching*, 9–10, 37; A.F. Raper, *The Tragedy of Lynching* (Chapel Hill: University of North Carolina Press, 1933), 35–36.

19. S. Lebsock, *The Free Women of Petersburg: Status and Culture in a Southern Town, 1784–1860* (New York: Norton, 1984), 248; see, also, G.C. Wright, *Racial Violence in Kentucky, 1865–1940* (Baton Rouge: Louisiana State University Press, 1990), 80–87.

20. On the white fear of black sexuality as a central element in white supremacy, see, W.D. Jordan, *White Over Black: American Attitudes Toward the Negro, 1550–1812* (Chapel Hill: University of North Carolina Press, 1968).

21. See, for example, Jordan, *White Over Black*; U.B. Phillips, *American Negro Slavery* (Baton Rouge: Louisiana State University Press, 1966; orig., 1918), 458–563, 511–572; *Negro Yearbook, 1931–1932*, 293–294.

22. *Cleveland Gazette*, January 16, 1892; quoted in I.D. Wells-Barnett, "A Red Record," in *On Lynchings* (Salem, NH: Ayer Publishers, 1991; orig., 1892), 60.

23. C.V. Woodward and E. Muhlenfeld (eds.) *The Private Mary Chestnut: The Unpublished War Diaries* (New York: Oxford University Press, 1984), x–xi, 42.

24. Wright, *Racial Violence in Kentucky*, 100–101.

25. P. Lewinson, *Race, Class & Party: A History of Negro Suffrage and White Politics in the South* (New York: Grosset & Dunlap, 1959; orig. 1932), 87–91; J.M. Kousser, *The Shaping of Southern Politics: Suffrage Restriction and the Establishment of the One-Party South* (New Haven, CT: Yale University Press, 1974), 232–233, 260.

26. Kousser, *The Shaping of Southern Politics*, 81.

27. Kousser, *The Shaping of Southern Politics*, 72, 80–81, 246, 263–64; statement of B.R. Tillman, *Congressional Record*, 59th Cong., 2d sess. (January 21, 1907) 41, 1441; Simkins, *Pitchfork Ben Tillman*, 1–2, 396–401.

28. *Greenwood Enterprise*, May 27, 1892; quoted in W.F. Holmes, *The White Chief: James Kimble Vardaman* (Baton Rouge: Louisiana State University Press, 1970), 36.

29. L. Goodwyn, *Democratic Promise: The Populist Movement in America* (New York: Oxford University Press, 1976), 298–300.

30. *Baton Rouge Daily Advocate*, February 4, 9, 18, 1896, May 1, 1896; *Pine Bluff Weekly Commercial*, July 17, 1892; quoted in Kousser, *The Shaping of Southern Politics*, 37–38, 160.

31. *Raleigh News and Observer*, July 8, 10, 21, 1900; quoted in Lewinson, *Race, Class and Party*, 95.

32. *St. Landry Clarion*, September 26, 1896; quoted in Ayers, *The Promise of the New South*, 155.
33. *Atlanta Journal*, August 1, 1906; quoted in Woodward, *Tom Watson*, 379.
34. *Winona Democrat* as reported in the *Indianola Enterprise*, June 26, 1903; quoted in N.R. McMillen, *Dark Journey: Black Mississippians in the Age of Jim Crow* (Urbana: University of Illinois Press, 1989), 396, fn. 41.
35. *Jackson Weekly Clarion-Ledger*, July 27, 1906; quoted in McMillen, *Dark Journey*, 226.
36. *Louisville Courier-Journal*, June 16, 1882; June 1, 1892; quoted in Wright, *Racial Violence in Kentucky*, 80–81.
37. *Louisville Courier-Journal*, September 12, 1885; quoted in Wright, *Racial Violence in Kentucky*, 81.
38. *Richland Beacon-News*, November 9, 1901; quoted in McMillen, *Dark Journey*, 234.
39. Independent publisher, Tyler, Texas; quoted in *Thirty Years of Lynching*, 12.
40. *Honey Grove Signal-Citizen*, May 16, 1930; quoted in Raper, *The Tragedy of Lynching*, 363.
41. *Houston Informer*, May 16, 1930. Quoted in A.F. Raper, *The Tragedy of Lynching* (Chapel Hill: University of North Carolina Press, 1933), 363–365.
42. *New York Times*, September 27, 1897; quoted in Wright, *Racial Violence in Kentucky*, 89.
43. *Troy Democrat*, April 26, 1895; quoted in J.W. Crudele, "A Lynching Bee: Butler County Style," *Alabama Historical Quarterly* 42 (Spring/Summer 1980), 66.
44. *Dallas Morning News* June 10, 1897; quoted in M.K. Belknap, *Federal Law and Southern Order* (Athens: University of Georgia Press, 1987), pp. 5–6; see, also, Wright, *Racial Violence in Kentucky*, 100.
45. W. White, *Rope and Faggot* (New York: Arno Press and the New York Times, 1969; orig. 1929), 224–225; J.H. Chadburn, *Lynching and the Law* (Chapel Hill: University of North Carolina Press, 1933, 13–14; J.R. McGovern, *Anatomy of a Lynching: The Killing of Claude Neal* (Baton Rouge: Louisiana State University Press, 1982), 11.
46. M.M. Barrett, "Recollections of My Boyhood: The Picnic at Pitman's Mill," *Georgia Department of Archives and History*, 49–50; quoted in Ayers, *The Promise of the New South*, 159.
47. C.S. Johnson, *Growing Up in the Black Belt* (Washington, DC: American Council on Education, 1941), 317–318 (emphasis added).
48. Quoted in A.B. Hart, "The Outcome of the Southern Race Question," *North American Review* 188 (June 1908), 56; see, also, J. Williamson, *The Crucible of Race* (New York: Oxford University Press, 1984), 187.

11

Segregation, Disfranchisement, and Legal Lynchings

"You couldn't smile at a white woman. If you did you'd be hung from a limb."
—Frank Houston, recalling his youth in Mississippi.[1]

"Insolence on the one side, and intolerance on the other, unnecessarily exhibited by the disturbing elements of both races have borne this fruit."
—James S. Hogg, governor of Texas, 1891[2]

"[A] legal hanging is sure to follow the holding of court."
—*Lincoln County Times*, 1908[3]

The clash of generations evident in the lynching epidemic portended anarchy and racial chaos in the South. In the midst of the epidemic, it began to occur to some Southern leaders that alternatives to mob violence had to be considered. Lynching, they realized, had outlived its usefulness, and now threatened to destabilize the racial caste system lynch mobs believed they were defending.

Three separate, but related, sets of policy initiatives emanated from this change in perspective: legal segregation, disfranchisement, and capital punishment. Each was intended to reduce racial violence and bring order to maintain *legally* the racial status quo. In so doing, each also reinforced and extended the black sense of injustice.

* * *

Segregation followed in the path of urbanization, growing population densities, and racial proximity, all of which heightened the potential for violence. As soon as the Civil War ended, a small but steady number of blacks began to break free from plantation labor to seek different lives in Southern towns and cities. By 1870, the percentage of blacks living in cities had doubled from 4.2 percent during the slave period to 8.5 percent. Migration tapered off in the 1870s, remaining at, or slightly below, that percentage for another decade. It resumed again in the 1880s and by 1890 the number of black city dwellers had grown to 12.4 percent.[4] By the turn of the century, 1.6 million of the country's eight million blacks, or twenty percent, had relocated to cities and towns, most of them in the South, where 90 percent of the black population still lived.[5]

Blacks who made the move to cities and towns, and remained, were usually younger, single men and women who left their families behind. Single people were better able to survive on the meager wages and uncertain employment cities offered. Most worked as manual laborers or domestic servants; few were able to establish themselves in other occupations. Unwelcome, poorly paid, and confronted with inadequate housing, and hostile police, for many the lure of the city soon lost its luster. The disillusioned returned to the countryside, rejoining the parents and children they commonly left behind. The more desperate or adventuresome remained, among them, those who were less inclined toward the deferential old ways of plantation life practiced by earlier generations.[6]

The growing numbers of this predominantly younger, postemancipation generation of blacks, and their displeasing proximity to whites, had an unsettling effect on urban race relations. Daily contact between the races in the less familiar and more ambiguously defined circumstances of city life increased the potential for misunderstandings and violence, especially between younger males.

As population densities in black districts grew, so did the risks for outnumbered whites who ventured into them. Mob violence in the countryside where black victims could be isolated was one thing, but such actions in cities and towns ran the risk of retaliation. Verbal confrontations and fist fights between blacks and whites occurred with a regularity unknown in rural areas. Racial altercations were commonplace, for example, on streetcars and trains, or wherever the two races met on now-contested urban territory.

On a tour of the South in 1891, English historian James Bryce observed the new mood among blacks and offered this European perspective: "This class of half-educated people," he wrote,

> who can read, but have yet learned to think, and are beginning to be averse to manual labor, increases daily, while the generation which had the deference, and often the affection, of the slave to his master, will soon have passed away. It is,

therefore, possible that the problem may within the next twenty or thirty years enter into a phase more threatening than the present.[7]

Even as Lord Bryce wrote these words, the lynching epidemic was raging. It was clear to other observers as well that some means short of mob violence was needed to contain this new threat to the racial status quo. The congressional investigation of Ku Klux Klan atrocities in the 1870s, for example, had revealed that the bloody race war Lincoln feared after emancipation was a real possibility if blacks ever decided to strike back. By the 1880s, it appeared that a new generation might. Even racial demogogues like James K. Vardaman of Mississippi, Ben Tillman of South Carolina, Cole Blease of Georgia, and Jeff Davis of Arkansas, to mention only a few, began to reconsider the implications of the continuing violence, while publicly defending it.[8]

Thus a counter-norm of nonviolence emerged, separating the races, restricting contact between volatile populations in situations where violence was likely to occur, seemed a logical first step in restoring and maintaining social order. In 1891, Texas Governor James S. Hogg explained that segregation was necessary to limit violent confrontations between insolent blacks and intolerant whites. The assessment was the same in Georgia where a state representative insisted that unless railroads were segregated, "little riots" would continue to occur between blacks and whites on trains and in railroad depots. Five black preachers were beaten by whites, he explained, when they refused to give up their seats in a first-class coach. Even greater violence was easy to imagine. The thought of white women, for example, traveling alone in the same railroad cars with black men was unthinkable to most white Southerners. Since both blacks and whites depended on railroads and streetcars, such considerations underscored the wisdom, in their view, of segregating public transportation.[9]

Separating the races was not, of course, a new idea. De facto racial segregation—or more accurately, racial exclusion—had emerged immediately after emancipation.[10] The first segregation laws appeared in the Black Codes of early Reconstruction. In 1870, not long after those codes were abolished by the Fourteenth Amendment and martial law, Tennessee became the first state to enact a law prohibiting interracial marriage. Other Southern states soon followed.

Although blacks resented being segregated in, or excluded from, public places like white-owned hotels and restaurants, it was something they could live with since they were not likely to patronize such places in any case. Moreover, in view of the tension and violence of the period, the vast majority of blacks preferred to distance themselves from whites as much as possible for safety's sake.

Racially restricted access to public transportation, however, was another matter. Blacks knew that segregation laws would mean being relegated to the least attractive and most uncomfortable accomodations on trains. They were correct in assuming that they would be assigned to "second-class" cars. Dilapidated and attached behind the locomotive and coal car, noise, heat, soot, and smoke were companions of passengers in those cars on every trip. It is little wonder that blacks expressed strong opposition to rail segregation.[11]

They were joined in their opposition by the railroads themselves, who objected to the added expense separate accomodations would create. Primarily for that reason, attempts to segregate public transportation by law, except in Tennessee,[12] were unsuccessful until the late 1880s. Segregationists finally prevailed, however, because the intimacy of rail travel, they convinced their opponents, invited social and sexual impropriety between the races. Whites enclosed in an area for extended periods of time in the unwanted company of blacks, they argued, was an invitation to mayhem.[13] Florida followed Tennessee's earlier lead, legally segregating its railways in 1887. Within four years Mississippi, Texas, Louisiana, Alabama, Arkansas, Kentucky, and Georgia followed. Constitutional challenges would occur, but states' rights advocates were by then confident that they could count on a favorable ruling from the U.S. Supreme Court. The court, after all, had already handed down major decisions restricting the "equal protection" provision of the Fourteenth Amendment.

Their confidence was justified in 1896 when the U.S. Supreme Court upheld Louisiana's railroad segregation law in its famous "separate but equal" ruling in *Plessy v. Ferguson*.[14] After that, the tempo of segregation accelerated as Southern state legislatures continued to buttress and expand their laws. In steady succession schools, theaters, hospitals, cemeteries, public restrooms, and drinking fountains were segregated in every Southern state.[15]

Custom and habit became law in these statutes, removing any lingering ambiguities in racial etiquette, and delineating in terms everyone could understand the penalties for black indiscretions. Such clarity, combined with the threat of fines and jail sentences for violators, were intended to deter the actions of those blacks inclined to test the limits of the system. Without such encroachments, it was assumed, violent confrontations were less likely.[16] In this sense, segregation was viewed by Southern political leaders as an important step into a new era of still repressive, but more tranquil, race relations.[17]

* * *

In similar fashion, disfranchisement, which accompanied segregation, was also intended to eliminate the threat of interracial political competition and, in so doing, the violence that often was its consequence. The problem, from this perspective, was the Fifteenth Amendment which had elevated black expectations about full citizenship beyond acceptable levels. "Too much liberty" and competition at the ballot box, one writer argued, led to violence. Political order required some modification of both.[18]

Moreover, it would not be difficult to accomplish that objective legally. Due to a significant loophole in the Fifteenth Amendment, which stated simply that the right to vote could not be "denied or abridged...on account of race, color, or previous condition of servitude," other restrictions were easily devised to accomplish the same purpose. Soon grandfather clauses, multiple ballot boxes, poll taxes, literacy tests, and "understanding" clauses eliminated all but a negligible percentage of black voters throughout the South.[19] Also, since elections were normally decided in Democratic primary elections, which were customarily and later legally restricted to whites only, the votes cast in general elections by this tiny number of blacks were meaningless. As a consequence, even few of those who could bothered to vote.[20] Until suffrage was restricted by these means, violence and economic coercion—or "more fundamental political processes," as political scientist V.O. Key, Jr. put it delicately—were the primary means used to discourage black voting. Although not quite the fait accompli Key described, the new formal restrictions formalized the process in a legal sense and, in so doing, eventually eliminated a major source of racial tension and continuing violence.[21]

Class, however, as well as race played a part in the drive to restrict suffrage in the South. The impetus for disfranchisement came from the wealthy who controlled state governments and had the most to lose should mob violence evolve into anarchy. Thus, Democrats representing the prosperous landowning class spearheaded the movement in state legislatures. Most of these men resided in "black belt" counties and traced their bloodlines to slaveholders. They were far removed economically and socially from the poor whites they looked down on, but who outnumbered them.[22] So it was that this group welcomed a reduction, as well, in the number of these potentially disruptive, "cracker" voters who had been so easily swayed, for example, by Populist candidates.

But it was, of course, black voters who were of overriding concern in the disfranchisement movement. Prominent politicians, for example, such as one from North Carolina who had once led a mob attack against blacks in Wilmington, were among those now saying that curbing such violence was necessary to "best conserve the commonwealth." Likewise, a Virginia senator expressed hope that denying the vote to blacks would enable his state to govern with "decency and with the association of that law and order which will command the respect...of the whole civilized world."[23]

With such objectives in mind, disfranchisement came in waves of political energy and purpose during the peak years of the lynching epidemic and continued over three decades. Accompanying new segregation laws, the first wave occurred between 1888 and 1893; another came in 1898. The flurry of suffrage restrictions enacted across the South after 1898 coincided with a United States Supreme Court decision approving stringent registration requirements that virtually eliminated black voters in Mississippi. The court's decision in *Williams v. Mississippi* (1898) was yet another in a series of decisions, beginning with the *Slaughterhouse Cases* (1873), that effectively denied blacks their civil and political rights by placing authority for protecting those rights with the states. By 1910 blacks had virtually disappeared from voter registration lists in the South. Surely it was not just coincidental that the number of lynchings began to decline steadily during the same decade.[24]

* * *

Southern concerns about the region's image in the "civilized world" also provided an important incentive to seek more palatable, but still intimidating, alternatives to mob violence. Violence and social instability were bad for business and economic development at a time when the South was anxious to attract outside investment to stimulate its troubled economy. Fears about possible federal intervention if the carnage continued were also growing. With memories of the "carpetbagger" governments of an earlier era still lingering, probably nothing worse could have been imagined by these militant states' righters than more meddling by the federal government.[25]

But public pressures in that direction were building. From the 1890s and on into the first decades of the twentieth century, newspaper coverage of the appalling savagery of Southern lynch mobs shocked the nation and the world. Stories carried in Chicago and New York newspapers, for example, made their readers aware that mutilating and burning victims alive had not ended with the Dark Ages on another continent.

Adding to the pressures were pamphlets distributed by antilynching groups like the newly formed National Association for the Advancement of Colored People and public speakers such as Ida Wells-Barnett, whose accounts of Southern atrocities stirred widening indignation and demands for remedial action. Condemning the lawlessness, one critic wrote,

> These tiny kingdoms can kill their subjects like hogs if they want to, and under State rights they know that there is no law on earth to prosecute them but their own law; no judge ever prosecutes himself.[26]

Even President Woodrow Wilson, a Virginian notably unsympathetic to blacks, was moved to compare lynching with the slaughter carried on by German armies during World War I.[27]

As the rest of the country spoke of industrial expansion, "progressivism," and a new century of progress, the image of the South as a grim and backward region, steeped in primordial savagery, remained fixed in the public mind. Apologists were forced to admit that lynching was a barbarous "crime against society," but some equivalent sanction was needed, they insisted, "to put an end to the ravishing of their women by an inferior race."[28] Without such a deterrent, another wrote, lynching would remain "an indirect act of self-defense" that was necessary "to hold in check the Negro in the South."[29]

But as pressures intensified, some Southern newspapers and civic leaders became increasingly uncomfortable with that kind of reasoning and its implications for the future. Interracial committees sprang up in a number of localities to address the lynching issue as well as other problems and to seek ways to establish better relations between the races. In 1919, a regional Commission on Interracial Cooperation was established in Atlanta for that purpose.[30] Simultaneously, efforts were made by many of the same parties to reassure increasingly restive blacks who, they worried, would leave the South, thus placing in greater peril its already precarious economy. Should that occur, they realized, the region would lose its low-wage labor, perhaps the major inducement it could offer to outside investors.

Carrot and stick methods were employed in the effort to reduce the threat of a black exodus. Promising change and a better life, blacks were reminded of better times and the comforts of the familiar rhythms and slower pace of Southern life. Pledges of better sanitation and schools, and higher wages, were common. Perhaps the most significant change, however, was in the perspective on lynching.[31]

Some newspapers like the tiny *Tifton Gazette* of Georgia, for example, addressed the issue squarely in these words,

> They have allowed negroes to be lynched, five at a time, on nothing stronger than suspicion; they have allowed whole sections to be depopulated of them; they have allowed them to be whitecapped and to be whipped, and their homes burned, with only the weakest and most spasmodic efforts to apprehend or punish those guilty—when any efforts were made at all. Loss of much of the State's best labor is one of the prices Georgia is paying for unchecked mob activity against negroes often charged only with ordinary crimes.[32]

By 1917, even the *Atlanta Constitution* had experienced a change of heart. This newspaper—perhaps the South's most influential, which had defended and even, on occasion, advocated mob violence—now called for blacks and whites to work together to resolve the issues that threatened the well-being of both races. So it was that its editors conceded that there had been, in fact, many cases of "unlawful deprivation of individual liberty" that blacks had suffered at the hands of white racists.[33] Elsewhere, other community leaders joined in the effort to placate and reassure blacks, enlisting the help of the Tuskegee Institute and even the Red Cross to convince them that things were bound to improve if only they remained patient. The change in mood and tactics could also be observed in a resurgence of Southern paternalism as newspapers in Mississippi, for example, regularly published letters from black leaders who had been persuaded to say that better wages and fairer treatment in the courts were on the way in that state.[34]

At the same time, however, punitive measures also came into play in the effort to dissuade blacks from leaving the region. One by one state legislatures passed, then strengthened, new emigrant-agent statutes to curb the activities of agents attempting to recruit black workers for Northern jobs. High licensing fees, tight restrictions on recruiting practices, and severe penalties for violators were intended to discourage recruiters. These regulations were accompanied by more stringent enforcement of antienticement laws and vagrancy statues, all with the same purpose: to limit black mobility.[35]

Concerns about the threat of a black exodus split white Southerners along class lines. Planters and industrialists who had an economic stake in cheap black labor, championed the effort to discourage black mobility by whatever means; those who had no stake were anxious for blacks to leave. For many white Southerners, historian William Cohen observed, the issue created a conflict between "dictates of the heart and demands of the head. Racism drew them toward ridding the land of blacks entirely, but economic calculation pulled them in the opposite direction." In most cases, however, economic interests prevailed.[36]

* * *

Since promises of better treatment meant little to blacks so long as the threat of lynch mobs remained, and since a significant segment of the white population was not inclined to give up the practice, capital punishment became the means selected to placate these two related, but very different, interests. For this reason, capital punishment became the means to supplant mob violence and, in the process, accomplish several key objectives: First, it was intended to offer what would prove to be an exceedingly hollow reassurance to fearful blacks that lynchings would cease, and due process and equal protection of the laws would become a reality in their lives; second, it would serve, as well, to fashion a more sanitized image of criminal justice in the region; and, finally it would accomplish both goals without compromising white expectations that violence remain the ultimate sanction in the arsenal of white supremacy.

So it was that court-ordered executions carried out under first local, then state, authority gradually took the place of lynchings in the early decades of the twentieth century.[37] Such "legal lynchings," as they were described by Southerners themselves, were commonly carried out after brief and superficial trials, before all-white juries, that made a mockery of justice. But, compared to the barbarism of lynching, capital punishment offered the appearance of civilized restraint and legality.

The decline of lynching and the eagerness with which judges began to impose the death penalty on black defendants are revealed in figure 11.1. Lynchings peaked in the 1890s with over eleven hundred victims. Then they declined steadily in each decade after that. At the same time, as anticipated, capital punishment began its predictable steep rise as public executioners took over the tasks of lynch mobs. The transition was reminiscent of the way uniformed police had replaced Ku Klux Klan terrorists a few decades before.

By the 1920s executions of blacks nationally exceeded lynchings for the first time as executioners claimed 481 victims to 315 for the lynch mobs in this grisly competition for black lives. The trend continued through the 1930s when 745 were executed and 119 were lynched.

FIGURE 11.1
Lynchings and Executions of Blacks in America, 1880–1959

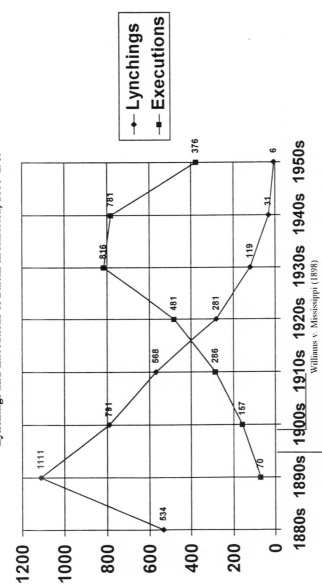

Sources: Bureaus of the Census, *Historical Statistics of the United States: Colonial Times to 1970* (Washington, DC: U.S. Government Printing Office, 1972), Series H 1155-1167, 1168-1170; Bureau of Justice Statistics, *Historical Corrections Statistics in the United States, 1850–1984* (Washington, DC: U.S. Government Printing Office, 1987), Tables 2-1, 2-2; Bureau of Justice Statistics, *Correctional Populations in the United States, 1930–1988*, Tables 7.26; *Statistical Abstract of the United States* (Washington, DC: U.S. Government Printing Office, 1989), 187.

Lynching continued to decline and reached single digits after the 1940s, continuing as disturbing but much less frequent events after that.[38]

Numerous studies have confirmed in meticulous detail the regional pattern of racial discrimination in death penalty cases. Southern and border states had the most extensive capital statutes, often stipulating the death penalty for robbery and burglary. Rape, unsurprisingly, meant almost certain death for a black defendant if the victim was white. Eighty-nine percent of those executed for rape have been black. In contrast, no white has ever been executed for raping a black woman.[39]

But a more graphic picture of the toll of black lives emerges when deaths by capital punishment are combined with those of lynching. Figure 11.2 reveals the grim realities of some eighty years of mob violence and racial discrimination in capital sentencing. Despite the fact that blacks represented approximately 10 percent of the national population during this period, they account for large majorities of those lynched and executed in every decade but the 1880s. Even in that decade, however, a disproportionately high 44 percent of those who died in this manner were black. In the first decade of the twentieth century they accounted for a staggering 81 percent. From the 1880s through the 1950s, 6,408 blacks were put to death by these means as compared to 4,022 whites. An average of 801 blacks were killed per decade through the combined efforts of public executioners and white lynch mobs. Put differently, this means that an average of eighty-three blacks died by one of these methods each year for nearly eighty years. The comparable averages for whites during the same period are 502 per decade and fifty-two per year. Recognition of this carnage and the discriminatory system of justice that provided its momentum are important reasons why the National Association for the Advancement of Colored People was established in 1909.

By the end of the 1930s, the death penalty already had a peculiarly Southern stamp. Archivist M. Watt Espy, Jr. has compiled a listing of executions under *state* authority from 1864 through 1982 from which Table 11.1 is drawn.[40] His research reveals that the same states that lynched thousands of blacks accomplished the same objective in the twentieth century with capital punishment. Although periods of record vary by state, and omit unrecorded executions carried out by local authorities, the racial pattern evident in these numbers leaves little doubt that capital punishment mirrors the regional subculture that fueled the scourge of lynching that preceded it. The disproportionality that is reflected in these figures speaks directly to the issue. Although blacks

FIGURE 11.2
Combined Lynchings and Executions by Race in America, 1882–1959

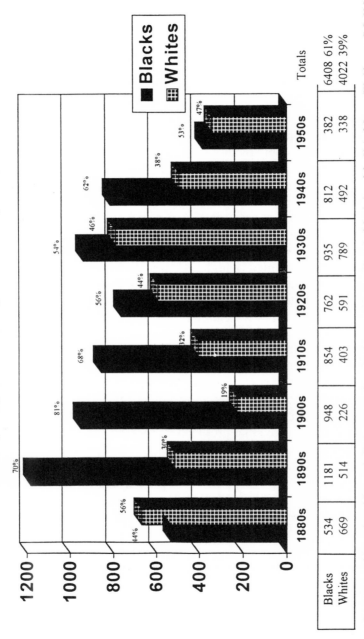

	1880s	1890s	1900s	1910s	1920s	1930s	1940s	1950s	Totals
Blacks	534	1181	948	854	762	935	812	382	6408 61%
Whites	669	514	226	403	591	789	492	338	4022 39%

Source: Department of Records and Research, Tuskegee Institute, Tuskegee, Alabama; *Historical Statistics of the United States* (Washington, DC: U.S. Department of Commerce, 1970), 422.

TABLE 11.1
State Executions by Race in the Former Slave States

State	Period of Record*	Non-Black	Black	Total	Percent Black
Alabama	1927–1965	27	126	153	82%
Arkansas	1913–1964	43	129	172	75%
Florida	1924–1979	64	134	198	67%
Georgia	1924–1964	83	339	422	80%
Kentucky	1911–1962	77	94	171	56%
Louisiana	1957–1961	1	10	11	91%
Maryland	1923–1961	17	62	79	78%
Mississippi	1955–1964	7	24	31	77%
Missouri	1938–1965	14	25	39	64%
N. Carolina	1901–1961	75	287	362	79%
S. Carolina	1912–1962	41	200	241	83%
Tennessee	1909–1960	43	91	134	68%
Texas	1924–1982	124	238	362	66%
Virginia	1908–1982	34	204	238	86%
Total		**650**	**1963**	**2613**	**75%**

*These are the only years when state records were kept. The figures do not reflect unknown numbers of executions that were imposed by local authorities. Records on the latter, when they were kept, are scattered throughout a myraid of county, prison and newspaper files that have yet to be examined. See, "Espy's Explanation of the Undated Procedure" in W.S. Bowers, *Legal Homicide: Death as Punishment in America, 1864–1982* (Boston: Northeastern University Press, 1984), 394–397, also Appendix A, 399–523 for the data upon which these calculations are based.

averaged approximately 26 percent of the population in the South after 1900, 75 percent of all persons put to death by its states' executioners were black.[41]

The race of the victim determined a defendant's fate. Over the course of nearly 15,000 documented executions in American history, whites were executed for killing blacks in only 29 cases. Of those cases, most involved defendants who had also killed whites; the remainder had killed slaves owned by someone else. It was not until February 18, 1936, in Raleigh, North Carolina that a white man was executed solely for murdering a black in the South.[42]

Like first the whipping, and then the lynching that took its place, capital punishment for blacks had little to do with retributive justice. Blacks who killed whites were almost certain to receive the death sentence, while *both* whites and blacks who killed blacks were much more likely to be treated leniently. The death penalty has always been imposed reluctantly on white defendants regardless of the victim's race. During the 1930s, when capital punishment reached record levels for both races, estimates suggest that death sentences were handed down in only one out of five first-degree murder cases involving white defendants. That such hesitancy was absent when black defendants were sentenced is beyond dispute.[43] The capriciousness of capital sentencing supports a familiar tenet—established centuries before and confirmed by recent research—that, be they defendants or victims, in Southern courts the lives of whites are worth more than the lives of blacks.[44] In the words of one expert,

> The fact that [the death penalty] has been used in a discriminatory way against the black man in America further demonstrates that it is not [imposed] as retribution for a given crime...but as retaliation against a selected group of offenders, without regard for retributive justice. Capital punishment used for crimes only, or chiefly, when they are committed by members of a racial minority is not retribution; it is minority group *oppression*.[45]

* * *

Southern political leaders were convinced that segregation and disfranchisement were necessary to limit mob violence and to ensure some semblance of racial civility in that troubled region. Moreover, they may have been right. At the same time, however, they also understood that "legal lynching" was essential to indulge the dark fears and yearnings that still remained in their white constituents. Southern culture did not change easily; racial injustice and violence continued, different only in form.

Notes

1. Oral history, Cleveland Payne private collection, Laurel, Mississippi; quoted in N.R. McMillen, *Dark Journey: Black Mississippians in the Age of Jim Crow* (Urbana: University of Illinois Press, 1989), 16.
2. Quoted in C.A. Lofgren, *The Plessy Case: A Legal-Historical Interpretation* (New York: Oxford University Press, 1987), 25.
3. Quoted in McMillen, *Dark Journey*, 209.
4. Between 1890 and 1900, for the first time in significant numbers, some 200,000 blacks also managed to make their way North where they settled mainly in towns and cities.

5. A. Davis, B.B. Gardner, and M.R. Gardner, *Deep South* (Los Angeles: University of California Press, 1988; orig., 1941), 341–342; H. Gannett, *Statistics of the Negroes in the United States*, Occasional Papers, No. 4 (Baltimore, MD: John F. Slater Fund, 1894), 15–16.

6. E. Foner, *Reconstruction, 1863–1877* (New York: Harper & Row, 1988), 396–398; G. Myrdal, *An American Dilemma: The Negro Problem and Modern Democracy* (New York: Harper & Row, 1944), 183; migration estimates based on E.J. Scott, *Negro Migration During the War* (New York: Oxford University Press, 1920), 59; W.E.B. DuBois, "The Negroes of Farmville, Virginia, A Social Study," *Department of Labor Bulletin* XIV (January 1898), 9.

7. J. Bryce, "Thoughts on the Negro Problem," 153 *North American Review* (1891), 650–651; see, also, Lofgren, *The Plessy Case*, 25–26.

8. See, for example, F.E. Simkins, *Pitchfork Ben Tillman* (Baton Rouge: Lousiana State University Press, 1967); and W.F. Holmes, *The White Chief, James Kimble Vardaman* (Baton Rouge: Louisiana State University Press, 1970).

9. Lofgren, *The Plessy Case*, 25–27.

10. H.N. Rabinowitz, *Race Relations in the Urban South*, esp., ch. 8.

11. H.N. Rabinowitz, "From Exclusion to Segregation: Southern Race Relations, 1865–1890," *Journal of American History* (September 1976), 342–345; and *Race Relations in the Urban South*, ch. 8.

12. In 1875, the first actual "Jim Crow" law segregating railroads and steetcars was enacted in Tennessee. Even before similar laws in other states were enacted, however, blacks were customarily assigned to "second class" cars.

13. See, for example, C. Carroll, *The Negro a Beast* (St. Louis, MO, 1900); Mrs. L.H. Harris, "A Southern Woman's View," *Independent* LI (May 18, 1899), 1354–1355; quoted in Frederickson, *The Black Image*, 277.

14. *Plessy v. Ferguson*, 163 U.S. 537 (1896).

15. C.V. Woodward, *Origins of the New South, 1877–1913* (Baton Rouge: Louisiana State University Press, 1951), 211–212.

16. Evidence from Arthur Raper's research on lynching in the 1930s, for example, concluded that blacks were safest where segregation was strictly enforced, and in greatest danger where interaction with whites was more frequent. The gradual urbanization of the black population, alone, probably contributed to the decline in lynching since it remained an almost exclusively rural phenomenon. See, A. Raper, *The Tragedy of Lynching* (Chapel Hill: University of North Carolina Press, 1933), 27–28; and H. Cantril, *The Psychology of Social Movements* (New York: John Wiley & Sons, 1963; orig., 1941), 85.

17. G.M. Frederickson, *The Black Image in the White Mind: The Debate on Afro-American Character and Destiny, 1817–1914* (New York: Harper & Row, 1971), 272–275.

18. C.H. Smith, "Have American Negroes Too Much Liberty?," *Forum* XVI (October 1893), 176–181; Frederickson, *The Black Image*, 273.

19. G.B. Tindall, *The Emergence of the New South* (Baton Rouge: Louisiana State University Press, 1967), 165; see, also, P. Lewinson, *Race, Class, and Party: A History of Negro Suffrage and White Politics in the South* (New York: Grosset & Dunlap, 1932).

20. Although Democratic white primaries almost completely excluded blacks, the actual impact on black political influence per se has probably been exaggerated. Most blacks who did vote continued to vote Republican until Franklin Roosevelt's reelection in 1936.

21. V.O. Key, Jr., *Southern Politics in State and Nation* (New York: Alfred A. Knopf, 1949), 533. See, also, J.M Kousser, *The Shaping of Southern Politics: Suffrage*

Restriction and the Establishment of the One-Party South (New Haven, CT: Yale University Press, 1974), 3–5. 244.

22. Kousser, *The Shaping of Southern Politics*, 246–50; Lewinson, *Race, Class, & Party*, 79–81.

23. Quoted in Kousser, *The Shaping of Southern Politics*, 20–21, 246–247, 263.

24. *Williams v. Mississippi*, 170 U.S. 213 (1898); *The Slaughter House Cases*, 16 Wallace 36 (1873); Kousser, *The Shaping of Southern Politics*, 20, 29–31, 238–246; Woodward, *Origins of the New South*, 321–349.

25. Frederickson, *The Black Image*, 221.

26. W.E. Wimpy, "Mob Lynching Lynches the Law," *Manufacturer's Record* LXXVI (December 25, 1919), 113; quoted in G.B. Tindall, *The Emergence of the New South, 1913–1945* (Baton Rouge: Louisiana State University Press, 1967), 172.

27. R.S. Baker and W.E. Dodd (eds.), *The Public Papers of Woodrow Wilson: War and Peace; Presidential Addresses and Public Papers, 1917–1924* (New York, 1927), I, 238; Tindall, *The Emergence of the New South*, 171–172.

28. A.G. Haygood, "The Black Shadow in the South," *Forum* XVI (October 1893), 167–169, 173; T.N. Page, *The Negro: The Southerner's Problem* (New York, 1904), 100; quoted in Frederickson, *The Black Image*, 274–275.

29. W.H. Collins, *The Truth about Lynching and the Negro in the South; in Which the Author Pleads That the South Be Made Safe for the White Race* (New York, 1918), 58, 70; quoted in Tindall, *The Emergence of the New South*, 170.

30. Tindall, *The Emergence of the New South*, 175–183.

31. W.W. Alexander, "Better Race Relations," *Southern Workman* 51 (1922), 362–364; Tindall, *The Emergence of the New South*, 179–183.

32. *Tifton Gazette*, quoted in Scott, *Negro Migration*, 79–80.

33. *Atlanta Constitution* quoted in Scott, *Negro Migration*, 79–80; see, also, 81–85.

34. W. Wilson, *Forced Labor in the United States* (New York: AMS Press, 1971; orig., 1933), 88.

35. W. Cohen, *At Freedom's Edge: Black Mobility and the Southern White Quest for Racial Control, 1861–1915* (Baton rouge: Louisiana State University Press), 232–247.

36. Cohen, *At Freedom's Edge*, 236–237.

37. Vermont was the first to impose executions under state authority in 1864. Executions were carried out by local authorities in the former slave states until the following years: Virginia, 1908; North Carolina, 1910; Kentucky, 1911; South Carolina, 1912; Arkansas, 1913; Tennessee, 1916; Maryland, 1923; Florida, 1924; Georgia, 1924; Texas, 1924; Alabama, 1927; Missouri, 1938; Mississippi, 1955; and Louisiana, 1957. Records were not available on Delaware. See, W.J. Bowers, *Legal Homicide: Death as Punishment in America, 1964 to 1982* (Boston: Northeastern University Press, 1984), 46–47.

38. As the public condemnation of lynching grew during this period, the practice became more surreptitious. A southern white informer described the change he observed in the 1930s:

> [F]or various reasons, lynching is entering a new and altogether dangerous phase. Lynchings in the past have been characterized by the mob, the faggot, the rope. Hundreds of people, often thousands, poured out to participate or witness the lynching of a man or woman accused of some crime, often of the most trivial nature and often without any real charge at all...
>
> Public opinion is beginning to turn against this sort of mob activity.... Lynching, they say, must go on, but it must be done quietly so as not to attract attention, draw publicity. Thus those who must rule by terror and intimidation turn to new methods. The old mob is disappearing but the work of the mob goes on. A

Negro is accused of some crime, real or alleged. A few white men gather, formulate their plans, seize the victim. In some lonely swamp a small body of men do the job formerly done by a vast, howling mob composed of men, women and children. The word is then passed that the matter has been handled to the satisfaction of those in charge of such matters.

Although fewer in number, and often more surreptitious in manner, still the savagery of the lynchings that did occur through the 1930s and 1940s approximated those of earlier years. During this "modern era," blow torches and boiling tar became instruments of death, supplementing the more traditional practices of sexual mutilation and dismemberment in this enduring legacy of human depravity. See, *Lynching Goes Underground*, an unpublished report prepared for "Senators Wagner and Capper and Representatives Gavagan and Fish," (January 1940), 7–9. fn. 40, quoted in G. Myrdal, *An American Dilemma: The Negro Problem and Modern Democray* (New York: Harper & Row, 1944), 1350, fn. 40; M.A Newton and J.A. Newton, *Racial and Religious Violence in America: A Chronology* (New York: Garland, 1991), 413, 419, 421; also, J.R. McGovern, *Anatomy of a Lynching: The Killing of Claude Neal* (Baton Rouge: Louisiana State University Press, 1982).

39. W.J. Bowers, *Executions in America* (Lexington, MA: D.C. Heath, 1974), 55–57, 191–193; H.A. Bedau (ed.), *The Death Penalty in America* (New York: Oxford University Press, 1982), 32.

40. Records of local executions are much more difficult to obtain and verify. Periods of record vary when executions were carried out under state authorities. There is no complete record of executions carried out under local authority. Espy's research continues.

41. These figures are drawn from the inventory compiled by M. Watt Espy, Jr. which appears in W.J. Bowers, *Legal Homicide: Death as Punishment in America, 1864–1982* (Boston: Northeastern University Press, 1984), Appendix A, 395–523. See, also, R.T. Bye, *Capital Punishment in the United States* (Philadelphia, PA: University of Pennsylvania, Ph.D. Thesis), published by The Committee on Philanthropic Labor of Philadelphia, 1919), 70–71; see, also, C.D. Phillips, "Social Structure and Social Control: Modeling the Discriminatory execution of Blacks in Georgia and North Carolina, 1925–35," *Social Forces* 65 (December 1986), 470.

42. For abundant evidence of racial discrimination in capital sentencing, see, the Brennan dissent in *McCleskey v. Kemp* 481 U.S. 279, 107 S.Ct. 1756 (1987); *Hearings*, U.S. House of Representatives, Subcommittee on Criminal Justice, 1st Sess., Ser. 142 (July 16, 1987), Testimony of M.L. Radelet, 18–19; M.L. Radelet and M. Mello, "Executing Those Who Kill Blacks: An Unusual Case Study," *Mercer Law Review* 37 (1986), 911–925; M.L. Radelet and M. Vandiver, "Race and Capital Punishment: An Overview of the Issues," *Crime and Social Justice* 25 (1986), 94–113; M. Radelet and G.L. Pierce, "Race and Prosecutorial Discretion in Homicide Cases," *Law & Society Review* 19, 4 (1985), 587–621; R. Paternoster, "Prosecutorial Discretion in Requesting the Death Penalty: A Case of Victim-Based Racial Discrimination," *Law & Society Review* 18, 3 (1984), 437–478; D.C. Baldus, C. Pulaski, and G. Woodworth, "Comparative Review of Death Sentences: An Empirical Study of the Georgia Experience," *Journal of Criminal Law & Criminology* 74, 3 (1983), 661–753; W.J. Bowers, "The Pervasiveness of Arbitrariness and Discrimination Under Post-*Furman* Capital Statutes," *Journal of Law and Criminology* 74, (1983), 1067–1100; G. Kleck, "Racial Discrimination in Criminal Sentencing: A Critical Evaluation of the Evidence with Additional Evidence on the Death Penalty," *American Socio-*

logical Review 46 (December 1981), 783–805; W. Espy, "The Death Penalty in America: What the Record Shows," *Christianity and Crisis,* 23 (June 1980), 191–195; *National Prisoner Statistics,* Capital Punishment (1979), 18; M.E. Wolfgang, "Racial Discrimination in the Death Sentence for Rape," in W.J. Bowers (ed.), *Executions in America* (Lexington, MA: D.C. Heath, 1974), 109–120; and A. Raper, "Race and Class Pressures" (unpublished manuscript, 1940), 166, quoted in Myrdal, *An American Dilemma,* 1345.

43. For this reason, in 1972, the Supreme Court declared a moratorium on executions until states revised their laws to meet new standards for fairness. The moratorium remained in effect until executions resumed in 1977. During that time, however, judges continued to hand down death sentences at former rates, contributing to a major backlog of those awaiting execution. See, *Furman v. Georgia* 408 U.S. 238, 92 S. Ct. 2726 (1972).

44. D.C. Baldus, G. Woodworth, and C. Pulaski, Jr., *Equal Justice and the Death Penalty: A Legal and Empirical Analysis* (Boston: Northeastern University Press, 1990); see, also, *National Prisoner Statistics,* 18; W.J. Bowers and G.L. Pierce, "Racial Discrimination and Criminal Homicide under Post-Furman Statutes," in H.A. Bedau (ed.) *The Death Penalty in America* (New York: Oxford University Press, 1982), 215.

45. Bowers, *Executions in America,* 191.

12

The Richest Soil, the Poorest People

"Slavery is just as much an 'institution' now as it was before the war. Only now it is done under the guise of Law."
—J.D. Lucas, Florida, 1907[1]

"He said if any of the hands got away or tried to get away, or did anything to me to kill them, and he said if I let one get away I would know what was coming to me."
—Claude Freeman, describing his instructions for supervising black laborers on a Jasper County, Georgia plantation, 1921[2]

In view of the oppression and violence suffered by black people during the post-Civil War period, one might ask why most remained in the South. It does seem odd that they did not leave, move north, or perhaps migrate west, as so many whites, European immigrants included, were doing during the last quarter of the nineteenth century. Was it because the evils of the South have been exaggerated? That life there for blacks wasn't as difficult as some have imagined?

The simple answer to both questions is no. Ninety percent of the black population remained in the South during this period because most could not leave. They were entrapped by an intricate web of criminal and contract labor law that was specifically designed to restrict their mobility both within and out of the South—and, in effect, reenslaved— not only untold numbers of black men, but their families as well.[3] Together such laws formed the legal foundation of a system of debt peonage that characterized large portions of the South's postemancipation agricultural economy.

This capricious system of justice left black males with little choice except either to obligate themselves to shamelessly exploitive labor contracts, or face the risks of unemployment, arbitrary arrest, and the horrors of convict labor. As a result, countless black husbands and fathers agreed to "X" contracts drawn up by white men who they knew were dishonest. Once obligated, most found it virtually impossible to escape the grip of these unscrupulous employers. Thus, from the end of the Civil War until well into the twentieth century, a large portion of the Southern economy was based an integrated system of convict labor, which supplied manpower primarily for public works and industry, and debt peonage, which became the mainstay of Southern agriculture.

State contract law provided a facade of legality for this elaborate system. Such laws included "false pretenses" clauses, for instance, that made breach of contract the equivalent of fraud, which was considered a criminal rather than a civil offense, and carried heavy fines and/or imprisonment. First enacted in Alabama in 1885, versions of such laws were quickly adopted by other Southern states to provide, as one scholar put it, "a veneer of legitimacy over legal proceedings that were nothing less than criminal prosecutions for breach of contract."[4] Alabama's contract/fraud law, for example, read as follows:

> Any person, who with intent to injure or defraud his employer, enters into a contract in writing for the performance of any act of service, and thereby obtains money or other personal property from such an employer, and with like intent, and without just cause, and without refunding such money, or paying for such property, refuses to perform such act or service, must on conviction be punished as if he had stolen it. And the refusal or failure of any person who enters into such a contract to perform such act or service, or refund such money or pay for such property, without just cause, shall be *prima facie* evidence of the intent to injure or defraud his employer.[5]

Additionally, "rules of evidence," such as Alabama's, prevented a defendant from testifying "to his uncommunicated motives, purpose, or intention." Consequently, breaking a contract under these circumstances was presumptive proof of fraud, and testimony to the contrary was inadmissable. What this meant, as Booker T. Washington complained, was

> that any white man, who cares to charge that a Colored man has promised to work for him and has not done so, or has gotten money from him and not paid it back, can have the Colored man sent to the chain gang.[6]

Anti-enticement laws added a final barrier which further limited a worker's choices and mobility. By 1875, every state but Virginia had passed such laws which made it a criminal offense for an employer to "entice" employees from their present employer by any means. The

Georgia law, for example, read that enticement was illegal whether "by offering higher wages or in any way whatever." Some states made it a crime for an employer even to aid or feed an employee under contract to someone else. The enticement statute in Louisiana went so far as to punish "any one who shall persuade or entice away, feed, harbor or secrete any person who leaves his or her employer." Anti-enticement laws were merely "race blind" echoes of the old fugitive slave laws and black codes of early Reconstruction. Their purpose was the same.[7]

Labor supply and demand did have a modulating effect on how strictly contracts and anti-enticement laws were enforced. When demand was low, enforcement was relaxed, and blacks were able to move from contract to contract and from one state to another, depending on growing seasons, weather, and the demand for labor in other areas. It was common, for example, for labor agents to round up, hire out, and fund the movement of large numbers of black laborers to contractors in areas where demand was greater. As during slavery, such large movements of labor were usually from the upper to the lower South, and from southeast to southwest. With only one exception, however, such movements occurred *within* the South, and rarely with any enduring benefits to the migrants, who remained confined to the most menial occupations, and poor.[8]

* * *

Immobilized by fear inspired by the certainty and severity of punishment for violators of this system, countless black laborers and their wives and children were forced to work indefinitely for planters who controlled most of the South's productive land. Confronted with the enormous difficulties involved in organizing large numbers of free blacks for the backbreaking gang labor large plantations required, these former slaveholders and descendants of slaveholders subdivided their holdings and leased smaller plots to black laborers and their families. The practice changed the face of Southern agriculture. By 1880, approximately 90 percent of the crops produced in the South were grown on small farms of thirty to fifty acres. Half of those farms were worked by sharecroppers or tenants and their wives and children. Most were required to grow cotton, and most never got out of debt. By 1900, debt peonage had replaced the plantation economy of slavery. The pattern of exploitation changed in form only. Instead of the lash-wielding master, it was now unscrupulous judges, nefarious contract laws, and the threat of convict labor from which one was likely never to return.[9]

The sharecropping system worked something like this: A farmer and his family would agree to work a small piece of land, perhaps forty acres or less, for a specified period of time and a share of profits. When the crop was sold, the landowner would claim his share, commonly 50 percent, and the sharecropper would be given the other half, *after* expenses were deducted by the landowner for a customary credit advance to cover the cropper's living expenses. Tenant farming differed in that the tenant simply leased the land at a set amount regardless of the crop yield. Because leases were fixed, tenancy tended to be less exploitative than sharecropping.[10]

On the surface these arrangements seemed to offer certain advantages to both farm workers and landowners. Sharecropping gave a person without resources a line of credit, a shanty to live in, land to grow vegetables and livestock, and a cash crop for income. But sharecropping proffered at least two important advantages to the now slaveless landowner. First, it bound the cropper to the land by contract, minimizing the risk of the lost labor of transient employees. Second, the landowner no longer bore any reponsibility for the health and welfare of his workers as a slaveholder had under the earlier system. Births, deaths, sickness, and health were no longer his concerns as long as a crop was produced. If hardships developed with croppers or tenants, they were simply replaced.

The system of sharecropping and tenancy also left blacks vulnerable to shameless credit manipulation by both landowners and merchants. Typically, the sharecropper's contract would include a provision stipulating that the landowner would provide the "furnish" in the form of food, clothing, seed, livestock feed, or whatever. These goods were supplied as advances from "commissary stores" that were sometimes owned by the landowner, or merchants with whom he dealt (and from whom he customarily received a cut from the profits he sent their way). Repayment was required at the "settle" when the crop was harvested. Price markups of 50 to 200 percent and interest charges of 25 to 75 percent, allegedly to minimize the risk of crop failures or non-payment, were common among merchants. Without the furnish, few blacks had the resources to "make a crop"; with it, many never got out of debt.[11]

Another consequence of the credit system was that food production dropped in the South as more acreage went into cotton.[12] The result was twofold: First, many families slipped deeper into debt to purchase food that they could have otherwise grown themselves; second, families who were denied credit went hungry, leaving many worse off than they had been as slaves. Some contracts even included provisions forbidding, or limiting, hunting privileges and the size of vegetable gardens to ensure that food would be purchased from the commissary.

In addition, the legislatures of most cotton-producing states drafted "crop lien" laws that gave landowners and merchants first claim on the crop. Thus, if the crop was poor, or prices were low, the sharecropper or tenant received only what, if anything, was left over after the landowner's claim had been met.[13] Instead of receiving hard-earned cash for their work, black tenants and sharecroppers often received a "balance due" slip, ensuring that they would be working the same land again the following year, or every year thereafter, until the debt was paid. As the process was repeated annually, countless black farmers slipped deeper and deeper into debt.[14]

Such practices meant that a man and his family could labor for years producing good crops and still have nothing but mounting debts to show for it. And debt, of course, was the objective of many landowners: it assured them control and the year-to-year stability and continuity they sought from their workers. By restoring the landholder's control of labor that had been lost briefly after emancipation, the new system virtually eliminated any potential for black advancement. Relatively few Southern blacks were able to use sharecropping as a stepping-stone to ownership as had white farmers in the Midwest during the same period. A condition of involuntary servitude, once more, dictated the terms of life for growing numbers of black farm laborers. By 1880 nearly 40 percent of Southern farms were worked by croppers and tenants.[15] The percentage continued to grow until the 1940s.[16]

A disproportionate number of the tenants and sharecroppers were black.[17] Most of them were concentrated in some two hundred counties that spread in a large inland crescent from Virginia to Texas. Described as the "Black Belt," the crescent contained the richest soil and the poorest people in the South. Fewer than 20 percent of them owned land and that percentage was not reached until the 1920s. Estimates indicate that nine out of ten of all black families were poor.[18] For many blacks, being poor meant owning *nothing*: no land, no cow, no hog, not even chickens to supply protein-deficient diets. Pellagra and rickets were common. Many were too poor even to own the tools they used in the fields. As such, they were captives in every sense of the word, utterly at the mercy of their employers.

Crop liens, credit advances, and a discriminatory system of criminal justice, held the system together and provided its energy. Landowners, creditors, and bondsmen became, in effect, the new masters of former slaves served by sheriff's deputies who acted as "patrollers" and "regulators." Arbitrary arrests, whippings, and murder remained the means of enforcement. Peonage immobilized entire families, often for generations, for debt was a family affair that, in this system, carried over from parent to child.

Concealed under the guise of ordinary, and perfectly legal, tenant, sharecropping, and labor contracts, there is no way to determine the full extent of peonage. Often the contracts were simply verbal agreements specifying the rent or share to be paid, the crops to be grown, and the amount of the "furnish," for most blacks remained illiterate. A tenant or sharecropper could be sure of nothing but the furnish in hand, everything else hinged on fate and the honesty of landholders and merchants, and, of course, the weather.[19]

In 1903, a white Alabaman wrote that "a system of enslavement of colored people in Alabama, begun [in Tallapoosa County] has now become a system in many parts of the state."[20] Four years later a federal investigator concluded that "the investigations [in Georgia, Mississippi, and Alabama] will prove that 33 1/3 percent of the planters operating from five to one-hundred plows, are holding their negro employees to a condition of peonage, and arresting and returning those that leave before indebtedness is paid." A year after that, the Justice Department acknowledged that official reports probably *underestimated* the encompassing nature of a system that was, by that time, *the* central feature of the South's agricultural economy.[21]

* * *

About the turn of the century, exposes began to appear as journalists such as Ray Stannard Baker and Oswald Garrison Villard, published articles about the evils of peonage. Stories that appeared in outlets like *The Nation*, *Outlook*, and the *New York Evening Post* often linked peonage and lynching as key elements in the South's exercise of totalitarian control over a black population it still held captive through contract law and debt. One important source of their information was black leader, Booker T. Washington, who also happened to enjoy the respect of Theodore Roosevelt who had become president when William McKinley was assassinated in 1901. With Washington's encouragement, Roosevelt asked his attorney general to provide a report on what was described as "a revolting system of enslaving helpless negro laborers."[22]

The handwritten letters from black victims that accumulated in Justice Department files from that time forward provide a sense of the desperate situation they faced. One letter signed by eight black laborers reads as follows:

> We poor colored men here in the State of Mississippi and poor women does ask the Civil Government to please please send us some one here to take us out of this place our wives and children are naked and Barefooted and we are the same they have here what is known as pennick [peonage] slavery they go to work and beat poor negroes with sticks and shoot them Just Like they were Wild Bears in the Woods and we make big crops here and they Wont settle with us they works us like dogs and mules and they just take our labor if you think we are lieing please send your men here and Just let them See our little Naked Children and wives and come and question with the Labor on the place When you send some one please send them to carry us away if you dont they will Shoot us down after they are gone, please Come and take us away from here.... We are just forced to make some complaint to ask for Help and if the Civil law dont Help us we are Bound to die for Need of Help.[23]

Although not all peons worked under the deplorable circumstances described in this letter, bad things usually happened wherever and whenever a peon tried to terminate his contract when a landowner objected. Persons who fled and were captured could expect a long prison sentence endured as convict labor, and even death. For example, in 1907 an Alabama federal judge received this anonymous letter:

> Sir:
>
> In the [railroad] cross tie camp of Henry Stephenson, of Enterprise, Ala. there are negroes being held in violation of the peonage laws of this country. One of these negroes escaped a few days ago, and this Mr. Henry Stephenson, followed him to the house where he had moved and after failing to persuade or force the negro to go back, he (Henry Stephenson) says, "well if you don't cut ties for me you wont cut them for any one unless you cut them in hell" at the same time placing a pistol to the negro's head, fired, and inflicted probably a fatal wound. There were several negro witnesses and one white man who was with Stephenson, and is probably biased in favor of Stephenson.... A little investigation will convince you that the above facts are true and perhaps the half has not been told.[24]

Another fear tormenting blacks was that even if one escaped, relatives left behind could be forced to work off the obligation. In 1908 an Oglethorp County (Georgia) planter named Dock Jones "bought Columbus Reed Dillard out of jail." In return, Dillard and his wife, Patience, were obligated to repay the fine by working on Jones' farm. Two years later with the fine still unpaid according to Jones' calculations, the Dillards ran off to Atlanta. Enraged, Jones abducted Columbus Dillard's younger two brothers and a sister and made them work off the remainder of the money he claimed was still owed him, even though they were but children. Local authorities saw nothing wrong with his actions and refused to intervene.[25]

Across the South local law enforcement could not be trusted to investigate peonage cases for they were an integral part of the system itself. And there was, of course, no recourse in state courts. Complaints fell on deaf ears, and to persist was to place oneself at risk, for the most powerful forces in Southern politics defended the system. The *Atlanta Constitution*, for example, insisted that "we do not for one moment believe that peonage, in the literal Mexican sense, has ever existed in a southern state." Drawing the familiar Constitutional distinction between state and individual actions, the same newspaper doubted that a federal Anti-Peonage Act had even the "slightest legal force against alleged *individual* peon-holders in a southern state."[26] What Yankees did not understand, the editorial continued, was that

> southerners know how best to get along with the negro for their mutual good...the negro agricultural laborer in the cotton belt is by temperament and the nature of his employment and environment very much of a dependent. If he were to receive his full wages in cash during the cropping season, he could not remain in the community without charity, or more shady means of support, through the winter. He lives to spend the "piece of money" he occasionally finds due him. [The system serves] to keep him in the community through the winter and so protect his family from starvation, the community from depredation, and insure some kind of help on the farm in the spring.[27]

* * *

The Justice Department's attempt to prosecute peonage cases after 1901 was limited and ineffective. Since those who profited from peonage were often wealthy men of considerable influence, prosecution was always difficult. It is not surprising that even well-intentioned federal prosecutors were hesitant to confront that kind of political power in Southern courts. For the less committed prosecutor, it was easier to look the other way.

Confronted with hostile white juries and black witnesses afraid to testify, the difficulties faced were daunting even to conscientious federal prosecutors. Customarily the prosecution's only witnesses were the black plaintiffs themselves. Other black witnesses were frightened, difficult to find, and when they could be located, often denied any knowledge. Win or lose, plaintiffs and witnesses knew they would be left behind to face the consequences when a trial or investigation was concluded and federal prosecutors moved on to other matters. In 1904, a U.S. Attorney in Georgia explained situation:

[T]hese peon holders have threatened them [black witnesses] that after the Federal Court adjourns at Athens last week that they, said slave-holders, will use all means to put in the chain gang every colored man, woman, and child who has complained to the Federal courts, and those they can't put in the chain gang will be reduced to peonage again, and those they can't put in peonage will be killed, and nobody will ever know what has become of them.[28]

Seven years later, another investigator reported that,

the public sentiment in regard to the peonage laws is in a most deploreable condition, many people not hesitating to say that the negroes will be compelled to work out labor contracts even if a few of them have to be lynched in order to terrorize the remaining ones into complying with these iniquitous contracts.[29]

Potential white prosecution witnesses were as intimidated as blacks, and usually unwilling, also, to expose themselves and their families to the considerable risks involved. "The majority of witnesses that the government will have to use," a federal investigator observed in 1913, "are so terrorized that it will be useless to have these cases tried in the immediate vicinity."[30] And in the absence of "reputable,"—that is, white—witnesses, prosecutors faced almost certain defeat wherever cases were tried in the South. "Convictions in peonage cases are very difficult to obtain," a U.S. Attorney explained, "and are only possible where the circumstances are very aggravated and the testimony is supported by white witnesses."[31]

Another indication of the degree to which intimidation was employed is the hostility that awaited federal investigators themselves. Viewed, like earlier agents of the Freedmen's Bureau, as unwelcome intruders into the sacrosanct domain of states' rights and white supremacy, leading Southern newspapers, for example, left no doubt about the animosity toward them.[32]

Thus it is not surprising that abundant evidence exposes the Justice Department's hesitancy to investigate the complaints that accumulated in their files during this period. Department documents reveal, for example, that it considered the involuntary servitude of black peons a "Southern" issue, and one best left to the states and the Democratic politicians who governed them. The Department's reluctance to prosecute peonage cases was evident in its first tentative forays. From the very beginning there was tacit, and sometimes explicit, recognition that peonage in the South was different; that it was a racial matter that federal authorities should avoid whenever possible. The Department's *Peonage Files* reveal an unmistakeable pattern of racial bias in the way it selected, investigated, and prosecuted cases. Of those cases it did prosecute successfully, sentences were usually light and then commonly commuted.[33] Complaints from European immigrants received prompt attention, those involving blacks were most often ignored. In 1908, for example, a Justice Department investigative report on peonage in Mississippi focused on the "ill treatment of Italians."[34]

* * *

Debt peonage remained well into the twentieth century because of black landlessness, Southern resistance, and federal indifference. Just as Southern lawmakers had redefined crime to supply black manpower for a profitable system of convict labor, so, too, did they use contract law to structure the system of debt peonage. The cycle was completed as grinding poverty forced many blacks into petty theft to meet needs that could be met no other way. The Thirteenth Amendment notwithstanding, involuntary servitude continued as a mainstay of the South's economy and a symbol of its culture. For blacks it was yet another bitter experience that deepened their distrust of law enforcement and the criminal justice system.

Notes

1. U.S. Department of Justice, *Peonage Files, 1900–1945* (Washington, DC: National Archives, Record Group 60), (microfilm), reel no. 14, 856–857. Hereafter cited as *Peonage Files*.
2. Testimony of Claude Freeman, *Georgia v. John S. Williams*, Newton Superior Court (1921), 89–90; quoted in P. Daniel, *The Shadow of Slavery: Peonage in the South 1901–1969* (Chicago: University of Illinois, 1972), 112.
3. J.M. Wiener, "Class Structure and Economic Development in the American South, 1865–1955," *American Historical Review* LXXXIV (1979), 983; also, Wiener, *Social Origins of the New South: Alabama, 1860–1885* (Baton Rouge: Louisiana State University Press, 1978), 66–73; and D.B. Billings, *Planters and the Making of the "New South": Class, Politics, and Development in North Carolina, 1865–1900* (Chapel Hill: University of North Carolina Press, 1979); W. Cohen, *At Freedom's Edge: Black Mobility and the Southern White Quest for Racial Control, 1861–1915* (Baton Rouge: Louisiana State University Press, 1991).
4. W. Cohen, "Negro Involuntary Servitude in the South, 1865–1940: A Preliminary Analysis," *Journal of Southern History* XLII (February 1976), 42–43.
5. *Alabama Criminal Codes* 4930 (1896), (1903).
6. Washington to O.G. Villard, September 7, 1908, Washington Papers; quoted in Daniel, *The Shadow of Slavery,* 67.
7. Quoted in Cohen, "Negro Involuntary Servitude," 35.
8. The only large scale black migration out of the South before World War I occurred in 1879–1880 when an estimated 25,000 migrated to Kansas. But most of those migrants came from Tennessee, Kentucky, and Missouri rather than the Deep South. See, W. Cohen, *At Freedom's Edge: Black Mobility and the Southern White Quest for Racial Control, 1861–1915* (Baton Rouge: Louisiana State University Press, 1991), esp. chapter 7.

9. R.L.Ransom and R. Sutch, *One Kind of Freedom: The Economic Consequences of Emancipation* (New York: Cambridge University Press, 1977), 68–80, 87–97.

10. Ransom and Sutch, *One Kind of Freedom*, 81–88; G.D. Jaynes, *Branches Without Roots: Genesis of the Black Working Class in the American South, 1862–1882* (New York: Oxford University Press, 1986), esp. 158–159, 180, 217, 291, 313.

11. T.D. Clark, "The Furnishing and Supply System in Southern Agriculture Since 1865," *Journal of Southern History* 12 (February 1946), 24–44.

12. R. Sutch and R. Ransom, "Debt Peonage in the Cotton South After the Civil War," *Journal of Economic History* 32 (September 1972), 641–669.

13. G.K. Holmes, "The Peons of the South," *Annals of the American Academy of Political and Social Sciences* 4 (September 1893), 265–274; W. Wilson, *Forced Labor in the United States* (New York: International Publishers, 1933), 86; W. Brown and M. Reynolds, "Debt Peonage Re-examined," *Journal of Economic History* 33 (December 1973), 862–871; G.B. Tindall, *The Emergence of the New South, 1913–1945* (Baton Rouge: Louisiana State University Press, 1967), 111–142, 409–410.

14. Although reliable figures are not available until the nineteen thirties, an 1933 study of farm households in Alabama revealed that 89 percent of their years spent in sharecropping ended in debt or only breaking even. Eighty percent of the three thousand families surveyed had accumulated more than a year's debt to landholders. See, H. Hoffsomer, *Landlord-Tenant Relations and Relief in Alabama*, (Washington, DC: FERA Research Bulletin Series II, no. 9, 1935), 2.

15. R.L. Sutch and R. Ransom, "The Ex-Slave in the Post-Bellum South: A Study of the Economic Impact of Racism in a Market Environment," *Journal of Economic History* 33 (March 1973), 131–148; Ransom and Sutch, *One Kind of Freedom*, 97–105, 179–186; C.S. Johnson, E.R. Embree, and W.W. Alexander, *The Collapse of Cotton Tenancy: Summary of Field Studies and Statistical Surveys, 1933–1935* (Chapel Hill: University of North Carolina, 1935), 4–5; Tindall, *The Emergence of the New South*, 125–126.

16. By 1920, the number of croppers and tenants had grown to 49.6 percent; by 1930, 55.5 percent. Forced labor was a hidden crime and reliable statistics do not exist, but it is reasonable to suspect that most of these croppers and tenants were bound to some degree by debt.

17. A.F. Raper, *Preface to Peasantry* (Chapel Hill: University of North Carolina Press, 1936), 3–9.

18. N. Fligstein, *Going North: Migration of Blacks and Whites from the South, 1900–1950* (New York: Academic Press, 1981), 163; N.R. McMillen, *Dark Journey: Black Mississippians in the Age of Jim Crow* (Urbana: University of Illinois Press, 1989), 144–146.

19. Raper, *Preface to Peasantry*, 218.

20. B.W. Walker to the U.S. Attorney General, May 14, 1903, *Peonage Files* (microfilm), reel no. 2, 20–24.

21. A.J. Hoyt to Attorney General, February 4, 1907, *Peonage Files* (microfilm) reel 13, 1073–1074; C.W. Russell, *Report on Peonage*, 1908, *Peonage Files* (microfilm) reel 5, 1040–1078.

22. "Illegal Forced Labor in Alabama," *Outlook* 74 (June 6, 1903), 301–302; quoted in Daniel, *The Shadow of Slavery*, 49; see, also, 44–50.

23. *Peonage Files*, (microfilm), reel no. 17, 156–157.

24. Letter to Judge Thomas G. Jones, December 19, 1907, *Peonage Files* (microfilm), reel no. 12, 759.

25. F.G. Tate to the Attorney General, August 15, 1910, *Peonage Files* (microfilm), reel no. 15, 898–899.
26. Debt peonage in America did not originate in the South. In 1867, Congress passed the Anti-Peonage Act that was a direct response to complaints about the terms of labor and debt in the territory of New Mexico. Peonage there had its origins in that region's earlier period of Spanish colonial rule.
27. *Atlanta Constitution*, April 18, 1904 (emphasis added); quoted in *Peonage Files* (microfilm), reel no. 1, 952–955.
28. *Peonage Files* (microfilm), reel 1, 957.
29. A. Akerman to Attorney General, August 24, 1911; quoted in Daniel, *The Shadow of Slavery*, 109.
30. Statement of U.S. Attorney Reese and Special Agent Allred, *Peonage Files* (microfilm), reel 13, 463.
31. Statement of H. Alexander, *Peonage Files* (microfilm), reel 17, 68–69.
32. In 1904, for example, the *Atlanta Constitution* railed that
    Until these peonage prosecutions were instituted, the average negro lived up to his supply contract without the necessity of recourse to the law. The farmer furnished him and he "worked it out." The effect of the [federal] prosecutions in question is to make the less honorable negroes repudiate their contracts in the spring, after having lived on the employer's bounty all winter and defy the farmer to legally make them work out the debt. The consequent demoralization of farm labor has alarmingly increased negro criminality, vagabondage and destitution, decreased southern agricultural production and the farmer's ability to live by the soil, and militated against a good feeling between the races and the south's internal development.
    ...Our local tribunals are able to take care of any case involving an unlawful deprivation of individual liberty, if such cases there be...and they can be depended upon to hew to the line of constitutionality and justice.
    In a sense, the *honor* of the south is involved in this matter, and, whatever the lessons of the civil war, the south clings tenaciously to what has been left of state sovereignty. See, *The Constitution* (Atlanta), April 18, 1904; reproduced in *Peonage Files* (microfilm), reel 1, 952–955 (emphasis added).
33. *Peonage Files* (microfilm) reel no. 1, 270–71, 957; reel no. 15, 669–71, 679–80, 689–90; see, also, *Clyatt v. United States* 197 U.S. 207 (1905); *Bailey v. Alabama* 219 U.S. 219 (1911); For discussions of these cases and other evidence on this point, see, B.C. Schmidt, Jr., "Principle and Prejudice: The Supreme Court and Race in the the Progressive Era," *WestLaw*, (1992), orig., *Columbia Law Review* (May 1982); D.A. Novack, *The Wheel of Servitude: Black Forced Labor After Slavery* (Lexington: University of Kentucky Press, 1978); N.V. Barley, *The Creation of Modern Georgia* (Athens: University of Georgia Press, 1990), 36–38; W. White, "The Negro and the Flood," 4–6, 10–11, *NAACP Files*, Box 380, quoted in McMillen, *Dark Journey*, 147–48. For one partial exception to the rule, see *Georgia v. John.S. Williams* (1921); also, W.A. Bootle to Attorney General, June 24, 1930, quoted in Daniel, *Shadow of Slavery*, at 130, see, also, 110–130.
34. In 1908, the Senate reluctantly began an investigation into peonage. Senators, however, did not want to confront the obvious race issue that Ray Stannard Baker and others had written so much about. Instead, the committee instructed the U.S Immigration Commission to investigate the extent to which *European* immigrants were being victimized by the practice. Stirred by the same forces, the Department of Justice also issued a *Report on Peonage* that year. Here, too, despite the countless blacks who were locked into the system, the report dealt

only obliguely with the race issue, focusing instead on a tiny aspect of the problem: the complaints made by, or in behalf of, German, Austrian, Italian, Bulgarian, and Russian Jewish immigrants, as well as "other foreigners," and "New York boys." See, C.W. Russell, *Report on Peonage* (Washington, DC: Department of Justice, 1908); see, also, *Peonage Files* (microfilm) reel 5, 1040–1078.

Part IV

The Urban Transformation

13

The Promised Land

*"They were a proud and selfish people, those
plantation owners, and I believe...that God finally
sent the boll weevil to jumble them. When the boll
weevil came, it ate right through thousands of fields
of cotton and most of those big plantations went
bankrupt. That part of the South went down and it has
never come back up. Thanks to the boll weevil, a lot
of those thieving plantation people died out, too."*
                                                        —Mahalia Jackson[1]

*Brady went down to the licensed saloon.
He thought he'd arrest him a rowdy coon.
...Said Duncan to Brady, "You done me wrong;
Come in my house when my game was going on,
Kicked in my windows, yes broke down my door."
Now Brady lays on the barroom floor.*
                   —"Duncan and Brady" Ballad, St. Louis, c. 1890s[2]

*"Our attention was called strikingly to the fact that at
the time of race rioting, the arrests made for rioting
by the police of colored rioters were far in excess of
the arrests made of white rioters. The failure of the
police to arrest impartially, at the time of the rioting,
whether from insufficient effort or otherwise, was a
mistake and had a tendency to further incite and
aggravate the colored population."*
                   —Coroner's jury, Chicago, November 3, 1919[3]

At the dawn of the twentieth century, the Southern black population
found itself immobilized and denied economic opportunity by an op-
pressive system of debt peonage. At the same time, segregation laws,
disfranchisement, and capital punishment together had served to con-
solidate and stabilize the political and social order of white supremacy

193

in the South. The indifference of federal authorities to these injustices completed what was a very ugly picture of American racism.

Soon, however, other powerful and unanticipated forces were unleashed that would alter the course of race relations and change the face of American society. Except for emancipation, itself, nothing has had a more profound effect on American race relations than the rapid urban transformation of the black population during the first half of the twentieth century.

In 1915, the same year that D.W. Griffith's triumphal film glorification of the Ku Klux Klan, *Birth of a Nation*, was playing to enthalled audiences,[4] nature had already begun a process that would loosen the bonds of peonage and the grip of white oppression. For the first time in their history on American soil, millions of blacks were able to leave the South, leaving behind, they hoped, the debt, impoverishment, and violence that had immobilized them for so long.

A curious set of circumstances, the boll weevil, bad weather, and a world war, struck debt peonage a telling blow. Nature buckled the South's economy, and the war created new jobs in the North and a shortage of white men to fill them. These forces shook the economic foundation of debt peonage in a way the Justice Department had not in its half-hearted investigative efforts at the turn of the century. Peonage continued in diminished form because poverty remained, but for millions of blacks plague and pestilence set in motion a major demographic transformation that can reasonably be considered a second emancipation. As landholders went bankrupt, tens of thousands of black farm laborers, many carrying all their worldly possessions in a single burlap sack, crowded onto segregated trains and began the trip north with the hope of better-paying jobs and what they hoped would be new lives in what they called "the Promised Land."

Incensed by lynching, lawlessness, and the South's heartless exploitation of black labor, black newspapers in the North urged blacks to flee. The nation's leading black newspaper, the *Chicago Defender*, with two-thirds of its circulation distributed across the South, was insistent in its appeals to blacks to move North:

> Every black man for the sake of his wife and daughters especially should leave even at a financial sacrifice every spot in the south where his worth is not appreciated enough to give him the standing of a man and a citizen in the community. We know full well that this would mean a depopulation of that section and if it were possible we would glory in its accomplishment...anywhere in God's country is far better than the southland.[5]

The boll weevil infestation that began in southern Texas in 1892 and gradually spread east and north across the South's most productive agricultural expanses was the major cause of what became known as the Great Migration. These voracious insects came in waves, along with rain and drought, to decimate cotton production in Louisiana, Mississippi, Alabama, Georgia, and Florida. In one Mississippi county, for example, annual cotton production dropped from 14,000 to 2,000 bales. The one-crop dependency and lack of diversity in farming made matters worse, creating a rippling effect of economic adversity that spread across the entire region. When credit dried up at the stores and banks, there was insufficent capital to take up the slack, leaving black tenants and sharecroppers without money or credit. For the first time since home rule had been restored in the South in 1877, hundreds of thousands of blacks were able to break free and leave their bankrupt employers. Labor contracts became meaningless and, with them, the debts owed by people without any possible means to pay them.

To some the movement had religious significance, an "exodus" of Biblical proportions, like the Israelites had made from Egypt, "crossing over Jordan" (the Ohio River) to "Beulah Land," or the "Promised Land" (of Northern cities). God had parted the Red Sea for the Israelites, black preachers claimed, and thousands of years later he had sent a plague of insects to free his black children in America.[6] Landed whites survived the scourge by planting food crops and living on savings. Large numbers of blacks, however, nearly 90 percent of whom were landless, left the farms they worked. Between 1910 and 1920, approximately 454,000 of them moved north, most from weevil infested areas.[7]

Once the bonds had been loosened, other reasons drew more north. Perhaps the most important one was the lure of industrial jobs. In 1914, European immigration totaled 1,218,480 as a steady flow of immigrants provided the manpower for the nation's rapidly expanding industrial economy. But by 1917, it had dropped to 295,403, the result of restrictions imposed in Europe as one country after another was drawn into World War I. At the same time, thousands of other immigrants, already in the country, quit their jobs and sailed back across the Atlantic to fight for their homelands and help families in distress. When the United States entered the war, thousands more young men were called into military service, leaving old jobs vacant and no one to fill new ones created by the war. For the first time in history, Northern industries began looking south for black workers. Newspaper ads, pamphlets, and recruiting agents appeared overnight at Southern churches and general stores, or wherever blacks congregated, inviting them to make the move north to better-paying industrial jobs.[8] But the welcome they received fell far short of expectations.

Blacks were unique among other ethnic groups in ways that set them apart even in the diverse ethnic environments of America's industrial cities. Unlike other non-European immigrant groups, blacks came quickly and in record numbers that could not be easily assimilated. Those numbers, the color of their skin, and the long history of racial hostility they had endured, made them, once again, highly visible targets of white discrimination and hostility.[9] Unlike disdained Eastern and Southern European immigrants, there was no Roman Catholic church, for example, with its parochial schools to welcome black children and to ease their transition into a society that was as strange to them as it was to Poles and Italians. Labor unions resisted their efforts to become members and, at the same time, tried to block their attempts to find nonunion employment. White workers viewed blacks as nothing more than strikebreakers and criminals. As a result, blacks were forcefully excluded from the mainstream of urban/industrial life. In what was already a hostile, biracial society, it is no wonder that they had enormous difficulty with problems they were poorly prepared to handle, and with which so few were willing to help.[10]

Such exclusion meant that they were not only denied jobs and incomes, but also the important lessons learned through work in an urban/industrial economy. As field hands and sharecroppers, they had lived in concert with the rhythms of seasons, weather, and hours of daylight, rather than the dictates of the time clock and the assembly line. Isolated and scorned by organized labor, they remained locked by custom and habit into the folkways and values of the preindustrial society from which they came, and which were no longer useful.[11]

American cities had become a volatile ethnic mix of competing groups even before blacks arrived in record numbers. Not only their color, but what would now be called the "life-styles" of blacks invited the hostility of people who were themselves recent immigrants and different also. It was as though blacks gave other contentious immigrant groups like the Poles, the Irish, and the Italians something that could unite them, for if they could agree on little else, they were united in their contempt for "niggers." Furthermore, the frustrations and festering resentments blacks took with them when they moved North left many poorly prepared to cope with such hostility and the new array of disappointments they encountered when they reached new destinations.

* * *

As black demographic status began to shift rapidly from rural to urban in the early decades of the twentieth century, so too did the form of mob violence that awaited them change from the lynchings of the Southern countryside to the race riots of Northern cities. Race riots, of course, were not new. They had occurred throughout American history. For obvious reasons, they were more common in Northern cities until after emancipation. Of the forty-four recorded race riots between 1820 and 1865, for example, only three occurred in Southern cities.

The most savage of the Civil War disturbances was the New York City draft riot of July 13–16, 1863. Angered by the prospect of being drafted into a war to free blacks they had no use for, working-class white males, many of them Irish immigrants, stormed an armory and then rampaged through the city attacking blacks and abolitionists and burning black property. Bullets and beatings claimed the lives of at least 105 black victims whose bodies were sometimes sexually mutilated and burned. Hundreds more were injured. Mobs burned black homes and churches and even razed an orphanage for black children, leaving no doubt that their intent was not only to destroy property, but also to drive blacks from the city.[12]

After the Civil War, major riots with similar consequences occurred in 1866 in Memphis and New Orleans, Philadelphia in 1871, Danville, Virginia in 1883, and Wilmington, North Carolina in 1898. The incidence of rioting shifted South after Appomattox. From 1865 to the end of the century, eighteen riots occurred, all but one in Southern cities.[13]

During the nineteenth century, race riots could be more accurately called pogroms, for in every instance violence was initiated by whites in response to some perceived or imagined threat posed by blacks in urban settings. In the Wilmington riot of 1898, for example, recent black political successes provided the spark for a riot that left at least thirty blacks dead. Not one white died in the assault as politically active blacks were either murdered or driven out of the city. The results of that episode were typical, extending a now familiar pattern of black casualties.[14]

The first major riot of the twentieth century occurred in Atlanta in 1906. It followed the familiar "nigger-baiting" gubernatorial campaigns of Hoke Smith and Clark Howell. At the same time Smith and Howell were trying to outdo one another with racial invective, newspapers fanned the embers of racial hatred by championing urban vagrancy drives to rid the city of "petty thieves and black beasts." "Drive Them To The Chain Gang" and, even "Kill The Vagrants" were shrill headlines that appeared in Atlanta's two major newspapers not long before the riot.[15]

As the physical proximity of blacks and whites narrowed on Atlanta's crowded streets, the same newspapers warned that social distance had to be maintained at any cost. White womanhood was at risk, they insisted, as an alleged new epidemic of rape threatened to engulf the city. The editor of the *Atlanta Georgian*, for example, wrote,

> The mere suggestion of the slightest familiarity of a black and filthy Negro with a refined and gentle Caucasian girl stirs the blood to fever heat, but the monstrous and unspeakable horror of a more serious and brutal assault wakes the blood to complete frenzy.

Another editorial warned that lynching was in store for any black who had "any contact under any circumstances by accident or design with a Southern woman."[16]

In the midst of this frenzy of fear and sexual hysteria created and fed by the media, the Atlanta riot began on September 22 when an estimated five thousand whites gathered near Decatur and Marietta Streets determined to cleanse the city of potential black rapists. Their numbers soon swelled to some ten thousand as armed young men intent on maiming or killing any black they could get their hands on surged through the city. Outnumbered blacks fought back briefly, but they were quickly overwhelmed. When order was finally restored five days later, twenty-five of them had been murdered, hundreds more had been injured, and thousands of others had been forced to flee the city.[17]

Within a decade after the Atlanta riot, the rapid urban transformation of the black population altered the regional locus of rioting. From that time to the present, race riots were likely to occur *anywhere*, South or North, wherever blacks concentrated in numbers that whites found threatening. From 1900 through the 1930s, nineteen major riots broke out, eleven of them in the North and eight in the South. As blacks moved north, mobs in East St. Louis, Philadelphia, and Chicago proved to be as ugly and vicious as they were in Atlanta and Wilmington. Animosity in the form of indignant landlords, dishonest merchants, hostile labor unions, and surly police officers awaited their arrival at the end of rail lines. Gangs of white youths cursed them, with only their strange new accents to distinguish them from mobs in Atlanta and New Orleans and other Southern cities.

* * *

The black response to mob violence changed, however, in the cities. Before the urban transformation, outnumbered and unarmed blacks had been hard-pressed to defend themselves against attacking mobs. But black resistance stiffened as their numbers grew and became more concentrated in urban neighborhoods. Soon they were standing their ground and contesting whites for control of disputed areas. Either group was just as likely to attack the other if racial boundaries were violated. In a pattern first observed in Southern cities, whites were as unsafe in black areas as blacks were in areas controlled by whites. The defiant black "outlaw" attitude that was first observed in the 1880s was evident whenever and wherever confrontations occurred as blacks began to arm themselves to challenge white intrusions. Black newspapers in the North became standard bearers for the new militancy, urging their readers to stand up to whites. Stop playing the white man's game, they advised; the only way to get respect from whites is to demand it.

No newspaper was more militant or more widely read than the *Chicago Defender*, which was founded in 1905 by Robert Abbot, a black Georgian well acquainted with Southern brutality. The newspaper's roving correspondents risked their lives covering the South to ensure that no racial atrocity was overlooked in a region that included more than fifteen hundred cities and towns. Calling Southern leaders "looters, grafters, lazy sinecurists, general 'no accounts,' persecutors, KILLERS OF NEGRO MEN, seducers, RAVISHERS OF NEGRO WOMEN," its goal was to make "the 'crackers' squirm under the lash" of national exposure.[18]

Another goal was to promote black pride. The need to fight back was a continuing theme in the *Defender's* pages: An "Eye for an Eye, and Tooth for a Tooth," began one editorial. "When the mob comes and you must die," it advised its readers in 1915, "take at least one with you." When mobs surround your home, it continued, "Call the white fiends to the door and shoot them down."[19] Blacks welcomed the newspaper's courage and unapologetic sense of racial pride and honor. Messages like these took hold in black communities anxious for change. Rioting white gangs in cities such as Chicago, Detroit, Philadelphia and Baltimore soon learned that they would have to contend with armed and, in a number of instances, organized black resistance.

* * *

In 1917, in the midst of the Great Migration, major riots broke out in East St. Louis, Philadelphia, Chester (Pennsylvania), and Houston. The most extensive of these, the East St. Louis disturbance, broke out in June when an aluminum company hired black workers to replace whites who had gone on strike. The response was swift as union representatives called on the mayor to stop further black hiring and migration into the city. Almost simultaneously, false rumors spread that blacks had attacked two white girls. An angry confrontation between blacks and police followed. It was not long before some three thousand whites were roaming the streets, beating blacks and crying for vengeance. Enraged whites drove automobiles through black neighborhoods, firing guns and hurling rocks into homes. When blacks returned the fire, police tried to disarm them. Then blacks opened fire on the police. In a matter of hours, East St. Louis became a battle zone. When order was finally restored, forty-eight people had been killed, hundreds injured, and more than three hundred buildings had been burned.[20]

There could be little doubt about the defiant mood of blacks later in that same year, when Houston police officers beat two black soldiers who had tried to prevent the arrest of a black woman, an alleged prostitute. When word of the brutal beatings reached the victims' segregated military base nearby, some one hundred and fifty black soldiers from the 24th Infantry seized rifles and ammunition and marched into the city seeking revenge. By the time the fighting ended, twelve whites and one black had been killed and nineteen others had been wounded, including five black soldiers. A few months later, thirteen black soldiers were hanged and forty-one others were sentenced to life imprisonment. Four others were given shorter sentences and five were acquitted. In a funeral sermon, a white Houston minister attributed the battle to nothing more than "bad niggers, vice, and booze." In the eyes of blacks everywhere, however, the soldiers were martyrs, the whole experience just one more bitter example of police brutality and racial injustice.[21]

* * *

Thoughout the following summer of 1918, sporadic racial violence continued in other cities as blacks pressed into poor and already over-crowded neighborhoods. Philadelphia, for example, was in the midst of absorbing a 58 percent increase in its black population that at that time already numbered nearly 134,000. The luckiest of these new immigrants found space in teeming, dilapidated tenements in crime-ridden areas; the less fortunate made due in makeshift shanties, tents, and boxcars along the tracks they had traveled. A report on black housing in Northern cities released in 1908, for example, concluded that "In more than one city the distinctively Negro Neighborhood is the same as, or next to, that district which seems, *by consent of civil authorities*, to be given up to vice."[22]

Blacks wanted to live in crime-free neighborhoods just as much as whites, but they were almost always denied the opportunity. When they did manage to move into decent housing they were usually forced out. Two black families, for example, had just moved into such a house on Pine Street in South Philadelphia when they were attacked by a mob. Irish thugs dragged their meager furnishings into the street and set them on fire. Such white-on-black violence was by then part of a familiar pattern in Northern cities, but police in Philadelphia were not prepared for the black response to it.

Philadelphia, like Chicago, had a black newspaper with an outspoken editor impatient with racial injustice. In an editorial entitled "Dixie Methods in Philadelphia," G. Grant Williams condemned the Pine Street outrage and similar attacks on blacks. But he did not stop there, as one might have expected a black editor to do in a bygone era of race relations. Instead, he urged his readers to arm themselves and fight back.

"You are not down in Dixie now and you need not fear the ragged rum-crazed hellion crew, prototypes of your old cracker enemies," Williams wrote:

> They are the enemies of all decent law-abiding citizens and the time has come to clean out this nest of dirty curs.... They may burn some of the property, but you burn their hides with any weapon that comes handy while they are engaged in that illegal pastime. We stand for law and order, decency and cleanliness, but...our patience runs out.
>
> Be at peace with all men at all times is our motto, if they will let you be; but when they tread upon your rights, fight them to the bitter end...we'll meet the rowdies of the town and give them shot and shell. These skunks...represent the scum of Erin's sod.[23]

A few weeks later, in the same city, a gang of white thugs attacked a black woman who had violated territorial claims when she purchased a home on the edge of a white neighborhood. When a rock smashed through her window, Adella Bond shot the assailant in the leg and called the police. The story of her predicament spread through the black community which immediately rallied to her support. Reports of the incident further incensed whites who countered with more assaults, but each was greeted with renewed black resistance, marking the beginnings of a series of violent racial skirmishes.

Two days after the assault on the Bond home, a white mob attacked a lone black man as he walked toward his home. The man shot and killed one of his attackers before he also was shot and wounded. Later the same day, a similar attack occurred in another part of town. This time the intended black victim drew a pistol and fled into a house. Daring his attackers to enter, they, instead, called the police. When police tried to drag the man from the building, he killed one and wounded another.

The emerging pattern of black self-defense evident in both these incidents enraged whites, who countered with further violence. Unwary blacks were attacked as they got off trolleys, or walked alone on the street. When six homes in a black neighborhood were set ablaze, police responded with a house-to-house search for the black "snipers" who had fired at the arsonists. The unmistakeable pattern of discrimination evident in the police response only fed black outrage.

"Why do your police arrest a colored man or woman for protecting their home?" the editor of the *Tribune* asked the mayor in an editorial, "The colored people of Philadelphia are law-abiding citizens and ask your protection, and if you don't protect them, they shall and will defend themselves." Before the siege ended, an unarmed black man was killed by police and hundreds more were injured. In the aftermath, black leaders labeled the actions of police a "disgrace." Police, it seemed to blacks, were the same North or South.[24]

* * *

That was certainly true in Chicago. Chicago was probably studied more closely by social scientists than any other city during this era. As the northern terminus of the Illinois Central Railroad, it was the most accessible Northern city for blacks leaving Louisiana, Mississippi, and Arkansas. Between 1916 and 1919, some 50,000 of them arrived in Chicago, making race relations, a study commission concluded, "Chicago's most serious municipal problem." Newly arrived blacks quickly found out why.[25]

As black numbers grew in that city, whites—especially the Irish and Poles who usually lived closest to them physically and economically—responded by reinforcing racial barriers. Competition for housing and living space were at the crux of an emerging racial crisis in Chicago. Certain neighborhoods, parks, playgrounds, and beaches were off-limits to blacks. When territorial claims were challenged, the result was almost always bloodshed as white gangs patrolled the borders of contested areas, ready to assault any black who strayed over the boundary. White police officers, who often lived in the same ethnic neighborhoods, stood as allies of gang members.

White "athletic clubs" commonly terrorized blacks who dared to enter the city's public parks. Fuller Park and the Armour Square recreation area, for example, just west of Wentworth Avenue, were controlled by the Irish and Poles from adjacent neighborhoods. When black youths tried to play baseball in Washington Park, they were continually harassed by white hoodlums who taunted them with cries of "Hey nigger," and stole and vandalized equipment to provoke fights. Blacks rapidly learned that few of the city's parks and beaches could be used safely. At the same time blacks were excluded from public facilities, white "neighborhood improvement societies" attacked black homes. Such urban terrorists were responsible for bombs that shattered black homes considered too close to other ethnic enclaves. Black families were the victims of fifty-eight such bombings between 1917 and 1921. That is, on average, more than one a month. In the words of one observer, "the South Side of Chicago became the battleground for racial war."[26]

The worst episode in the ongoing struggle began on July 27, 1919 when racial tensions exploded in a rampage of violence. The riot followed the drowning of a black youth who had unknowingly drifted across an invisible boundary that defined a "whites only" swimming area in Lake Michigan. Whites pelted the helpless boy with rocks as he clung desperately to a railroad tie before finally slipping beneath the surface. News of the murder spread quickly and an angry crowd gathered as blacks demanded that police arrest those responsible. When police arrested instead a black protestor, blacks turned on the police.

In the mayhem that followed, black and white mobs fought pitched battles in the streets, others stormed buildings, killing or maiming any person of a different race unlucky enough to draw their attention. Homes were attacked and burned; windows were broken and stores ransacked and looted as angry crowds surged back and forth through the city. Blacks torched forty-nine houses in an immigrant neighborhood near the Stock Yards, leaving nearly a thousand homeless. Generations of racial hatred spilled out in the screams and curses that filled Chicago streets. When authorities finally regained control four days later, thirty-eight people had been killed (fifteen whites and twenty-three blacks) and 537 had been injured (178 whites, 342 blacks, and seventeen others whose race was unknown).[27] The rioting sent another unmistakeable signal to whites that times had changed: blacks would no longer tolerate atrocities as they had so often in the South. Like their counterparts in Philadelphia a year before, win or lose, they would strike back. By this time blacks understood that in the North, just like the South, calling the police was too often a self-defeating exercise.

* * *

After seven major race riots in 1919, urban riots became less frequent in the 1920s with disturbances occurring only in Chicago, again in 1920, and Tulsa, Oklahoma in 1921. The greater sensitivity and awareness of public officials in the wake of the frightening and costly earlier disturbances probably accounts, in part, for the change. The calm continued during the Great Depression of the 1930s as many of the jobs blacks and whites had earlier competed with one another for disappeared. Job shortages also slowed the flow of migration north. The some-348,000 blacks who did migrate represented less than half the number of the previous decade. This easing of population pressure also appeared to reduce racial tensions. A single riot in Harlem in 1935 marked the only major racial disturbance of the decade.

In every race riot of this period, it is important to note, discriminatory law enforcement and police brutality were the precipitating events. It did not matter whether it was Atlanta or Philadelphia, Wilmington or Detroit, New Orleans or Chicago, police behaved as though black guilt and white innocence could be assumed. W.E.B. DuBois made this assessment of police conduct in 1940:

> [Black] districts are not usually protected by the police rather victimized and tyranized over by them. No one who does not know can realize what tyranny a low-grade white policeman can exercise in a colored neighborhood. In court his unsupported word cannot be disputed and the only defense against him is often mayhem and assassination by black criminals, with resultant hue and cry.[28]

Policemen everywhere were viewed by blacks with suspicion, contempt, and fear. There was no trust, and it cut both ways. In this context, one can understand, perhaps, why in black folklore women wore red to celebrate the deaths of bullying policemen:

> When King Brady was on de beat,
> He 'lowed no ladies to walk de street;
> Now King Brady is daid an' gone,
> An' de ladies walk de street all night long.
> When dey heard King Brady was daid,
> Dey all went home an' dressed in red;
> Come back dancin' an' singin' a song —
> King Brady went to hell wid a stetson on.[29]

* * *

Between 1915 and 1940, the black population living outside the South more than doubled to over 2.5 million. This represented 21 percent of the total number of blacks living on American soil. More than half of these were migrants who had crowded into the slums of just seven cities: New York, Chicago, St.Louis, Detroit, Cleveland, Philadelphia, and Pittsburgh. In that year, New York alone accounted for over sixteen percent of the non-Southern black population. Already in motion were new forces that would ensure that the trend would accelerate in the coming decades. The result was a remarkable transformation of the black population from South to North, and rural to urban, in less than a half century.[30]

But the Promised Land of black hopes and dreams was for many a bitter and disillusioning experience. Mob violence, police brutality, and discrimination against them continued in the cities of the North. "I learned when I was 10 or 11 not to turn my back on a cop," former Detroit mayor Coleman Young said, recalling his youth in that city during the 1930s.[31] If there was trouble, it was better just to settle things yourself.

Notes

1. M. Jackson, *Movin' on Up* (New York: Hawthorn Books, 1966), 13–14.
2. H.M. Belden and A.P. Hudson (eds.), *Folk Ballads From North Carolina, The Frank C. Grown Collection of North Carolina Folklore* 7 vols. (Durham, NC: Duke University Press, 1952), 671–72.
3. Chicago Commission on Race Relations, *The Negro in Chicago: A Study of Race Relations and a Race Riot in 1919* (Chicago: University of Chicago Press, 1922), 36.
4. There was a resurgence in the Ku Klux Klan's popularity in the 1920s reflected in growth both in its membership and its repectability as a patriotic organization. Always strong in the South, its membership flourished during this period in states such as Pennsylvania, Ohio, and Indiana, peaking at an estimated five million in 1925, the same year some 40,000 of its members met and marched in Washington, DC. During this period it helped to elect more than twenty governors and senators, not only in the South, but in California, Colorado, and Oregon as well. See, *The Ku Klux Klan: A History of Racism and Violence* (Montgomery, AL: Southern Poverty Law Center, 1991), 14–18.
5. Chicago *Defender*, October 7, 1916, September 22, 1917; see, also, J.R. Grossman, *Land of Hope: Chicago, Black Southerners, and the Great Migration* (Chicago: University of Chicago Press, 1989), 83–90; Chicago Commission, *The Negro in Chicago*, 87–92; S. Marullo, "The Migration of Blacks to the North, 1911–1918," *Journal of Black Studies* 15 (1985), 291–306.
6. Marullo, "The Migration of Blacks to the North," 291–306; A. Davis, B.B. Gardner, and M.R. Gardner, *Deep South* (Chicago: University of Chicago Press, 1941), 255–262; "Report on Negro Migration from Alabama" in E.J. Scott, *Negro Migration During the War* (New York: Oxford University Press, 1920), 14–15, 45.

7. A. Davis, B.B. Gardner, and M.R. Gardner, *Deep South* (Los Angeles: University of California Press, 1988; orig., 1941), 255–262, 338–341, 373–374; C.G. Woodson, *A Century of Negro Migration* (New York: Russell & Russell, 1918), 167–173; A.F. Raper, *Preface to Peasantry: A Tale of Two Black Belt Counties* (Chapel Hill: University of North Carolina Press, 1936), 201–216; N. Fligstein, *Going North: Migration of Blacks and Whites from the South, 1900–1950* (New York: Academic Press, 1981), 15–16, 98–105, 120–136.

8. Marullo, "The Migration of Blacks to the North," 291–306; Chicago Commission, *The Negro in Chicago*, 79–84; S.C. Drake, and H.R. Cayton, *Black Metropolis: A Study of Negro Life in a Northern City* (New York: Harcourt, Brace, 1945), 58–59; Scott, *Negro Migration*, 16–17, 51–54.

9. On the problems of the size of the black migation and the difficulties in assimilation compared to other immigrant groups, see, S. Lieberson, *A Piece of the Pie: Blacks and White Immigrants Since 1880* (Berkeley: University of California, 1980), 376–381.

10. See, for example, W.M. Tuttle, Jr., "Labor Conflict and Racial Violence: The Black Worker in Chicago, 1894–1919," *Labor History* 10, 3 (Summer 1969), 408–432; K.L. Kusmer, *A Ghetto Takes Shape: Black Cleveland, 1870–1930* (Urbana: University of Illinois Press, 1978), 67–75.

11. On the exclusion from the socialization provided by the urban/industrial economy, see, R. Lane, *Roots of Violence in Black Philadelphia, 1860–1900* (Cambridge, MA: Harvard University Press, 1986), 3, 5, 16, 37–38, 134, 140–143. See, also, A.H. Spear, *Black Chicago: The Making of a Negro Ghetto, 1890–1920* (Chicago: University of Chicago Press, 1976), 49.

12. I. Bernstein, *The New York City Draft Riots* (New York: Oxford University Press, 1990), 3–42.

13. Calculations in this chapter are based on data drawn from the *Report of the National Advisory Commission on Civil Disorders* (New York: Bantam, 1968); see, also, R.M. Brown, *Strain of Violence* (New York: Oxford University Press, 1975), 320–326; and M. Newton and J.A. Newton, *Racial & Religious Violence in America: A Chronology* (New York: Garland, 1991).

14. H.G. Edmonds, *The Negro and Fusion Politics in North Carolina: 1894–1901* (Chapel Hill: University of North Carolina Press, 1951), ch. 11.

15. *Atlanta Georgian*, August 21 and September 18, 1906; quoted in C. Crowe, "Racial Violence and Social Reform—Origins of the Atlanta Riot of 1906," *Journal of Negro History* 53, 3 (July 1968), 247.

16. *Atlanta News*, July 27 and September 1, 1906; quoted in Crowe, "Racial Violence and Social Reform," 250.

17. C. Crowe, "Racial Massacre in Atlanta, September 22, 1906," *Journal of Negro History* 54, 2 (April 1969), 150–173.

18. *Chicago Defender*, January 8, February 19, April 1, August 5, 1916; see, also, Grossman, *Land of Hope: Chicago*, 74–79.

19. *Chicago Defender*, January 23, March 27, October 30, 1915; January 8, 1916; see, also, Grossman, *Land of Hope*, 82.

20. "East St. Louis Riots: Report of the Special Committee," in A.D. Grimshaw (ed.) *Racial Violence in the United States* (Chicago: Aldine, 1969), 61–73; *Report of the National Advisory commission on Civil Disorders* (New York: New York Times/Bantam, 1968), 217–218; hereafter cited as *Kerner Report*.

21. *Houston Daily Post*, August 28, 1917; see, also, E.A. Schuler, "The Houston Race Riot, 1917," in Grimshaw, *Racial Violence*, 73–87.

22. R.R. Wright, Jr., "Recent Improvement in Housing among Negroes in the North,' *Southern Workman*, 37 (November 1908), 602 (emphasis added); see, also, Kusmer, *A Ghetto Takes Shape*, 48–49.

23. *Philadelphia Tribune*, July 6, 1918; quoted in V.P. Franklin, "The Philadelphia Race Riot of 1918," *Pennsylvania Magazine of History and Biography* (July 1975), 338–339.

24. Franklin, "The Philadelphia Race Riot," 339–343; *Philadelphia Tribune*, August 3, 1918, quoted by Franklin, 343–344.

25. Chicago Commission, *The Negro in Chicago*, 122–123; Spear, *Black Chicago*, 129–130; Brown, *Strain of Violence*, 212–213.

26. Spear, *Black Chicago*, 201, 288–295.

27. Chicago Commission, *The Negro in Chicago*, 1–5; see, also, W.M. Tuttle, *Race Riot: Chicago in the Red Summer of 1919* (New York: Atheneum, 1970).

28. W.E.B. DuBois, *Dusk of Dawn* (New York: Harcourt, Brace, 1940), 182–183.

29. J.W. Roberts, *From Trickster to Badman: The Black Folk Hero in Slavery and Freedom* (Philadelphia: University of Pennsylvania Press, 1989), 209–210.

30. C.L. Beale, "Leaving the Farm," in H. Hughes (ed.), *Population Growth and the Complex Society* (Boston: Allyn and Bacon, 1972), 84; *Kerner Report*, 240; W.E.B. Du Bois, "A Nation within the Nation," *Current History* (June 1935), 265; G. Myrdal, *An American Dilemma: The Negro Problem and Modern Democracy* (New York: Harper & Brothers, 1944), 191–197.

31. *The Quotations of Mayor Coleman A. Young* (Detroit, MI: Droog Press, 1991), 64.

14

Black-On-Black Homicide, 1900–1939

*"We have very little crime. Of course, Negroes knife each
other occasionally, but there is little real crime. I mean
Negroes against whites or whites against each other."*
—A white woman, Natchez, Mississippi, 1930s[1]

"Dere's so much cuttin' and killin' goin' on."
—A black woman, Alabama, 1930[2]

*Frankie went down to the coke joint
And she rung the coke-joint bell,
She says, 'If I find that mistreatin' bastard in here,
I'm going to kill him, sure as hell,
Because he's my my man, and he's been doing me wrong.*
—Frankie, 1930s[3]

*Well I'd rather my man would hit me
Than for him to just up and quit me,
Ain't nobody's business if I do.
I swear I won't call no coppa,
If I'm beat up by my Poppa
Ain't nobody's business if I do.*
—Billie Holiday, 1930s[4]

As bad as the urban race riots and police brutality of Northern cities
were, by far the heaviest toll of black lives during the urban transformation was due to blacks themselves. As population densities in black slums
climbed, so did domestic violence among the black lower class.[5] It was
as though the *bottom edge* of black society began to shred during this
period as its members turned increasingly against one another in response
to daily frustrations and disappointments that were unrelenting, and too
often overwhelming. It is this exceedingly distressed segment of American society that is the focus of this and the remaining chapters.

* * *

209

Southern blacks were, of course, already well aware before they moved north that few whites cared whether they lived or died, or what they did to one another. So long as the victims were black, even the courts cared little who was murdered, raped, or robbed, or by whom. Unless, of course, such crimes affected white interests. In the South, black-on-black offenses were considered "negro peccadilloes," and a waste of judicial time and money. Southern prosecutors and defense attorneys alike trivialized black-on-black crime, suggesting as one did disdainfully in court that a criminal case *only* involved "these niggers." Thus the term "Negro law" emerged after emancipation to describe such judicial indifference and the existence of a different standard of justice. A Mississippi judge was typical of Southern jurists, advising that such crimes were "wisely ignored," or best settled "out of court" by blacks themselves. And many blacks did settle disputes themselves in virtually every Southern community. Shootings and slashings were common, especially in "jook joints" and saloons on Saturday afternoons and evenings.[6] It was easier, and less frustrating, to settle disputes personally.

The tradition may have had its roots in slavery where the frustrations of bondage, one observer remarked, had resulted in a sometimes "unbounded insolence and tyranny" that slaves exhibited toward one another. Anger and resentment were endemic, never far beneath the surface of daily life. "Everybody in the South wants the privilege of whipping someone else," Frederick Douglass wrote of the experience.[7] After emancipation, without slaveholders to hold the competition in check to protect their investments, it became deadly.

But the warped system of criminal justice that replaced the slaveholders' authority was probably the most important reason for the violence. It had three destructive and enduring consequences: First, it provided what was, in effect, a grant of immunity for crimes committed against black victims; second, it condoned and encouraged black-on-black violence as a means of settling disputes; third, it contributed directly to disruption, disunity, and rising rates of violent crime within the black community and, not incidentally, black families.

* * *

Southern newspapers reflected the indifference of whites to the obvious scourge of black-on-black crime. In contrast to the hyperbole and extensive coverage that characterized reports of black-on-white crime, such crimes were usually mentioned with disdain in a breezy, sometimes jocular, fashion that characterized some descriptions of lynchings. The *Montgomery Advertiser*, for example, reported this account in 1905:

> Selma, July 30—The usual Saturday night killing was reported on the steets this morning at an early hour. Saturday night a week ago the shooting scrapes were on the eastern outskirts of the city. Last night the one pulled off was on the western outskirts. As in the previous shootings, negroes were engaged, and as is usually the case, the event happened at a church supper.

Another story describes a ruckus in Livingstone, Alabama:

> Negroes got in a general fight on the Willingham place last Saturday night. One was knocked down and another one was stabbed. They kept up noise enough to have killed ten.[8]

But most of the time black-on-black crime was not reported at all. Domestic disputes, for example, were not considered newsworthy. "One nigger cuts another's throat about the former's wife and that is the last heard of it," the *Hattiesburg Progress* (Mississippi) admitted. Nor did anyone want to read about "nigger crap shooters [who] kill each other in different parts of the state nearly every day."[9] The deaths of black men who fought and murdered one another regularly in railroad, logging, and turpentine camps also received little notice in newspapers. Labor camp homicides were rarely investigated by authorities. If in the instance the victim happened to be a valued employee, charges might be brought by the victim's white employer. After all, as a black attorney explained it, "The average white jury would take it for granted that the killing of a white man's nigger is a more serious offense than the killing of a plain, every-day black man." The seriousness of black-on-black crime was almost solely determined by its impact on white interests. Trial records reveal that "Whose nigger are you?" or "Whose nigger was he?" were common questions asked by magistrates.[10]

For example, in the 1930s John Dollard's research in Indianola, Mississippi revealed that there was often a tradeoff of sorts between landowners and tenant farmers that protected blacks from certain laws whites considered unimportant because violating them had little impact on the white community. Dollard noted that as long as blacks worked hard, landowners saw to it that the laws regarding "polygamy, bigamy, adultery, and assaultive behavior" were not enforced against them. Landowners went so far, Dollard wrote,

> even [to] prevent community peace officers from interfering under the threat of electoral retaliation. Whether planned or not, it seems that direct and instinctual

gratification is offered to lower-class Negroes in exchange for the money and mastery which are the chief cultural values of whites. It is not difficult to see how a *different* kind of collective conscience has been standardized in the Negro group and how the person trying to act according to wider [social and moral] standards would lack support from his social environment.[11]

In 1903, the *Jackson Clarion Ledger* (Mississippi) offered this assessment of black-on-black crime:

Perhaps not one-third of the murder[ers] are ever arrested. It is like dog chewing on dog and the white people are not interested in the matter. Only another dead nigger—that's all.[12]

It was a view reflected in white newspapers and by white law enforcement across the South.

* * *

This disdain and indifference of white authorities had a profound effect on the way blacks thought about law enforcement and their relations with one another. It sanctioned, for example, growing domestic turmoil in black households as violence became a common means of settling disputes within lower-class families. In the words of one investigator,

many of the Negroes have long since concluded that their best course is to keep clear of legal complications wherever possible. To go to court for any cause would be to solicit *more* trouble than the matter at issue might be worth. Since no Negro can expect to find justice by due process of law, it is better in the long run to suffer one's loss—*or to adjust it oneself.* From this angle, the "lawlessness" sometimes ascribed to the Negro may be viewed as being rather his private and individual "law enforcement."[13]

Another investigator wrote in 1930 that,

Negroes reported that they, feeling that the authorities would not protect them, had provided for their own protection oftentimes resulting in a ready use of firearms in trivial matters. Moreover, Negroes are often allowed without interference from police, to commit crimes on one another, which, when committed against white people, result in severe court sentences, if not death at the hands of a mob. Many Southern leaders, white and Negro, feel strongly that the inadequate police provided within the Negro communities virtually breeds crime.[14]

As much as blacks hated the police and distrusted the courts by this time, they were, perhaps, even more contemptuous of members of their own race who collaborated with authorities. "The feeling against going to court has in it an element of race-solidarity," wrote another observer. "Some Negroes will criticize one of the race who takes legal action against another Negro."[15] So in this respect, right and wrong had been reversed in Southern black culture. "The Negro who works with the police," a report on black criminality noted, "becomes a party to the 'crime' of subjecting a member of his group to an unfriendly court. He is by definition [a] hunted man, a traitor to his own race—and his life may be the price."[16] As one white prosecutor told a Mississippi jury, "This bad nigger killed a good nigger. The dead nigger was a white man's nigger, and these bad niggers like to kill that kind."[17]

A study of six hundred black families completed in Alabama during the 1930s described how deeply these attitudes were ingrained in the culture. "There is a tradition of violence which seems to mark personal relations to a high degree," sociologist Charles S. Johnson wrote,

> Social control in this community is related only vaguely to law. The courts are *outside* of the scheme of life; adjustments of relations in the past has been very largely the province of the white planter. Such unanimity of sentiment on law as exists is a common disposition to remain as far as possible out of contact with the courts whether as plaintiff or accused.... [I]n the younger generation...the adjust-ment of disputes becomes a matter of the individual involved. Instead of providing security as the arbitrator of personal differences, the courts are an institution to be feared.... Thus, differences tend to be settled on a *personal and face-to-face* basis. This sentiment helps further to account for the prevalence of weapons of defense.... The violence of life was an inescapable fact in a large number of families.[18]

Violence was the most likely outcome of anger in the *lower-class* black community. It was abrupt, frequently deadly, and not unexpected. The words of black men and women themselves, as expressed in con-versations Johnson had with them, suggest that domestic violence was accepted fatalistically. It was simply part of the inevitable rhythms of daily life and, often, premature death:

Carrie, a black woman horribly scarred by a blow to the mouth, ex-plained to an interviewer how it happened:

> My husband did it—jest jealous-hearted. He hit me right up there with a fence post and it wasn't about nothing...[later] He said he didn't believe I was doing all them things he 'cused me of, but he would git in behind me for fear.

Another woman explained why she had left her husband:

> Tom Bright was my husband, but he fight me so I just couldn't live with him. He treat me so bad. I didn't do nothing a-tall. I [used to] cook his breakfast and he'd come home [after being gone all night] with a big stick and beat me. Said I didn't have breakfast done.... One time I went away to mamma's and come back I found some women in my house. When I come in he got mad and went to cussin', so I packed up and went back home.

A mother told an interviewer how she had learned of her daughter's murder:

> I was sitting on the bed in one room and all of a sudden Jake Johnson run in and said, 'Willa's done been killed.' I run out there and there she was all heaped on the bed—limp. The house was so full, but I just screamed and run to her. I picked her up in my arms and her brains was all shot out in her hair. When I put her down I was covered with blood and I couldn't do nothing but scream. Some nigger come in there to kill his wife cause she was going running 'round with other men, but he missed her and put a steel bullet in my baby. This was the dress she got killed in.

Sometimes the motives were unclear as in this statement of a sister explaining her brother's death:

> My brother got killed out there by the creek. He was coming home from a ball game one evening and two boys grabbed him. I spose they got to fussing and the boys got mad and kilt him. We found him dead over there .... They caught the boys.... One was a little boy 'bout twelve.

The same uncertainty was there when a mother told an interviewer simply that, "My other boy got kilt. He was jest stabbed to death."

"My boy got killed in Birmingham. They say he got shot—I don't know," another said of her son.[19]

Johnson who, like his subjects, was black, believed they were typical of lower-class blacks living under similar circumstances throughout the South. His conclusions, as well as Dollard's reached in studies done in the 1930s could not have surprised W.E.B. DuBois who had anticipated such trends at the turn of the century. He recognized that there was no reason to believe that such fatalism would recede in Northern cities. Nor is it any wonder why blacks would continue to ignore the police and to settle disputes among one another personally. Even the sense of "guilt" was distorted in the moral vacuum of Southern injustice. It was this perspective and these feelings that many blacks took with them to Northern cities in the form of folk tales and songs. But, more ominously, it could also be observed in attitude, habit, and violent behavior, primarily toward one another.[20]

* * *

Wherever statistics were recorded, by the 1930s black males were fighting and killing one another with withering frequency, and at rates far exceeding whites. Nowhere was the carnage more evident than in the swelling ghettos of American cities.[21] As earlier chapters have shown, comparisons between black and white homicide rates in the nineteenth century are misleading because white homicide rates did not take into account the thousands of blacks who were lynched and murdered with impunity by whites. This bias was most apparent in the South where all but 10 percent of the black population lived and where white-on-black violence was, by any standard, extraordinary. The editor of the black *Savannah Tribune* was correct when he complained in 1893 that, "Some of our white exchanges are always very eager to gloat about the large amount of crime committed by the colored people [but] if the crimes committed by whites were recorded and…punished accordingly, they would doubly offset that of the colored people."[22] A researcher acknowledged in 1930 that "There is a much higher Negro rate for homicides than white." But, he added, "It is difficult to secure dependable data on Negro crime, because (a) general crime records are poor and comparative figures less dependable, and (b) racial factors enter, influencing the agencies of law enforcement most frequently to the disadvantage of the Negro and Negro records of crime."[23]

Even with that important qualification, however, there is compelling evidence that the urban transformation contributed substantially to rising rates of violence within black communities. In a group already culturally predisposed to settle matters personally and violently, dramatic increases in population density, alone, ensured as much. Evidence from a wide variety of sources consistently reveals that domestic violence within the black community rose sharply in the early twentieth century, especially in urban areas.[24]

In nineteenth-century Philadelphia, for example, black homicides occurred at a rate of 7.5 per 100,000 compared to a white rate of 2.8. At the turn of the century, homicide rates among blacks were almost three times higher than whites. The same pattern could be observed in New York City where black rates of homicide were more than twice the rates of whites from 1865 to 1900. In Philadelphia during the 1920s, the black homicide rate was twelve times the rate for whites. By that decade, national estimates suggest that blacks were killing one another at nearly seven times the rate for whites.[25]

Between 1918 and 1927, in the midst of the Great Migration, the national mean annual homicide rate for blacks was thirty-seven deaths per 100,000 persons, compared to a white rate of five. The trend continued, reaching unprecedented levels in the 1930s. By that time, the national homicide rate for black males was over seventy-five deaths per 100,000 population. White male homicide rates nationally also peaked at that time, but they were much lower at fewer than ten deaths per 100,000 population. This rate was even lower than the approximately fifteen deaths per 100,000 rate for black females.[26]

The figures were even more alarming during this period in cities where blacks were concentrating. In 1925, for example, the black homicide rate in Chicago was 103 murdered per 100,000 persons, as compared to eleven for whites. This, despite Chicago's reputation for organized *white* crime and gangsterism. In Cincinnati, the black rate was 190 per 100,000; in East St. Louis it was 229; in Miami it was a staggering 276. The racial differentials were stark: In New York, as well, black homicide rates were twelve times higher than white rates, and the pattern was evident in virtually every city with a large black population. Homicide was two to five times more prevalent in urban areas for both races, but even the relatively lower black rates in rural areas exceeded, by far, the homicide rates of white urban dwellers.[27]

The extraordinary levels of violence among blacks set them apart from every other ethnic group. Scholars have pointed out that, unlike native-born whites and European immigrants, blacks did not go through a cycle of violent crime that declined after the Civil War. Homicide rates for Italian and Irish immigrants, for example, were often high during their first years on American soil, but then dropped within a generation to near or below city and national averages. In contrast, black rates of violent crime climbed steadily through the last quarter of the nineteenth century. With only brief reversals, they continued to climb in the twentieth.[28]

* * *

Men, regardless of race, have always fought and killed for money and women. Gambling proved to be a popular and dangerous pastime in Southern black communities. Cards and dice were common sources of mayhem, for example, among black laborers on railroad construction gangs. The same was true wherever black men eagerly bet money they could not afford to lose. Among "the lower class of Negroes," an observer wrote in 1908,

> a predilection for petty gambling amounts almost to a passion.... Around these tables, especially on Saturday nights and Sundays, gather crowds of men and boys of all ages, scarcely one in five without a knife or pistol. It takes but a word to bring both into the game.[29]

Dollard noted the same tendencies in Indianola, Mississippi. "Gambling between [lower-class] Negro men," he wrote, "is a frequent occasion for violent expressions, especially when strangers meet over the gambling table." The deadly competition continued with the move North as ever greater numbers of idle strangers congregated in pool halls, saloons, and street corners to bet everything they had on the turn of a card or the roll of the dice.[30] In Cleveland, Central Avenue in the black ghetto had already become an area of heavy gambling and much violence by 1915. The same pattern was repeated in virtually every large city as black numbers grew. Like domestic violence, as long as vice was contained in black districts, it was tolerated by the police. Containment meant that a flourishing variety of illegal activities, like prostitution and drug dealing, became more concentrated, and deadly. Frustration and despondency in Cleveland's ghetto, like those in other cities, soon spawned, a historian of the period wrote, "a deviant subculture involving gambling, excessive drinking, and sexual promiscuity" among that city's black lower class.[31]

But gambling was not nearly so dangerous as was sex. In 1899, DuBois was distressed to observe that among Philadelphia's black lower class, "The lax moral habits of the slave regime still show themselves in a large amount of cohabitation without marriage." Such relationships, he wrote, were subject to "whim or desire" and changing circumstances as blacks, men especially, exhibited a "lack of respect for the marriage bond [and] inconsiderate entrance into it."[32]

Schooled in the uncertainty that social and economic instability assured, marriage vows were a problematic consideration among the lower class. As a consequence, continually shifting sexual boundaries were too often defined as they had been during slave times by honor, pride, and force instead of by legal and moral obligation. Unrelenting sexual competition, jealousy, and domestic violence were their by-products.

As were illegitimate children. A pregnancy could solidify a relationship or end it. Illegitimacy and desertion were high among the black lower class, DuBois guessed, for there were no reliable records at that time. "Economic stress, a high death rate [among men] and lax morality," he wrote at the turn of the century, accounted for the high number of black women without husbands—40 percent of whom were between the ages of thirty and forty and most remained sexually active. "There can be no doubt," he concluded,

> but what sexual looseness is to-day the prevailing sin of the mass of the Negro population, and that its prevalence can be traced to bad home life in most cases. Children are allowed on the street night and day unattended; loose talk is often indulged in; the sin is seldom if ever denounced in the churches...the most crime

is committed when sexual excess is more frequent, and when there has not been developed fully the feeling of responsibility and personal worth.[33]

In the world created by slaveholders, women were property—virtually the only, and probably the most satisfying, possession available to a male slave. The pattern continued. Even in Northern cities of the early twentieth century, black females remained one of the few objects of value an impoverished, uneducated, black male could readily possess and control. Like the wives of African chieftains, the number of females a man controlled provided evidence, for all to see, of his personal worth. And the status to be gained from possessing a woman other men wanted probably sharpened the competition between them as much as sexual gratification. Indeed, for too many young, black males of this period, manhood itself, as well as respect, depended on the number of women one could claim.[34]

* * *

In addition to Southern traditions of gambling and intense sexual competition, overcrowding, along with the unprecedented availability of alcohol and handguns, provided a new and even more deadly edge to black violence in the city. Most blacks who traveled north remained as they had been—desperately poor. Some things did change, however, for unlike the ramshackled shanties at the edges of cotton fields they had gladly forsaken, they now found themselves squeezed into dilapidated tenement buildings and makeshift, inadequate, housing of all sorts. Black families had been long accustomed to limited quarters, usually one-room dwellings with little privacy. But welcome respites were often close by in the rural South, sometimes in the cool shade of live oak trees, or maybe along grassy riverbanks. Such opportunities for solitude and seclusion were merely memories in the city. Families and strangers mixed in changing blends as people sought shelter from the rain and cold of the industrial North. Many people, some family, others strangers, just "lodgers," who roamed from one residence to another, were forced to live together in the same tiny rooms above noisy, teeming streets. They had to share everything, from cooking utensils to toilet facilities and beds.

Even when good intentions and moral commitments were present, the unwanted intimacy of crowded tenements, often without locks or even partitions to separate families from strangers and men from women, enhanced the opportunities for casual or forced sex. In these circumstances it was easy to be pulled loose from one's ethical moorings, and both men and women were easy marks for sexual predators. A day at work or even a trip to the grocery store could trigger anxieties about the company being kept by someone left behind. An unexpected return, a chance meeting in a stairwell, or outside a bedroom door, could be deadly; it often was. In the crowded ghettoes, sexual competition was intense, compressed and distilled into dark hatreds and bitter rivalries that often ended in bloodshed. Living conditions grew worse with each new wave of migration from the South. An investigation of housing in Newark, New Jersey, offered this description of one section of that city in 1917:

> In the last two weeks the Negro Welfare Committee, with the help of an investigation of 120 self-supporting families, all of whom were found in the worst sections of the city, showed that 166 adults—only twenty of whom are over forty years of age—and 134 children, a total of 300 souls are all crowded into insanitary (sic) dark quarters, averaging four and two-sevenths persons to a room.

Elsewhere in the same study, investigators made notations like these:

> Three families in four rooms...doors off hinges, water in cellar, two families in five rooms.... Indescribable; so dark they must keep the light burning all day.... Unused to city life, crowded into dark rooms, their clothing and household utensils unsuitable...stoves too small to heat even tiny rooms.[35]

Even before the major surge in population after 1915 made living conditions much worse, DuBois' study of black housing in Philadelphia at the turn of the century revealed, for example, that only 14 percent of the families he studied had access to toilet facilities. Of those, he continued, "Many share the use of one bathroom with one or more other families. The bathtubs usually are not supplied with hot water and very often have no water-connection at all."[36] Inadequate plumbing, poor ventilation, and the absence of public restrooms added to the filth and discomfort as toilets, when they did work, were shared not only by the tenants, but the public at large. One was never sure who or what activity might be encountered in a bathroom. Frequently families had to pay up to 75 percent of their total income for rent and the privilege of using a filthy toilet. Under these circumstances, nonpayment and frequent moves were common. Fifteen years later, conditions had not improved.[37]

High rents meant it was usually necessary to sublet rooms to strangers. Under such conditions, a person guarded what little one possessed, and carefully monitored who it was shared with. Arguments about who was responsible for the rent, concerns about who might consume the groceries one had bought, and worries about "lodgers" who sometimes became rivals in romance added to the stress. DuBois' description of living conditions in Philadelphia were echoed in every subsequent study done in other cities.[38]

Abundant research has shown that crowded and inadequate living conditions greatly diminish the moral, mental, and physical health of those forced to live in those circumstances. Overcrowding is associated with irritability, communicable diseases, prostitution, juvenile delinquency, domestic violence, and crime in general. Moreover, family controls are weakened because both adults and children who live in such stressful conditions seek relief and privacy wherever they can find it. In American cities in the first half of the twentieth century, that usually meant vice-ridden and dangerous streets.[39]

DuBois described the dynamics of street violence at that time:

> Affairs will be gliding on lazily some summer afternoon at the corner of Seventh and Lombard streets; a few loafers on the corners, a prostitute here and there, and the Jew and Italian plying their trades. Suddenly there is an oath, a sharp altercation, a blow; then a hurried rush of feet, the silent door of a neighboring club closes, and when the policeman arrives only the victim lies bleeding on the sidewalk; or at midnight the drowsy quiet will be suddenly broken by the cries and quarreling of a half-drunken gambling table; then comes the sharp, quick crack of pistol shots—a scurrying in the darkness, and only the wounded man lies awaiting the patrol-wagon.[40]

As cities filled to overflowing with new arrivals, such scenes became commonplace. The unprecedented ease with which blacks could obtain handguns in the city also contributed substantially to the deadly nature of the violence. After living for centuries unarmed and vulnerable, for the first time in their history on American soil blacks could easily arm themselves with something other than knives and straight razors. And, without police protection one could count on, it was a good idea—especially a handgun that could be carried out of sight in a pocket or tucked under a belt. In the early twentieth century, manufacturers like Smith and Wesson, Harrington and Richardson, and Colt were turning out tens of thousands of handguns on factory assembly lines. In hardware stores and pawn shops handguns were no more expensive than a pocket watch, and were available to anyone who could pay the few dollars for them. Handguns quickly became the weapon of choice among blacks.

Handguns were nearly as easy to obtain as a fifth of liquor. The two often went together. Often fatally. Unlike the "dry" South, where a person had to know a bootlegger or operate a still to obtain strong drink, there seemed to be saloons and liquor stores on every block in the growing black districts of Northern cities. Alcohol could be purchased almost anytime, day or night. And those who sold it were more than pleased to accomodate the black trade. Even during prohibition, liquor continue to flow. "Bathtub" gin was as familiar to blacks as it was to whites. The new ease with which alcoholic beverages could be obtained signalled a major increase in black consumption. As probably never before, alcohol became a way for many blacks to blur the impact of the enormous difficulties they faced.[41]

Just as alcohol provided a release, it also elevated passions, and handguns surely provided a sense of empowerment to black males already primed to handle grievances personally. Nowhere, not even in the frontier West, did the term the "great equalizer" have greater resonance than in the streets and alleys of American cities. Armed, angry, and drunk; this deadly combination would soon account for more black lives lost in a shorter period of time than lynching and capital punishment combined.

* * *

The nihilistic quality that characterized much of the violence of the black lower class provided testimony to the utter chaos and complete hopelessness of so many lives. A free-floating sense of persecution and rage defined the outlook of many. Normally fear and guilt temper human aggression. But, for some, those emotions disappeared, swept away in the dehumanizing tides of American racism. Like mistreated dogs that have turned mean, some black males had become unpredictable and dangerous predators.

Richard Wright was once asked where he got the idea for the treacherous black killer, Bigger Thomas, the central character in his classic novel, *Native Son*. "The birth of Bigger Thomas," Wright replied in 1940,

goes back to my childhood, and there was not just one Bigger, but many of them, more than I could count and more than you suspect.... When I was a bareheaded, barefoot kid in Jackson, Mississippi, there was a boy who terrorized me and all of the boys I played with. If we were playing games, he would saunter up and snatch from us our balls, bats, spinning tops, and marbles. We would stand around pouting, sniffling, trying to keep back our tears, begging for our playthings. But Bigger would refuse. We never demanded that he give them back; we were afraid and Bigger was bad. We had seen him clout boys when he was angry and we did not want to run that risk. We never recovered our toys unless we flattered him and made him feel that he was superior to us. Then, perhaps, if he felt like it, he condescended, threw them at us and then gave each of us a swift kick in the bargain, just to make us feel his utter contempt.

"His life was a *continuous challenge* to others," Wright continued,

At all times he took his way, right or wrong, and those who contradicted him had to fight. And never was he happier than when he had someone cornered and at his mercy; it seemed that the deepest meaning in this squalid life was in him at such times.[42]

Hopeless men like Bigger Thomas, historian Lawrence W. Levine wrote of this era,

never really tried to change anything. They were pure force, pure vengeance; explosions of fury and futility. They were not given any socially redeeming characteristics simply because in them there was no hope of social redemption.[43]

No hope of social redemption. Like a cancer of the human spirit, the anger and hopelessness of lower-class black males would take a devastating toll on the black community, eroding its vitality, draining away from too many of its homes and families the strength they needed to survive. In a world without moral meaning, it was as though the new freedom of Northern cities had for them come to mean only a license to kill anyone whose existence became bothersome or inconvenient. After generations of victimization and despair, the anger of lower-class black males began to turn inward, producing a plague of violence that in the last decade of the twentieth century threatens the existence of the black community.

Notes

1. Quoted in A. Davis, B.B. Gardner and M.R. Gardner, *Deep South* (Chicago: University of Chicago, 1941), 499.
2. Quoted in C.S. Johnson, *Shadow of the Plantation* (Chicago: University of Chicago Press, 1934), 189.
3. Collection of G. Legman, as recorded in Kansas City by Palmer Jones in A. Lomax, *The Folksongs of North America* (Garden City, NY: Doubleday, 1960), 570.
4. Billie Holiday, "Ain't Nobody's Business," Lyrics by B. White, Decca Studio Orchestra with Lester Young (no date). Compiled and remastered by Steve Hoffman from original Decca session tapes, Verve/Polygram, 1989 (C.D. ISMCA).
5. W.E.B. DuBois, *The Philadelphia Negro: A Social Study* (New York: Schocken, 1967, orig., 1899), 235–238; E.F. Frazier, *The Negro in the United States* (New York: Macmillan, rev. ed., 1957), 638–644; H.C. Brearly, *Homicide in the United States* (Chapel Hill: University of North Carolina Press, 1932), 97–100.

6. M.N. Work, "Negro Criminality in the South," *Annals* 49 (September 1913), 74–79; G.N. Sisk, "Crime and Justice in the Alabama Black Belt, 1875–1917," *MidAmerica* 40 (1958), 106–113; Davis et al., *Deep South*, 504. Mississippi Judge Percy Bell quoted in N.R. McMillen, *Dark Journey: Black Mississippians in the Age of Jim Crow* (Urbana: University of Illinois Press, 1989), 202, 386, fn. 15; see, also, G.B. Tindall, *South Carolina Negroes, 1877–1900* (Columbia: University of South Carolina Press, 1952), 186–188, 263.

7. Journal of F.A. Kemble, 239; quoted in K.A. Stampp, *The Peculiar Institution: Slavery in the Ante-Bellum South* (New York: Vintage, 1956), 335; F. Douglass, *My Bondage and My Freedom* (New York and Auburn: Miller, Orton, Mulligan, 1855), 69–75, 129–132.

8. *Montgomery Advertiser*, July 31, 1905; *Our Southern Home*, March 8, 1905; quoted in G.S. Sisk, "Crime and Justice in the Alabama Black Belt, 1875–1917," *Mid America* 40 (1958), 107.

9. *Hattiesburg Progress*, taken from Jackson *Weekly Clarion-Ledger*, January 22, 1903; quoted in McMillen, *Dark Journey,* 204.

10. *Collins v. Mississippi*, 100 Miss. 435 at 437 (1911); quoted in McMillen, *Dark Journey*, 203; see, also, 205.

11. J. Dollard, *Caste and Class in a Southern Town* (Madison: University of Wisconsin Press, 1988, orig., 1937), 418–419 (my emphasis); see also, 279–286, as well as, Johnson, *Shadow of the Plantation*, 52–53, 189–192; A.F. Raper, *The Tragedy of Lynching* (Chapel Hill: University of North Carolina, 1933), 33.

12. *Hattisburg Progress* quoted in the *Jackson Weekly Clarion-Ledger*, January 22, 1903; quoted in McMillen, *Dark Journey*, 204, 386, fn. 21.

13. H. Powdermaker, *After Freedom* (New York: Viking, 1939), 126 (emphasis added); see, also, R.R. Moton, *What the Negro Thinks* (Garden City, NY: Doubleday, Doran, 1929), 154–155; and G. Myrdal, *An American Dilemma: The Negro Problem and Modern Democracy* (New York: Harper & Brothers, 1944), 535–557, 1336.

14. Raper, *The Tragedy*, 34–35.

15. Powdermaker, *After Freedom*, 126.

16. A. Raper, "Race and Class Pressures," (unpublished manuscript, 1940), 21–22, quoted in Myrdal, *An American Dilemma*, 1341.

17. *Collins v. Mississippi* (1911), 435 at 437, quoted in McMillen, *Dark Journey*, 203.

18. Johnson, *Shadow of the Plantation*, 189–191 (emphasis added).

19. DuBois, *The Souls of Black Folk* (New York: New American Library, 1969; orig. 1903), 199–202; Dollard, *Caste and Class*, 279–286; and Johnson, *Shadow of the Plantation*, 51–53, 189–191.

20. Du Bois, *The Souls of Black Folk*, 199–202; M.F. Berry and J.W. Blassingame, *Long Memory: The Black Experience in America* (New York: Oxford University Press, 1982), 227.

21. W.E.B. Du Bois, *Some Notes on Crime* (Atlanta, 1904), 2–9; Frazier, *The Negro in the United States*, 640–645, 649–653.

22. *Savannah Tribune*, July 22, 1893; quoted in E.L. Ayers, *Vengeance and Justice: Crime and Punishment in the 19th Century American South* (New York: Oxford University Press, 1984), 228.

23. C.S. Johnson, *The Negro in American Civilization* (New York: Henry Holt, 1930), 316.

24. Part, but not all, of this increase may reflect more accurate reporting of black-on-black crime in areas outside of the South where much of it was ignored. There are only two sources of national data on homicide rates: the *Vital Statis-*

tics collected by the National Center for Health Statistics and the *Uniform Crime Reports* compiled by the Federal Bureau of Investigation. Neither source has reliable national data before 1933 because not all states and municipalities participated until that time. Even information in the FBI's *Uniform Crime Reports* after that time tends to be spotty in that the information published year-to-year varies. Despite problems in reporting, cities provide the best, and only, sources of information on homicides before 1933. For a discussion of these issues, see, D.F. Hawkins, *Homicide Among Black Americans* (Lanham, MD: University Press of America, 1986), 3–11.

25. H. Gannett, *Statistics of the Negroes in the United States* (Baltimore, MD: John F. Slater Fund, 1894), 24–25; Bureau of the Census, *Negro Population, 1790–1915* (Washington, DC, 1918), 436–447; Bureau of the Census, *Prisoners and Juvenile Delinquents in the United States, 1910* (Washington, DC, 1918), 87–105, 416–418, 528–529. Calculations based on data presented in E.H. Monkkonen, "Diverging Homicide Rates: England and the United States, 1850–1875," in T.R. Gurr (ed.) *Violence in America: The History of Crime*, v. 1 (Newbury Park, CA: Sage, 1989), 86–88; see, also, R. Lane, *Violent Death in the City: Suicide, Accident and Murder in 19th Century Philadelphia* (Cambridge, MA: Harvard University Press, 1979), 113.

26. A.J. Klebba, "Homicide Trends in the United States, 1900–1974," *Public Health Reports* 90, 3 (May/June 1975), 195–204; P.C. Holinger, *Violent Deaths in the United States: An Epidemiological Study of Suicide, Homicide, and Accidents* (New York: Guilford Press, 1987); A.J. Reiss, Jr. and J.A. Roth (eds.) *Understanding and Preventing Violence* (Washington, DC: National Academy Press, 1993), 50–51.

27. R. Lane, *Roots of Violence in Black Philadelphia, 1860–1900* (Cambridge, MA: Harvard University Press, 1986), esp. 95–133; H.C. Brearley, *Homicide in the United States* (Chapel Hill: University of North Carolina Press, 1932), 97–100; M.N. Work, *Negro Year Book, 1914–1915* (Tuskegee, AL: Tuskegee Institute, 1914), 314, 350; T.R. Gurr, "Historical Trends in Violent Crime: Europe and the United States," in Gurr (ed.) *Violence in America*, 38–40; W.E.B. Du Bois, *The Philadelphia Negro: A Social Study* (New York: Schocken, 1967, orig. 1899), 235–238.

28. Lane, *Roots of Violence*, 2–3.

29. A.H. Stone, *Studies in the American Race Problem* (New York: Doubleday, Doran, 1908), 107; quoted in Dollard, *Caste and Class*, 272; see, also, Tindall, *South Carolina Negroes*, 186–188.

30. Dollard, *Caste and Class*, 272.

31. K.L. Kusmer, *A Ghetto Takes Shape: Black Cleveland, 1870–1930* (Urbana: University of Illinois Press, 1978), 111.

32. Du Bois, *The Philadelphia Negro*, 67; for similar observations, see Dollard, *Caste and Class*, 268–278.

33. DuBois, *The Philadelphia Negro*, 56, 72.

34. H.C. Brearley, "The Pattern of Violence," in W.T. Couch (ed.), *The Culture of the South* (Chapel Hill: University of North Carolina Press, 1935), 690–91; see, also, Ayers, *Vengeance and Justice*, 234–35.

35. "Cotton Pickers in Northern Cities," *The Survey*, February 17, 1917; quoted in E.J. Scott, *Negro Migration During the War* (New York: Oxford University Press, 1920), 139–140; see, also, 100, 105–106, 121–122, 135–136, 141–142.

36. Du Bois, *The Philadelphia Negro*, 290–299.

37. Commission on Race Relations, *The Negro in Chicago*, 152–230; Myrdal, *An American Dilemma*, 375–379; S.C. Drake and H.R. Cayton, *Black Metropolis:*

A Study of Negro Life in a Northern City (New York: Harcourt, Brace, 1945), 61, 202–203; G. Osofsky, *Harlem: The Making of a Ghetto, Negro New York, 1890–1930* (New York: Harper & Row, 1966); Kusmer, *A Ghetto Takes Shape*, 165–173; P. Gottlieb, *Making Their Own Way: Southern Blacks' Migration to Pittsburgh, 1916–1930* (Chicago: University of Illinois Press, 1987), 63–88; and S. Lieberson, *A Piece of the Pie: Black and White Immigrants Since 1880* (Berkeley: University of California Press, 1980), 376–381.

38. See, for example, E.F. Frazier, *The Negro in the United States* (New York: Macmillan, rev. ed., 1957), 634–636.

39. See, for example, Frazier, *The Negro in the United States*, 634–636; Myrdal, *An American Dilemma*, 375–379, 1290; S. Riemer, "Maladjustment to the Family Home," *American Sociological Review* 10 (1945), 642–648; W. Loring, "Housing Characteristics and Social Disorganization," *Social Problems* 3 (1955), 160–168; L. Rainwater, "Fear and the House-as-Haven in the Lower Class," *Journal of the American Institute of Planners* 32 ((1966), 23–31; D.M. Fanning, "Families in Flats," *British Medical Journal* (1967), 382–386; R.E. Mitchell, "Some Social Implications of High Density Housing," *American Sociological Review* 36 (1971), 18–29; R. Gillis, "Population Density and Social Pathology," *Social Forces* 53 (1973), 306–314; and Lieberson, *A Piece of the Pie*, 376–381.

40. Du Bois, *The Philadelphia Negro*, 312.

41. Du Bois, *The Philadelphia Negro*, 277.

42. R. Wright, "How 'Bigger' Was Born," in *Native Son* (New York: HarperPerennial Edition, 1993, orig., 1940), 506–507 (emphasis added).

43. L.W. Levine, *Black Culture and Black Consciousness: Afro-American Thought From Slavery to Freedom* (New York: Oxford University Press, 1977), 420. On the same point see, also, R.D. Abrahams, *Deep Down in the Jungle...Negro Narratives from the Streets of Philadelphia* (Chicago: Aldine, rev. ed. 1970), 65–66; and B. Jackson, *"Get Your Ass in the Water and Swim Like Me": Narrative Poetry from Black Oral Tradition* (Cambridge: Harvard University Press, 1974), 30–35.

15

Dark Ghettos

*"[T]he first impulse of the best, the wisest and the richest is
to segregate themselves from the mass."*
—W.E.B. Du Bois describing the attitudes of the
black middle class in Philadelphia, 1890s.[1]

*"[T]hey enjoy liquor brawls...have large families and can't
take care of them...children run wild, with little respect
for parents."*
—Comments of upper-class blacks about
the lower class in Chicago, 1930s.[2]

We was fighting like hell till everything went black.
One of those sneaky cops come up and shot me in the back.
I've got a tombstone disposition, graveyard mind.
*I know I'm a bad motherfucker, that's why I don't mind
dying.*
—"Ballad of the Great MacDaddy," Philadelphia, 1950s[3]

The rapid transition from South to North, rural to urban, and plantation to factory, produced the first large-scale social stratification in the
black community. There had been little economic diversity among blacks
in the South. Most were poor and few were educated. Research by both
W.E.B. Du Bois and E. Franklin Frazier, revealed that moral and behavioral considerations, along with white ancestry, were more important in making social distinctions in the black community than income
and education. Frazier notes, for example, that in rural communities of
the South, higher social status was based primarily on stable family life
and church membership.[4] It was this incipient black middle class, many
of whom had been educated in small black schools like Tuskeegee and
Morehouse, and who had struggled to overcome the South's rigid racial caste system, that slowly began to flourish in Northern cities.

But the deluge of millions of Southern black migrants that continued through the 1920s placed great strains on those of the same race
who had earlier managed to carve out a social and economic niche for
themselves in cities. With little opportunity awaiting them, newly arrived migrants made familiar problems worse.[5] It was the small numbers of middle-class blacks, however, who were most troubled, just as
whites, as impoverished and poorly educated blacks moved into already crowded black districts. According to Du Bois, "moral considerations," continued to be a central concern of the evolving black middle
class. He was well aware, however, that morality often followed money,
and that poverty provided the spawning grounds for the indiscriminate
sex, venereal disease, alcoholism, and high rates of domestic violence
of the black lower class that the middle class so abhorred at the turn of
the century.[6]

Even before the Great Migration began, Du Bois observed that
middle-class blacks in Philadelphia sought to insulate themselves as
much as possible from the lower class that compromised their lives in
crowded, segregated neighborhoods. In 1899 he wrote:

> they [the middle class] are not the leaders or the ideal-makers of their own group
> in thought, work, or morals. They teach the masses to a very small extent, mingle
> with them but little, do not largely hire their labor. Instead then of social classes
> held together by strong ties of mutual interest we have in the case of the Negroes,
> classes who have much to keep them apart, and only community of blood and
> color prejudice to bind them together...the first impulse of the best, the wisest
> and the richest is to segregate themselves from the mass.[7]

Escaping the "mass" that threatened to envelope the black middle
class was difficult. Housing discrimination presented a major impedi-
ment to their flight to safer, more agreeable neighborhoods. Voicing
such concerns in 1904, a black physician complained,

> Those of the race who are desirous of improving their general condition are pre-
> vented to a great extent by being compelled to live with those of their color who
> are shiftless, dissolute and immoral.... Prejudice of landlords and agents render it
> almost impossible for [the middle-class black] to take up his residence in a more
> select quarter of the city...no matter...how much cultivation and refinement he
> may possess.[8]

But despite these obstacles, the relatively greater degree of economic
and social freedom blacks found in cities outside the South served to
accelerate and widen class differences. By the time of the First World
War, class distinctions based on occupation and income had become

obvious even in the South. The growth of the black middle class from that time was not spectacular, but it was steady and significant, especially in the service sector of local economies as black grocery stores, bars, restaurants, beauty parlors, barber shops, and funeral homes opened and prospered in segregated black neighborhoods. One national estimate suggested that from 1898 to 1930 black businesses had grown from 1,900 to 70,000. Smaller gains were made in white-collar employment as blacks made inroads into banking, insurance, real estate, and the professions. Still more than two-thirds of the black population remained at the bottom of the social structure.[9]

As the urban black middle class slowly grew and prospered, it continued to place great emphasis on "civilized behavior" and a disciplined use of the wealth it had struggled to accumulate. Religion and the family remained central features of its values and affairs.[10] This emphasis on proper and conventional behavior was evident in the responses of middle-class blacks who were interviewed as part of Drake's and Cayton's study of Chicago's black community in the 1930s. Questions about their impressions of the black lower class evoked these comments:

> "I would put illiteracy first."
>
> "[they] have large families and can't take care of them."
>
> "dirty homes—dirty children—dirty people."
>
> "ranges from the respectable individual to the rowdy who beats his wife to make her respect him."
>
> "sex behavior is loose and overt. "
>
> "immorality is one of the criteria of lower-class behavior...on the whole, you don't find the strict morality that exists in the middle class."
>
> "they drink excessively...they enjoy liquor brawls."
>
> "razors and knives as weapons are always associated in my mind with lower-class persons."
>
> "their present position is often due to their former environment in the South."[11]

W.E.B. Du Bois shared such assessments. He worried that the growing black lower class would result in "grave physical, economic and moral disorder" that would adversely affect all blacks. Voicing similar concerns, a black newspaper editor complained that "the white people draw the line at the wrong point and put all of us in the same class."[12] The black upper and middle classes had no objections to a line being drawn, he implied, *where* was the only issue. Middle-class blacks wanted as little to do with the lower classes of both races as their businesses and professions would permit. It was not the poverty that bothered them, for few blacks had not, at some time, been poor. Rather it was the "ig-norance," "boisterousness," "uncouthness," and "low behavior" that offended Drake's and Cayton's respondents most. The loose morals and violence that characterized the life of the lower class frightened them. Their disdain and fear, and the social stratification it reflects, served to isolate lower-class blacks in the cities in a way that they had never been in the rural South.[13]

* * *

The social isolation and problems of black lower-class life contin-ued to worsen and became more concentrated during the Great Depres-sion. Even as joblessness slowed temporarily the flow of black migration north, other forces were at work that would cause it to resume and widen to flood proportions. Franklin D. Roosevelt's election as presi-dent in 1932 signalled a major shift in national politics and priorities. His New Deal policies account for the beginnings of the Second Great Migration that began in the 1940s and continued through the 1960s. Determined to ease the hardship brought on by the Depression, Roosevelt immediately began to inundate Congress with policy initiatives to stimu-late the economy. Among them was the establishment of the Agricul-tural Adjustment Administration (AAA), whose purpose it was to regulate and stimulate the agricultural economy. In a move to reduce production and raise the price of cotton in the late summer of 1933, the AAA began paying farmers to plow up their unharvested cotton. The following year it paid subsidies to farmers for taking cotton and other surplus crop acreage out of production. Black laborers were the first to lose their jobs as thousands of sharecroppers and tenants were forced off land that now, under government decree, lay dormant.[14]

In this manner, the federal government soon replaced the tenant farmer and sharecropper as the most significant renter of cotton acre-age. In the 1930s alone, some 175,000 black farmers and their families were forced off the land as a result of the crop subsidy program. Added to this number were 223,000 more who found themselves jobless for related reasons. Whites were less hard hit, for while 15 percent of white tenants were also forced off the land, white farm ownership actually increased 12 percent during this period as a good number with money left cities and towns to purchase devalued land and wait out the De-pression as subsistence farmers. Also, when the Federal Emergency Relief Administration and Civilian Conservation Corps moved in to assist the poor and unemployed, whites were always given preference over blacks; the agency's administrators shared the view of one who explained that "most any nigger who wants to work can get something to do."[15]

Throughout his administration, Roosevelt stood back warily from civil rights issues for fear of antagonizing Southern Democrats, both voters and congressional leaders, whose support he needed to advance his controversial agenda. Despite the intense lobbying by the National Association for the Advancement of Colored People, for example, the president refused to endorse federal antilynching legislation that was introduced in 1933 and again in 1934, 1935, 1936, 1937, and 1938.[16] Thus, it would be a mistake to view Roosevelt's executive order in 1941, that prohibited racial discimination in war-related industries, as a presidential initiative to open up industrial jobs to displaced black farm laborers. Rather the president did all he could to avoid an action that few in his administration supported. Executive Order 8802 was issued only under threat of "the greatest demonstration of Negro mass power for our economic liberation ever conceived," if he refused.[17] Still Roosevelt's reluctant action in 1941 provided a significant new inducement for Southern blacks to seek jobs in the industrial centers of the North and Midwest as the nation mobilized for World War II. The regular employment and higher pay of such jobs enabled many blue-collar blacks to rise to the edge of middle-class status and respectability during the 1940s.[18]

At the same time unprecedented employment opportunities became available for blacks in war-related industries, other initiatives by the president were continuing to change the face of Southern agriculture. While displacing farm laborers, the administration's crop subsidy program had worked well for large landholders and banks. Cotton prices doubled within a few years after the program went into effect, but those dollars did not trickle down to sharecroppers and field hands as some imagined they would. Instead, crop subsidies were used to mechanize Southern agriculture. Federal money bought tractors that gradually replaced mules and hoes, and the men and women who toiled with them. The invention of the mechanical cotton picker followed, displacing still more workers and bringing an end to debt peonage in its traditional sharecropping guise.[19] Some 1,468,000 unemployed black farm laborers migrated out of the South in the 1940s alone. At the same time new federal irrigation projects opened up vast areas of the arid Southwest to agriculture, shifting cotton and produce production, and with it black laborers, in that direction. These "pickers" eventually filtered into west-

ern cities as tractors also replaced them . In the 1950s, the use of herbi-
cides for weed control eliminated still more agricultural jobs. That decade another 1,473,000 blacks left Southern farms for America's big
cities. The flow continued into the 1960s as an additional 1,380,000
moved north. Thus between 1940 and 1970, some 4,321,000 blacks
flooded into already overcrowded and problem-ridden slums of American cities.[20]

* * *

Even before Roosevelt was elected, the problems of slums, overcrowding, and inadequate housing were drawing national attention. His
administration sought federal solutions to a housing crisis that was
clearly beyond the capacity of cities alone to resolve. In the midst of a
resurging wartime economy, urban slums remained stagnant focal points
of crime, disease, and hopelessness. Housing shortages were critical,
for example, in Philadelphia between 1920 and 1930, as the city's black
population increased 63.5 percent from 134,229 to 269,559. The problems that W.E.B. Du Bois described in Philadelphia's black community at the turn of the century had grown accordingly in every city where
blacks had concentrated in large numbers.[21]

Yet even though Roosevelt's secretary of the interior, Harold Ickes,
acknowledged in 1936 that blacks had been "denied the human right of
proper habitation," blacks did not fare well in the administration's plans
for housing.[22] Between 1935 and 1950, for example, Federal Housing
Administration (FHA) regulations made racial discrimination a *condition* of federal assistance. "If a neighborhood is to retain stability," its
manual read, "it is necessary that properties shall be continued to be
occupied by the *same* social and racial classes." Among the "adverse
influences" to be avoided, it continued, was the "infiltration of inhar-
monious racial or nationality groups." Natural barriers such as rivers,
streams, and ravines as well as busy highways and racial convenants
were suggested as ways to exclude "incompatible racial elements." Such
suggestions were welcomed by state and local government officials
who shared the same concerns and objectives.[23]

In 1941, with these racial restrictions in force, the FHA announced a
proposal on "urban development" that was designed to deal with the
need to rehabilitate and redevelop problem areas. Eight years later, these
ideas took shape in the form of the Housing Act of 1949. The act authorized one billion dollars in federal loans and five hundred million more
in federal grants to remove and prevent urban blight and to stimulate

residential development and improvement. Congress amended the act in 1954 to include the term "urban renewal" rather than urban development to encompass the idea of restoration of historic buildings and the rehabilitation of neighborhoods. More amendments and bills were passed, and by 1960 urban renewal was well underway in a number of cities.[24]

With a pattern of housing segregation already well established, it is little wonder that urban renewal proved to be a disaster for the poor as rundown homes and tenements were torn down to make room for new expressways, luxury apartments, and commercial development. Too often federal bulldozers reduced rundown neighborhoods to nothing more than a rubble-strewn wastelands punctuated by a few "historic" buildings that had been preserved or "gentrified" for wealthy investors. Additionally, the FHA failed miserably to provide adequate alternative housing for those it displaced.[25] The federal government's commitment to urban renewal continued to exacerbate the problems of poor blacks through the Truman, Eisenhower, and Kennedy administrations. Despite President John F. Kennedy's executive order in 1962, which outlawed discrimination in federally assisted housing, the damage already done to impoverished blacks was virtually irreversible.

* * *

And the problems grew worse. The federal government's ill-conceived solution for the poor it had displaced was the construction of high-density public housing projects. The effect was to squeeze increasing numbers of displaced and homeless people often into even worse circumstances than they left. By the time President Lyndon Johnson introduced his Model Cities legislation in 1965, thousands of poor black families had been relocated by then into federally funded public housing projects and were already suffering the consequences.

Strong public opposition prevented dispersion and relocation of public housing beyond the de facto boundaries of segregated slums. Declining property values, the threat of interracial sex, and crime characterized the fears of whites opposed to using public housing as a means to desegregate cities and to dilute an increasingly self-destructive subculture of the black lower class.

By the 1960s, public housing projects were viewed by everyone, black and white alike, as welfare centers, at best; at worst, as growth areas for the problems they had been intended to eliminate. The early hope that public housing would serve temporarily as a way station on the road to economic recovery and better lives had long been abandoned. These stark monotonous row houses and high rises only compressed problems and made them worse. Crowded, noisy, and graffiti-splashed buildings were already little more than segregated breeding grounds for domestic violence and family disintegration.[26]

Landlords became known as "slumlords" during this period as they exploited people who had nowhere else to go with rent increases for dwellings that were often in worse condition than those they had been forced to leave. In Chicago, for example, rents paid by relocated blacks rose from 16.6 to 26.3 percent; in San Francisco, they rose from 17 to 23 percent. In Chicago those percentages meant that 41 percent of those relocated to substandard housing were paying eighty dollars more a month in rent; 19 percent were paying at least ninety dollars more; and 8 percent were paying more than one hundred dollars. For those in the lowest income brackets (approximately 35 percent of those relocated), such increases consumed an average 45.9 percent of their incomes. Regardless of city, the hardest hit were poor blacks, and seventy percent of those relocated were black.[27]

Studies in forty-one cities from 1958 and 1961, for example, revealed that between 60 and 70 percent of the dispossessed were relocated to what in effect were other slums. New substandard housing for which they paid higher rents only created greater disappointment, more frustration, and deeper resentment. Dislocation of this sort meant disruption, not improvement, in their lives, leaving people with a sense of loss, of being taken, of being disconnected and rootless. Too many public housing projects had become nothing more than stigmatized enclaves where frustration and despair were daily companions. It is little wonder that these structures deteriorated with such spectacular rapidity. Within ten years of its 10,000 person occupancy, for example, the Pruitt-Igoe public housing project in St. Louis "[had] simply become a more visible kind of slum," its residents living in a worsening state of moral and spiritual decay. Its demolition in 1976 symbolized the failure of such projects.[28]

Furthermore, between 1940 and 1960, rising birth- and fertility rates compounded the problem of overcrowding and stress in black districts brought on by record migration and housing shortages. Blacks experienced a "baby boom" following the end of World War II that exceeded that of whites. At the same time, an upward trend began in the number of children born to unmarried women, marking with yet another statistic the deteriorating circumstances and marital prospects of lower-class black women.[29] Both demographic trends resulted in a numerical expansion of the black lower class and the violent subculture that was its most ruinous affliction.

In the early sixties, those black "boom" babies were reaching their trouble-prone teen years in slums and housing projects that were already crime-ridden. Further overcrowding, a rapidly growing younger population being raised by growing numbers of single mothers, and the emotional baggage of the past meant problems would become even more concentrated and worsen.[30] Estimates suggest that between one-third and one-half of the increase in crime and racial violence in the 1960s can be explained simply by the growth in the number young, black males.[31] One must qualify that explanation by saying, however, that these were youngsters born into an *already* hostile urban environment whose violent subculture growing numbers of them inevitably embraced.

"Sometimes walking among the ruined shacks and lives of the worst Harlem slum," black writer LeRoi Jones wrote in 1962,

> there is a feeling that just around the next corner you'll find yourself in South Chicago or South Philadelphia, maybe even Newark's Third Ward. In these places life, and its possibility, has been distorted almost identically. And the distortion is as old as its sources: the fear, frustration, and hatred that Negroes have always been heir to in America. It is just that in the cities, which were once the black man's twentieth century "Jordan," promise is a dying bitch with rotting eyes. And the stink of her dying is a deadly killing fume.[32]

* * *

By the time of President Kennedy's assassination in 1963, the federal government had become the largest slumlord in America. Viewed as a locale for "undesireables," public housing was built as far as feasible from the centers of finance and power—and, most importantly jobs, as companies relocated and employment shifted to outlying areas. Police reports indicate that these projects had already become stultifying bulwarks of urban segregation and flash points of crime and domestic violence.[33] Names of projects like Cabrini Green, Robert Taylor Homes, Pruitt-Igoe, and many others in virtually every large city became synomous with drugs, shootings, rapes, and illegitimacy. High-rises to hell, they must have seemed to the thousands trapped inside them. One observer, for example, described Philadelphia as a society segregated into "vicious islands of mutually suspicious residents: a city sundered into warring 'racial worlds.'"[34] When the rioting began in Harlem and Philadelphia in 1964, that judgment as well as Le Roi Jones's, were confirmed.

Notes

1. W.E.B. Du Bois, *The Philadelphia Negro: A Social Study* (New York: Schocken, 1967, orig., 1899), 317.
2. Quoted in S.C. Drake and H.R. Cayton, *Black Metropolis: A Study of Negro Life in a Northern City* (New York: Harcourt Brace, 1945), 560–561.
3. R.D. Abrahams, *Deep Down in the Jungle: Negro Narrative Folklore from the Streets of Philadelphia* (Chicago: Aldine, rev. ed. 1970), 162–163.
4. E.F. Frazier, *The Negro in the United States* (New York: Macmillan, rev. ed., 1957), 275–279; W.E.B. Du Bois, *The Negro in the Black Belt: Some Social Sketches* Bulletin No. 22 (Washington, DC: U.S. Department of Labor, 1902).
5. S. Lieberson, *A Piece of the Pie: Blacks and White Immigrants Since 1880* (Berkeley: University of California Press, 1980), 365–381.
6. Du Bois, *The Philadelphia Negro*, 310–311.
7. Du Bois, *The Philadelphia Negro*, 317.
8. George C. Hall, Speech before the Frederick Douglass Center, reprinted in the Chicago *Broad Ax*, December 31, 1904, quoted in A.H. Spear, *Black Chicago: The Making of A Negro Ghetto, 1890–1920* (Chicago: University of Chicago Press, 1967), 73.
9. A.L. Harris, *The Negro as Capitalist* (Philadelphia, PA, 1936), 53–54; E.F. Frazier, *The Negro Family in the United States* (Chicago: University of Chicago Press, 1939), 317–318; Frazier, *The Negro in the United States*, 303–305.
10. E.F. Frazier, *The Negro in the United States*, 283; and his *Black Bourgeoisie: The Rise of a New Middle Class* (New York: The Free Press, 1957), 19–23.
11. Drake and Cayton, *Black Metropolis*, 559–562.
12. Quoted in Frazier, *The Negro Family*, 326 (emphasis added).
13. Drake and Cayton, *Black Metropolis*, 559.
14. A.F. Raper, *Preface to Peasantry: A Tale of Two Black Belt Counties* (Chapel Hill: Univeristy of North Carolina Press, 1936), 243–249, 258–259; G.B. Tindall, *The Emergence of the New South, 1913–1945* (Baton Rouge: Louisiana State University Press, 1967), 391–432.
15. Quoted in N. Fligstein, *Going North: Migration of Blacks and Whites from the South, 1900–1950* (New York: Academic Press, 1981), 163; see, also, Tindall, *The Emergence of the New South*, 391–432.
16. It must be said in Roosevelt's defense that while ducking civil rights issues himself for political reasons, he gave a free hand to both his Interior Secretary, Harold Ickes, and his wife, Eleanor, to speak out on race issues with unprecedented candor and force. In the words of one scholar, "By never silencing or otherwise reigning in Ickes [or his wife] on the extremely touchy issue of race relations, Roosevelt in effect lent tacit support to [their] efforts. It was not an inconsequential strategy on the president's part." See, J.N. Clarke, *Roosevelt's Warrior: Harold L. Ickes and the New Deal* (Baltimore, MD: Johns Hopkins University Press, 1996), 182.
17. *Chicago Defender*, June 21, 1941, quoted in H. Sitkoff, *A New Deal for Blacks* (New York: Oxford University Press, 1978), 320.
18. Sitkoff, *A New Deal for Blacks*, 314–325.
19. Peonage would continue, however, in modified form among migrant laborers well into the 1970s.
20. R. Farley and W.R. Allen, *The Color Line and the Quality of Life in America* (New York: Oxford University Press, 1989), 112–117; Raper, *Preface to Peasantry*, 252–253; Fligstein, *Going North*, 142, 147–149, 163; C.H. Hamilton, "The Negro Leaves the South," *Demography* 1,1 (1964), 273–295; H.C. Dillingham

and D.F. Sly, "The Mechanical Cotton-Picker, Negro Migration, and the Integration Movement," *Human Organization* (Winter 1966), 344–351; Tindall, *The Emergence of the New South*, 430–432; *Report of the National Advisory Commission on Civil Disorders* (New York: New York Times/Bantam, 1968), 239–243; hereafter cited as *Kerner Report*.

21. Frazier, *The Negro in the United States*, 634–636.
22. M.W. Straus to S.T. Early, June 16, 1936, Franklin D. Roosevelt Library, File 466-B. This source was pointed out to me by J.N. Clarke in the course of her research for *Roosevelt's Warrior*.
23. J.F. Bauman, *Public Housing, Race, and Renewal: Urban Planning in Philadelphia, 1920–1974* (Philadelphia, PA: Temple University Press, 1987), 26–29; Federal Housing Authority *Manual*, (1936), Sects. 937, 225, 229 (1938), Sect. 935; quoted in C. Abrams, "The Housing Problem and the Negro," in T. Parsons and K.B. Clark (eds.), *The Negro American* (Boston: Beacon, 1967), 517, 523–524, n. 2; D.S. Massey and N.A. Denton, *American Apartheid: Segregation and the Making of the Underclass* (Cambridge, MA: Harvard University Press, 1993), 58–59.
24. A.A. Foard and H. Fefferman, "Federal Urban Renewal Legislation," in J.Q. Wilson (ed.) *Urban Renewal: The Record and the Controversy* (Cambridge, MA: MIT Press, 1966), 72–125.
25. Massey and Denton, *American Apartheid*, 55–58.
26. Bauman, *Public Housing, Race, and Renewal*, 160–208; Massey and Denton, *American Apartheid*, 56–57.
27. C. Hartman, "The Housing of Relocated Families," in Wilson (ed.), *Urban Renewal*, 311–313; F.F. Piven and R.A. Cloward, *Regulating the Poor: The Functions of Public Welfare* (New York: Vintage, 1971), 241.
28. M. Fried, "Grieving for a Lost Home: Psychological Costs of Relocation," and H.J. Gans, "The Failure of Urban Renewal," in Wilson (ed.), *Urban Renewal*, 359–361, 539–540; L. Rainwater, *Behind Ghetto Walls: Black Family Life in a Federal Slum* (Chicago: Aldine, 1970), 408–409.
29. S.J. Ventura, J.A. Martin, T.J. Mathews, and S.C. Clarke, "Advance Report of Final Natality Statistics, 1994," *Monthly Vital Statistics Report* 44, 11, (Hyattsville, MD: National Center for Health Statistics, 1996), 28.
30. Farley and Allen, *The Color Line*, 58–62, 76–83; *Kerner Report*, 269; C. Jencks and P.E. Peterson, *The Urban Underclass* (Washington, DC: The Brookings Institution, 1991), 81–82.
31. C. Jencks, "Is the American Underclass Growing," in Jencks and Peterson (eds.) *The Urban Underclass*, 81–82.
32. L. Jones (aka, Imamu Amiri Baraka), *Home* (New York: Charles Morrow, 1966), 94–95.
33. D. Roncek, R. Bell, and J.M.A. Francik, "Housing Projects and Crime: Testing a Proximity Hypothesis," *Social Problems* 29 (1981), 151–166; D. Roncek, "Dangerous Places: Crime and Residential Environmnet," *Social Forces* 60 (1981), 74–96.
34. D. Clark, "Racial Change in Philadelphia," (mimeograph), Philadelphia Housing Association, quoted in Bauman, *Public Housing, Race, and Renewal*, 168–169.

16

Killing Fumes

"Bloodshed.... You don't have a peaceful revolution. You don't have a turn-the-other-cheek revolution. There's no such thing as a nonviolent revolution.... Revolution is bloody. Revolution is hostile. Revolution knows no compromise. Revolution overturns and destroys everything that gets in its way."

—Malcolm X, 1963[1]

"I became a rapist.... Rape was a revolutionary act. It delighted me that I was defying and trampling upon the white man's law, upon his system of values, and that I was defiling his women...I was getting revenge."

—Eldridge Cleaver, 1968[2]

The deadly killing fume, LeRoi Jones described, was evident in virtually every black slum in the country. By the time of the Watts riot in 1965, not only Los Angeles but every city where significant numbers of blacks lived had become a ticking timebomb of fear, frustration, and hatred. The problems and frustrations blacks had endured for generations were now compacted in a highly volatile mass in the core of the nation's major cities. Isolated and confined within stifling ghettos, hostile policemen were one of the few contacts the black lower class had with white society. Urban blacks were stirred less by the successes of the civil rights movement, which eluded them completely, than the savagery they witnessed inflicted by Southern whites, especially men who wore uniforms and badges. Unlike earlier periods of vicious racial violence, illuminated first by bonfires and lanterns and later by the headlights of pickup trucks, many of these brutal scenes were televised across America for all to see. Public opinion research indicates that these shocking revelations of Southern custom and practice were a significant factor in stirring an indifferent electorate to support major reforms in civil rights in 1964 and 1965.[3]

These recurring scenes of snarling dogs, tear gas, and police officers swinging clubs down on the heads of kneeling victims contributed to a sense of black outrage that spilled into the streets of Harlem in 1964 after police shot and wounded a twelve-year-old child. A year later, nearly ten thousand blacks rampaged through South-Central Los Angeles after police used what witnesses considered excessive force when arresting a drunk driver who was black. Thirty-five people died, most of them shot while looting, thousands were arrested, and forty million dollars in property was destroyed before the rioting ending. These riots marked the beginning of another significant change in American race relations.[4]

Every urban race riot in the twentieth century had been precipitated in the same manner as those in Harlem and Watts: Police officers using excessive force to arrest blacks for minor offenses. Such scenes had grown too familiar in black neighborhoods. Reports of major riots of the 1960s in Newark, Detroit and other cities too numerous to mention, as well as Harlem and Watts, revealed the same pattern of provocation. A criminologist described the view from black slums in 1968 this way: "[T]he law [is] not of their making nor to their interest; the law is that of [a] foreign power and the police [are] an army of occupation." No segment of the white community was hated more.[5] Records and classifications vary, but between 1963 and 1969 nearly five hundred race riots broke out in American cities. The riots were unprecedented in their scope and destructiveness. It was as though violence and destruction had become ends in themselves with no other purpose anyone could discern.[6]

* * *

Although blacks of both sexes and all ages participated in the rioting, the typical rioter was a young, black male, aged fifteen to thirty, who was single. About three-quarters had been raised by two parents and about the same number had grown up in the North. Over half had been born in the city where they had rioted. Approximately 60 percent had not finished high school and about 70 percent were employed at least part of the time, but often in low-skill, low-wage jobs. Such characteristics did not distinguish them in any interpretable way from those who did not riot. An analysis of the 1960s riots revealed that the single best predictor of riot occurrence was simply the size of the black population. The finding seemed to confirm the presence of a mood of profound alienation that most blacks, regardless of background, shared.[7]

"It takes no one to stir up the sociological dynamite that stems from unemployment, bad housing, and inferior education already in the ghettos," Malcolm X explained not long before his death in 1965, "This explosively criminal condition has existed for so long, it needs no fuse; it fuses itself; it spontaneously combusts from within itself."[8]

The typical rioter, as Malcolm X anticipated, was angrier and better informed about current affairs than those who did not riot. Being better informed only heightened his cynicism and contempt. Who was he angry with? The same people his ancestors had learned to hate: first and foremost, the police, and then, in descending order, politicians, local governments, and white people in general. More than half of those arrested in Newark, for example, said they did not think the country was worth fighting for. Over half of those surveyed in both Newark and Detroit admitted that at times they hated white people. Young black males who had the most frequent contact with police officers were the most disaffected group. They insisted that their actions were justified, expressed no remorse for their rioting, nor did they expect or fear sanctions from the black community.[9]

There was little need to. Most blacks, regardless of background and, like the rioters themselves, blamed the police for the riots. As early as 1957, a poll conducted in Detroit revealed that two-thirds of the black repondents complained of discrimination and mistreatment at the hands of police officers. Ten years later, 58 percent made the same complaint. Nor was Detroit unusual. A national Louis Harris poll in 1967 reported that blacks felt "two to one that police brutality is a major cause [of the riots]." It was a belief most whites rejected. Fewer than one in five whites, the poll revealed, "believe that there is any police brutality to Negroes." Another national survey in 1969 revealed that among blacks under thirty years of age, 58 percent believed that "Police brutality is a fact of life." Every poll taken during this period showed that blacks looked upon police officers in much the same way earlier generations had viewed the Ku Klux Klan. Klansmen and "Kops," as it was spelled on the walls of burnt-out buildings, were both symbols of racism and brutality.[10]

Blacks had learned long before that it was futile to complain to authorities about police practices, for the system had always been rigged against them. In Detroit, for example, the local chapter of the NAACP filed 172 complaints with the Detroit Police Commissioner during a three-year period, from 1957 to 1960; in only one case was an officer found at fault. So intense and widespread was the hostility toward the police that one researcher described it as part of a "riot ideology" among inner-city blacks. The frustrating circumstances of their lives they attributed overwhelmingly to the hostility and injustice of white society, and police officers—as they had always been—were its enforcers. Whether it was an ideology or not, it was a widely shared perspective that provided the rationale, not only for unlawful behavior and mass violence, but for direct attacks on police officers themselves.[11]

* * *

In the midst of the Watts riot of 1965, a black youth told a reporter, "We in a war. Or hasn't anybody told you that?" "The cops think we're scared of them because they got the guns," another said at an inquiry into the violence, "but you can only die once: If I get a few of them I don't mind dying."[12]

Getting "a few of them" became a goal of many more angry black males in 1966 as paramilitary organizations began to appear in black districts across the country. Between 1960 and 1975, there were at least 1,722 racial clashes between blacks and whites that resulted in loss of life and/or property.[13] Formed initially to combat police brutality and provide protection for black neighborhoods, black paramilitary organizations quickly became locked into what can reasonably be described as a guerrilla war with police. The Black Panther organization in Oakland, California, for example, formed armed patrols to monitor police activities in black neighborhoods. They made their objectives clear. Authorities were warned of retaliation if blacks continued to be harassed and victimized by the police. Adopting the motto of Chinese revolutionary Mao Tse-Tung, "Power flows from the barrel of a gun," the new militants armed themselves and, in the process, captured the imagination of the black lower class they sprang from and claimed to represent.

These swaggering, goateed, beret-wearing young men in African hairstyles rejected the nonviolent posture of the civil rights movement, scoffed at its Christian leaders, and demanded "Black Power." Men like Malcolm X, Huey Newton, Bobby Seale, and Stokely Carmichael, representing militant organizations such as the Black Muslims, Black Panthers, and the Black United Front spoke for the urban masses in ways that traditional Southern civil rights leaders did not. Frustrated, angry, and left virtually untouched by civil rights reforms, urban blacks responded enthusiastically to the militants' message of black pride, racial separation, and the Islamic eye-for-an-eye perspective on racial injustice.[14]

The resonance of this new militancy among inner-city blacks, and the willingness to act on it, became evident most dramatically in 1968, after the assassination of Martin Luther King, Jr. It was as though King's death—a Christian minister, a heroic figure to millions of blacks who had preached and lived nonviolence—at the hands of a remorseless white man, had drained away the last bit of hope many blacks had for peaceful social change. The sorrow and anger that followed King's death is difficult to exaggerate.[15] Many blacks mistakenly believed the FBI had been involved in the conspiracy that ended King's life, but there were good reasons to believe the Bureau's investigation of the assassination had been prematurely concluded once his assassin, James Earl Ray, was arrested; strong suspicions remained that Ray had not acted alone.[16] Once again, law enforcement was viewed on the wrong side of justice.

Increasingly, whites became targets of this swelling black rage. In the year preceeding the assassination, for example, there were 142 documented instances of group violence between blacks and whites. In the twenty months following it, from April 1968 through 1969, that number leaped to 659. Riots accounted for much, but by no means all, of this violence. As the rioting began to subside, what is also evident in these numbers is what can be described as an undeclared war that had begun between black militants and the police.

For the first time in American history, black militants and paramilitary organizations began a sustained effort to single out police officers and white supremacist organizations for attack. During a four-day period in August 1968, for example, black gunmen terrorized the Detroit suburb of Inkster, killing one policeman and wounding two others as well as a passing motorist. In Chicago, police raided Black Panther headquarters the following year, killing two and wounding four others in what NAACP investigators described as a "search and destroy" mission. In 1970 three Berkeley, California patrolmen were assassinated in separate incidents by black militants. Other cities like Philadelphia, New York, San Francisco, Oakland, and Los Angeles became killing zones as they never had before, for police venturing into black areas.[17]

Any provocation by the police was likely to trigger a violent response. Blacks not only began to resist arrest, but sniper fire aimed at patrol cars in contested neighborhoods, and drive-by shootings at officers and police stations, became an occupational hazard for patrolmen now confronted with organized and well-armed forces intent on destroying them. Newton and Newton's chronology of racial violence from 1968 through the 1970s is punctuated with hundreds of incidents like those above in cities across the country. Except for Miami, police had *less* to fear in southern cities.[18]

This guerilla warfare continued through 1973. By that time, massive police intervention in the forms of surveillance, infiltration, arrests,

and what most blacks believed were political assassinations, had deci-
mated the Black Panthers and had virtually wiped out the leadership of
other militant organizations as well. As police began to gain the advantage in this struggle, yet another pattern of interracial violence emerged.
Shifting their attacks from the police and white supremacist organizations, organizations like the Black Liberation Army and the Symbionese
Liberation Army adopted new strategies of random terror, singling out
banks and white businesses. These attacks seemed to have more to do
with instilling fear and, perhaps, to satisfying a gnawing desire for vengeance, than they did financial gain.

Other acts of racial violence were less organized, more opportunistic, but just as deadly, and the victims were ordinary people. In Boston,
a white woman was doused with gasoline and burned to death by black
youths when her car broke down in a black neighborhood. Two days
later, in the same city, a white man was stoned and stabbed to death by
black teenagers while fishing near a public housing project. In November, five white students were wounded by black gunmen in a drive-by
shooting at a Pontiac, Michigan high school.[19]

Although the attacks in Boston appeared to have been unplanned
and probably more opportunistic, the shooting at the Michigan high
school must have been planned. Moreover, police in San Francisco were
convinced that the random violence on whites in that area was the work
of an organized black terrorist group called the Death Angels which
had split from the Black Muslims. The killing spree, labeled "Zebra"
attacks by the police for their black-on-white pattern, appear to have
begun on October 23, 1973 with a Nat Turner-like machete attack on a
white couple. The deadly attacks that continued for another six months
included sexual assault, torture, and dismemberment. There were
twenty-three victims in the Zebra killing spree, although San Francisco
police guessed the Death Angels might have been responsible for the
murders of more than eighty white people.[20]

Five years later, in 1978, similar attacks began to occur in Illinois
and Nebraska as another black terrorist group, the Mau Maus, claimed
at least eight white victims in five separate unprovoked attacks. Eight
black males were eventually arrested for the crimes, two of whom were
found strangled in their cells, the remaining six receiving life sentences.
In addition, muggings and rapes became more common in large cities
as the early political idealism of groups like the Black Panthers gave
way to the nihilistic rage captured in the words of Elridge Cleaver at
the beginning of this chapter. To most Americans, it seemed that the

color of violent crime was black. It appeared that to many inner-city blacks the distinction between *crime* and a *war* with police had become indistinguishable.[21]

* * *

Like Richard Wright's fictional killer, Bigger Thomas, for those beyond the reach of respectability, frustration is great and the constraints on anger are weak. Psychiatrists William Grier and Price Cobbs wrote in 1968, that lower-class, black males

> are angry and hostile. They strike fear into everyone with their uncompromising rejection of restraint or inhibition. They may seem at one moment meek and compromised—and in the next a terrifying killer. Because of his experience in this country, every black man harbors a potential "bad nigger" inside him.... The more one approaches the American ideal of respectability, the more this hostility must be repressed. The bad nigger is a defiant nigger, a reminder of what manhood could be.[22]

So it was with black males who rioted and battled police in the 1960s and 1970s. But the anger they focused on whites during this period represents only a fraction of the horrific toll they continued to inflict on one another. Another casualty was their sharply deteriorating relationships with women. As the next chapter reveals, anger destroys relationships and families as surely as it does lives.

Notes

1. Quoted in B. Perry, *Malcolm: The Life of a Man Who Changed Black America* (Barrytown, NY: Station Hill, 1991), 237.
2. E. Cleaver, *Soul on Ice* (New York: Dell, 1968), 14.
3. See, for example, R. Weisbrot, *Freedom Bound: A History of America's Civil Rights Movement* (New York: W.W. Norton, 1990).
4. M. Newton and J.A. Newton, *Racial & Religious Violence in America: A Chronology* (New York: Garland, 1991), 471, 487; *Kerner Report*, 206, 224.
5. J. Lohman, "Law Enforcement and the Police," in L.H. Masotti and D.R. Bowen (eds.) *Riots and Rebellion: Civil Violence in the Urban Community* (Beverly Hills, CA: Sage, 1968), 360.
6. R.M. Brown, *Strain of Violence: Historical Studies of American Violence and Racism* (New York: Oxford University Press, 1975), appendix 4.
7. S. Spilerman, "The Causes of Racial Disturbances: A Comparison of Alternative Explanations," *American Sociological Review* 35 (August 1970), 627–649; *Kerner Report*, 172–174. For the argument that unemployment rates of nonwhites may be somewhat more important than Spilerman's analysis suggests, see, D.J. Meyers, "Racial Rioting in the 1960s: An Event History Analysis of Local Conditions," *American Sociological Review* 62 (February 1997), 94–112.
8. Quoted in A. Haley, *The Autobiography of Malcolm X* (New York: Grove Press, 1964), 366.

9. *Kerner Report*, 176–178; A. Campbell and H. Schuman, "Racial Attitudes in Fifteen American Cities," in *Supplemental Studies for the National Advisory Commission on Civil Disorder* (Washington, DC: U.S. Government Printing Office, 1968); "A Report of Attitudes of Negroes in Various Cities," *Hearings* Before the Subcommittee on Executive Reorganization of the Committee on Government Operations, United States Senate, 89th Cong., Sec. Sess., *Federal Role in Urban Affairs*, P.6, Exh. 124, 1383–1423; N.S. Caplan and J.M. Paige, "A Study of Ghetto Rioters," *Scientific American* 219 (August 1968), 15–21; R.J. Murphy and J.M. Watson, "The Structure of Discontent," and W.J. Raine, "The Perception of Police Brutality in South Central Los Angeles," in N.E. Cohens (ed.), *The Los Angeles Riots: A Socio-Psychological Study* (New York: Praeger, 1970); D.O. Sears, "Black Attitudes Toward the Political System in the Aftermath of the Watts Insurrections," *Midwest Journal of Political Science* 73 (1969), 261–284; H.E. Ransford, "Isolation, Powerlessness, and Violence: A Study of Attitudes and Participation in the Watts Riot," *American Journal of Sociology* 73 (1968), 581–591; J.R. Forward and J.R. Williams, "Internal-External Control in Black Militancy," *Journal of Social Issues* 26 (1970), 75–92; T. Crawford and M. Naditch, "Relative Deprivation, Powerlessness, and Militancy: The Psychology of Social Protest," *Psychiatry* 33 (1970), 208–223; J.W. Clarke, "Race and Political Behavior," in K.S. Miller and R.M. Dreger, *Comparative Studies of Blacks and Whites in the United States* (New York: Seminar Press, 1973), 528–538.

10. A. Kornhauser, *Detroit: As the People See It* (Detroit, MI: Wayne State University Press, 1957), 123–124; *Detroit News*, February 4, 1965; *Newsweek*, August 21, 1967; J.W. Clarke, "Race and Political Behavior," in Miller and Dreger (eds.) *Comparative Studies*, 517–541; *Kerner Report*, 206, 224, 268, 284, 301–312.

11. B. Levy, "Cops in the Ghetto: A Problem of the Police System," in Masotti and Bowen (eds.), *Riots and Rebellion*, 350; T.M. Tomlinson, "The Development of a Riot Ideology Among Urban Negroes," *American Behavioral Scientist* 11 (1968), 27–31.

12. Quoted in "The Hard-Core Ghetto Mood," *Newsweek*, August 21, 1967, 20; and *Report of the Governor's Commission on the Los Angeles Riot* (Sacramento, CA, 1966), 1: 16.

13. Newton and Newton, *Racial Violence*, 448–603.

14. R. Weisbrot, *Freedom Bound: A History of America's Civil Rights Movement* (New York: Penquin, 1991), 236–242, 253.

15. See, for example, J.W. Clarke and J.W. Soule, "How Southern Children Felt About King's Death," *Trans-Action* 5 (October 1968), 35–40.

16. *Report of the Department of Justice Task Force to Review the FBI Martin Luther King, Jr. Security and Assassination Investigations* (Washington, DC: U.S. Department of Justice, January 11, 1977); see. also, U.S. Congress, House Select Committee on Assassinations, *Hearings on the Investigation of the Assassination of Martin Luther King, Jr.*, 95th Cong., 2d Sess., 1978, vols. 1–12; and J.W. Clarke, *American Assassins: The Darker Side of Politics* (Princeton, NJ: Princeton University Press, 1982), 239–257.

17. Newton and Newton, *Racial Violence*, 496–568.

18. Newton and Newton, *Racial and Religious Violence*, 496–611.

19. Newton and Newton, *Racial Violence*, 594.

20. Newton and Newton, *Racial Violence*, 594–597.

21. Newton and Newton, *Racial Violence*, 611.

22. W.H. Grier and P.M. Cobbs, *Black Rage* (New York: Basic Books, 1968), 65–66.

Part V

Consequences

17

Vanishing Families

"Better leave this marryin' business alone, Honey, 'cause these men will git you a house full of chillun den up and leave you."

—Mary Robinson, Alabama, c. 1930[1]

"He's nice all right, but I ain't thinking 'bout marrying. Soon as you marry a man he starts mistreating you, and I'm not going to be mistreated no more."

—Artie Joe McDaniel, Alabama, c. 1930[2]

"Shit, nigger, as many niggers as I have fucked I can look at a man right away and tell what size dick he's got."

—Josephine, a St. Louis public housing resident, c. 1966[3]

"The dark ghetto is institutionalized pathology," psychologist Kenneth B. Clark wrote in 1965,

> it is chronic, self-perpetuating pathology.... Not only is the pathology of the ghetto self-perpetuating, but one kind of pathology breeds another. The child born in the ghetto is more likely to come into a world of broken homes and illegitimacy; and this family and social instability is conducive to delinquency, drug addiction, and criminal violence. Neither instability nor crime can be controlled by the police or by the reliance on the alleged deterring forces of legal punishment, for the individual crimes are to be understood more as symptoms of the contagious disease of the community itself than as the result of inherent criminal or deliberate viciousness.[4]

Since Clark wrote these words, the slums and ghettos have become known as the "inner city" and its residents are now described as the "underclass." The underclass is defined by poverty, high rates of joblessness, teenage pregnancy, illegitimacy, female-headed families, welfare dependency, and violent crime. It is disproportionately black.[5] For these reasons, sociologist William Julius Wilson has also described the underclass as "the truly disadvantaged." There can be no doubt, Wilson writes, that it is "a heterogeneous grouping of inner-city families whose behavior contrasts sharply with that of mainstream America."[6] And, one should emphasize, the middle- and upper- classes of their own race. The size of the black underclass remains elusive and must be estimated from a variety of troubling statistics, but possibly 20 percent of the total black population, or some five to six million people, may be a reasonable estimate.

Whether the afflictions of this underclass are attributed to a "contagious disease of the community," as Clark suggested, the "subculture of violence" that Wolfgang and Ferracutti described during the same period, or "behavior [that] contrasts sharply with that of mainstream America," as Wilson put it more delicately some twenty years later, the symptoms are very familiar. Moreover, they have grown worse.[7] Juvenile violence, police and mental health reports of the remorseless nature of such crimes, and the popularity of gangsta rap music which glorifies and condones it, confirm the seriousness of the problem.

In 1965, the same year that Kenneth Clark published his bleak assessment of America's "dark ghettos," the Department of Labor published a report on the condition of black families. This well-known report, written by Daniel Patrick Moynihan, described how nearly a quarter of black families were headed by single women—more than double the percentage for whites. The trend in single-parent black families, Moynihan explained, began to rise in 1940 and continued upward while the trend among whites remained relatively unchanged, or dropped slightly, during the same period. At the same time, rates of black illegitimacy climbed from 16.8 percent of all births in 1940 to 23.6 percent in 1963. The illegitimacy rate for whites also rose, but from a dramatically lower base of 2 percent in 1940 to 3.07 percent in 1963. The breakdown of black families, Moynihan concluded, had produced a "startling" and growing dependency on public welfare since 1945.[8]

Moynihan's monograph also revealed other disturbing facts about black families. To wit, the poorer a black single mother was, the more children she was likely to have. The problem of father absence, he found, was worst in cities. In New York City, for example, 30.2 percent of black families were without fathers in 1960. More than one-third of urban nonwhite children were living in broken homes, and the figure was only slightly lower in rural areas.[9]

The Moynihan Report described what was to be the first ripples of a tidal wave of calamity that would by the end of the century threaten to destroy both marriage and the nuclear family among lower-class blacks. For despite the efforts since then to shore up "at-risk" families with family assistance, educational and training programs, birth control, and family planning assistance, the numbers have grown to an extent few could have anticipated. As the percentage of black single-parent families approached 60 percent, a Brookings Institution study concluded in 1991 that "socioeconomic factors *cannot* account for the drastic decreases in [black] marriage rates during the past thirty years...family trends, once set in motion," Robert D. Mare and Christopher Winship conclude, "may continue by their own momentum."[10]

* * *

Destructive policies and customs set the trends in black family life in motion; now cultural factors account for their continuing momentum. Foremost among these damaging influences is the violence blacks have endured for generations. Recall that as many as a quarter to one-third of black families were shattered by slave sales, and probably at least as many were destroyed by the violence and bloodshed that followed emancipation.[11] The Klan's explicit assaults on black families, for example, were devastating. And countless black fathers were separated from their families by predatory systems of justice. Southern law enforcement—arbitrary arrests, excessively punitive sentencing, convict labor, lynchings, and capital punishment added to the terrible toll of Southern custom and policy on black males—and, it is critical to emphasize, the families they left behind.

Some scholars, such as Moynihan, have suggested that the extended family and kinship patterns that have been observed in black families for so long—as opposed to the more familiar nuclear and conjugal pattern of Europeans and white Americans—are symptomatic of this history of oppression. Others have proposed that such racial distinctions reflect, instead, a different cultural tradition that can be traced back to roots in sub-Saharan Africa.[12]

Whether the cultural origins are to be found in either sub-Saharan Africa or the American South, or both, it is a fact that black families were seriously victimized by the extraordinary violence and predatory law enforcement that took husbands and fathers away from their families after emancipation in 1865. Social dislocation added to the problem as husbands left spouses, and parents left their children, to roam from place to place seeking employment and new lives. That as many as two-thirds or three-fourths of black families survived all this is remarkable. But that does not lessen the social and cultural significance of the estimated one-quarter to one-third of those families that did not.[13]

Additionally, there is much evidence to suggest that something about the responsibilities and respect that men had for women changed among lower-class blacks during the urban transformation. Moreover, that change in values set in motion trends that continue. Even before the first Great Migration began in 1915, the newfound social mobility, the transcience that became its most obvious manifestation, as well as the poverty that was its constant companion, greatly diminished the obligation of black men and women to one another, as it did fathers to their children.[14]

In the rural South, sociologist E. Franklin Frazier noted, parental discipline and the church encouraged marriage and responsible parenthood even while tolerating premarital sex and out-of-wedlock pregnancy. In the city, he concluded, premarital sex and pregnancy continued, but social controls rapidly disappeared as "thousands of men and women...cut themselves loose from family and friends and sought work and adventure as solitary wanderers from place to place." The result among the black lower class, he wrote, was "free sex behavior and spontaneous matings which these roving men and homeless women form during their wanderings." Another result, of course, were the fatherless children that sprang from such couplings.[15]

But more recent research suggests that these tendencies were already present among the poorest blacks in the rural South even before they migrated north. At the turn of the century, for example, black women in *rural* areas were over three times more likely than white women to head households and have children out of wedlock. In the cities, the disparities increased to five times the rate for white women. Black women also were nearly four times as likely as white women to have their children raised by someone else, usually a relative, as a result of living and working apart from them. The racial distinctions in childrearing were greatest in cities but left no doubt, as one report described it, of "the existence of pervasive racial differences" regardless of location.[16]

At first glance, historian Herbert Gutman's study of black families seems to dispute this. His research in Buffalo, New York City, Mobile, Alabama, and small communities in South Carolina extends from 1750 to 1925. He concludes that most black families were headed by both a male and a female throughout this period. But Gutman's data also reveal that the pairs were not always a husband and wife, or a father with his own children. Moreover, Guttman's own evidence indicates that at any point in the 175 years encompassed in his study, between a quarter and a third of black families in every locale he studied were headed by females living apart from the fathers of their children. This is precisely the number of single-parent families revealed in Stephen Crawford's analysis of slave interviews.[17]

Subsequent research based on previously unanalysed nineteenth- and twentieth-century census data supports the conclusion that the high incidence of black children being raised without one or both parents is not a recent phenomenon. During the period from 1880 to 1960, historian Steven Ruggles concluded, approximately 30 percent of black children up to the age of fourteen were raised without one or both parents. The comparable figure for whites was 10 percent. Thus for more than a century black children were two to three times more likely to find themselves in these circumstances than were white children.[18]

Two studies also challenge Frazier's contention that urbanization per se was the major reason for black family instability. In separate research conducted in the 1930s, both the Johnson and Dollard studies (described earlier) reported widespread social disorganization among lower-class black families in the small Alabama and Mississippi communities they studied. Both, for example, remarked upon the prevalence of venereal disease, promiscuity, and marital instability, as well as high rates of domestic violence.[19]

"Sex, as such," Johnson wrote, "appears to be a thing apart from marriage.... The legal relationship had little to do with romantic life." Premarital sex and illegitimacy were common and not stigmatized by blacks, especially the lower class, Johnson explained,

> When pregnancy [occurs], pressure is not strong enough to compel the father either to marry the mother or support the child. The girl does not lose status, perceptibly, nor are her chances for marrying seriously threatened. An incidental compensation for this lack of censuring public opinion is the freedom for children thus born from warping social condemnation. There is, in a sense, no such thing as illegitimacy in this community.[20]

Dollard reached the same conclusion because, he concluded, sexual freedom was one of the few freedoms blacks were ever permitted to enjoy in the South. But the frequent corollaries of such freedom—competition, infidelity, jealousy, and desertion, both Johnson and Dollard found—were the major sources of domestic violence.[21]

* * *

The pattern continued in Northern cities, extending though the Second Great Migration that began during World War II. The stresses created by the crush of millions of poor, rural blacks into already congested and problem-ridden slums only hastened the destruction of black families already teetering at the edge of collapse. The upward trend in black single-parent families and illegitimacy rates mirror the flow of that migration. In spite of the enormous difficulties they faced in the urban transition, most black families—approximately 75 percent — were able to hold themselves together until the early 1960s. Then the strains became too great and the bonds of marriage and parental responsibility for growing numbers—usually the poorest—began to unravel. The consequences would metastisize and continue to spread like a disease of the spirit.

The numbers are staggering and reveal the many dimensions of the problem. Between 1965, when the Department of Labor published Moynihan's report, and 1990, the number of black families headed by women has more than doubled—to 56.2 percent. The comparable figure for whites is 17.3 percent. In addition, 63.7 percent of black babies were born out of wedlock in 1990; the comparable figure for whites is 14.9 percent. Out of every thousand black teenage girls, 186 become pregnant; the comparable figure for white teenagers is 93. Over 55 percent of the black mothers in single-parent families have never been married and will probably never marry; the comparable figure for whites is 18.1 percent. More than half of all black children are raised without fathers; the figure for whites is 14 percent. Black single mothers and their babies are twice as likely as whites to be poor and in poor health, and just as likely as whites (approximitely 39 percent) to be receiving government assistance. Black women are much more likely than white women to continue to have children throughout their reproductive years so that families composed of children, mothers, and grandmothers are the fastest growing family "unit" among blacks, increasing threefold since 1970.[22] Although teenage birth rates declined by 17 percent in the early 1990s, those rates remain high, with some 70 percent of black babies born out of wedlock in 1995.[23]

Additionally, the extraordinarily high rates of crime and violence that characterize life in American inner cities strongly suggest that the civil rights reforms of the 1960s had little impact on those isolated in these areas except to heighten frustrations with unfulfilled hopes for change. The paradox of the civil rights era is that the removal of legal barriers to social and economic advancement were accompanied by technological changes that largely nullified their effect. The invention of the transistor, and the nation's abrupt and concerted response to cold war anxieties and Russian advances in technology, symbolized in the launching of Sputnik in 1957, changed the face of American technology, industry, and education within a decade. The demand for manual labor and low-skill industrial jobs that had, until then, been the salvation of other immigrants to the United States rapidly disappeared. With such opportunities no longer available, the result was growing joblessness and frustration among lower-class blacks who were now concentrated as never before in inner cities.

At the same time as industrial jobs were disappearing, higher birth rates and in-migration created a dramatic increase in the number of young men seeking jobs in the 1960s. Males born in 1946, for example, would have been eighteen years of age in 1964 and in need of a job. But instead of finding jobs, too many black youths of this and following generations remained idle, adding to the already volatile pool of young black males trapped without employment in increasingly segregated and socially isolated city slums. The numbers and idleness of young, black males continued to increase between 1960 and 1975 as a result of advancing skill requirements for jobs that many could not meet. Deprived of educational opportunities by law and discrimination in the South, poorly educated blacks found themselves in government and corporate training programs staring blankly at a bewildering world of numbers and symbolic logic displayed on computer screens.

A large proportion of the blank faces belonged to young men between the ages of eighteen and twenty-five; many were from the South, and over 50 percent of whom had never attended high school. Even the best educated of their number often found they had educational levels below the average in the non-Southern cities to which they migrated.[24] Even so, there is some evidence to indicate that the new migrants may have fared somewhat better in finding employment than their counterparts born in the North. Southern migrants, for example, may have been less selective in accepting work than Northern blacks whose job expectations were higher.[25] As a consequence, they also may have been more motivated and, therefore, trainable. But the results were the same. Despite unprecedented opportunities for "equal" employment, and the best intentions of liberal politicians, millions of blacks simply lacked the basic skills required for employment in a technology-driven economy. And the unskilled, minimum-wage jobs that were available in the service sector barely paid enough to support an individual, let alone a family.

Middle-class blacks who did have the skills and values to press ahead when discriminatory barriers were lifted in the 1960s did so, according

to sociologist William Julius Wilson, thus contributing further to the growing social isolation of the black underclass.[26] Subsequent analysis of census data by demographers Douglas S. Massey and Nancy A. Denton,
however, reveals that this increased segregation along *class* lines within
the black community was slight and is not reflected geographically as
clearly as Wilson has suggested. Their research indicates that relatively
small numbers of middle-class blacks did flee the ghetto in the 1970s,
but soon found themselves once again in racially segregated neighborhoods. Black communities regardless of class remain racially segregated,
Massey and Denton explain with convincing documentation, due to the
tendency of whites to flee neighborhoods that are turning black. "To the
extent that middle-class blacks left poor ghetto areas," they write, "their
departure exacerbated a geographic concentration of poverty that was
already built structurally into the black community through its segregation from the rest of society." Furthermore, because other racial groups
ordinarily refuse to move into poor and crime-ridden black neighborhoods, housing vacancies are simply filled by more poor blacks. Thus,
according to Massey and Denton, it is the in-migration of lower-class
blacks who have no where else to go, rather than the out-migration of the
black middle class, that is the most important reason for the social isolation of the black underclass, an isolation which has increased in the last
last quarter of the twentieth century.[27] The same demographic trends have
concentrated and perpetuated, as well, the effects of its self-destructive
subculture of violence.[28]

Another major consequence of these trends, according to Wilson, is
that the pool of "marriageable" black men (i.e., those having a steady
job, predictable income, and what might be called "family" values) in
these areas has grown smaller every year since the 1960s, while the
number of black males without those qualities has increased propor-
tionately. Accordingly, marriage rates for black men and women, in
every age category, have dropped steadily since 1960. Although white
marriage rates have also dropped, the decline is much less dramatic, so
that the racial difference in rates has widened. Wilson argues that black
women are not marrying because the low education levels and poor
earning potential of black men make them less attractive as marriage
partners. For the same reason, he argues, growing numbers of black
children are being born out of wedlock to fathers most may never know.[29]

Other recent research, however, again challenges Wilson's hypothesis, suggesting instead that although steady employment and a good
education enhance the chances of a black man marrying, these are not

the determining factors in their "marriageability," as Wilson believes. Another study, this one done by the Brookings Institution, concludes that "four-fifths of the decline in marriage rates among mature black men would have occurred even if their employment status had not changed at all." A second related study concluded that "changes in marriage rates were largely the result of factors *not measured* in the census."[30]

* * *

One important factor "not measured in the census" is the evolving subculture of violence that has shaped and molded lower-class black values and behavior. That subculture began to destroy relationships as well as lives, as we have seen, even before the urban transformation. The domestic violence that has plagued lower-class, black family life preceded, by generations, the much-criticized welfare system that was established with the passage of the Social Security Act of 1935. The trend in violence simply continued, accelerating in the 1960s. By the mid-1980s, most black children were being born to increasingly younger single women and were being raised without fathers.

Lower-class black males make poor husbands and fathers, not only because they are jobless and without predictable incomes, as Wilson contends, but also because they are irresponsible and often cruel to the women who bear their children. Their unreliable and irresponsibile behavior is also a major reason employers are reluctant to hire them. The problem, as an abundance of neglected research demonstrates, was not caused by the welfare system; rather, federal family assistance programs, such as Aid to Dependent Children, which was expanded in 1950 to provide for the essential expenses of mothers as well as their dependent children,[31] gave black women an opportunity to avoid, or break free from, brutalizing marriages to irresponsible and abusive males. For that reason—and not simply the employment problems black males confronted—welfare rolls grew significantly after that.

Sexual relationships of course continue outside of marriage and so, also, does the violence that often accompanies them. Black women are still two to four times more likely to be beaten by their partners than are white women.[32] These battering males live by the "street" code of conduct that evolved out of the Southern experience. That code emphasizes personal respect, or "honor" as it was called in the last century, and militates against long-term relationships and commitments, even to one's children. Denied the ordinary means of achieving social status, young, lower-class, black males still rely on physical courage and sexual exploits to gain the respect they desire. Out-of-wedlock births and homicide statistics measure its force. Being disrespected, or "dissed," in street language, requires retaliation of the most convincing kind. Harming or killing rivals, and raping and impregnating the women in dispute are common. Challenges are frequent and no insult can be ignored, for courage, physical toughness, and sexual dominance are central in the lower-class black male's "quest for manhood" and for his ability to survive in a hostile world.[33]

"Even before an underclass black male inherits the economic problems that have contributed to the low level of involvement for his father in family affairs," one scholar writes, "he is socialized to expect that men demonstrate their manhood in the streets, not the home."[34] Thus manhood hinges on sexual exploitation and is defined by the number of women with whom one has had sex, and the children that can be claimed as a result. One's affection for and sense of obligation to either mother or child are secondary. For this reason, sexual competition and violence remain, as they have been since emancipation, highly visible and closely intertwined in the black lower class. Because black males still see little opportunity for success by conventional means, they are denied, in the words of sociologist Elijah Anderson, "the traditional American mark of manhood," the dual roles of provider and protector. As a consequence, he writes,

> the young men's peer group emphasizes sexual prowess as a mark of manhood, at times including babies as its evidence. A sexual game emerges and becomes elaborated, with girls becoming lured by the boys' often vague but convincing promises of love and marriage. As the girls submit, they often end up pregnant and abandoned, but eligible for a limited but sometimes steady income in the form of welfare, which may allow them to establish their own households and, at times, attract other men, in need of money.[35]

And so in this manipulative world, women become the sole providers, not only for the children they bear, but also for the smooth-talking derelicts that impregnate them and thus command the respect of their male rivals and peers. "Respect is like money," a nineteen-year-old black male explained, "You got to have it. No respect, no cooperation; no cooperation, no money."[36]

To enjoy respect, one must also display a certain contempt for women. Such contempt was evident in male behavior, as the Johnson and Dollard studies revealed in the 1930s, long before some rap musicians made it fashionable, and captured the imagination of a new generation of black males in the 1980s. "Playing the dozens," for example, the common, sometimes rhymed, verbal insults, and "yo mama" taunts exchanged between jousting black males that preceded rap in the 1950s and 1960s, were heavily laden with contempt for women.[37]

While not the cause of this contempt, the growing welfare dependency of black mothers—and the new independence it gave them, especially in the 1960s—probably made matters worse for the irresponsible men they no longer sought as providers. Making women scapegoats may have been a way black males used to cope with their own growing sense of inadequacy as fathers and husbands.

Three decades later, the contempt for women has been raised to an art form; it is a central, and profitable, element in a subculture of black violence. Nowhere is this misogynistic mood more evident (except perhaps on police blotters and hospital emergency room records) than in gangsta rap music. This music, first chanted on street corners by black teens in the 1980s, reflects the soul of a youthful underclass. Gangsta rap got its name and became commercially successful in 1989 with the release of an album, "Straight Outta Compton," by the rap group N.W.A. (Niggaz With Attitude). That group's popular "One Less Bitch," for example, describes in angry and boastful words how a young woman is kidnapped, gang-raped, and murdered. Another song, "She Swallowed It," provides instructions on how to force women to perform oral sex by first punching them in the face. Still another, "A Bitch Iz a Bitch" depicts black women as scheming exploiters who deserve the violence they suffer.[38]

A Bay Area rapper, Ant Banks, who describes himself as a "big dick gangsta," has recorded a song, "Only Out to Fuck," which advises, "Fuck that love-affair shit. Just hit it, split it, quit it and forget it." Rapper Dr. Dre sings a song with the words, "Bitches ain't shit but ho's and tricks." A female rapper, M.C. Lyte, sings a song titled, "Ruffneck" that claims boys who rub their genitals, urinate in public, and indulge in rough sex turn her on. It is not so strange, perhaps, that "killing the pussy" is now a popular way for black youths to describe making love. The music mirrors the brutality and unregulated sexuality of a violent subculture.[39]

* * *

In this crude world of sexual excess and violence, male status is not attached to either parental or sexual responsibilities. Children are little more than trophies, objects of pride only to the degree they provide evidence of an absent father's sexual prowess and, consequently, his status among his peers as a man. "I got strong sperm," a young black man boasted to television journalist, Bill Moyers, about the half-dozen children he had fathered by different women. He had trouble remembering names and ages. "That's all we be doing, makin' babies," another young man, with a large radio pressed against his ear, told Moyers.[40]

In the same bleak, hostile world, Moyers was told by young mothers that giving birth is one of the few ways they could experience real love—from the babies they bear. It is also one of the few ways lower-class females can gain social status, for a woman without babies may appear unwanted and unattractive. A swollen stomach and an infant in arms demonstrates, for all to see, her value as a desirable and fertile female.

But it is also clear that the hostility of males is reciprocated; black females often have little respect for the men who father their children. When Moyers asked a teenage mother about the father's role in helping her raise their infant daughter, she scoffed, "He can't even take of himself." But within months of the first child's birth, she was pregnant again, continuing further what has become a familiar pattern of behavior.[41]

In this fashion a subculture of unregulated sexuality, parental irresponsibility, and violence have grown into the major domestic crisis of the 1990s. In the midst of this chaos, females bear sole responsibility for their homes and children, while males prance and preen, and battle one another for respect and turf, like warriors in urban tribal societies.

Notes

1. Quoted in C.S. Johnson, *Shadow of the Plantation* (Chicago: University of Chicago Press, 1934), 44.
2. Quoted in Johnson, *Shadow of the Plantation*, 83.
3. Quoted in L. Rainwater, *Behind Ghetto Walls: Black Family Life in a Federal Slum* (Chicago: Aldine, 1970), 334.
4. K.B. Clark, *Dark Ghetto: Dilemmas of Social Power* (New York: Harper & Row, 1965), 81.
5. D.G. Glasgow, *The Black Underclass: Poverty, Unemployment and the Entrapment of Ghetto Youth* (New York: Vintage, 1980); K. Auletta, *The Underclass* (New York: Vintage, 1982).
6. W.J. Wilson, *The Truly Disadvantaged: The Inner City, the Underclass, and Public Policy* (Chicago: University of Chicago Press, 1987), 6; and, *The Declining Significance of Race* (Chicago: University of Chicago Press, 1978), 131–132.
7. M.E. Wolfgang and F. Ferracutti, *The Subculture of Violence: Toward an Integrated Theory in Criminology* (London: Tavistock, 1967), 264, 298–299.

8. D.P. Moynihan, *The Negro Family: The Case for National Action* (Washington, DC: U.S. Department of Labor, March 1965), 6–12; hereafter cited as *Moynihan Report*.

9. *Moynihan Report*, 8–11, 18; see, also, R.D. Mare and C. Winship, "Socioeconomic Change and the Decline of Marriage for Blacks and Whites," in C. Jencks and P.E. Peterson (eds.) *The Urban Underclass* (Washington, DC: Brookings Institution, 1991), 175, 182–184.

10. Mare and Winship, "Socioeconomic Change and the Decline of Marriage," 195.

11. P.J. Parish, *Slavery: History and Historians* (New York: Harper & Row, 1989), 86; see, also, A. Manfra and R.R. Dykstra, "Serial Marriage and the Origins of the Black Stepfamily: The Rowanty Evidence," *Journal of American History* 72 (1985): 18–44.

12. For varying perspectives on this question, see, E.F. Frazier, *The Negro Family in the United States* (Chicago: University of Chicago Press, 1966, orig., 1939), esp. 5–6, 8, 15–32, 33–49; S.P. Morgan, A. McDaniel, A.T. Miller, and S.H. Preston, "Racial Differences in Household and Family Structure at the Turn of the Century," (Philadelphia: University of Pennsylvania, Population Studies Center, 1990), 25; N. Sudarkasa, "Interpreting the African Heritage in Afro-American Family Organization," in McAdoo (ed.), *Black Families* (Beverly Hills, CA: Sage, 1981), 37–53; E.N. Goody, *Parenthood and Social Reproduction: Fostering and Occupational Roles in West Africa* (Cambridge: Cambridge University Press, 1982); U.C. Isiugo-Abanihe, "Child Fosterage in West Africa," *Population and Development Review* 11 (1985), 53–74; H. Page, "Childbearing versus Childrearing: Coresidence of Mother and Child in Sub-Saharan Africa"; and C. Bledsoe and U.C. Isiugo-Abanihe, "Strategies of Child-Fosterage Among Mende Grannies in Sierra Leone" in R. Lesthaghe (ed.), *Reproductive and Social Organization in Sub-Saharan Africa* (Berkeley: University of California Press, 1989), 401–436 and 442–469; A.S. Parent, Jr. and S.B. Wallace, "Childhood and Sexual Identity Under Slavery," *Journal of the History of Sexuality* 3 (1993), 363–401. See, also, R. Staples, "Sexual Harassment: Its History, Definition and Prevalence in the Black Community," *Western Journal of Black Studies* 17 (Fall 1993), 143–149.

13. In 1944 Gunnar Myrdal, for example, estimated that 29.6 percent of black families were "broken," meaning that such families for whatever reason, desertion, divorce, death, were headed by single persons, usually women. See, Myrdal, *An American Dilemma: The Negro Problem and Modern Democracy* (New York: Harper & Row, 1944), 934.

14. See, for example, Frazier, *The Negro Family*, 5–49; E.H. Pleck, *Black Migration and Poverty, Boston 1865–1900* (New York: Academic Press, 1979), 198–203.

15. Frazier, *The Negro Family*, 210–211.

16. Manfra and Dykstra, "Serial Marriage", 18–44; and Morgan et al., "Racial Differences in Household and Family Structure," esp., 21–27.

17. H. G. Gutman, *The Black Family in Slavery and Freedom, 1750–1925* (New York: Random House, 1976), 432–456, appendix A; S.C. Crawford, *Quantified Memory: A Study of the WPA and Fisk University Slave Narrative Collections* (unpublished Ph.D. dissertation, University of Chicago, 1980), 241.

18. S. Ruggles, "The Origins of African American Family Structure," *American Sociological Review* 59 (1994), 136–151 at 136 and 141. See, also, L. Gordon and S. McLanahan, "Single Parenthood in 1900," *Journal of Family History* 16 (1991), 97–116; and P.S. Morgan, A. McDaniel, A.T. Miller, and S.H. Preston, "Racial Differences in Household Structure at the Turn of the Century," *American Journal of Sociology* 98 (1993), 798–828.

19. Johnson, *Shadow of the Plantation*, 188–192; J. Dollard, *Caste and Class in a Southern Town* (Madison: University of Wisconsin Press, 1988; orig., 1937), 392–402.

20. Johnson, *Shadow of the Plantation*, 49, 53; see, also, Dollard, *Caste and Class*, 396–397.

21. Johnson, *Shadow of the Plantation*, 51–53; Dollard, *Caste and Class*, 392–402.

22. R. Farley and W.R. Allen, *The Color Line and the Quality of Life in America* (New York: Oxford University Press, 1989), 160–187; Hacker, *Two Nations*, 67–87, 92, 228–233.

23. S.A. Holmes, "Quality of Life is Up for Many Blacks, Data Say," *New York Times*, November 18, 1996, A1.

24. C.H. Hamilton, "The Negro Leaves the South," *Demography* 1, 1 (1964), 293–295.

25. See, for example, L.H. Long, "Poverty Status and Receipt of Welfare Among Migrants and NonMigrants in Large Cities," *American Sociological Review* 39 (February 1974), 46–56; R.L. Crain and C.S. Weisman, *Discrimination, Personality, and Achievement* (New York: Seminar Press, 1972), 140.

26. Wilson, *The Truly Disadvantaged*, esp. 49–56. For a modest extention of the same argument, see his *When Work Disappears: The World of the New Urban Poor* (New York: Alfred A. Knopf, 1996).

27. Massey and Denton, *American Apartheid*, 145–147.

28. E.S. Shihaadeh and N. Glynn, "Segregation and Crime: The Effect of Black Social Isolation on the Rates of Black Urban Violence," *Social Forces* 74 (June 1996), 1325–1352; and R.B. Felson, A.E. Liska, S.J. South, and T.L. McNulty, "The Subculture of Violence and Delinquency: Individual vs. School Context Effects," *Social Forces* 73 (September 1994), 155–173.

29. Wilson, *The Truly Disadvantaged*, 81–106.

30. Mare and Winship, "Socioeconomic Change and the Decline of Marriage," 175–202, esp., 182–184, 188, 194; D.T. Ellwood and J. Crane, "Family Change Among Black Americans: What Do We Know?" *Journal of Economic Perspective* 4, 4 (Fall 1990), 65–84 (emphasis added).

31. At that time the program's name was changed to Aid to Families with Dependent Children. In the 1960s, AFDC was buttressed with the Food Stamp Program (1964), Medicaid (1965), and the Child Nutrition Act (1966).

32. R.L. Hampton, R.J. Gelles, and J. Harrop, "Is Violence in Black Families Increasing? A Comparison of 1975 and 1985 National Survey Rates," in R.L. Hampton (ed.), *Black Family Violence: Current Research and Theory* (Lexington, MA: Lexington Books, 1991), 16.

33. On the enduring centrality of sex in lower-class black culture, see, also, U. Hannerz, *Soulside* (New York: Columbia University Press, 1969), 457–458.

34. Cazenave, "Black Men in America," 180; see also, L. Dickson, "The Future of Marriage and Family in Black America," *Journal of Black Studies* 23 (June 1993), 472–491, esp., 481; R. Staples, "Social Inequality and Black Sexual Pathology," *The Black Scholar* 21 (Summer 1990), 29–38.

35. E. Anderson, "Sex Codes and Family Life among Poor Inner-City Youths," *The Annals* (January 1989), 59.

36. N.A. Cazenave, "Black Men in America—The Quest for 'Manhood,'" in McAdoo (ed.), *Black Families*, 176–184: quote from D. Terry, "Fear and Ghosts: The World of Marcus, 19," *The New York Times*, April 11, 1993, 1; on the importance of respect, see, also, E. Anderson, *Streetwise: Race, Class, and Change in an Urban Community* (Chicago: University of Chicago Press, 1990).

37. Consider, for example, this rhyme from that period:

> I was walking through the jungle
> With my dick in my hand
> I was the baddest mother fucker
> In the jungle land
> I looked up in the tree
> And what did I see?
> *Your* little black mama
> Trying to piss on me.
> I picked up a rock
> And hit her in the cock
> And knocked that bitch
> A half a block.
> I hate to talk about *your* Mama
> She's a sweet old soul.
> She got a rap-pa-tap-pa tap dick
> And a pussy hole.
> Listen Mother Fucker
> You a two-timing bitch
> You got a ring around your pussy
> Make an old man rich.

Quoted in L. Rainwater, *Behind Ghetto Walls: Black Family Life in a Federal Slum* (Chicago: Aldine, 1970), 278.

38. M.S. Skinner, "The Music of Hate," *Arizona Daily Star* (October 17, 1993), 1E; N.W.A. and the Posse, "A Bitch Iz A Bitch" (Hollywood. CA: Priority Records, Ruthless Attack Muzick, 1989, ASCAP). Skinner, "The Music of Hate," 1E.

39. Skinner, "The Music of Hate," 1E.

40. *CBS Reports*, "The Vanishing Family: Crisis in Black America," Bill Moyers, producer (1986).

41. *CBS Reports*, "The Vanishing Family." See, also, Dickson, "The Future of Marriage and Family in Black America," 481; and U.S. Bureau of the Census, *Household and Family Characteristics*, March 1985 (Current Population Reports, Popluation Characteristics, Series P-20, No. 411).

18

Urban Tribal Societies

"We are breeding a society that will destroy itself."
—George Jackson, psychiatrist, Howard University, 1986[1]

"Violence is normal in the world of today's adolescent. Even worse, it is glamorous and appealing."
—Deborah Meier, secondary school principal, East Harlem, 1989.[2]

"The streets are scary 'cause a gun is real easy to get.... It scares me in a way because nobody wants to fight anymore. It's not, you know, we go blow for blow. Now it's 'I'll shoot you and get it over with.'"
—Zaire, a teenager, 1993.[3]

"You know, like your mother's probably whoring around or something like that. She ain't giving you that hug and that love. Every human being needs love. So if you get it from your brothers...you form a gang."
—Bernardo, a teenager, 1993[4]

Mutual contempt. With each generation since 1960 relationships between lower-class black men and women have grown more hostile. Black marriages continue to collapse, but more significantly, they are failing to occur; meanwhile the births continue. As a consequence, in the thirty years since the Moynihan study, significant numbers of at least two, maybe three, troubled generations of lower-class black children have reached adolescence without adequate parenting, without knowing what its like to have a father—or to be one. As might have been predicted, each of these generations has become more violent toward one another, more promiscuous, and more neglectful of its own children. Violence breeds violence. The damage has been so great that even young women who are inclined to care for their children often fail because they have never learned how to care.

A significant body of psychological theory and evidence reveals that a child's conscience emerges out of the attachments it forms with its parents. When that attachment is warm and nurturing, the child feels loved and secure. Under these circumstances, a bond of trust and mutual love is established between parent and child during infancy. It is that sense of cherished attachment to its parents that precedes the lessons that teach it self-discipline and a sense of personal responsibility for its actions. Not wanting to disappoint those it loves, pleasing them begins to take precedence over satisfying its own impulses and desires. It is in this manner that parents teach their children the standards of appropriate and moral behavior.[5] Ideally, they are toilet trained, taught to eat meals regularly, to go to bed on time, and to respect the rights of others by their own mothers and fathers before they enter school.

With or without actual punishment, shame is the penalty a child endures when it disappoints or disobeys the parents it loves. As standards of acceptable conduct become internalized, transgressions produce disappointmentment in itself, or feelings of guilt. Without parental love and discipline, these important inhibitions are much less likely to develop. The simple lessons of early childhood are gradually transformed into standards of moral conduct that apply to all areas of its behavior, and are likely to endure throughout its life. Thus, the core of a child's conscience has been formed when the awareness of its obligation to others, and sense of responsibility for its own actions, are sufficiently strong to deter it from wrongdoing even when detection and punishment could be avoided. Abundant research suggests that if those values are not learned during the preschool years, a child's future difficulties as an adult are virtually assured.[6]

The difficulties associated with not learning these important lessons worsen not only with each succeeding generation but, within families, with each succeeding child as well. As too many single, black females continue to have babies thoughout their reproductive years, a new baby frequently results in a mother's neglect, or abuse, of the older siblings. Anthropologist Arthur Hippler's study of black lower-class families in the Bay Area in the early 1970s, for example, revealed that when a child as young as two years becomes mobile and bothersome to a mother with a new baby, it is frequently "locked out" of the house, except for meals. Hippler writes:

> Comments directed at the older child in such situations, such as "Get out of here—You bother me," "You're nothin' but a lot of trouble," and "I'm gonna beat you if

you don't quit botherin' me," are so common as to be almost completely interchangeable from family to family.

Hippler explained that "locking out" enables the mother to turn her attention to the more rewarding and less demanding experience of a new baby or other interests. Often the practice is purely arbitrary. "A sudden irritation with the child, the appearance of a visitor, or a particular television program—almost anything," he writes, "may trigger the desire to lock children out." In another study of lower-class black residents of the now-demolished Pruitt-Igoe public housing project in St. Louis, sociologist Lee Rainwater also observed that, "Adult interest and interaction with children declines rather sharply as they move toward the school years."[7]

A mother's hostility and rejection are not the only thing a toddler neglected in this manner must deal with. Locking out children leads, Hippler continues, "to a certain amount of relatively public defecation and urination by young children," which invites the ridicule and scorn of those who witness it. If toilet training is as critical to a child's self-image and its ultimate ability to deal with authority, as Sigmund Freud and Benjamin Spock believed, it is little wonder that such children have trouble with both, especially as those qualities bear on their inborn sexuality and aggression.

Reported child abuse has increased steadily since 1976. The best research suggests that although most abused children (71 percent) do not become violent offenders, a significant number (29 percent) do. Moreover, most adult violent offenders are abused or neglected children. There is compelling evidence that violence breeds violence among black inner-city families. Young, black males who have been abused and neglected are the highest risk group for adult violent crime.[8]

Child neglect and abuse are crimes that are difficult to discover and prevent. Legal and clinical distinctions between the two may be useful in some contexts, but they tend to blur the devastating impact both have on children. Children suffer from neglect almost as frequently as they suffer from abuse.[9] A survey of the fifty states in 1992 revealed that nearly three million children had been victimized. The most frequent forms of maltreatment are neglect (49 percent), physical abuse (23 percent), sexual abuse (14 percent), miscellaneous abuse (9 percent), and emotional abuse (5 percent). While most victims are white (55 percent), a disproportionate number are black (26 percent), and the pattern, as figure 18.1 reveals, is found in all regions of the country. Like other types of violent crime, child neglect and abuse are an inherent part of the subculture of violence.[10]

FIGURE 18.1

Black Population and Black Child Neglect/Abuse in Selected States

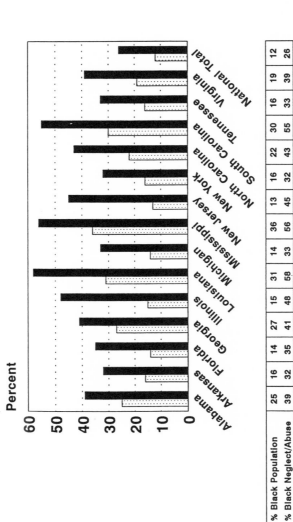

	Alabama	Arkansas	Florida	Georgia	Illinois	Louisiana	Michigan	Mississippi	New Jersey	North Carolina	South Carolina	Tennessee	Virginia	National Total
% Black Population	25	16	14	27	15	31	14	36	13	16	22	30	16	19	12
% Black Neglect/Abuse	39	32	35	41	48	58	33	56	45	32	43	55	33	39	26

☐ % Black Population ■ % Black Neglect/Abuse

Sources: U.S. Bureau of Census, *1990 Census of Population and Housing* (Washington D.C.: U.S. Government Printing Office, 1992); U.S. Department of Health and Human Services, National Center on Child Abuse and Neglect, *Child Maltreatment 1992: Reports from the States* (Washington, D.C.: U.S. Government Printing Office, 1994).

Most abuse is committed by parents (79 percent), or other members of the victim's family (12 percent), with the remainder (7 percent) attributed to foster parents or other "caregivers." Both fathers and mothers abuse their children.[11] Black children in poor, large (four or more children) families are the most likely victims of abuse. One national study reported that "severe parent-to-child violence was 114 percent greater in black families than in white families (221 incidents per 100,000 compared with 103 per 100,000)."[12] The younger the mother at the birth of her first child, the greater the risk that she will abuse her children. Fifty-two percent of the victims were between four and seven years of age; 27 percent were ages three and under. Little girls are somewhat more likely to be abused (53 percent), especially sexually, than little boys (46 percent). But boys are twice as likely to die from abuse and neglect as girls. Most die before the age of three, usually from brain damage due to battering or shaking, often as result of being disciplined for misbehavior.

Unlike abuse, some neglect is unintentional, a byproduct of ignorance among mothers who, as children, never received adequate parenting themselves. Educational, nutritional, and medical neglect, for example, are common in such families. Regardless of intent, however, children who survive these experiences bear emotional, intellectual, and sometimes physical, scars for the rest of their lives.[13]

It is difficult for a single person without sufficient time, energy, and money to raise a family, who is also living in substandard housing in a crime-ridden neighborhood, to teach her children the standards of appropriate behavior. It is almost certain not to happen if she is fourteen or fifteen years old, or younger, and has never known her father, or been taught these lessons herself. Children who bear children often have neither the desire nor the ability to nurture their offspring. Before long their needs and energies are, once again, biologically and temperamentally focused on attracting other mates, not parenting.

In addition, women who lurch from pregnancy to pregnancy in the haze and stupors of drug and alcohol addiction cannot nurture and discipline children, and are the most likely to neglect and abuse them. In addition to substance abuse, studies reveal that abusive black mothers report feelings of isolation during their own childhoods and adult lives, poor attachments to their parents, repeated foster care placements as children, poor relationships with men, and severe depression.[14] Their children, born to fathers who often are not part of anyone's memory, frequently enter a chaotic world undersized and already temperamentally and intellectually impaired due to *in utero* drug addiction and alcoholism. For example, estimates suggest that 5 percent of the black children born in New York, and 15 percent in the District of Columbia, had been exposed to cocaine in the womb.[15] If one took into account alcohol and other drugs, the estimates would be even higher.

In these circumstances, already severely handicapped and emotionally troubled children are abandoned to fend for themselves on the streets. There they are "raised" by other children who have themselves been raised without parents in the same streets. Their role models are the players in a subculture of violence—drug dealers, pimps, prostitutes, and street thugs—for there is no one else, except, perhaps, the glittering sports heroes and entertainers they see on television and smiling down from billboards, but whose lives are so far removed from the realities of their own. By the time such disadvantaged children reach the first grade, it is already too late to help many of them, especially the second or third generation of those who have grown up in this manner, especially those who end up—as almost all will—in overcrowded and disorderly classrooms. Public schools are poorly prepared to handle the enormous disciplinary problems of unsocialized children, and can do little to alter a course already set before they enter school.

* * *

Infancy and the period of nurturance that accompanies it are very brief for such children, many of whom are literally turned loose before they are toilet trained. Thus as early as their preschool years, many inner-city children learn a cardinal rule of survival: ignore others and "go for yourself." It is a perspective, like most things learned during early childhood, that remains.[16] As a result, each new generation of neglected children since the 1960s has been taught no alternative to this self-centered, inconsiderate, and often destructive pattern of behavior. They live, as one black writer described them, with "free-floating, non-specific feelings of anger" that can explode—just like their mothers'—at any moment and toward anyone who annoys them.[17]

Such children, raised without fathers by overextended and/or incompetent mothers, are placed at enormous risk for all kinds of misfortune. Girls, for example, are more likely to have difficulties in school, become delinquent, drop out, get pregnant, and live on welfare. The fate of boys is similar except many of them will end their lives in prison cells or early graves. In this manner, the problems of abuse and neglect are magnified, extended, and grow worse with each new generation.

This is true regardless of race, but nowhere are these problems more evident than in black inner cities.[18]

It is not surprising that a proliferation of youth gangs has accompanied the trend in child neglect and abuse. The rivalries that rage between them extend a pattern of inner-city violence that began, for many, in infancy. There is abundant evidence that links broken homes, juvenile delinquency, drugs, gang membership, and a subculture of violence.[19]

Black gangs, of course, have been around for as long as black males have lived in cities. But in the early years of this century they were virtually unnoticed by the general public since they functioned primarily as social organizations. Nor was there at that time the extradordinary number of parentless black children roaming city streets. It was in the 1960s that modern black gangs began to evolve, supplanting not only vanishing families, but also the paramilitary organizations of the preceding generation. Less political, more hedonistic, and more violent, gangs like the Bloods and Crips quickly assumed greater importance among a younger generation of black males than even the much-admired Black Panthers.

But instead of unifying young people against the common white enemy, as the Panthers tried to do, gangs began to battle one another, usually for the spoils of disintegrating neighborhoods. In Los Angeles, the Crips and, somewhat later, the Bloods soon found themselves in a war over territory and drug markets. As drug use has increased, so have gangs and weaponry. By the 1990s the Crips and Bloods are only two of countless organized gangs that are battling one another in cities across the country. In Chicago alone, more than forty major street gangs compete with the powerful Gangster Disciples for control of neighborhoods and drug markets.[20]

Drug dealing has honed a new and deadly edge to the struggle for control of inner-city streets and neighborhoods. For many unemployed and impoverished young blacks, the lure of making hundreds of dollars or more a week selling crack cocaine on the street is compelling. It also provides an equally strong incentive to join a gang and to carry guns that now, with money made from drugs, are affordable, required for protection, and convey status in a violent subculture.[21] Even young people who are not directly involved with gangs or the drug trade recognize the status that carrying a weapon conveys. These circumstances have lengthened the lists of casualties as expensive and devastatingly effective large caliber, semi-automatic weapons have replaced the crude "zip guns" and knives of a bygone era of gang violence. Most victims of gang violence now die from multiple gunshot wounds. Staccato bursts of gunfire regularly create chaos in black neighborhoods as stray bullets hiss and whine toward unknowing victims. Street gangs thrive on the fear such mayhem creates. As the black outlaws of the last century learned, fear commands recognition and respect when all else has failed.

Gangs also fill the void left by negligent parents, in effect, becoming surrogate families to many youngsters who feel abandoned by their parents. Young people may find gangs attractive for a variety of reasons, but a study in Los Angeles revealed that a majority of street gang members were teenagers from "broken homes without a strong male authority figure," or homes "where both parents work, and the gang member has little or no supervision." Most were described as "underachievers with a poor self-image and low self-esteem."[22] Another study of Crips and Bloods members offered similar conclusions: almost all had grown up in "dangerous family environments" where there was no "comfort, protection, and warmth." Beneath the swagger and posturing, these studies show, many gang members are neglected and abused children.[23]

To such troubled and neglected youngsters, gangs provide what their families never did: feelings of acceptance and belonging. Graffiti, secret hand signs, tattoos, and fashion all signify that cherished sense of belonging. Unlike absent, neglectful, and abusive parents, gangs provide structure in chaotic lives by setting out understandable expectations and well-defined standards of behavior. The rewards and punishments which accompany these standards fix personal responsibility and instill discipline. Loyalty and respect, above all else, are valued by gang members, perhaps because it was loyalty and respect, not to mention love, that so many of them never got from their parents. Some drive-by shootings, for example, are nothing more than initiation rites performed in rituals of tribal allegiance. A young victim dies for no other reason than the killer was challenged to demonstrate his courage and loyalty to the gang. Much like executioners in other wars, anger is not a requirement, for many young killers are simply *conforming* to a subculture that condones violence and demands compliance.[24]

* * *

Troubled, insecure juveniles are often drawn early to gang involvement and the dangerous activities that accompany it. And the trend is likely to continue since a history of juvenile violence is the best predictor of adult violence. Based on an extensive longitudinal study, psychologist David Farrington concluded,

It seems clear that the courses of adult criminal convictions can be traced back to childhood. The best predictors at age 21–24 years were convictions at age 17–20 and convictions at age 14–16. The best predictors of convictions at age 14–16 were convictions at age 10–13 and daring behavior at age 8–10. And the best predictors of convictions at age 10–13 was troublesome behavior at age 8–10.[25]

As a consequence, inner-city public schools are now one of the most dangerous sites in America. Metal detectors at the entrances, children who "dress down" to avoid attack, and teachers who are afraid to discipline unruly students, describe the state of many inner-city schools. The threat of virtually random violence has become a constant companion to black children of all ages, not only in school, but wherever they congregate. In one study, for example, 73 percent of the eighth graders surveyed in a Chicago neighborhood reported that they had seen someone shot, stabbed, robbed, or killed. In Washington, DC, a similar survey of first and second graders revealed that 45 percent had witnessed muggings, 31 percent had seen someone shot, and 39 percent had seen a dead body in the street.[26] A majority of those who carry guns claim they do so to protect themselves.[27]

A fourth-grader in Chicago explained that he preferred to play in the recreation area of a McDonald's restaurant because, "There's a giant hamburger, and you can go inside of it. And it's made out of steel so no bullets can't get through."[28] "You have to be so aware of what's around you all the time," a young girl said of her Brooklyn school and neighborhood, "And if you're not, you're putting yourself in danger."[29] Similar assessments have been made of city schools, playgrounds, and public parks in Detroit, Newark, Miami, Baltimore, and Washington, DC.

It is difficult to imagine the stress of living in neighborhoods fraught with such danger. "You got to watch your back all the time," another Chicago youngster said. "There's never no time to rest.... If you ain't careful, living around here can drive you crazy."[30] If a few months in a war zone can produce "post-traumatic stress disorder" in trained soldiers, imagine the effect of such fears on children who have known nothing else.[31]

Still, police protection is something few will consider, for the contempt so many lower-class black males show toward females is also directed toward police officers. Once more, the lyrics of gangsta rap music reveal its depths. N.W.A.'s hit "Gangsta, Gangsta," for example, is an ode to the young, black offenders who account for a huge share of the alarming crime statistics. It provides a vivid description of the brutality of life and the hostility toward police officers in South-Central

Los Angeles. "Fuck tha Police" is the title of another piece on this album. Other rappers, such as Public Enemy and Ice-T, elaborated on the anticop theme with hit songs like "911 is a Joke" and "Cop Killer." In his popular "Deep Cover," Snoop Doggy Dogg gloats over a cop killing with the words "It's 1-8-7 on an undercover cop," sung in a singsong drawl. The police code for homicide is 187.[32]

For some rap stars, like Snoop Doggy Dogg, the late Tupac Shakur, and the Notorious B.I.G., life and art have converged in their own violent encounters with the law and, perhaps, with one another. Shakur, who recorded his music on the "Death Row" label, died from wounds sustained in a drive-by shooting in 1996. The Notorious B.I.G., with whose wife Shakur had boasted of having an affair, was a suspect in the murder. Best known for his "Ready to Die" release, B.I.G. proved it six months later when he was killed by shots fired from a passing car. Before their murders, both had faced charges of drug dealing, sexual assault, aggravated assault, and attempted murder.[33]

If you are black, however, it matters not whether one is a rap star or just an ordinary youth; any encounter with the law often deepens the contempt for police officers and the criminal justice system reflected in the music of rappers like Shakur and B.I.G. Palpable in the modern inner city, such contempt builds on the experiences of a dark and brutal past.[34]

"Once they get a badge and a gun.... They got all the authority in the world," a seventeen-year-old black youth said of his experiences with the police in the Bronx. "They really disgust me. They cruise right behind you. You're looking at them, and they are looking at you. But if you look back at them, they want to get out of the car and search you and rough you up a little and throw you against the wall.... They are no better than us. Cops are just [another] gang."[35]

In addition to the animosity shown toward them, police officers are regularly struck by the absence of remorse and shame expressed by the young, black killers they arrest. "In my personal conversations with young people who have been involved in violence," the police chief of Washington, D.C. said, "there is no remorse, there is not the first tear, there is no sense that this is wrong." Neither are mental health professionals any longer surprised to observe how human life has been trivialized among black youngsters they interview and counsel. Black children have killed one another, for example, to obtain a pair of athletic shoes or a soft-leather jacket.[36]

Hopelessness breeds danger because it often purges concerns for personal safety as well as empathy for one's victims. The threat of punishment means little to a teenager without hope. For many inner-city youngsters, the dreariness and limitations of everyday life, as well as the dismal future they face, reduces whatever deterrent effect incarceration may have had. Three meals a day, a bed at night, television, and weight rooms to build their physiques and enhance their sexuality hardly serve as deterrents to this generation. In these circumstances, many young men become risk-takers who will bet ten years of their lives on the contents of a cash register drawer, or the whole works on a few moments of excitement, and a chance for glory, in a gun battle.[37]

Within the inner-city, black males who have "done time" acquire status in the eyes of their peers. Being considered "bad" or dangerous elevates one's status in a violent subculture just as it did in the late nineteenth century. Although the roots of the system run deep in Southern culture and the black outlaw tradition, the ethos is easy to recognize in young men generations removed from the Southern experience. A black high school principal explained why being considered dangerous is so "glamorous and appealing" to black teenagers:

> Boys will acknowledge that their ideal of manliness exudes violence. The girls are caught in a double bind: they're expected to adopt a veneer of toughness along with traditional female docility. To be a man is to sneer in the face of the weak. To be a woman is to worry about your man's needs.... To let down your guard [is] an invitation to danger or cruel jests, at the very least. Weakness [is] equated with sissiness. To be a thoughtful person [is] to invite a rep for being a homosexual...poor kids seem more prone to the view that this is the way the world is...or should be.[38]

While researching material for the film, *Menace II Society*, director Allen Hughes questioned a young black killer in South-Central Los Angeles about what he was thinking when he pulled the trigger that ended the life of another young man.

"Did you see him drop?" Hughes asked:

> When the blood came out, what were you doing then, when you were going "whomp"? I asked about every little step, and he said, "I went home, I laid down, went to sleep. Didn't lose one wink."[39]

* * *

Didn't lose one wink. Such indifference to human life is the defining characteristic of a sociopath. Criminal records reveal that remorseless killers of all races are commonly linked together by histories of parental neglect and abuse.[40] Fearless, free-floating anger. Danger. Watch your back all the time. All are words that describe the lives of too many inner-city black children. Accumulating research reveals evidence of post-traumatic stress disorder, depression, emotional distress, and behavioral problems among black children who have endured—both as victims and witnesses—these circumstances all their lives.[41] "People be fighting in front of me," a black teenager said, describing his recurring dream, "they just keep fighting. It just seems like nobody's winning. I know I have to get out of there."[42]

"There" is a war zone and the chaotic breeding grounds for succeeding generations of remorseless young killers and their traumatized victims. There in black, inner-city streets and schools, a subculture of violence, generations deep, dictates the daily routines of life and death. "What's a kid need to know to be smart on the street, to be a man?" a young black man was asked. "To be hateful. To be mean. Don't care about the next person," he answered immediately. "If you get in my way, I don't go around you, I go over you."[43]

The defining characteristics of the black underclass are not only its "weak attachment to the labor market" and its "social isolation," as sociologist William Julius Wilson has argued. Included also are the neglect of its children and their tragic violence toward one another. Since 1965, both have altered and claimed lives in ways that the very real problems of joblessness and social isolation never have.[44]

As the twentieth century draws to a close, black violent crime has evolved into an eerie sociopathic pattern reminiscent of Nat Turner's rampage as well as of white lynch mobs. Seemingly unrestrained by shame, guilt, or community pressure, black street crime has a terrifying, random, self-destructiveness about it. Those qualities extend a trend whose beginnings W.E.B. Du Bois and Richard Wright attributed to the conscience-numbing viciousness of slavery's aftermath, and which John Dollard described later, in the 1930s, as a "frontier psychology" and an "idealization of violence" among the lower-class blacks denied protection of the law in a small Mississippi town.[45] In the 1990s, drug dealing, modern weaponry, and organized gangs that depend on both have honed an edge to the meaning of the idealization of violence among inner-city youth that probably goes beyond anything that Du Bois, Wright, and Dollard could have imagined.

Notes

1. *CBS Reports*, "The Vanishing Family: Crisis in Black America," Bill Moyers, producer (1986).
2. "Down These Mean Streets: Violence By And Against America's Children," *Hearings*, U.S. House of Representatives, Select Committee on Children, Youth,

and Families, 101 Cong. 1st sess., May 16, 1989, Statement of Deborah Meier, 57; hereafter cited as *Hearings*.

3. Quoted in D. Terry "Young People Is Killing Young People," *The New York Times* (April 11, 1993), A11.

4. Quoted in J. Tierney "You Do What You Have to Do," *The New York Times* (April 13, 1993), A12.

5. M.S. Ainsworth, M.C. Blehar, E. Waters, and S. Wall, *Patterns of Attachment* (Hillsdale, NJ: L. Erlbaum Associates, 1978); W. Damon, *The Moral Child: Nurturing Children's Natural Moral Growth* (New York: The Free Press, 1988).

6. See, for example, E. Staub, "A Conception of the Determinants and Development of Altrusism and Aggression: Motives, the Self, and the Environment," in C. Zahn-Waxler, E.M. Cummings, and R. Iannotti (eds.), *Altruism and Aggression: Biological and Social Origins* (Cambridge: Cambridge University Press, 1986), 135–164; N. Eisenberg and P.A. Miller, "The Relation of Empathy to Prosocial and Related Behaviors," *Psychological Bulletin* 93 (1987), 100–131; J. Gibbs, "The Need to Facilitate Empathy as Well as Sociomoral Reasoning," in W. Kurtines and J. Gewirtz (eds.), *Moral Development Through Social Interaction* (New York: John Wiley and Sons, 1987); T. Hirschi, *Causes of Delinguency* (Berkeley, CA: University California Press, 1969), esp. pp. 86–94.

7. A.E. Hippler, *Hunter's Point: A Black Ghetto* (New York: Basic Books, 1974), 24–27; L. Rainwater, *Behind Ghetto Walls: Black Family Life in a Federal Slum* (Chicago: Aldine, 1970), 219. See, also, P. Gray-Ray and M.C. Ray, "Juvenile Delinquency in the Black Community," *Youth and Society* 22 (September 1990), 67–84; R. Loeber and T.J. Dishion, "Boys Who Fight at Home and School: Conditions Influencing Cross-Setting Consistency," *Journal of Consulting and Clinical Psychology* 52 (1984), 759–768; and M.S. Fleisher, *Beggars and Thieves: Lives of Urban Street Criminals* (University of Wisconsin Press, 1995).

8. C.S. Widom, "Victims of Childhood Sexual Abuse—Later Criminal Consequences," *National Institute of Justice: Research in Brief* (March 1995), 1–7; National Center on Child Abuse and Neglect [NCCAN], *Child Maltreatment 1992: Reports From the States to the National Center of Child Abuse and Neglect* (Washington, DC: U.S. Department of Health and Human Services, 1994), 9; NCCAN, *Study of the National Incidence and Prevalence of Child Abuse and Neglect* (Washington, DC: U.S. Department of Health and Human Services, 1987), 7.1–7.3; C.S. Clark, "Child Sexual Abuse," *CQ Researcher* 3 (January 15, 1993), 39; C.S. Widom, "Child Abuse, Neglect, and Violent Criminal Behavior," *Criminology* 27 (1989), 251–271; D. Hoffman-Plotkin and C. Twentyman, "A Multimodel Assessment of Behavioral and Cognitive Deficits in Abused and Neglected Preschoolers," *Child Development* 55 (1984), 794–802; B. Egeland, "The Consequences of Physical and Emotional Neglect on the Development of Young Children," *Research Symposium on Child Neglect* (Washington, DC: National Center on Child Abuse and Neglect, 1988); J. Sexton, "Young Criminals' Prey: Usually Young," *New York Times* (December 1, 1994), A1, 12. For a complete review of the literature on child abuse and subsequent violence, see, C.P. Widom, "Does Violence Beget Violence? A Critical Examination of the Literature," *Psychological Bulletin* 106 (1989), 3–28; D.O. Lewis, E. Moy, L.D. Jackson, R. Aaronson, N.S. Restifo, S. Serra, and A. Simos, "Biopsychological Characteristics of Children Who Later Murder," *American Journal of Psychiatry* 142 (1985), 1161–1167.

9. Because of data coordination problems at the state level, national reporting on child deaths is incomplete and imprecise. The most recent estimates suggest a range of 949 to 2,022 deaths per year from 1979 to 1988. Forty-four states reported a total of 1,068 child deaths from abuse and neglect in 1992. No racial

classifications were reported. See, *Child Maltreatment 1992: Reports From the States to the National Center on Child Abuse and Neglect* (Washington, DC: U.S. Department of Health and Human Services, 1994), pp. 18–19.

10. National Center for Child Abuse and Neglect, *Child Maltreatment, 1992*, 9, 14, 18; R.L. Hampton, R.J. Gelles, and J. Harrop, "Is Violence in Black Families Increasing? A Comparison of 1975 and 1985 National Survey Rates," in R.L. Hampton (ed.) *Black Family Violence: Current Research and Theory* (Lexington, MA: Lexington Books, 1991), 3–18.

11. L. Margolin, "Beyond Maternal Blame: Physical Child Abuse as a Phenomenon of Gender," *Journal of Family Issues* 13 (September 1992), 410–423).

12. R.L. Hampton and R.J. Gelles, "A Profile of Violence Toward Black Children," in R.L. Hampton (ed.) *Black Family Violence: Current Research and Theory* (Lexington, MA: Lexington Books, 1991), 33.

13. National Center for Child Abuse and Neglect, *Child Maltreatment, 1992*, 19; C.D. Connelly and M.A. Straus, "Mother's Age and Risk for Physical Abuse," *Child Abuse and Neglect* 16 (1992), 709–718; J. Pierpont and J. Poertner, "Active Surveillance of Child Abuse Fatalities," *Child Abuse and Neglect* 16 (1992), 3–10; D. Boyer and D. Fine, "Sexual Abuse as a Factor in Adolescent Pregnancy and Child Maltreatment," *Family Planning Perspectives* 24 (January-February 1992), 4–11; M. Straus and R. Gelles, *Physical Violence in American Families: Risk Factors and Adaptations to Violence 8,145 Families* (New Brunswick, NJ: Transaction Publishers, 1990); American Humane Association, *Highlights of Official Child Neglect and Abuse Reporting: 1986*, 24; L. Margolin, "Fatal Child Neglect," *Child Welfare* 69 (1990), 309–319; J.D. Alfaro, *Studying Child Maltreatment Fatalities: A Synthesis of Nine Projects* (unpublished); K.K. Christoffel, "Violent Death and Injury in US Children and Adolescents," *American Journal of Diseases of Childhood* 144 (1990), 697–706; P. Crittenden and S. Craig, "Developmental Trends in the Nature of Child Homicide," *Journal of Interpersonal Violence* 5 (1990), 202–216; see, also, National Center on Child Abuse and Neglect, *Child Neglect*, 1, 21; National Center on Child Abuse and Neglect, *A Study of the National Incidence and Prevalence of Child Abuse and Neglect* (Washington, DC: U.S. Department of Health and Human Services, 1987), 7.1–7.7.

14. S.J. Zuravin and R.H. Starr, Jr., "Psychosocial Characteristics of Mothers of Physically Abused and Neglected Children: Do They Differ by Race?" in R.L. Hampton (ed.), *Black Family Violence: Current Researach and Theory* (Lexington, MA: Lexington Books, 1991), 65.

15. "Abuse, Neglect Rising in D.C.—Drugs Ravage Home Life," *Washington Post* (September 10, 1989), A1; "Children of Cocaine," *Washington Post*, Sunday Editorial Section (September 17, 1989).

16. Hippler, *Hunter's Point*, 27; Rainwater, *Behind Ghetto Walls*, 218–221.

17. D. Prothrow-Smith (with M. Weissman), *Deadly Consequences* (New York: Harper Perennial, 1991), 6–7.

18. R. Hampton, "Family Violence and Homicides in the Black Community: Are They Linked?" in R. Hampton (ed.) *Violence in the Black Family: Correlates and Consequences* (Lexington, MA: Lexington Books, 1987), 135–156; E. Stark and A. Flitcraft, "Spouse Abuse," in M. Rosenberg and J. Mercy (eds.) *Violence in America: A Public Health Approach* (New York: Oxford University Press, 1991) 123–157; see, also, *Hearings*, Statement of Karl Zinsmeister, 127.

19. R.B. Felson, A.E. Liska, S.J. South, and T.L. McNulty, "The Subculture of Violence and Delinquency: Individual vs. School Context Effects," *Social Forces* 73 (September 1994), 155–173; T.P. Thornberry, M.D. Krohn, A.J. Lizotte, and

D. Chard-wierschem, "The Role of Juvenile Gangs in Facilitating Delinquent Behavior," *Journal of Research in Crime and Delinquency* 30, 1, (February 1993), 55–87, esp. 79; R.J. Sampson, "Urban Black Violence: The Effect of Male Joblessness and Family Disruption," *American Journal of Sociology* 93, 2 (September 1987), 348–382.

20. J. Marynik and D. Hudson, "Crips and Bloods: A Brief Description," 1–5, and "Black Gangs and Narcotics," 1–2, in Los Angeles County Sheriff's Department, *Third Annual Gang Symposium*, September 19, 1991); cited hereafter as *Gang Symposium*; C.R. Block and R. Block, "Street Gang Crime in Chicago," *National Institute of Justice* (December 1993), 1–11.

21. See, for example, A. Blumstein, "Violence By Young People: Why the Deadly Nexus?" *National Institute of Justice Journal* (August 1995); R. Dembo, P. Hughes, L. Jackson, and T. Mieczkowski, "Crack Cocaine Dealing By Adolescents in Two Public Housing Projects: A Pilot Study," *Human Organization* 52 (1993), 89–96.

22. "Black Gangs," 3 and "Los Angeles Street Gang Drug Dealers," 1–7 in *Gang Symposium*; see, also, C.H. Conley, *Street Gangs: Current Knowledge and Strategies* (Washington: National Institute of Justice, 1993), 16–18; W. McCord and J. McCord, *Origins of Crime: A New Evaluation of the Cambridge-Somerville Study* (New York: Columbia University Press, 1959); T. Hirschi, *Causes of Delinquency* (Berkeley: University of California Press, 1969); D.J. West and D.P. Farrington, *Who Becomes Delinquent?* (London: Heinemann Educational Books, 1973).

23. M. Fleisher, *Sentenced to Life* (forthcoming); quoted in K.N. Wright, *Family Life, Delinquency, and Crime: A Policymaker's Guide* (Washington: U.S. Department of Justice, May 1994), 15.

24. Felson et al., "The Subculture of Violence," 170; see, also, Stanley Milgram, *Obedience to Authority* (New York: Harper & Row, 1975).

25. D.P. Farrington, "Stepping Stones to Adult Criminal Careers," in D. Olweus, J. Block, and M. Radke-Yarrow (eds.), *Development of Antisocial and Prosocial Behavior: Research, Theories, and Issues* (Orlando: Harcourt Brace Jovanovich Academic Press, 1986), 373; see, also, P.H. Tolan, "Implications of Age of Onset for Delinquency Risk," *Journal of Abnormal Psychology* 16 (1987), 47–65; and C.S. Widom, "Child Abuse, Neglect, and Violent Criminal Behavior," *Criminology* 27 (1989), 251–271.

26. B. Shakoor and D. Chalmers, "Co-Victimization of African American Children Who Witness Violence: Effects on Cognitive, Emotional, and Behavioral Development," *Journal of the National Medical Association* 83 (1991), 233–37; J. Richters and P. Martinez, "The NIMH Community Violence Project: I. Children as Victims and Witnesses to Violence," *Psychiatry* 56 (1994), 7–21.

27. J.F. Sheley and J.D. Wright, "Gun Acquisition and Possession in Selected Juvenile Samples," *National Institute of Justice* (December 1993), 1–11; J.F. Sheley, Z. McGee, and J. Wright, "Gun-Related Violence In and Around Inner-City Schools," *American Journal of Diseases of Childhood* 146 (1992), 677–82; Centers for Disease Control, "Weapon-Carrying Among High School Students," *Journal of the American Medical Association* 266 (1991), 2342; J. Menacker, W. Weldon, and E. Hurwitz, "Community Influences on School Crime and Violence," *Urban Education* 25 (1990), 68–80; *Uniform Crime Reports* (Washington, DC: Federal Bureau of Investigation, 1980–1992); "Coroner's Report," in *Gang Symposium*.

28. Quoted in I. Wilkerson, "First Born, Fast Grown: The Manful Life of Nicholas 10," *New York Times* (April 4, 1993), A1.

29. Quoted in "Young People Is Killing Young People," *New York Times* (April 11, 1993), A11.

30. Quoted in D. Terry, "Fear and Ghosts: The World of Marcus, 19," *New York Times* (April 11, 1993), A11.

31. See, for example, E.J. Jenkins, "Violence Exposure, Psychological Distress and Risk Behaviors in a Sample of Inner-City Youth," in National Institute of Justice, C. Block and R. Black (eds.), *Trends, Risks and Interventions in Lethal Violence: Proceedings of the Third Annual Spring Symposium of the Homicide Research Working Group* (Washington, DC: U.S. Department of Justice, July 1995), 287–298; L. Terr, "Childhood Traumas: An Outline and Overview," *American Journal of Psychiatry* 48 (1991), 10–20; R. Pynoos and K. Nader, "Children's Exposure to Violence and Traumatic Death," *Psychiatric Annals* 20 (1986), 334–344.

32. M.S. Skinner, "The Music of Hate," *Arizona Daily Star* (October 17, 1993), E1; J. Leland, "Criminal Records: Gangsta Rap and the Culture of Violence," *Newsweek* (November 29, 1993), 63.

33. C. Jones, "For A Rapper, Life and Art Converge in Violence," *New York Times* (December 1, 1994), A1; M. Marriott, "Before He Was B.I.G., Rap Star Was Shadowed by Trouble, *New York Times* (March 17, 1997), A13.

34. Tupac Shakur's mother, for example, Afeni Shakur, was among the "New York 21," a group of Black Panthers who were accused of conspiring to bomb police stations and department stores in 1971. Her son was born a month after she was acquitted.

35. Quote from M. Marriott, "Provider, Protector and Felon: Freddie, 17," *New York Times* (April 18, 1993), A1.

36. J. Lauritsen, J. Laub, and R. Sampson, "Convention and Delinquent Activities: Implications for the Prevention of Violent Victimization Among Adolescents," *Violence and Victims* 7 (1992), 91–108; S. Roberts, "Murder, Mayhem, and Other Joys of Youth," *Journal of NIH Research* 2 (1990), 67–72; G. Escobar, "Washington Area's 703 Homicides in 1990 Set a Record," *Washington Post* (January 2, 1991), A1.

37. L. Dickson, "The Future of Marriage and Family in Black America," *Journal of Black Studies* 23 (June 1993), 477–478; W.M. Blake and C.A. Darling, "The Dilemmas of the African American Male," *Journal of Black Studies* 24 (June 1994), 402–416; see, also, R. Staples, "Black Male Genocide: A Final Solution to the Race Problem in America," *The Black Scholar* 18 (May-June 1987), 2–12.

38. *Hearings*, Statement of Deborah Meier, 57–58.

39. Quoted in H.L. Gates, Jr., "Niggaz With Latitude," *New Yorker* (March 21, 1994), 147.

40. D.O. Lewis, E. Moy, L.D. Jackson, R. Aaronson, N.S. Restifo, S. Serra, and A. Simos, "Biopsychological Characteristics of Children Who Later Murder: A Prospective Study," *American Journal of Psychiatry* 142 (1985), 1161–1167.

41. R. Durant, C. Cadenhead, R. Pendergrast, G. Slavens, and C. Linder, "Factors Associated With the Use of Violence Among Urban Black Adolescents," *American Journal of Public Health* 84 (1994), 612–17; K. Fitzpatrick, "Exposure to Violence and the Presence of Depression Among Low-Income, African-American Youth," *Journal of Consulting and Clinical Psychology* 13 (1993), 528–31; K. Fitzpatraick and J. Boldizar, "The Prevalence and Consequences of Exposure to Violence Among African-American Yourth," *Journal of the American Academy of Child and Adolescent Psychiatry* 32 (1993), 424–30; P. Martinez and J. Richters, "The NIMH Community Violence Project: II. Children's Dis-

tress Symptoms Associated With Violence Exposure," *Psychiatry* 56 (1994), 22–35; J. Osofsky, S. Wewers, D. Hann, and A. Fick, "Chronic Community Violence: What Is Happening to Our Children?" *Psychiatry* 56 (1994), 36–45; H. Schubiner, R. Scott, and A. Tzelepis, "Exposure To Violence Among Inner-City Youth," *Journal of Adolescent Health* 14 (1993), 214–19.

42. Quoted in S. Rimer, "Shawn, 17: Running Past Many Obstacles," *New York Times* (April 25, 1993), A1.

43. *CBS Reports*, "The Vanishing Family."

44. W.J. Wilson, *The Truly Disadvantaged: The Inner City, the Underclass, and Public Policy* (Chicago: University of Chicago Press, 1987); see, also, his, "Public Policy Research and *The Truly Disadvantaged*," in C. Jencks and P.E. Peterson (eds.) *The Urban Underclass* (Washington, DC: The Brookings Institution, 1991), esp. 471–476.

45. W.E.B. Du Bois, *The Souls of Black Folk* (New York: New American Library, 1969, orig. 1953), 200–201; J. Dollard, *Caste and Class in a Southern Town* (Madison: University of Wisconsin Press, 1987; orig. 1937), 279–280.

19

Conclusions

"The black man has been separated and made to live in his own country of color. If you are black the only roads into the mainland of American life are through subservience, cowardice, and loss of manhood. Those are the white man's roads. It is time we built our own...Let no one convince any black man that he is an American like anybody else."
—LeRoi Jones, 1962–63[1]

"The divide of race has been America's constant curse."
—President Bill Clinton, January 20, 1997

As the twentieth century draws to a close, the prescience of Thomas Jefferson's sense of foreboding about American race relations has been confirmed. On January 20, 1997, nearly two hundred years after he expressed these concerns, his namesake, President William Jefferson Clinton, echoed them in his Second Inaugural Address.

"The divide of race has been America's constant curse," the President said. "Prejudice and contempt, cloaked in the pretense of religious or political conviction," still threaten the nation. "...We cannot, we will not, succumb to the dark impulses that lurk in the far regions of the soul everywhere."[2]

Despite recent advances in civil rights and economic opportunity, slavery and its brutal aftermath have left not only "lineaments of wrath", but open sores that mar the countenance of American society. Each of the preceding chapters has described a portion of what Jefferson called the "odious peculiarities" of white supremacy and the effects these have had on black victims. Established as soon as slaves were brought ashore in the seventeenth century, that violent, racist subculture continued to flourish well into the twentieth before the strict enforcement of new federal laws removed the tools used to sustain it. But there is ample evidence, as President Clinton acknowledged, that the emotions that gave that subculture life remain in a nation still gravely divided by the burden of race.[3]

These same chapters also have shown how a black subculture of violence has evolved over generations in response to the systematic injustice that is white supremacy's defining quality. The defining quality of the violent subculture of the black underclass, however, is its self-destructiveness. Despite year-to-year fluctuations in violent crime rates, evidence presented in Chapter One leaves little doubt that the problem remains, growing worse among young people, with the prospect of more ominous things to come as a new generation comes of age in the approaching century.[4]

The essential elements of both these two mutually reinforcing subcultures were described in Wolfgang's and Ferracuti's subculture of violence theory. The cross-validating evidence supporting the theory is substantial.

* * *

Change in American race relations has been slow but inevitable. No civilized nation, especially one with democratic pretensions, could ignore indefinitely the injustice and savagery inflicted on the black inhabitants of a region within its borders. But it was a plague of insects, not the electorate or its leaders, that finally precipitated a second Emancipation as millions of blacks began to flee the South early in the twentieth century. Until the Great Migration began, there appeared to be little likelihood that race relations would improve. After that, the tireless efforts of brave men and women, and organizations like the NAACP, gradually convinced the U.S. Supreme Court to reconsider earlier rulings that had stripped meaning from the Fourteenth and Fifteenth Amendments and, in effect, had legitimized the racial caste system imposed by whites.

Those reconsiderations in criminal trials in the 1920s and 1930s began to whittle away at the injustice of Southern courts. The *Scottsboro Case,*[5] for example, placed racial injustice in the starkest light possible before the nation and the world. The trial revealed the desperate circumstances blacks still faced in Southern courts where guilt was presumed and death too often the penalty. Other decisions during the same period aroused public awareness and revived the struggle for racial justice.[6]

Although debt peonage and convict leasing gradually disappeared in the twentieth century, remnants of both remained in migrant worker

camps, state prisons, county prison farms, and the stark impoverishment of countless black households. Records show that rampant brutality continued in Louisiana, Mississippi, and Arkansas prisons, for
example, until well into the 1960s until reforms finally were enacted.[7]

Those reforms were but one element in the NAACP's long struggle
to end racial injustice. After a series of precedent-setting victories in
criminal justice, school segregation, and voting rights cases, it won a
major victory in the Supreme Court's landmark *Brown* decision in
1954.[8] Striking down the "separate but equal" standard, the court ruled
that racial segregation in the public schools was unconstitutional. In
1957, federal troops were sent to Little Rock, Arkansas to enforce
school desegregation orders. This action by President Dwight
Eisenhower marked the *first* time since the Compromise of 1877 that
federal troops were used to protect the lives and civil rights of blacks
in the South.

The *Brown* decision sparked a Civil Rights Movement whose major
accomplishments were the Civil Rights Act of 1964 and the Voting
Rights Act of 1965. Those laws, the Twenty-Fourth Amendment that
eliminated the poll tax, and other implementing legislation changed
the political and social landscape of the South.[9] As blacks registered to
vote in unprecedented numbers, even southern politicians, who cherished reelection above all else, were hesitant to ignore their wishes.
Due process and equal protection of the laws became—for the *first*
time in history—a realistic possibility, if not a certainty, for black Americans. Racial discrimination—whether practiced by states or individuals—in education, employment, housing, and voting was made
punishable under tough new federal laws.

Also in the 1960s, landmark decisions by the Supreme Court in the
area of criminal justice restored rights to the accused at the same time
they restricted the role and discretion of the police, prosecutors, and
judges who had preyed upon blacks since the Civil War. In 1972, for
example, the NAACP was successful in persuading the Court to declare a moratorium on the death penalty until states met its new standards of fairness.[10] Although racial discrimination in sentencing and
other areas of concern did not end, it became much more risky, and
potentially costly, for those who practiced it. Even though southern
juries continued to acquit the white murderers of blacks,[11] those killers,
from that point forward, could then be subject to federal prosecution
for violating the civil rights of their slain victims. As a result of such
strong and determined federal intervention during the 1960s and 1970s,

the regional subculture of white supremacy and violence was significantly weakened.[12]

Even so, the legacy lives on in the troubled relationship between blacks and the police throughout the country. Most blacks, regardless of social class, differ from whites in their profound distrust of the police. They are outraged by what they see as the impunity enjoyed by police officers who harm and kill black men. In 1992, the largest urban riot in American history occurred in Los Angeles after police officers, who had beaten a defenseless black man senseless in a sadistic ritual worthy of a lynch mob, were acquitted by an all-white jury.[13] Similar incidents where black men have been brutalized or killed under questionable circumstances by policemen continue to outrage blacks in Miami, St. Petersburg, Chicago, Brooklyn, Charlotte, and Leland, Mississippi, to name only a few. In New York City, an investigation by Amnesty International revealed that charges of police brutality rose from 977 in 1987 to more than 2,000 in 1994. A disproportionate number of victims were black and an overwhelming number of the police officers involved were white.[14] Contacts between white policemen and black males remain, as they have historically, flashpoints in American race relations.

Culture is shaped, in part, by the tools used to sustain it. Despite severe and continuing problems in the nation's inner cities, the federal government succeeded in altering the white supremacist culture of the South, and the vestiges of that culture elsewhere, by removing many of the tools used to perpetuate it. Although the underlying problem remains, the higher probability that racial crimes will be punished has greatly reduced their occurrence. Structural reforms of this sort worked, however, only because potential offenders had much to lose if they broke the law. Fear of prosecution and conviction, not moral principles as Myrdal imagined in 1944,[15] were the new elements introduced in the 1960s that, over the next several decades, gradually constrained and substantially altered America's subculture of white supremacy. But serious problems remain and, as President Clinton insisted, they can be ignored only at grave risk.

* * *

It is *not* possible, however, in the same way, to change a violent black subculture that is essentially self-destructive, whose members have much less to lose. Fines mean little to people who cannot pay. The threat of imprisonment—a place to sleep, regular meals, television—

has little deterrent value to a person already living a precarious existence on the streets. Nor, except for the offender, does capital punishment deter, when the chances of being killed by a rival gang member,
or during a drug deal, are daily realities.

Nowhere are the failings of the present system more clearly demonstrated than in black inner-city schools. In these dangerous, failing institutions, academic success has become an invitation to ridicule or
worse. The good grades of the few motivated students represent "disre-
spect to the rest of us," one gang leader said in explaining his contempt
for such "goodies." "Everyone knows they're trying to be white, to get
ahead in the white man's world."[16]

It would be a mistake to assume that the behavior of black children
today, who have no personal memory and probably little knowledge
of the experiences of their forebears, is unaffected by the history of
victimization that has been described in these pages. The mood of
distrust and anger toward whites, so evident in the words and actions
of inner-city blacks, has carried over from generation to generation.
That contempt for white mainstream values and culture is so deeply
entrenched among inner-city children, a black marketing research firm
discovered in 1992, that many of them would rather risk death than
be ostracized by their peers for endorsing values that are perceived as
white. The values that are rejected by these nine-to fifteen-year-old
children, however, are those that most parents try to impress upon
their children. They include refraining from drugs, doing well in
school, abstaining from sex or being sexually responsible, and re-
specting the right of others to make their own choices on those matters without intimidation and fear. The survey showed that even when
black celebrities endorse such values, these youngsters, while sometimes admiring the celebrities, ridicule their messages as merely playing the "white man's game."[17]

So, too, are appeals to traditional African-American sensibilities
"likely to be ineffective" on this current generation of black children,
the report concluded. When asked about Martin Luther King, Jr., for
example, a boy replied, "Yeah, he was a great man and all, but I'm sick
of hearing about Martin Luther King. Just 'cause I'm black, why do I
have to know about all this black stuff?" Most of the respondents did
not know what the acronym NAACP stood for, nor did they care.[18]

What these young people embrace, the survey revealed, is a "street
culture" that reflects "a chilling disbelief in the future" and, consequently, a strong propensity to live for the moment through "macho"

risk-taking with drugs, sexual promiscuity, and violence. The report concluded that,

> African-American inner city teenagers are far more certain of who they are *not* than who they are, and their efforts at self-definition, even those they know to be antisocial and self-destructive, are defended on grounds that they are, at least, authentic...Mainstream society has vitually no credibility with these young people; they are alienated from their own heritage, and their *subculture* tolerates self-destructive behavior and encourages taking risks.[19]

Such is the state of the third and fourth generations of children growing up in a hostile society without parental guidance. Feral children multiplying recklessly in a subculture of violence threaten to destroy the black community from within.

The violent subculture of the black underclass includes not only identifiable behavior patterns and values, but also rituals and artistic activities that set it apart from the mainstream. Some are goal-directed, but others serve simply to make sense out of past experiences and everyday lives. The nihilistic themes contained in gangsta rap music and the heroic status accorded its performers fulfill both functions for the underclass, and define as well as any scholarly work has the values and elements of status within the subculture.[20] Its anger, estrangement, and glorification of rapists and street killers describe not only the moral and social turmoil of the inner city, but reflect, as well, the long legacy of injustice chronicled in these pages.

Whether values and behavior patterns are dysfunctional or self-defeating is irrelevant to the larger issue of their existence. Cultures differ not in their rationality, but in their utility as means to cope with, and understand, particular problems. The strategies that have evolved over many generations in the black underclass make no pretense toward problem solving. *Coping* rather than problem solving describes its prescriptions and its behavior. The problems it faces persist from generation to generation, accompanied by a fatalistic acceptance of their inevitability and intractable nature. That fatalism defines the boundaries of rationality for those who are trapped and socialized within it.[21]

* * *

A subculture of violence that was molded in a crucible of racial oppression, then hardened over generations into a way of life, probably cannot be changed by conventional means of social reform. Contrary to some observers,[22] education and employment alone provide solutions only for those who *value* training and jobs. Both have worked, for example, since the 1960s for a black middle class that already possessed both the skills and desire required to push forward and succeed after discriminatory laws and practices were removed. But the underclass, without the skills to take advantage of these reforms, now adamantly rejects the *values* that must accompany them as a matter of principle and racial pride. Attempts to change the subculture with *only* the lure of education and *only* the promise of jobs is sure to fail just as they have in the past.[23]

The most fundamental, and critical, problem today facing the underclass, and, perhaps, society at large, is the breakdown in childcare and discipline that has accompanied the collapse of black family structure since the 1960s. Without families there can be no social order, and the sexual chaos and violence of the inner city confirm that. Although abundant research indicates that marital conflict is a more powerful predictor of delinquency than having only a single parent, the two, unfortunately, cannot often be separated in the black lower class. Whether a man and woman are married matters little to the children who live in the same household and suffer the battles, as well as the neglect and abuse, that frequently emanate from them.[24]

The typical black welfare family is a mother with children who has never married. Research by Mary Jo Bane and David T. Ellwood concluded that welfare dependency could be eliminated, "If we could prevent the formation of single-parent families..."[25] Although there is some evidence that welfare programs may have reduced the female incentive to marry,[26] this conclusion, alone, obscures a more important, underlying problem: The most important disincentive to black marriage is the hostility and distrust that characterize male/female relationships in the black underclass. The threat of domestic violence haunts the lives of lower-class black women and their children. Blacks account for more than 45 percent of all spousal homicides; the rates for such crimes are nearly nine times higher than white rates.[27] Among female crime victims, lower-income, young, black women, who have never married, are the most likely to be harmed or killed by male intimates, acquaintances, and strangers alike. Battering frequently precedes death, and as often as not it is the male abuser who dies in the struggle.[28] It does not require too much imagination to realize that a government check, regularly delivered, might be more attractive than an irresponsible, abusive male who neither respects you, nor provides for your children.

* * *

In 1996, Congress passed historic legislation that ended the federal welfare system that has sustained poor mothers and their children since 1935. Although it is too early to assess its ultimate impact, initial projections indicate that federal welfare spending could be cut by as much as $55 billion during the first six years of its implementation. Those who will be hit hardest by these cuts are the poorest twenty percent, who are disproportionately black, that need it most. Henceforth, federal block grants for welfare will be administered by the individual states in whatever manner they see fit, most guided by the objective that recipients be required to join education, training and employment programs that will lead to financial self-sufficiency.

As laudable as those "welfare to work" goals may be, too little attention has been given to the child-care burden this will create for the mothers affected. It is likely that even the most successful participants in such programs will in the end get the same kind of low-paying, odd-hours jobs that people coming off welfare usually get. Hardly the kind of employment that will enable them to earn livable wages, not to mention assume the additional costs of transportation and day care for their children. The potential consequences of such added burdens and the stress that accompanies them could be most damaging to the millions of needy children seemingly left out of these considerations. Unless important adjustments are made to compensate for this oversight, the unsupervised children of those mothers who are unable to afford day care will be placed at even greater risk.[29]

Moreover, there is no evidence to suggest that welfare reform—well-intentioned though it is—will reduce the problem of domestic violence that is intergenerational in character, and which gives rise to welfare dependency. When government assistance is finally withdrawn after two years, as required, many mothers and children will be left vulnerable to the predatory males against whom the old system offered a shield. It is not welfare dependency that is destroying lower-class black families; dependency is but a symptom of the real cause—*domestic abuse and violence*.

America's racial problem in the 1990s is exceedingly complex and multifaceted: First is the continuing animosity, estrangement, and distrust that characterize relations between whites and blacks, especially on matters involving the criminal justice system. Although the worst white-on-black injustices have greatly diminished in number, the gulf that has historically divided the races on this most fundamental matter remains; as long as it does, there can be no shared feeling of community.

A related issue is the distrust and fear that compromise relationships between black males and females. A subculture that derides conventional family life and commends sexual exploitation and violence will ultimately destroy itself.[30] The most tragic victims are the children who issue from the transient couplings that have replaced marriage among the black lower class. They, in turn, are likely to become poor parents and victimizers themselves in a tragic generational cycle of behavior that perpetuates the subculture of violence.

As their numbers increase, as they did in the 1960s, so will the violence. Current research indicates that about 30 percent of the approximately 754,000 black children who were neglected and abused in 1992 (the most recent data available) will probably become adult violent offenders; males are at highest risk.[31] If this estimate is correct, it means that, for this reason alone, as many as 218,660 new violent offenders will add more names to the already long list of victims. But if welfare reform exacerbates the problem of child care, a possibly far greater number of neglected children will enter their childbearing years without ever having learned how to be responsible, caring parents themselves.[32]

Efforts to break this destructive intergenerational pattern have been unsuccessful for a variety of reasons. Intervention programs for child neglect and abuse are ineffective, in large part, because they focus on parents rather than children.[33] The history of countless cases indicates that efforts to "reunify" such families too frequently sacrifice children to the problems of unreformable parents, or next of kin, many of whom are afflicted with the same problems. Because of the shortage of black foster homes, and the resistance of some black organizations to having black children placed in white homes, black children are the most frequent victims of misguided decisions that place them in the custody of relatives who are poorly prepared to handle such responsibilties.

By the time a child of an abused, drug-addicted mother is bounced from one relative or foster home to another, while the mother fails at one rehabilitation program after another, he/she has probably suffered predictable, and irreparable, psychological damage. The conscience-forming attachments that should have developed between such mothers and their children are either warped or non-existent. It makes no sense to subject children to what amounts to an alternative form of abuse for years on end while efforts are made to reunite a "family" whose destructiveness is likely to continue. Meanwhile, state child protection service agencies are overwhelmed with burgeoning caseloads for which they have neither the personnel nor resources to investigate.[34]

Ironically, growing awareness and fear of the AIDS epidemic may be reflected in recent declines in teenage pregnancies. Still, without continuing efforts to discourage irresponsible reproductive behavior and parenting, accompanied by more comprehensive programs to care for, and socialize, the tragically disadvantaged children born into these circumstances,[35] the racial crisis Jefferson feared, de Tocqueville anticipated, and President Clinton has acknowledged in 1997 as the nation's overriding domestic problem, will continue to worsen. A projected twenty-three percent increase in the teenage population within the first decade of the twenty-first century virtually assures that.

An accumulation of historical and recent evidence suggests that *fear* and *distrust* are probably the most important reasons why growing numbers of black females do not marry, and also why their children flee to the street. Without acknowledging this crucial dimension of the child-care problem—and understanding the historical reasons for it—both those who blame male joblessness and those damning the welfare system miss the point.

In the same sense, even though increased police surveillance and presence may have reduced crime recently in New York City, Boston, Houston, and Kansas City,[36] the underlying causes remain and the long-term viability of that solution is open to question. In Los Angeles, for example, research conducted between 1990 and 1994 reveals that its law enforcement agencies are simply overwhelmed by the epidemic of violence and cannot keep pace. Inadequate investigations by the police, and plea bargains negotiated by prosecutors without sufficient evidence to try cases, account for the nearly 70 percent of that city's murder investigations that fail to lead to arrests and convictions.[37]

Despite recent declines in violent crime, the United States continues to have a far higher rate of violent crime than any comparable European or Asian country. At the same time it incarcerates more of its citizens than any nation in the world. Moreover, nearly half of them are black, as are more than forty percent of those awaiting execution. Does this racial disproportionality reflect actual crimes committed, as most whites believe, or discriminatory law enforcement and discrepancies in sentencing—especially for drug-related crimes—which is the position of most blacks?[38]

The racial divide is undeniable as are its potentially incendiary political implications: Any proposed policy to reduce violent crime must take into account that it will affect blacks disproportionately; it must confront directly what one observer has called "the hidden burden of race."[39]

* * *

There is, of course, a profound irony in this tragic situation. It has only been during the last thirty years that the black community has experienced, for the first time in American history, some semblance of the rights it had been denied for more than three centuries. But those civil rights reforms, as we have seen, were too late and too little to correct the damaging effects of countless generations of cruelty and injustice.

As the nation approaches a new century, the evidence presented in these pages suggests that in order to contain and break the cycle of violence that is destroying lives and families, nothing short of a moral transformation is required. Black leaders as different in perspective as W.E.B. Du Bois, Malcolm X, Colin Powell, and Jesse Jackson have acknowledged this. Without a rededication to spousal and parental responsibilities, all have agreed, government programs alone—no matter how essential, how benevolent, or how punitive—will fail, and the future of the black community and even American democracy will remain in jeopardy.

In 1995, Louis Farrakhan, controversial leader of the black separatist Nation of Islam, led a "million man march" on the nation's capital. Although ridiculed by the media, condemned by the leadership of both political parties, and even by prominent spokesmen of his own race for his outspoken anti-Semitism, Farrakhan's purpose at this rally was different. Calling for "solidarity," he confronted the cultural issue directly, challenging the vast throng of black males before him to rededicate themselves to family and community responsibilities as "new black men." "Go back home," he urged his listeners, "and turn our communities into productive places." Another speaker called for his black brothers to "lay down our Uzis and Tech-9's and not kill each other any more."[40] Whatever else might be accomplished through government programs to change the quality and course of American race relations, these pleas for a moral transformation should not be ignored.

Notes

1. L. Jones, (aka, I.A. Baraka) *Home* (New York: William Morrow, 1966), 85, 165.
2. President William Jefferson Clinton, *Second Inaugural Address*, January 20, 1997.

3. See, for example, D.O. Sears, C. Van Laar, M. Carrillo, and R. Kosterman, "Is It Really Racism? The Origins of White Americans' Opposition to Race-Targeted Policies;" and L. Sigelman and S.A. Tuch, "Metastereotypes: Blacks' Perceptions of Whites' Stereotypes of Blacks," *Public Opinion Quarterly* 61 (Spring 1997), 16–54; 87–102.

4. Federal Bureau of Investigation, *Uniform Crime Reports, January-June 1995* (Washington, DC: U.S. Department of Justice, December 1995).

5. *Powell v. Alabama*, 287 U.S. 56 (1932).

6. D.T. Carter, *Scottsboro: The Tragedy of the American South* (Baton Rouge: Louisiana State University Press, 1979; J. Goodman, *Stories of Scottsboro* (New York: Pantheon, 1994); *Moore v. Dempsey*, 261 U.S. 86 (1923); *Powell v. Alabama*, 287 U.S. 56 (1932); *Brown v. Mississippi*, 297 U.S. 278 (1936). See, also, R.C. Cortner, *A Mob Intent on Death* (Middletown, CT: Wesleyan University Press, 1979), and *A "Scottsboro" Case in Mississippi* (Jackson, Miss.: University Press of Mississippi, 1986); R.L. Zangrando, *The NAACP Crusade Against Lynching, 1909–1950* (Philadelphia: Temple University Press, 1980.

7. See, "The Delta Prisons: Punishment for Profit," *Special Report of the Southern Regional Council*, March 1968; P. Atkinson, "Our Paroles, Pardons," New Orleans *Times Picayune*, February 12–21, 1967; C.M. Hargroder, "A Look At Angola," New Orleans *Times-Picayune*, April 9–16, 1967. See, also, D.E. Kneeland, "Mississippi Prison, a Symbol of Horror, Is Reforming Quietly," *New York Times*, February 14, 1968, A28; J.C. Mouledous, "Sociological Perspectives on a Prison Social System," (M.A. Thesis, Louisiana State University, 1962), 80–84; M.T. Carleton, *Politics and Punishment: The History of the Louisiana Prison System* (Baton Rouge: Louisiana State University Press, 1971); and D.M. Oshinsky, *Worse Than Slavery: Parchment Farm and the Ordeal of Jim Crow Justice* (New York: The Free Press, 1996).

8. *Brown v. Board of Education of Topeka* 347 U.S. 483 (1954).

9. E. Black and M. Black, *Politics and Society in the South* (Cambridge: Harvard University Press, 1987).

10. *Furman v. Georgia* 408 U.S. 238 (1972). See, also, W.J. Bowers, *Legal Homicide: Death as Punishment in America* (Boston: Northeastern University Press, 1984), esp., ch. 3: and R. Paternoster, *Capital Punishment in America* (New York: Lexington Books, 1991), esp., ch.4.

11. D.C. Baldus, G. Woodworth, and C. Pulaski, Jr., *Equal Justice and the Death Penalty: A Legal and Empirical Analysis* (Boston: Northeastern University Press, 1990); see, also, F. Mars, *Witness in Philadelphia* (Baton Rouge: Louisiana State University Press, 1977).

12. See, for example, D. King, *Separate and Unequal: Blacks and the United States Federal Government* (New York: Oxford University Press, 1995).

13. See, for example, *Report of the Independent Commission of the Los Angeles Police Department* (Los Angeles, 1991), esp., 69–91; B. Stumbo, "Daryl Gates: A Portrait of Frustration," *Los Angeles Times*, August 15 and 16, 1982; J.G. Dunne, "Law and Disorder in L.A.," *New York Review of Books*, October 10 and October 24, 1991, 23, 62.

14. Amnesty International, "Police Brutality and Excessive Force in the New York City Police Department," (June 1996).

15. G. Myrdal, *An American Dilemma: The Negro Problem in American Democracy* (New York: Harper & Brothers, 1944).

16. Quoted in R. Suskind, "Against All Odds: In Rough City School, Top Students Struggle To Learn—and Escape," *Wall Street Journal*, May 26, 1994, A1; see, also, R.B. Felson, A.E. Liska, S.J. South, and T.L. McNulty, "The Subculture of

Violence and Delinquency: Individual vs. School Effects," *Social Forces* 73 (September 1994), 155–173.

17. "Reaching the Hip-Hop Generation," *The MEE Report*, prepared for the Robert Wood Johnson Foundation (Philadelphia: MEE Productions, 1992), vii–ix.

18. *The MEE Report*, viii.

19. *The MEE Report*, vi–viii, xii (emphasis added).

20. See, for example, "Rappers, Black Muslims Honor Slain Shakur as 'a Child of God'," *Arizona Daily Star*, September 23, 1996, A9; and M. Datcher, "Shakur's Death Impossible for Many to Accept," *Arizona Daily Star*, December 10, 1996, A15.

21. See, for example, J.D. Greenstone, "Culture, Rationality, and the Underclass," in C. Jencks and P.E. Peterson (eds.), *The Urban Underclass* (Washington: Brookings Institution, 1991, 399–408; see, also, U. Hannerz, *Soulside: Inquiries into Ghetto Culture and Community* (New York: Columbia University Press, 1969).

22. See, for example, W.J. Wilson, *When Work Disappears: The World of the New Urban Poor* (New York: Knopf, 1996). For a somewhat contradictory earlier view by the same author, see, W.J. Wilson, *The Declining Significance of Race* (Chicago: University of Chicago Press, 1978).

23. See, for example, two family biographies: L. Dash, *Rosa Lee: A Mother and Her Family in Urban America* (New York: Basic Books, 1996); and F. Butterfield, *All God's Children: The Bosket Family and the American Tradition of Violence* (New York: Knopf, 1995).

24. R. Hampton, "Family Violence and Homicides in the Black Community: Are They Linked? in R. Hampton (ed.) *Violence in the Black Family: Correlates and Consequences* (Lexington, MA: Lexington Books, 1987), 135–156; N. Long and R. Forehand, "The Effects of Parental Divorce and Parental Conflict on Children: An Overview," *Developmental and Behavioral Pediatrics* 8 (1987), 292–296; R.E. Emery, *Marriage, Divorce, and Children's Adjustment* (Newbury Park, CA: Sage, 1988); C. Harlow, *Female Victims of Violent Crime* (Washington, DC: U.S. Department of Justice, Bureau of Justice Statistics, 1991); E. Stark and A. Flitcraft, "Spouse Abuse," in M. Rosenberg and J. Mercy (eds.) *Violence in America: A Public Health Approach* (New York: Oxford University Press, 1991), 123–156; A.J. Cherlin, F.F. Furstenberg, Jr., L. Chase-Lansdale, K.E. Kiernan, P.K. Robins, D.R. Morrison, and J.O. Teitler, "Longitudinal Studies of Effects of Divorce on Children in Great Britain and the United States," *Science* 252 (June 1991), 1386–1389; R.L. Hampton and R.J. Gelles, "A Profile of Violence Toward Black Children," in R.L. Hampton (ed.), *Black Family Violence: Current Research and Theory* (Lexington, MA: Lexington Books, 1991), 30.

25. M.J. Bane and D.T. Ellwood, *Welfare Realities: From Rhetoric to Reform* (Cambridge, MA: Harvard University Press, 1994), 55.

26. U.S. Bureau of Census, Current Population Reports, Series P20-484, *Marital Status and Living Arrangements, 1950–1995* (1996); see, also, C. Murray, *Losing Ground: American Social Policy, 1950–1980* (New York: Basic Books, 1984).

27. A. Goetting, "Patterns of Homicide Among Women," *Journal of Interpersonal Violence* 3 (1988), 3–20; J. Mercy and L. Saltzman, "Fatal Violence Among Spouses in the United States, 1976–1985," *American Journal of Public Health* 79 (1989), 595–99; E. Stark, "Rethinking Homicide: Violence, Race, and the Politics of Gender," *International Journal of Health Services* 20 (1990), 3–26; C.E. Marsh, "Sexual Assault and Domestic Violence in the African American Community," *Western Journal of Black Studies* 17 (1993), 149–155; R.L. Hampton and R.J. Gelles, "Violence Toward Black Women in a Nationally Represen-

tative Sample of Black Families," *Journal of Comparative Family Studies* 25 (1994), 105–119.

28. Mercy and Saltzman, "Fatal Violence Among Spouses," 595–99; R. Bachman, "Violence Against Women: A National Crime Victimization Report," U.S. Department of Justice: Bureau of Justice Statistics (January 1994), 1, 7; P.S. Plass, "African American Homicide: Patterns in Partner, Parent, and Child Victimization, 1985–1987," *Journal of Black Studies* 23 (1993), 515–538. See, also, J. Asbury, "Afican-American Women in Violent Relationships: An Exploration of Cultural Differences, in R. Hampton (ed.) *Violence in the Black Family: Correlates and Consequences* (Lexington, MA: Lexington Books, 1987), 89–106; E. Stark and A. Flitcraft, "Spouse Abuse," in M. Rosenberg and J. Mercy (eds.) *Violence in America*, 123–157.

29. See, for example, A.T. Geronimus, J. Bound, T.A. Waidmann, M.M. Hillemeier, and P.B. Burns, "Excess Mortality Among Blacks and Whites in the United States," *The New England Journal of Medicine* 335, 21 (November 21, 1996), 1552–1558; R.J. Sampson and J.H. Laub, "Urban Poverty and the Family Context of Delinquency: A New Look at Structure and Process in a Classic Study," *Child Development* 65, 2 (April 1994), 2; R. Sharpe, "Latchkey Kids in '91 Exceeded 1.6 Million, Census Bureau Finds: More Than 50,000 Children Younger Than 12 Were Home Alone After School," *Wall Street Journal*, May 20, 1994, A5; S. Greenbaum, "Drugs, Deliquency and Other Data," *Juvenile Justice* II, 1 (Spring/Summer 1993), 2.

30. See, for example, R. Staples, "Sexual Harassment: Its History, Definition and Prevalence in the Black Community," *Western Journal of Black Studies* 17 (Fall 1993), 143–149; and his "Social Inequality and Black Sexual Pathology," *The Black Scholar* 21 (Summer 1990), 29–38.

31. C.S. Widom, "Child Abuse, Neglect, and Violent Criminal Behavior," *Criminology* 27, 2 (1989), 251–271; see, also, R.L. Hampton and R.J. Gelles, "A Profile of Violence Toward Black Children," in R.L. Hampton (ed.), *Black Family Violence: Current Research and Theory* (Lexington, MA: Lexington Books, 1991), 30; and J.A. Fox and G. Pierce, "American Killers Are Getting Younger," *USA Today* (Magazine), 122, 2548 (January 1994), 24.

32. U.S. Department of Health and Human Services, National Center on Child Abuse and Neglect. *Child Maltreatment 1992: Reports From the States to the National Center on Child Abuse and Neglect* (Washington: U.S.Goverment Printing Office, 1994), 9.

33. K. Watson, *Substitute Care Providers: Helping Abused and Neglected Children* (Washington, DC: U.S. Department of Health and Human Services, National Center on Child Neglect and Abuse, 1994), 4; D. DePanfilis and M.K. Salus, *Child Protective Services: A Guide for Caseworkers* (Washington, DC: U.S. Department of Health and Human Services, National Center on Child Abuse and Neglect, 1994), 5.

34. P.M. Crittenden and M.D.S. Ainsworth, "Child Maltreatment and Attachment Theory," in D. Cicchetti and V. Carolson, *Child Maltreatment* (Cambridge: Cambridge University Press, 1989), 432–464; see, also, T. Weisenburger, "Neglected Children of Arizona: State Agency Protects Itself, Not Its Kids," *Arizona Daily Star*, September 25, 1994, F1; and M. Bustamante, "1,500 CPS Cases Go Unprobed," *Tucson Citizen*, January 29, 1997, A1.

35. See, for example, articles by D.T. Lykken, B.M. Roth, J.C. Westman, H.G. Schneiderman, W.M. Epstein, W.A. Donohue, and R.A. Gordon, "Licensing Parents," *Society* 34 (November/December 1996).

36. Council of Crime in America, *The State of Violent Crime in America* (January 1996), 56–58; F. Butterfield, "In Boston, Nothing is Something," *New York Times* November 21, 1996, A8; J. Traub, "New York Story: Behind the City's Falling Murder Rate," *The New Republic*, January 17, 1997, 12–15; and G.L. Kelling and C.M. Coles, *Fixing Broken Windows: Restoring Order and Reducing Crime in Our Communities* (New York: The Free Press, 1996).

37. F.N. Tulsky and T. Rohrlich, "Only 1 in 3 Killings In L.A. County Led to Any Punishment," *Los Angeles Times*, December 1, 1996, A1.

38. M. Mauer, "Young Black Men and the Criminal Justice System: A Growing National Problem," (Washington, DC: The Sentencing Project, February 1990); *idem., Americans Behind Bars: The International Use of Incarceration, 1992– 1993* (Washington, DC: The Sentencing Project, 1994). *idem., Young Black Men and the Criminal Justice System: Five Years Later* (Washington, DC: The Sentencing Project, 1995); and Bureau of Justice Statistics, *Capital Punishment 1995* (Washington, DC: U.S. Department of Justice, December 1996).

39. H.G. Schneiderman, "Antisocial Personalities, Antidemocratic Solutions," *Society* (November/December 1996), 51–57; see, also, Sears, et al., "Is It Really Racism?" 16–53; and Sigelman and Tuch, "Metastereotypes," 87–101.

40. Quoted in R.W. Apple, Jr., "Ardor and Ambiguity," *New York Times*, October 17, 1995, A1; and F.X. Clines, "Throngs Hear Call for Solidarity of 'New Black Man,'" *New York Times*, October 17, 1995, A1.

Selected Bibliography

Manuscripts and Collections

Berlin, I., B.J. Fields, T. Glymph, J.P. Reidy and L.S. Rowland. 1985. Eds. *Freedom: A Documentary History of Slavery*, Series I, Volume I, *The Destruction of Slavery*. Cambridge: Cambridge University Press.

Berlin, I., T. Glymph, S.F. Miller, J.P. Reidy, L.S. Rowland and J. Saville, eds. 1990. *Freedom: A Documentary History of Emancipation, 1861–1867*, Series I, Volume III, *The Wartime Genesis of Free Labor: The Lower South*. Cambridge: Cambridge University Press.

Berlin, I., J.P. Reidy and L.S. Rowland, eds. 1982. *Freedom: A Documentary History of Emancipation, 1861–1867*, Series II, *The Black Military Experience*. Cambridge: Cambridge University Press.

Department of Records and Research. *Lynching Files*. Tuskegee, AL: Tuskegee Institute.

Gannett, H., *Statistics of the Negroes in the United States* Occasional Papers, No. 4 (Baltimore, MD: Trustees of the John F. Slater Fund, 1894).

Rawick, G.P., ed. 1977. *The American Slave: A Composite Autobiography*. Westport, CT: Greenwood Press.

Sanborn, F. M. "Negro Crime," in W.E.B. Dubois, ed. 1904. *Proceedings of the Ninth Atlanta Conference for the Study of Negro Problems* 9. Atlanta, GA: Atlanta University Press; reprinted as *Some Notes on Negro Crime, Particularly in Georgia*. New York: Octagon, 1968.

Government Documents and Publications

Annual Report of the Prison Inspector of Alabama, 1914.

Bachman, R. 1994. "Violence Against Women: A National Crime Victimization Report," U.S. Department of Justice: Bureau of Justice Statistics (January).

Baker, R.S. and W.E. Dodd, eds. 1927. *The Public Papers of Woodrow Wilson: War and Peace; Presidential Addresses and Public Papers, 1917–1924*. New York.

Bastian, L. 1995. "Criminal Victimization 1993," Bureau of Justice Statistics Bulletin (May).

Biennial Report, Board of Control, State Penitentiary. 1914. New Orleans, LA.

Block, C.R. and R. Block. 1993. "Street Gang Crime in Chicago," *National Institute of Justice* (December).

Blumstein, A. 1995. "Violence by Young People: Why the Deadly Nexus." *National Institute of Justice Journal* (August). Washington, DC: U.S. Department of Justice.

Bureau of Justice Statistics. 1973–1975. *National Crime Victimization Survey.* Washington, DC: U.S. Department of Justice.

Bureau of Justice Statistics. 1993. *Capital Punishment 1992.* Washington, DC: U.S. Department of Justice (December).

Bureau of Justice Statistics. 1994. *Crime Data Brief: Violent Crime.* Washington, DC: U.S. Department of Justice (April).

Bureau of Justice Statistics. 1994. *Crime Data Brief: Young Black Male Victims.* Washington, DC: U.S. Department of Justice (December).

Bureau of Justice Statistics. 1994. *National Crime Victimization Survey: Violence Against Women.* Washington, DC: U.S. Department of Justice.

Bureau of Justice Statistics. 1996. *Capital Punishment 1995.* Washington, DC: U.S. Department of Justice (December).

Campbell, A. and H. Schuman. 1968. "Racial Attitudes in Fifteen American Cities," in *Supplemental Studies for the National Advisory Commission on Civil Disorder.* Washington, DC: U.S. Government Printing Office.

Centers for Disease Control. 1986. *Human Surveillance: High Risk Racial and Ethnic Groups, 1970–1983.* Atlanta, GA: U.S. Public Health Service.

Chicago Commission on Race Relations. 1922. *The Negro in Chicago: A Study of Race Relations and a Race Riot in 1919.* Chicago: University of Chicago Press.

Clinton, W.J. 1997. *Second Inaugural Address* (January 20).

Congressional Record, 59th Cong., 2d sess. (January 21, 1907).

Conley, C.H. 1993. *Street Gangs: Current Knowledge and Strategies.* Washington, DC: National Institute of Justice.

"Continuing Cruelties in the Convict Chain Gangs and Camps of the Southern United States." 1902. London: The Howard Association, Bishopsgate Without.

DePanfilis, D. and M.K. Salus. 1994. *Child Protective Services: A Guide for Caseworkers.* Washington, DC: U.S. Department of Health and Human Services, National Center on Child Abuse and Neglect.

DuBois, W.E.B. 1898. "The Negroes of Farmville, Virginia, A Social Study," *Department of Labor Bulletin* XIV (January): 9.

DuBois, W.E.B. 1902. *The Negro in the Black Belt: Some Social Sketches*, Bulletin No. 22. Washington, DC: U.S. Department of Labor.

Egeland, B. 1988. "The Consequences of Physical and Emotional Neglect on the Development of Young Children," *Research Symposium on Child Neglect.* Washington, DC: National Center on Child Abuse and Neglect.

Federal Bureau of Investigation. 1932–1994. *Uniform Crime Reports in the United States.* Washington, DC: U.S. Government Printing Office.

Federal Housing Authority *Manual.* 1936. Washington, DC: U.S. Government Printing Office.

First Annual Report of the Department for the Inspection of Jails and Alms-Houses, 1909. 1910. Montgomery, AL.

Gilliard, D.K. and A.J. Beck. 1994. "Prisoners in 1993," *Bureau of Justice Statistics Bulletin* (June).

Harlow, C. 1991. *Female Victims of Violent Crime.* Washington, DC: U.S. Department of Justice, Bureau of Justice Statistics.

Hoffsomer, H. 1935 *Landlord-Tenant Relations and Relief in Alabama.* Washington, DC: FERA Research Bulletin Series II, No. 9.

Journal of Proceedings of the House of Representatives of the General Assembly, 1902. 1902. Baton Rouge, LA.

Maguire, K. and A.L. Pastore, eds. 1994. *Sourcebook of Criminal Justice Statistics 1993.* Washington, DC: U.S. Department of Justice, Bureau of Justice Statistics.

Maguire, K. and A.L. Pastore, eds. 1995. *Sourcebook of Criminal Justice Statistics 1994.* Washington, DC: U.S. Department of Justice, Bureau of Justice Statistics.

Monahan, J. 1981. *The Clinical Prediction of Violent Behavior.* Rockville, MD: National Institutes of Mental Health.

Moynihan, D.P. 1965. *The Negro Family: The Case for National Action.* Washington, DC: U.S. Department of Labor (March).

National Center for Child Neglect and Abuse. 1987. *Study of the National Incidence and Prevalence of Child Abuse and Neglect.* Washington, DC: U.S. Department of Health and Human Services.

National Center on Child Abuse and Neglect. 1994. *Child Maltreatment 1992: Reports From the States to the National Center of Child Abuse and Neglect.* Washington, DC: U.S. Department of Health and Human Services.

National Institute of Justice. 1995. Block, C. and R. Block, eds. *Trends, Risks, and Interventions in Lethal Violence: Proceedings of the Third Annual Spring Symposium of the Homicide Research Working Group* (July). Washington, DC: U.S. Department of Justice.

National Prisoner Statistics, Capital Punishment. 1979. Washington DC: U.S. Department of Justice.

Office of Juvenile Justice and Delinquency Prevention. 1995. *Juvenile Offenders and Victims: A Focus on Violence* (May). Washington, DC: U.S. Department of Justice.

Report of the Department of Justice Task Force to Review the FBI Martin Luther King, Jr. Security and Assassination Investigations. 1977. Washington, DC: U.S. Department of Justice.

Report of the Board of Inspectors of Convicts, 1902. 1902. Montgomery, AL.

Report of the Governor's Commission on the Los Angeles Riot. 1966. Sacramento, CA.

Report of the Independent Commission of the Los Angeles Police Department. 1991. Los Angeles, CA.

Report of the Inspectors of Convicts, 1890. 1890. Montgomery, AL.

Report of the Joint Select Committee to Inquire into The Condition of Affairs in The Late Insurrectionary States, 42d Cong. 2d Sess., 13 vols., February 19, 1872.

Report of the National Advisory Committee on Civil Disorders. 1968. New York: Bantam.

Report of the Secretary's Task Force on Black and Minority Health. Executive Summary 1985. Washington, DC: Department of Health and Human Services. Executive Summary.

Report of the Sheriff of Jefferson County, Alabama, 1917.

Riedel, M., M.A. Zahn, and L.F. Mock. 1985. *The Nature and Patterns of American Homicide.* Washington, DC: National Institute of Justice (May).

Russell, C.W. 1908. *Report on Peonage.* Washington, DC: Department of Justice.

Sheley, J.F. and J.D. Wright. 1993. "Gun Acquisition and Possession in Selected Juvenile Samples," *National Institute of Justice* (December): 1–11.

Southern Regional Council. 1968. *Special Report: The Delta Prisons: Punishment for Profit* (March).

Sparks, R.F. 1982. *Research on the Victims of Crime: Accomplishments, Issues, and New Directions.* Rockville, MD: Department of Health and Human Services, National Institutes of Mental Health.

State of Louisiana, *Board of Control, State Penitentiary, Annual Report—Calendar Year 1901.* 1902. New Orleans, LA.

Third Annual Gang Symposium. 1991. Los Angeles County Sheriff's Department.

U.S. Bureau of the Census. 1918. *Negro Population, 1790–1915.* Washington, DC.

U.S. Bureau of the Census. 1918. *Prisoners and Juvenile Delinquents in the United States, 1910.* Washington, DC.

U.S. Bureau of the Census. 1985. *Household and Family Characteristics.* Current Population Reports, Populuation Characteristics (March), Series P-20, No. 411.

U.S. Bureau of the Census. 1994. *Current Population Reports.* Series P20-484, "Marital Status and Living Arrangements, 1950–1995" (March).

U.S. Commissioner of Labor. 1886. *Second Annual Report: Convict Labor.* Washington, DC: U.S. Department of Labor.

U.S. Commission of Labor. 1906. *Twentieth Annual Report of the Commissioner of Labor, 1905.* Washington, DC: U.S. Department of Labor.

U.S. Congress, House. *House Reports.* Joint Committee on the Conduct and Expenditures of the War. "Fort Pillow Massacre." 38th Cong., 1st sess., 1864, no. 65.

U.S. Congress, House *Joint Select Committee to Inquire into the Condition of Affairs in the Late Insurrectionary States*, 42d Cong., 2d sess., 1872, vols. 1–13.

U.S. Congress, House. Select Committee on Assassinations. *Hearings on the Investigation of the Assassination of Martin Luther King, Jr.*, 95th Cong., 2d Sess., 1978, vols. 1–12.

U.S. Congress, House. Subcommittee on Criminal Justice. *Hearings*, 1st Sess., 1987, Ser. 142, July 16.

U.S. Congress, House. Select Committee on Children, Youth, and Families: Down These Mean Streets: Violence By And Against America's Children. *Hearings*, 101 Cong. 1st sess., 1989, May 16.

U.S. Congress, Senate. *Final Report of the American Freedmen's Inquiry Commission to the Secretary of War.* 38th Cong., 1st sess., 1864, June 22.

U.S. Congress, Senate. Subcommittee on Executive Reorganization of the Committee on Government Operation. "A Report of Attitudes of Negroes in Various Cities." *Hearings*, 89th Cong., Sec. Sess., 1968.

U.S. Congress, Senate. *Report 693.* The Removal of the Negroes from the Southern States to the Northern States. 46th Cong., 2d sess., 1880.

U.S. Department of Justice, *Peonage Files, 1900–1945* Washington, DC: National Archives, Record Group 60 (microfilm).

U.S. Department of Justice, Federal Bureau of Investigation. 1993. *Age-Specific Arrest Rates and Race-Specific Arrest Rates for Selected Offenses, 1965–1992.* Washington, DC: FBI Uniform Crime Reports.

Ventura, S.J., J.A. Martin, T.J. Mathews, and S.C. Clarke. 1996. "Advance Report of Final Natality Statistics, 1994. *Monthly Vital Statistics Report.* 44, 11. Hyattsville, MD: National Center for Health Statistics.

Watson, K. 1994. *Substitute Care Providers: Helping Abused and Neglected Children.* Washington, DC: U.S. Department of Health and Human Services, National Center on Child Neglect and Abuse.

Widom, C.S. 1995. "Victims of Childhood Sexual Abuse—Later Criminal Consequences," *National Institute of Justice: Research in Brief* (March).

Wines, F.H. 1891. "Twenty Years' Growth of the American Prison System," *Proceedings of the Annual Congress of the National Prison Association,* September 25–30, 1890. Pittsburgh, PA: Shaw Brothers.

Wines, F.H. 1906. *Detailed Report upon the Penal and other State Institutions Upon Thirty-Nine Parish Jails, for the Prison Reform Association of Louisiana.* New Orleans, LA.

Wines, F.H. 1906. "The Prisons of Louisiana," *Proceedings of the Annual Congress of the National Prison Association.* Indianapolis, IN: W.B. Burford.

Wright, K.N. 1994. *Family Life, Delinquency, and Crime: A Policymaker's Guide.* Washington, DC: U.S. Department of Justice (May).

Zawitz, M.W., P.A. Klaus, R. Bachman, L.D. Bastian, M.M, DeBerry, Jr., M.R. Rand, and B.M. Taylor. 1993. *Highlights from 20 Years of Surveying Crime Victims: The National Crime Victimization Survey, 1973–92.* Washington, DC: Bureau of Justice Statistics.

Newspapers, Periodicals, and Annuals

Arizona Daily Star
Arkansas Gazette
Atlanta Constitution
Atlanta Georgian
Atlanta Journal
Atlanta News
Atlanta Weekly Defiance
Baton Rouge Daily Advocate
Boston Journal
Chicago Broad Ax
Chicago Defender
Christian Recorder
Cleveland Gazette
Columbus (Georgia) *Enquirer Sun*
Dallas Morning News
Detroit News
Indianola (Mississippi) *Enterprise*
Fisk Herald
Greenwood (Mississippi) *Enterprise*
Hattiesburg (Mississippi) *Progress*
Honey Grove (Texas) *Signal-Citizen*
Houston Daily Post
Houston Informer
Jackson (Mississippi) *Weekly Clarion-Ledger*
Los Angeles Times
Louisville Courier-Journal
Mobile (Alabama) *Register*
Montgomery (Alabama) *Advertiser*
Nashville Tribune
New Orleans Times Picayune
New Orleans Tribune
New Republic
Newsweek
New York Times
New York Tribune
Our Southern Home
Philadelphia Tribune
Pine Bluff (Arkansas) *Weekly Commercial*
Raleigh (North Carolina) *News and Observer*
Richland (Louisiana) *Beacon-News*
Richmond (Virginia) *Planet*
Savannah (Georgia) *Morning News*

Savannah (Georgia) *Tribune*
St. Landry (Louisiana) *Clarion*
Tifton (Georgia) *Gazette*
Time
Troy (Alabama) *Democrat*
Tucson (Arizona) *Citizen*
USA Today
Vicksburg (Mississippi) *Daily Commerical*
Wall Street Journal
Washington Post

Contemporary Publications and Published Documents

Amnesty International. 1996. "Police Brutality and Excessive Force in the New York City Police Department" (June).

American Humane Association. 1986. *Highlights of Official Child Neglect and Abuse Reporting: 1986.*

Black Community Crusade for Children. 1994. *Overwhelming Majority of Black Adults Fear For Children's Safety and Future.* Children's Defense Fund (May 26).

"Cotton Pickers in Northern Cities." 1917. *The Survey* (February 17).

Council on Crime in America. 1996. *The State of Violent Crime in America* (January).

M. Mauer. 1990. *Young Black Men and the Criminal Justice System: A Growing National Problem.* Washington, DC: The Sentencing Project (February).

M. Mauer. 1994. *Americans Behind Bars: The International Use of Incarceration, 1992–1993.* Washington, DC: The Sentencing Project.

M. Mauer. 1997. *Intended and Unintended Consequences: State Racial Disparities in Imprisonment.* Washington, DC: The Sentencing Project (January).

National Association for the Advancement of Colored People. 1969, orig., 1919. *Thirty Years of Lynching in the United States, 1889–1918.* New York: Negro Universities Press.

Negro Yearbook: An Annual Encyclopedia of the Negro, 1914–1915. Tuskegee, AL: Tuskeegee Institute and the Negro Yearbook Publishing Company.

Negro Yearbook: An Annual Encyclopedia of the Negro, 1925–1926. Tuskegee, AL: Tuskeegee Institute and the Negro Yearbook Publishing Company.

Negro Yearbook: An Annual Encyclopedia of the Negro, 1931–1932. Tuskegee, AL: Tuskeegee Institute and the Negro Yearbook Publishing Company.

Proceedings of the Annual Congress of the National Prison Association, November 16–20, 1889, 1890. Chicago: Knight & Leonard, Printers.

Proceedings of the Annual Congress of the National Prison Association, September 25–30, 1890, 1891. Pittsburgh, PA: Shaw Brothers.

"Reaching the Hip-Hop Generation." 1992. *The MEE Report*, prepared for the Robert Wood Johnson Foundation. Philadelphia, PA: MEE Productions.

Southern Poverty Law Center. 1991. *The Ku Klux Klan: A History of Racism and Violence*. 1991. Montgomery, AL.

Weatherford, W.D. 1916. "Lynching: Removing Its Causes," address delivered before the Southern Sociological Congress, New Orleans (April 14).

Books

Abrahams, R.D. 1970 (rev. ed.). *Deep Down in the Jungle: Negro Narrative Folklore from the Streets of Philadelphia*. Chicago: Aldine.

Ainsworth, M.S., M.C. Blehar, E. Waters, and S. Wall. 1978. *Patterns of Attachment*. Hillsdale, NJ: L. Erlbaum Associates.

Allen, W.F., C.P. Ware, and L.M. Garrison. 1951; orig., 1867. *Slave Songs of the United States*. New York: A. Simpson & Co.

Anderson, E. 1990. *Streetwise: Race, Class, and Change in an Urban Community*. Chicago: University of Chicago Press.

Aptheker, H. 1987; orig., 1943. *American Negro Slave Revolts*. New York: International Publishers.

Archer, W. 1970; orig., 1910. *Through Afro-America*. Westport, CT: Negro Universities Press.

Auletta, K. 1982. *The Underclass*. New York: Vintage.

Ayers, E.L. 1984. *Vengeance and Justice: Crime and Punishment in the 19th Century American South*. New York: Oxford University Press.

Ayers, E.L. 1992. *The Promise of the New South*. New York: Oxford University Press.

Bailey, T.P. 1969; orig., 1914. *Race Orthodoxy in the South*. New York: Negro Universities Press.

Baker, R.S. 1973; orig., 1908. *Following the Color Line*. Williamstown, MA: Corner House.

Baldus, D.C., G. Woodworth, and C. Pulaski, Jr. 1990. *Equal Justice and the Death Penalty: A Legal and Empirical Analysis*. Boston: Northeastern University Press.

Bane, M.J. and D.T. Ellwood. 1994. *Welfare Realities: From Rhetoric to Reform*. Cambridge, MA: Harvard University Press.

Barringer, P.B. 1900. *The American Negro: His Past and Future*. Raleigh, NC: Edwards & Broughton.

Bartley, N.V. *The Creation of Modern Georgia*. Athens: University of Georgia Press, 1990.

Basler, R.P., ed. 1946. *Abraham Lincoln: His Speeches and Writings*. Cleveland, OH: World Publishing.

Basler, R.P., ed. 1953. *The Collected Works of Abraham Lincoln*. New Brunswick, NJ: Rutgers University Press.

Bauman, J.F. 1987. *Public Housing, Race, and Renewal: Urban Planning in Philadelphia, 1920–1974*. Philadelphia, PA: Temple University Press.

Beale, H.K., ed. 1960. *Diary of Gideon Welles, Secretary of the Navy Under Lincoln and Johnson*. New York.

Bedau, H.A., ed. 1982. *The Death Penalty in America*. New York: Oxford University Press.

Belden, H.M. and A.P. Hudson, eds. 1952. *Folk Ballads From North Carolina, The Frank C. Grown Collection of North Carolina Folklore*, 7 vols. Durham, NC: Duke University Press.

Belknap, M.K. 1987. *Federal Law and Southern Order*. Athens: University of Georgia Press.

Bernstein, I. 1990. *The New York City Draft Riots*. New York: Oxford University Press.

Berry, M.F. and J.W. Blassingame. 1982. *Long Memory: The Black Experience in America*. New York: Oxford University Press.

Billings, D.B. 1979. *Planters and the Making of the "New South": Class, Politics, and Development in North Carolina, 1865–1900*. Chapel Hill: University of North Carolina Press.

Black, E. and M. Black. 1987. *Politics and Society in the South*. Cambridge, MA: Harvard University Press.

Blassingame, J.W. 1977. *Slave Testimony: Two Centuries of Letters, Speeches, Interviews, and Autobiographies*. Baton Rouge: Louisiana State University Press.

Blassingame, J.W. 1979. *The Slave Community*. New York: Oxford University Press.

Bowers, W.J. 1974. *Executions in America*. Lexington, MA: D.C. Heath.

Bowers, W.J. 1984. *Legal Homicide: Death as Punishment in America*. Boston: Northeastern University Press.

Braithwaite, J. 1979. *Inequality, Crime, and Public Policy*. Boston: Routledge & Kegan Paul.

Brearly, H.C. 1932. *Homicide in the United States*. Chapel Hill: University of North Carolina.

Brodie, F. 1966. *Thaddeus Stevens: Scourge of the South*. New York: W.W. Norton.

Brown, J. 1972; orig., 1855. *Slave Life in Georgia*. F.N. Boney, ed. Savannah, GA: Beehive Press.

Brown, R.M. 1975. *Strain of Violence: Historical Studies of American Violence and Vigilantism*. New York: Oxford University Press.

Brown, W.W. 1969; orig., 1880. *My Southern Home*. Boston, New York: Negro Universities Press.

Bruce, P.A. 1989. *The Plantation Negro as a Freeman: Observations on His Character, Condition, and Prospects in Virginia*. New York: G.P. Putnam's Sons.

Brundage, W.F. 1993. *Lynching in the New South: Georgia and Virginia, 1880–1930*. Champaign: University of Illinois Press.

Butler, B.F. 1892. *Autobiography and Personal Reminiscences of Major-General Benjamin F. Butler*. Boston: A.M Thayer.

Butler, J. 1990. *Awash in a Sea of Faith: Christianizing the American People*. Cambridge, MA: Harvard University Press.

Butterfield, F. 1995. *All God's Children: The Bosket Family and the American Tradition of Violence*. New York: Alfred A. Knopf.

Bye, R.T. 1919. *Capital Punishment in the United States*. Philadelphia, PA: The Committee on Philanthropic Labor of Philadelphia.

Cable, G.W. 1885. *The Silent South*. New York: Charles Scribner's Sons.

Cantril, H. 1963; orig., 1941. *The Psychology of Social Movements*. New York: John Wiley & Sons.

Carleton, M.T. 1971. *Politics and Punishment: The History of the Louisiana State Penal System*. Baton Rouge: Louisiana State University Press.

Carroll, C. 1900. *The Negro a Beast*. St. Louis, MO.

Carter, D.T. 1979. *Scottsboro: The Tragedy of the American South*. Baton Rouge: Louisiana State University Press.

Cash, W.J. 1969; orig., 1941. *The Mind of the South*. New York: Vintage.

Chadburn, J.H. 1933. *Lynching and the Law*. Chapel Hill: University of North Carolina Press.

Chestnut, M. 1984. *The Private Mary Chestnut: The Unpublished Civil War Diaries*, C.V. Woodward and E. Muhlenfeld, eds. New York: Oxford University Press.

Childs, A.R., ed. 1947. *The Private Journal of Henry William Ravenel 1859–1887*. Columbia, SC.

Cicchetti, D. and V. Carolson. 1989. *Child Maltreatment*. Cambridge: Cambridge University Press.

Clark, K.B. 1965. *Dark Ghetto: Dilemmas of Social Power*. New York: Harper & Row.

Clarke, J.N. 1996. *Roosevelt's Warrior: Harold L. Ickes and the New Deal*. Baltimore, MD: Johns Hopkins University Press.

Clarke, J.W. 1982. *American Assassins: The Darker Side of Politics*. Princeton, NJ: Princeton University Press.

Clarke, J.W. 1990. *On Being Mad Or Merely Angry: John W. Hinckley and Other Dangerous People*. Princeton, NJ: Princeton University Press.

Cleaver, E. 1968. *Soul on Ice*. New York: Dell.

Cohen, W. 1991. *At Freedom's Edge: Black Mobility and the Southern White Quest for Racial Control*. Baton Rouge: Louisiana State University Press.

Cohens, N.E., ed. 1970. *The Los Angeles Riots: A Socio-Psychological Study*. New York: Praeger.

Collins, W.H. 1918. *The Truth about Lynching and the Negro in the South; in Which the Author Pleads That the South Be Made Safe for the White Race*. New York.

Cortner, R.C. 1986. *A "Scottsboro" Case in Mississippi*. Jackson: University Press of Mississippi.

Cortner, R.C. 1988. *A Mob Intent on Death*. Middletown, CT: Wesleyan University Press.

Cose, E. 1994. *The Rage of a Privileged Class*. New York: HarperCollins.

Couch, W.T., ed. 1935. *The Culture of the South*. Chapel Hill: University of North Carolina Press.

Courtwright, D.T. 1996. *Violent Land: Single Men and Social Disorder from the Frontier to the Inner City*. Cambridge, MA: Harvard University Press.

Crain, R.L. and C.S. Weisman. 1972. *Discrimination, Personality, and Achievement*. New York: Seminar Press.

Cutler, J.E. 1905. *Lynch-Law: An Investigation into the History of Lynching in the United States*. New York: Longmans, Green.

Daly, M. and M. Wilson. 1988. *Homicide*. New York: Aldine de Gruyter.

Damon, W. 1988. *The Moral Child: Nurturing Children's Natural Moral Growth*. New York: The Free Press.

Daniel, P. 1972. *The Shadow of Slavery: Peonage in the South 1901–1969*. Chicago: University of Illinois Press.

Dash, L. 1996. *Rosa Lee: A Mother and Her Family in Urban America*. New York: Basic Books.

David, P.A. 1976. *Reckoning With Slavery: A Critical Study in the Quantitative History of American Negro Slavery*. New York: Oxford University Press.

Davis, A., B.B. Gardner, and M.R. Gardner. 1988; orig., 1941. *Deep South*. Los Angeles: University of California Press.

Davis, E.A., ed. 1967. *Plantation Life in the Florida Parishes of Louisiana, 1836–1846 as Reflected in the Diary of Bennet H. Barrow*. New York: AMS Press.

Davis, E.A., and W.R. Hogan. 1954. *The Barber of Natchez*. Baton Rouge: Louisiana State University Press.

De Tocqueville, A. 1969; orig., 1838. *Democracy in America*. New York: Doubleday Anchor.

Dennett, J.R. 1965; orig., 1865–66. *The South As It Is: 1865–1866*. New York: Viking.

DeSantis, V.P. 1959. *Republicans Face the Southern Question: The New Departure Years, 1877–1897*. Baltimore, MD: Johns Hopkins University Press.

Dollard, J. 1988; orig., 1937. *Caste and Class in a Southern Town*. Madison: University of Wisconsin Press.

Donald, D. 1961. *Lincoln Reconsidered*. New York: Vintage.

Douglass, F. 1855. *My Bondage and My Freedom*. New York: Miller, Orton, Mulligan.

Drake, S.C. and H.R. Cayton. 1945. *Black Metropolis: A Study of Negro Life in a Northern City*. New York: Harcourt, Brace.

Du Bois, W.E.B. 1904. *Some Notes on Crime*. Atlanta.

Du Bois, W.E.B. 1924. *The Gift of Black Folk*. Boston: Stratford.

Du Bois, W.E.B. 1940. *Dusk of Dawn*. New York: Harcourt, Brace.

Du Bois, W.E.B. 1962; orig., 1935. *Black Reconstruction in America: 1860–1880*. New York: Atheneum.

Du Bois, W.E.B. 1967; orig., 1899. *The Philadelphia Negro: A Social Study*. New York: Schocken.

Du Bois, W.E.B. 1982; orig., 1903. *The Souls of Black Folk*. New York: New American Library.

Du Bose, J.W. 1940. *Alabama's Tragic Decade, 1861–1874*. J.K. Greer, ed. Birmingham, AL: Webb.

Edmonds, H.G. 1951. *The Negro and Fusion Politics in North Carolina: 1894–1901*. Chapel Hill: University of North Carolina Press.

Emery, R.E. 1988. *Marriage, Divorce, and Children's Adjustment*. Newbury Park, CA: Sage.

Farley, R. and W.R. Allen. 1989. *The Color Line and the Quality of Life in America*. New York: Oxford University Press.

Flanigan, D.J. 1987. *The Criminal Law of Slavery and Freedom, 1800–1868*. New York: Garland.

Fleisher, M.S. 1995. *Beggars and Thieves: Lives of Urban Street Criminals*. Madison: University of Wisconsin Press.

Fligstein, N. 1981. *Going North: Migration of Blacks and Whites from the South, 1900–1950*. New York: Academic Press.

Flynn, C.L. 1983. *White Land, Black Labor: Caste and Class in Late Nineteenth Century Georgia*. Baton Rouge: Louisiana State University Press.

Fogel, R.W. and S.L. Engerman. 1974. *Time on the Cross: The Economics of American Negro Slavery*. Boston: Little, Brown.

Foner, E. 1988. *Reconstruction: America's Unfinished Revolution, 1863–1877*. New York: Harper & Row.

Fosdick, R. 1972; orig., 1920. *American Police Systems*. Montclair, NJ: Patterson Smith.

Frazier, E.F. 1939. *The Negro Family in the United States*. Chicago: University of Chicago Press.

Frazier, E.F. 1957. *Black Bourgeoisie: The Rise of a New Middle Class*. New York: The Free Press.

Frazier, E.F. 1957 (rev.ed.). *The Negro in the United States*. New York: Macmillan.

Frederickson, G.M. 1971. *The Black Image in the White Mind: The Debate on Afro-American Character and Destiny, 1817–1914*. New York: Harper & Row.

Frederickson, G.M. 1988. *The Arrogance of Race: Historical Perspectives on Slavery, Racism, and Social Inequality*. Middletown, CT: Wesleyan University Press.

Freud, S. 1962. *Civilization and Its Discontents*. New York: W.W. Norton.

Gannett, H. 1894. *Statistics of the Negroes in the United States*. Baltimore, MD: John F. Slater Fund.

Genovese, E.D. 1976. *Roll Jordan Roll: The World the Slaves Made*. New York: Vintage.

Genovese, E.D. 1979. *From Rebellion to Revolution: Afro-American Slave Revolts in the Making of the Modern World*. Baton Rouge: Louisiana State University Press.

Glasgow, D.G. 1980. *The Black Underclass: Poverty, Unemployment and the Entrapment of Ghetto Youth*. New York: Vintage.

Goodman, J. 1994. *Stories of Scottsboro*. New York: Pantheon.

Goodwyn, L. 1976. *Democratic Promise: The Populist Movement in America*. New York: Oxford University Press.

Goody, E.N. 1982. *Parenthood and Social Reproduction: Fostering and Occupational Roles in West Africa*. Cambridge: Cambridge University Press.

Gottlieb, P. 1987. *Making Their Own Way: Southern Blacks' Migration to Pittsburgh, 1916–1930*. Chicago: University of Illinois Press.

Green, F.M., ed. 1949. *Essays in Southern History*. Westport, CT: Greenwood.

Grier, W. and P.M. Cobbs. 1968. *Black Rage*. New York: Basic Books.

Grimshaw, A. 1969. *Racial Violence in the United States*. Chicago: Aldine.

Grossman, J.R. 1989. *Land of Hope: Chicago, Black Southerners, and the Great Migration*. Chicago: University of Chicago Press.

Gurr, T.R., ed. 1989. *Violence in America: The History of Crime*, v. 1. Newbury Park, CA: Sage.

Gutman, H.G. 1975. *Slavery and the Numbers Game*. Urbana: University of Illinois Press.

Gutman, H.G. 1977. *The Black Family in Slavery and Freedom, 1750–1925*. New York: Vintage.

Hacker, A. 1992. *Two Nations*. New York: Charles Scribner's Sons.

Hair, W.H. 1969. *Bourbonism and Agrarian Protest: Louisiana Politics, 1877–1900*. Baton Rouge: Louisiana State University Press.

Haley, A. 1964. *The Autobiography of Malcolm X*. New York: Grove Press.

Hampton, R., ed. 1987. *Violence in the Black Family: Correlates and Consequences*. Lexington, MA: Lexington Books.

Hampton, R.L, ed. 1991. *Black Family Violence: Current Research and Theory*. Lexington, MA: Lexington Books.

Hannerz, U. 1969. *Soulside: Inquiries into Ghetto Culture and Community*. New York: Columbia University Press.

Harris, A.L. 1968; orig., 1936. *The Negro as Capitalist*. College Park, MD: McGrath.

Hawkins, D.F., ed. 1986. *Homicide Among Black Americans*. New York: University Press of America.

Henson, J. 1858. *Truth Stranger Than Fiction: Father Henson's Story of His Own Life*. Boston: J.P. Jewett.

Higginbotham, A.L. 1978. *In the Matter of Color: Race and the American Legal Process*. New York: Oxford University Press.

Hindus, M.S. 1980. *Prison and Plantation: Crime, Justice, and Authority in Massachusetts and South Carolina, 1767–1878*. Chapel Hill: University of North Carolina Press.

Hippler, A.E. 1974. *Hunter's Point: A Black Ghetto*. New York: Basic Books.

Hirschi, T. 1969. *Causes of Delinquency*. Berkeley: University California Press.

Hobsbawm, E. 1969. *Bandits*. London: Weidenfeld & Nicolson.

Hochschild, J.L. 1995. *Facing Up to the American Dream: Race, Class, and the Soul of the Nation*. Princeton, NJ: Princeton University Press.

Holinger, P.C. 1987. *Violent Deaths in the US: An Epidemiologic Study of Suicide, Homicide and Accidents*. New York: Guilford Press.

Holmes, W.F. 1970. *The White Chief James Kimble Vardaman*. Baton Rouge: Louisiana State University Press.

Howard, O.O. 1907. *Autobiography of Oliver Otis Howard*, 2 vols. New York: Baker & Taylor.

Howell, D.W., ed. 1995. *I Was A Slave: True Life Stories Told by Former American Slaves in the 1930s*. Washington, DC: American Legacy.

Hughes, H., ed. 1972. *Population Growth and the Complex Society*. Boston: Allyn and Bacon.

Hughes, H.S. 1958. *Consciousness and Society: The Reorientation of Social Thought, 1890–1930*. New York: Vintage.

Jackson, B. 1972. *Wake Up Dead Man: Afro-American Worksongs from Texas Prisons*. Cambridge, MA: Harvard University Press.

Jackson, B. 1974. *"Get Your Ass in the Water and Swim Like Me": Narrative Poetry from Black Oral Tradition*. Cambridge, MA: Harvard University Press.

Jackson, M. 1966. *Movin' on Up*. New York: Hawthorn Books.

Jaynes, G.D. 1986. *Branches Without Roots: Genesis of the Black Working Class in the American South, 1862–1882*. New York: Oxford University Press.

Jefferson, T. 1801. *Notes on the State of Virginia*. Boston: Printed by David Carlisle for Thomas & Andrews et al.

Jencks, C. and P.E. Peterson. 1991. *The Urban Underclass*. Washington, DC: The Brookings Institution.

Johnson, C.S. 1930. *The Negro in American Civilization*. New York: Henry Holt.

Johnson, C.S. 1941. *Growing Up in the Black Belt*. Washington, DC: American Council on Education.

Johnson, C.S. 1941. *Shadow of the Plantation*. Chicago: University of Chicago Press.

Johnson, C.S., E.R. Embree, and W.W. Alexander. 1935. *The Collapse of Cotton Tenancy: Summary of Field Studies and Statistical Surveys, 1933–1935*. Chapel Hill: University of North Carolina.

Johnston, H.H. 1969; orig., 1910. *The Negro in the New World*. New York: Johnson Reprint Corp.

Jones, C.C. 1969; orig., 1842. *The Religious Instruction of the Negroes in the United States*. New York: Negro Universities Press.

Jones, L. (aka, Imamu Amiri Baraka). 1966. *Home*. New York: Charles Morrow.

Jordan, W.E. 1968. *White Over Black: American Attitudes Toward the Negro, 1550–1812*. Chapel Hill: University of North Carolina Press.

Joyner, C. 1984. *Down by the Riverside: A South Carolina Slave Community*. Urbana: University of Illinois Press.

Katz, W.L., ed. 1969. *Five Slave Narratives*. New York.

Keeler, C.O. 1907. *The Crime of Crimes; or, the Convict System Unmasked*. Washington, DC: Pentecostal Era.

Kelling, G.L. and C.M. Coles. 1996. *Fixing Broken Windows: Restoring Order and Reducing Violent Crime in Our Communities*. New York: The Free Press.

Kennedy, R.M. 1925. *Mellows: A Chronicle of Unknown Singers*. New York (publisher unknown).

Key, V.O., Jr. 1949. *Southern Politics in State and Nation*. New York: Alfred A. Knopf.

King, D. 1995. *Separate and Unequal: Blacks and the United States Federal Goverment*. New York: Oxford University Press.

Kornhauser, A. 1957. *Detroit: As the People See It*. Detroit, MI: Wayne State University Press.

Kousser, J.M. 1974. *The Shaping of Southern Politics: Suffrage Restrictions and the Establishment of the One-Party South*. New Haven, CT: Yale University Press.

Kurtines, W. and J. Gewirtz., eds. 1987. *Moral Development Through Social Interaction*. New York: John Wiley and Sons.

Kusmer, K.L. 1978. *A Ghetto Takes Shape: Black Cleveland, 1870–1930*. Urbana: University of Illinois Press.

Lane, R. 1979. *Violent Death in the City: Suicide, Accident and Murder in 19th Century Philadelphia*. Cambridge, MA: Harvard University.

Lane, R. 1986. *Roots of Violence in Black Philadelphia, 1860–1900*. Cambridge, MA: Harvard University Press.

Lavender, D. 1970. *The Great Persuader*. Garden City, NY: Doubleday.

Lebsock, S. 1984. *The Free Women of Petersburg: Status and Culture in a Southern Town, 1784–1860*. New York: Norton.

Lesthaghe, R., ed. 1989. *Reproductive and Social Organization in Sub-Saharan Africa*. Berkeley: University of California Press.

Levine, L.W. 1977. *Black Culture and Black Consciousness: Afro-American Folk Thought From Slavery to Freedom*. New York: Oxford University Press.

Lewinson, P. 1959; orig., 1932. *Race, Class & Party: A History of Negro Suffrage and White Politics in the South*. New York: Grosset & Dunlap.

Lieberson, S. 1980. *A Piece of the Pie: Blacks and White Immigrants Since 1880*. Berkeley: University of California Press.

Lindsley, J.B. 1974; orig., 1886. *Our Prison Discipline and Penal Legislation, with Special Reference to the State of Tennessee*. Spartanburg, SC: Reprint Co.

Litwak, L.F. 1979. *Been in the Storm so Long: The Aftermath of Slavery*. New York: Random House.

Lofgren, C.A. 1987. *The Plessy Case: A Legal-Historical Interpretation*. New York: Oxford University Press.

Lomax, A. 1948. *A Common Ground* (publisher unknown).

Lomax, A. 1960. *The Folksongs of North America*. Garden City, NY: Doubleday.

Mars, F. 1977. *Witness in Philadelphia*. Baton Rouge: Louisiana State University Press.

Masotti, L.H. and D.R. Bowen, eds. 1968. *Riots and Rebellion: Civil Violence in the Urban Community*. Beverly Hills, CA: Sage.

Massey, D.S. and N.A. Denton. 1993. *American Apartheid: Segregation and the Making of the Underclass*. Cambridge, MA: Harvard University Press.

McAdoo, H., ed. 1981. *Black Families*. Beverly Hills, CA: Sage.

McCord, W. and J. McCord. 1959. *Origins of Crime: A New Evaluation of the Cambridge-Somerville Study*. New York: Columbia University Press.

McGovern, J.R. 1982. *Anatomy of a Lynching: The Killing of Claude Neal*. Baton Rouge: Louisiana State University Press.

McKelvey, B. 1977. *American Prisons: A History of Good Intentions*. Montclair, NJ: Patterson Smith.

McMillen, N.R. 1989. *Dark Journey: Black Mississippians in the Age of Jim Crow*. Chicago: University of Illinois Press.

McPherson, J.M. 1991; orig., 1965. *The Negro's Civil War*. New York: Ballantine.

Mellon, J., ed. 1988. *Bullwhip Days: The Slaves Remember*. New York: Weidenfeld & Nicholson.

Milgram, S. 1975. *Obedience to Authority*. New York: Harper & Row.

Miller, K. 1969; orig., 1908. *Race Adjustment*. New York: Arno Press.

Miller, K.S. and R.M. Dreger. 1973. *Comparative Studies of Blacks and Whites in the United States*. New York: Seminar Press.

Moton, R.R. 1929. *What the Negro Thinks*. Garden City, NY: Doubleday, Doran.

Mullin, G.W. 1972. *Flight and Rebellion: Slave Resistance in Eighteenth-Century Virginia*. New York: Oxford University Press.

Murphy, E.G. 1909. *The Basis of Ascendancy*. New York: Longmans, Green, and Co.

Murphy, E.G. 1969; orig., 1904. *Problems of the Present South*. New York: Negro Universities Press.

Murray, C. 1984. *Losing Ground: American Social Policy, 1950–1980*. New York: Basic Books.

Murray, C. and R. Herrnstein. 1994. *The Bell Curve*. New York: The Free Press.

Myrdal, G. 1944. *An American Dilemma: The Negro Problem and Modern Democracy*. New York: Harper & Brothers.

Nevins, A. 1936. *Hamilton Fish: The Inner History of the Grant Administration*. New York: Dodd, Mead.

Newton, M. and J.A. Newton. 1991. *Racial & Religious Violence in America: A Chronology*. New York: Garland.

Northup, S. 1968; orig., 1853. *Twelve Years a Slave*. Baton Rouge: Louisiana State University Press.

Oakes, J. 1983. *The Ruling Race: A History of American Slaveholders*. New York: Vintage.

Oates, S.B. 1985. *Abraham Lincoln*. New York: Meridian.

Olmsted, F.L. 1968; orig., 1856. *A Journey in the Seaboard Slave States in the Years 1853–1854*. New York: Negro Universities Press.

Olmsted, F.L. 1970; orig., 1860. *A Journey in the Back Country*. New York: Schocken.

Olweus, D., J. Block, and M. Radke-Yarrow, eds. 1986. *Development of Antisocial and Prosocial Behavior: Research, Theories, and Issues*. Orlando, FL: Harcourt Brace Jovanovich Academic Press.

Oshinsky, D.M. 1996. *"Worse Than Slavery": Parchment Farm and the Ordeal of Jim Crow Justice*. New York: The Free Press.

Osofsky, G. 1966. *Harlem: The Making of a Ghetto, Negro New York, 1890–1930*. New York: Harper & Row.

Page, T.N. 1904. *The Negro: The Southerner's Problem*. New York: Charles Scribner's Sons.

Parish, P.J. 1989. *Slavery: History and Historians*. New York: Harper & Row.

Parsons, T. and K.B. Clark, eds. 1967. *The Negro American*. Boston: Beacon.

Paternoster, R. 1991. *Capital Punishment in America*. New York: Lexington Books.

Perry, B. 1991. *Malcolm: The Life of a Man Who Changed Black America*. Barrytown, NY: Station Hill.

Phillips, U.B. 1966; orig., 1918. *American Negro Slavery*. Baton Rouge: Louisiana State University Press.

Piven, F.F. and R.A. Cloward. 1971. *Regulating the Poor: The Functions of Public Welfare*. New York: Vintage.

Pleck, E.H. 1979. *Black Migration and Poverty, Boston 1865–1900*. New York: Academic Press.

Powdermaker, H. 1939. *After Freedom*. New York: Viking.

Powell, J.C. 1976; orig., 1891. *The American Siberia; or Fourteen Years' Experience in a Southern Convict Camp*. Gainesville: University of Florida Press.

Prothrow-Smith, D. (with M. Weissman). 1991. *Deadly Consequences*. New York: Harper Perennial.

Quinby, W.F. 1876. *Mongrelism*. Wilmington, NC: James & Webb.

Rabinowitz, H.N. 1980. *Race Relations in the Urban South, 1865–1890*. Chicago: University of Illinois Press.

Raboteau, A.J. 1978. *Slave Religion*. New York: Oxford University Press.

Rainwater, L. 1970. *Behind Ghetto Walls: Black Family Life in a Federal Slum*. Chicago: Aldine.

Ransom, R.L. and R. Sutch. 1977. *One Kind of Freedom: The Economic Consequences of Emancipation*. New York: Cambridge University Press.

Raper, A.F. 1933. *The Tragedy of Lynching*. Chapel Hill: University of North Carolina Press.

Raper, A.F. 1936. *Preface to Peasantry: A Tale of Two Black Belt Counties*. Chapel Hill: University of North Carolina Press.

Reid, W. 1965; orig., 1866. *After the War: A Southern Tour, 1865–1866*. New York: Harper & Row.

Reiss, A.J. Jr. and J.A. Roth, eds. 1993. *Understanding and Preventing Violence*. Washington, DC: National Academy Press.

Roberts, J.W. 1989. *From Trickster to Badman: The Black Folk Hero in Slavery and Freedom*. Philadelphia: University of Pennsylvania Press.

Rosenberg, M. and J. Mercy, eds. 1991. *Violence in America: A Public Health Approach*. New York: Oxford University Press.

Royster, C. 1991. *The Destructive War*. New York: Alfred A. Knopf.

Runciman, W. G., ed. 1978. *Max Weber: Selections in Translation*. Cambridge: Cambridge University Press.

Scott, E.J. 1920. *Negro Migration During the War*. New York: Oxford University Press.

Sefton, J.E. 1967. *The United States Army and Reconstruction, 1865–1877*. Baton Rouge: Louisiana State University Press.

Shklar, J.N. 1990. *The Faces of Injustice*. New Haven, CT: Yale University Press.

Simkins, F. E. 1967. *Pitchfork Ben Tillman*. Baton Rouge: Louisiana State University Press.

Sitkoff, H. 1978. *A New Deal for Blacks*. New York: Oxford University Press.

Sitterson, J.C. 1953. *Sugar Country: The Cane Sugar Industry in the South, 1753–1950*. Lexington: University of Kentucky Press.

Slaughter, T.P. 1991. *Bloody Dawn: The Christiana Riot and Racial Violence in the Antebellum North*. New York: Oxford University Press.

Sparks, W.H. 1870. *The Memories of Fifty Years*. Philadelphia.

Spear, A.H. 1976. *Black Chicago: The Making of a Negro Ghetto, 1890–1920*. Chicago: University of Chicago Press.

Stampp, K.M. 1956. *The Peculiar Institution: Slavery in the AnteBellum South*. New York: Vintage.

Stampp, K.M. 1965. *The Era of Reconstruction, 1865–1877.* New York: Alfred A. Knopf.

Stearns, C. 1969; orig., 1872. *The Black Man of the South and the Rebels.* New York: Kraus Reprint Co.

Stirling, J. 1857. *Letters from the Slave States.* London: J.W. Parker.

Stone, A.H. 1908. *Studies in the American Race Problem.* New York: Doubleday, Doran.

Straus, M. and R. Gelles. 1990. *Physical Violence in American Families: Risk Factors and Adaptations to Violence 8,145 Families.* New Brunswick, NJ: Transaction Publications.

Stroyer, J. 1879. *Sketches of My Life in the South,* in W.L. Katz, ed. 1969. *Five Slave Narratives.* New York.

Swint, H.L. 1941. *The Northern Teacher in the South, 1862–1870.* Nashville, TN.

Tannenbaum, F. 1924. *Darker Phases of the South:* n.p.

Taylor, J.G. 1974. *Louisiana Reconstructed, 1863–1877.* Baton Rouge: Louisiana State University Press.

Thompson, S. 1975; orig., 1916. *Publications of the Texas Folklore Society.* Dallas, TX: Southern Methodist University Press.

Tindall, G.B. 1952. *South Carolina Negroes, 1877–1900.* New York: Columbia University Press.

Tindall, G.B. 1967. *The Emergence of the New South, 1913–1945.* Baton Rouge: Louisiana State University Press.

Tolnay, S.E. and E.M. Beck. 1995. *A Festival of Violence: An Analysis of Southern Lynchings, 1882–1930.* Urbana: University of Illinois Press.

Trealease, A.W. 1971. *White Terror: The Ku Klux Klan Conspiracy and Southern Reconstruction.* New York: Harper & Row.

Tremain, H.E. 1905. *Two Days of War: A Gettysburg Narrative and Other Excursions.* New York: n.p.

Tunnell, T. 1984. *Crucible of Reconstruction: War, Radicalism, and Race in Louisiana.* Baton Rouge: Louisiana State University Press.

Tuttle, W.M. 1970. *Race Riot: Chicago in the Red Summer of 1919.* New York: Atheneum.

Wade, R.C. 1964. *Slavery in the Cities.* New York: Oxford University Press.

Waskow, A.I. 1966. *From Race Riot to Sit-In: 1919 and the 1960s.* New York: Doubleday.

Weatherford, W.D. and C.S. Johnson. 1969; orig., 1934. *Race Relations.* New York: Negro Universities Press.

Weiner, N.A. and M.E. Wolfgang, eds. 1989. *Pathways to Criminal Violence.* Newbury Park, CA: Sage.

Weinstein, A., F.O. Gatell, and D. Sarasohn, eds. 1979. *American Negro Slavery.* New York: Oxford University Press.

Weisbrot, R. 1991. *Freedom Bound: A History of America's Civil Rights Movement.* New York: Penguin.

Weld, T.D. 1839. *American Slavery As It Is: Testimony of A Thousand Witnesses*. New York: American Anti-Slavery Society.

Wells-Barnett, I.B. 1991; orig., 1892. *On Lynching*. Salem, NH: Ayer.

West, D.J. and D.P. Farrington. 1973. *Who Becomes Delinquent?* London: Heinemann Educational Books.

Wharton, V.L. 1947. *The Negro in Mississippi, 1865–1890*. Chapel Hill: University of North Carolina Press.

White, W. 1969; orig., 1929. *Rope and Faggot*. New York: Arno Press and the New York Times.

Williamson, J. 1984. *The Crucible of Race: Black-White Relations in the American South Since Emancipation*. New York: Oxford University Press.

Williamson, J. 1986. *A Rage for Order*. New York: Oxford University Press.

Wilson, E.O. 1978. *On Human Nature*. Cambridge, MA: Harvard University Press.

Wilson, J.Q., ed. 1966. *Urban Renewal: The Record and the Controversy*. Cambridge, MA: MIT Press.

Wilson, J.Q. and R.J. Herrnstein. 1985. *Crime and Human Nature: The Definitive Study of the Causes of Crime*. New York: Simon & Schuster.

Wilson, W. 1933. *Forced Labor in the United States*. New York: International Publishers.

Wilson, W.J. 1996. *When Work Disappears: The World of the New Urban Poor*. New York: Alfred A. Knopf.

Wilson, W.J. 1978. *The Declining Significance of Race: Blacks and Changing American Institutions*. Chicago: University of Chicago Press.

Wilson, W.J. 1987. *The Truly Disadvantaged: The Inner City, the Underclass, and Public Policy*. Chicago: University of Chicago Press.

Wilson, W.J. 1996. *When Work Disappears: The World of the New Urban Poor*. New York: Alfred A. Knopf.

Wines, E.C. 1880. *State of Prisons and Child Saving Institutions*. New York: Cambridge University Press and J. Wilson & Sons.

Wolfgang, M.E. 1958. *Patterns of Criminal Homicide*. Philadelphia: University of Pennsylvania Press.

Wolfgang, M.E. and F. Ferracutti. 1967. *The Subculture of Violence: Toward an Integrated Theory in Criminology*. London: Tavistock.

Woodson, C.G. 1918. *A Century of Negro Migration*. New York: Russell & Russell, 1918.

Woodward, C.V. 1970; orig., 1938. *Tom Watson: Agrarian Rebel*. New York: Oxford University Press.

Woodward, C.V. 1971; orig., 1951. *Origins of the New South, 1877–1913*. Baton Rouge: Louisiana State University Press.

Woodward, C.V. 1991; orig., 1951. *Reunion and Reaction: The Compromise of 1877 and the End of Reconstruction*. New York: Oxford University Press.

Wright, G.C. 1990. *Racial Violence in Kentucky, 1865–1940*. Baton Rouge: Louisiana State University Press.

Wright, R. 1994. *The Moral Animal: Evolutionary Psychology and Everyday Life*. New York: Pantheon.

Wyatt-Brown, B. 1982. *Southern Honor: Ethics and Behavior in the Old South*. New York: Oxford University Press.

Wyatt-Brown, B. 1986. *Honor and Violence in the Old South*. New York: Oxford University Press.

Yetman, N.R., ed. 1970. *Life Under the "Peculiar Institution": Selections from the Slave Narrative Collection*. New York: Holt, Rinehart and Winston.

Young, C.A. 1991. *The Quotations of Mayor Coleman A. Young*. Detroit, MI: Droog Press.

Zahn-Waxler, C., E.M. Cummings, and R. Iannotti, eds. 1986. *Altruism and Aggression: Biological and Social Origins*. Cambridge: Cambridge University Press.

Zangrando, R.L. 1980. *The NAACP Crusade Against Lynching, 1909–1950*. Philadelphia, PA: Temple University Press.

Articles and Book Chapters

Abrams, C. 1967. "The Housing Problem and the Negro," in Parsons, T. and K.B. Clark, eds. 1967. *The Negro American*. Boston: Beacon.

Alexander, W.W. 1922. "Better Race Relations," *Southern Workman* 51: 362–364.

Anderson, E. 1989. "Sex Codes and Family Life among Poor Inner-City Youths," *The Annals* (January): 59.

Asbury, J. 1987. "African-American Women in Violent Relationships: An Exploration of Cultural Differences, in Hampton, R., ed. 1987. *Violence in the Black Family: Correlates and Consequences*. Lexington, MA: Lexington Books.

Baldus, D.C., C. Pulaski, and G. Woodworth. 1983. "Comparative Review of Death Sentences: An Empirical Study of the Georgia Experience," *Journal of Criminal Law & Criminology* 74 (3): 661–753.

Balkwell, J. 1990. "Ethnic Inequality and the Rate of Homicide," *Social Forces* 69 (September): 53–70.

Ball-Rokeach, S.J. 1973. "Values and Violence: A Test of the Subculture of Violence Theory," *American Sociological Review* 38 (December): 736–749.

Bass, N. 1972. "Essay on the Treatment and Management of Slaves," Southern Central Agricultural Society, *Transactions, 1851–1856*.

Beck, E.M. and S.E. Tolnay. 1990. "The Killing Fields of the Deep South: The Market for Cotton and the Lynching of Blacks, 1882–1930, *American Sociological Review* 55 (August): 526–539.

Bernard, T.J. 1990. "Angry Aggression Among the `Truly Disadvantaged,'" *Criminology* 28 (February): 73–96.

Blake, W.M. and C.A. Darling. 1994. "The Dilemma of the African-American Male," *Journal of Black Studies* 24 (June): 402–416.

Blau, J.R. and P.M. Blau. 1982. "The Cost of Inequality: Metropolitan Structure and Violent Crime," *American Sociological Review* 47: 114–129

Bledsoe, C. and U.C. Isiugo-Abanihe. "Strategies of Child-Fosterage Among Mende Grannies in Sierra Leone" in Lesthaghe, R., ed. 1989. *Reproductive and Social Organization in Sub-Saharan Africa*. Berkeley: University of California Press.

Bowers, W.J. 1983. "The Pervasiveness of Arbitrariness and Discrimination Under Post-*Furman* Capital Statutes," *Journal of Law and Criminology* 74: 1067–1100.

Bowers, W.J. and G.L. Pierce. 1982. "Racial Discrimination and Criminal Homicide under Post-Furman Statutes," in Bedau, H.A., ed. 1982. *The Death Penalty in America*. New York: Oxford University Press.

Boyer, D. and D. Fine. 1992. "Sexual Abuse as a Factor in Adolescent Pregnancy and Child Maltreatment," *Family Planning Perspectives* 24 (January-February): 4–11.

Brearley, H.C. 1935. "The Pattern of Violence," in Couch, W.T. 1935. Ed. *The Culture of the South*. Chapel Hill: University of North Carolina Press.

Brewer, J.M. 1932. "Juneteenth," in Dobie, F., ed. *Tone the Bell Easy* (Texas Folklore Society).

Brown, W. and M. Reynolds. 1973. "Debt Peonage Re-examined," *Journal of Economic History* 33 (December): 862–871.

Bryce, J. 1891. "Thoughts on the Negro Problem," *North American Review* 153: 650–51.

Caplan, N.S. and J.M. Paige. 1968. "A Study of Ghetto Rioters," *Scientific American* 219 (August): 15–21.

Carpenter, J.A. 1962. "Atrocities in the Reconstruction Period," *Journal of Negro History* 47 (October): 234–247.

Cazenave, N.A. 1991. "Black Men in America—The Quest for `Manhood,'" in McAdoo, H., ed. 1981. *Black Families*. Beverly Hills, CA: Sage.

Centers for Disease Control. 1990. "Homicide Among Young Black Males—United States , 1978–1987." *Morbidity and Mortality Weekly Report* 39: 869–73.

Centers for Disease Control. 1991. "Weapon-Carrying Among High School Students," *Journal of the American Medical Association* 266.

Cherlin, A.J., F.F. Furstenberg, Jr., L. Chase-Lansdale, K.E. Kiernan, P.K. Robins, D.R. Morrison, and J.O. Teitler. 1991. "Longitudinal Studies of Effects of Divorce on Children in Great Britain and the United States," *Science* 252 (June): 1386–1389.

Chilton, R. 1995. "Homicide Arrest Trends and the Impact of Demographic Changes on a Set of U.S. Central Cities," in National Institute of Justice, C. Block and R. Block, eds. *Trends, Risks, and Interventions in Lethal Violence: Proceedings of the Third Annual Spring Symposium of the Ho-*

micide Research Working Group (July). Washington, DC: U.S. Department of Justice.

Christoffel, K.K. 1990. "Violent Death and Injury in US Children and Adolescents," *American Journal of Diseases of Childhood* 144: 697–706.

Clark, C.S. 1993. "Child Sexual Abuse," *CQ Researcher* 3 (January): 39.

Clark, T.D. 1946. "The Furnishing and Supply System in Southern Agriculture Since 1865," *Journal of Southern History* 12 (February): 24–44.

Clarke, J.W. 1973. "Race and Political Behavior," in Miller, K.S. and R.M. Dreger. 1973. *Comparative Studies of Blacks and Whites in the United States*. New York: Seminar Press.

Clarke, J.W. 1996. "Black-on-Black Violence," *Society* 33 (July/August): 46–50.

Clarke, J.W. and J.W. Soule. 1968. "How Southern Children Felt About King's Death," *Trans-Action* 5 (October): 35–40.

Clarke, L. 1846. "Questions and Answers," in *Interesting Memoirs and Documents Relating to American Slavery*. London.

Cohen, W. 1976. "Negro Involuntary Servitude in the South, 1865–1940: A Preliminary Analysis," *Journal of Southern History* XLII (February): 42–43.

Connelly, C.D. and M.A. Straus. 1992. "Mother's Age and Risk for Physical Abuse," *Child Abuse and Neglect* 16: 709–718.

Corzine, J., J. Creech, and L. Corzine. 1983. "Black Concentration and Lynchings in the South: Testing Blalock's Power-Threat Hypothesis," *Social Inquiry* 61 (March): 774–796.

Crawford, T. and M. Naditch. 1970. "Relative Deprivation, Powerlessness, and Militancy: The Psychology of Social Protest," *Psychiatry* 33: 208–223.

Crittenden, P.M. and M.D.S. Ainsworth. 1989. "Child Maltreatment and Attachment Theory," in Cicchetti, D. and V. Carolson. 1989. *Child Maltreatment*. Cambridge: Cambridge University Press.

Crittenden, P. and S. Craig. 1990. "Developmental Trends in the Nature of Child Homicide," *Journal of Interpersonal Violence* 5: 202–216.

Crouch, B.A. 1984. "A Spirit of Lawlessness: White Violence; Texas Blacks, 1865–1868," *Journal of Social History* 18 (Winter): 217–232.

Crouch, B.A. and L.J. Schultz. 1970. "Crisis in Color: Racial Separation in Texas During Reconstruction," *Civil War History* 16: 37–49.

Crowe, C. 1968. "Racial Violence and Social Reform—Origins of the Atlanta Riot of 1906," *Journal of Negro History* 53.

Crowe, C. 1969. "Racial Massacre in Atlanta, September 22, 1906," *Journal of Negro History* 54: 150–173.

Crudele, J.W. 1980. "A Lynching Bee: Butler County Style," *Alabama Historical Quarterly* 42 (Spring/Summer) 66.

Currie, J.T. 1980. "From Slavery to Freedom in Mississippi's Legal System," *Journal of Negro History* 65 (Spring): 114–115.

Daly, M. and M. Wilson. 1989. "Homicide and Cultural Evolution," *Ethology and Sociobiology* 10: 99–110.

Daniel, P. 1975. "The Tennessee Convict War," *Tennessee Historical Quarterly.* 34 (3): 273–292.

Dembo, R., P. Hughes, L. Jackson, and T. Mieczkowski. 1993. "Crack Cocaine Dealing By Adolescents in Two Public Housing Projects: A Pilot Study," *Human Organization* 52: 89–96.

Dickson, L. 1993. "The Future of Marriage and Family in Black America," *Journal of Black Studies* 23 (June): 472–491.

Dillingham, H.C. and D.F. Sly. 1966. "The Mechanical Cotton-Picker, Negro Migration, and the Integration Movement," *Human Organization* (Winter): 344–351.

Doerner, W.G. 1975. "A Regional Analysis of Homicide Rates in the United States," *Criminology* 13 (May): 90–101.

Dorman, J.H. 1977. "The Persistent Spectre: Slave Rebellion in Territorial Louisiana," *Louisiana History* XVIII (Fall): 389–404.

DuBois, W.E.B. 1900. "The Religion of the American Negro," *New World* IX (December): 618.

DuBois, W.E.B. 1934. "Postscripts of W.E.B. DuBois: Roosevelt," *The Crisis* XLI: 20.

DuBois, W.E.B. 1935. "A Nation within the Nation," *Current History* (June): 265.

Dunne, J.G. 1991. "Law and Disorder in L.A.," *New York Review of Books* (10 and 24 October).

Durant, R., C. Cadenhead, R. Pendergrast, G. Slavens, and C. Linder. 1994. "Factors Associated With the Use of Violence Among Urban Black Adolescents," *American Journal of Public Health* 84: 612–17.

Editors. 1877. "South Carolina Morals," *Atlantic Monthly* 33 (April): 470.

Eisenberg, N. and P.A. Miller. 1987. "The Relation of Empathy to Prosocial and Related Behaviors," *Psychological Bulletin* 93: 100–131.

Ellwood, D.T. and J. Crane. 1990. "Family Change Among Black Americans: What Do We Know?" *Journal of Economic Perspective* 4 (Fall): 65–84.

Erlanger, H.S. 1974. "The Empirical Status of the Subculture of Violence Thesis," *Social Problems* 22 (December): 280–292.

Espy, W. 1980. "The Death Penalty in America: What the Record Shows," *Christianity and Crisis*, 23 (June): 191–195.

Fanning, D.M. 1967. "Families in Flats," *British Medical Journal*, 382–386.

Farley, R. 1980. "Homicide Trends in the United States," *Demography* 17 (May): 177–188.

Farley, R. 1986. "Homicide Trends in the United States," in D.F. Hawkins, ed., *Homicide Among Black Americans.* New York: University Press of America.

Farrington, D.P. 1986. "Stepping Stones to Adult Criminal Careers," in Olweus, D., J. Block, and M. Radke-Yarrow, eds. 1986. *Development of Antisocial and Prosocial Behavior: Research, Theories, and Issues*. Orlando, FL: Harcourt Brace Jovanovich Academic Press.

Felson, R.B., A.E. Liska, S.J. South and T.L. McNulty. 1994. "The Subculture of Violence and Delinquency: Individual vs. School Context Effects," *Social Forces* 73 (September): 155–73.

Fine, G.A. and S. Kleinman. 1979. "Rethinking Subculture: An Interactionist Analysis," *American Journal of Sociology* 85 (July): 1–20.

Fingerhut, L.A. and J.C. Kleinman. 1990. "International and Interstate Comparisons of Homicide Among Young Males," *Journal of the American Medical Association* 263 (June 27): 3292–3295.

Fitzpatrick, K. 1993. "Exposure to Violence and the Presence of Depression Among Low-Income, African-American Youth," *Journal of Consulting and Clinical Psychology* 13: 528–31.

Fitzpatrick, K. and J. Boldizar. 1993. "The Prevalence and Consequences of Exposure to Violence Among African-American Yourth," *Journal of the American Academy of Child and Adolescent Psychiatry* 32: 424–30.

Foard, A.A. and H. Fefferman. 1966. "Federal Urban Renewal Legislation," in Wilson, J.Q., ed. 1966. *Urban Renewal: The Record and the Controversy*. Cambridge, MA: MIT Press.

Foreman, P.B. and J.R. Tatum. 1938. "A Short History of Mississippi's State Penal System," *Mississippi Law Journal* (April): 263.

Forward, J.R. and J.R. Williams. 1970. "Internal-External Control in Black Militancy," *Journal of Social Issues* 26: 75–92.

Franklin, J.H. 1974. "The Enforcement of the Civil Rights Act of 1875," *Prologue* 6 (Winter): 225–235.

Franklin, V.P. 1975. "The Philadelphia Race Riot of 1918," *Pennsylvania Magazine of History and Biography* (July): 338–339.

Frederickson, G.M. 1975. "A Man but Not a Brother: Abraham Lincoln and Racial Equality," *Journal of Southern History* XLI (February): 57.

Fried, M. 1966. "Grieving for a Lost Home: Psychological Costs of Relocation," in Wilson, J.Q., ed. 1966. *Urban Renewal: The Record and the Controversy*. Cambridge, MA: MIT Press.

Gans, H.J. 1966. "The Failure of Urban Renewal," in Wilson, J.Q., ed. 1966. *Urban Renewal: The Record and the Controversy*. Cambridge, MA: MIT Press.

Gastil, R.D. 1971. "Homicide and a Regional Culture of Violence," *American Sociological Review* 36 (June): 412–427.

Gates, H.L. Jr. 1994. "Niggaz With Latitude," *New Yorker*, 21 (March): 143–148.

Geronimus, A.T., J. Bound, T.A. Waidmann, M.M. Hillemeier, and P.B. Burns. 1996. "Excess Mortality Among Blacks and Whites in the United States." *New England Journal of Medicine*, 335 (November 21).

Gibbs, J. 1987. "The Need to Facilitate Empathy as Well as Sociomoral Reasoning," in Kurtines, W. and J. Gewirtz, eds. 1987. *Moral Development Through Social Interaction*. New York: John Wiley and Sons.

Gillis, R. 1973. "Population Density and Social Pathology," *Social Forces* 53: 306–314.

Goetting, A. 1988. "Patterns of Homicide Among Women," *Journal of Interpersonal Violence* 3: 3–20.

Gordon, L. and S. McLanahan. 1991. "Single Parenthood in 1900," *Journal of Family History* 16: 97–116.

Gray-Ray, P. and M.C. Ray. 1990. "Juvenile Delinquency in the Black Community," *Youth and Society* 22 (September): 67–84.

Green, F.M. 1949. "Some Aspects of the Convict Lease System in the Southern States," in F.M. Green, ed. 1949. *Essays in Southern History*. Westport, CT: Greenwood.

Greenbaum, S. 1993. "Drugs, Delinquency, and Other Data," *Juvenile Justice* II (Spring/Summer).

Greenstone, J.D. 1991. "Culture, Rationality, and the Underclass," in Jencks, C. and P.E. Peterson. 1991. *The Urban Underclass*. Washington, DC: The Brookings Institution.

Griffith, E.E.H. and C.C. Bell. 1989. "Recent Trends in Suicide and Homicide Among Blacks," *Journal of the American Medical Association* 262 (October 27) 5.

Gurr, T.R. 1989. "Historical Trends in Violent Crime: Europe and the United States," in Gurr, T.R., ed. 1989. *Violence in America: The History of Crime*, v. 1. Newbury Park, CA: Sage.

Gutman, H.G. 1979. "Slave Work Habits and the Protestant Ethic," in *American Negro Slavery*, eds. A. Weinstein, F.O. Gatell, and D. Sarasohn. New York: Oxford University Press.

Hackney, S. 1979. "Southern Violence," *American Historical Review* 74: 906–925.

Hall, K.L. 1984. "Political Power and Constitutional Legitimacy: The South Carolina Ku Klux Klan Trials, 1871–1872," *Emory Law Journal* 33 (Fall): 921–951.

Hamilton, C.H. 1964. "The Negro Leaves the South," *Demography* 1 (1): 273–295.

Hampton, R. 1987. "Family Violence and Homicides in the Black Community: Are They Linked?" in Hampton, R., ed. 1987. *Violence in the Black Family: Correlates and Consequences*. Lexington, MA: Lexington Books.

Hampton, R.L. and R.J. Gelles. 1991. "A Profile of Violence Toward Black Children," in Hampton, R.L, ed. 1991. *Black Family Violence: Current Research and Theory*. Lexington, MA: Lexington Books.

Hampton, R.L. and R.J. Gelles. 1994. "Violence Toward Black Women in a Nationally Representative Sample of Black Families," *Journal of Comparative Family Studies* 25: 105–119.

Hampton, R.L., R.J. Gelles, and J. Harrop. 1991. "Is Violence in Black Families Increasing? A Comparison of 1975 and 1985 National Survey Rates," in Hampton, R.L., ed. 1991. *Black Family Violence: Current Research and Theory.* Lexington, MA: Lexington Books.

Harris, Mrs. L. H. 1899. "A Southern Woman's View," *Independent* LI (May): 1354–55.

Hart, A.B. 1908. "The Outcome of the Southern Race Question," *North American Review* 188 (June): 56.

Hartman, C. 1966. "The Housing of Relocated Families," in Wilson, J.Q., ed. 1966. *Urban Renewal: The Record and the Controversy.* Cambridge, MA: MIT Press.

Haskell, T.L. 1975. "The True and Tragical History of *Time on the Cross.*" *New York Review of Books* (October).

Hawkins, D.F. 1986. "Black and White Homicide Differentials: Alternatives to an Inadequate Theory," in *Homicide Among Black Americans*, D.F. Hawkins, ed. New York: University Press of America.

Haygood, A.G. 1893. "The Black Shadow in the South," *Forum* XVI (October): 167–173.

Henry, W.A. III. 1994. "Pride and Prejudice." *Time* (28 February).

Hoffman-Plotkin, D. and C. Twentyman. 1984. "A Multimodel Assessment of Behavioral and Cognitive Deficits in Abused and Neglected Preschoolers," *Child Development* 55: 794–802.

Holmes, G.K. 1893. "The Peons of the South," *Annals of the American Academy of Political and Social Sciences* 4 (September): 265–274.

Holmes, J.D.L. 1970. "The Abortive Slave Revolt at Point Coupee, Louisiana, 1795," *Louisiana History* XI (Fall): 341–62.

Holmes, W. 1973. "The Arkansas Cotton Pickers Strike of 1891 and the Demise of the Colored Farmers Alliance," *Arkansas Historical Quarterly* XXXII (Summer): 107–119.

Howard, V.B. 1973. "The Black Testimony Controversy in Kentucky, 1866–1872," *Journal of Negro History* 58: 140–165.

Humphrey, J.A. and S. Palmer. 1986. "Race, Sex, and Criminal Homicide: Offender-Victim Relationships," in Hawkins, D.F., ed. 1986. *Homicide Among Black Americans.* New York: University Press of America.

Hutson, A.C., Jr. 1936. "The Overthrow of the Convict Lease System in Tennessee," *Publications*, East Tennessee Historical Society (8).

Inverarity, J.M. 1976. "Populism and Lynching in Louisiana, 1889–1896: A Test of Erikson's Theory of the Relationship Between Boundary Crises and Repressive Justice," *American Sociological Review* 41 (April): 262–280.

Isiugo-Abanihe, U.C. 1985. "Child Fosterage in West Africa," *Population and Development Review* 11: 53–74.

Jencks, C.1991. "Is the American Underclass Growing," in Jencks, C. and P.E. Peterson. 1991. *The Urban Underclass.* Washington, DC: The Brookings Institution.

Klebba, A.J. 1975. "Homicide Trends in the United States, 1900–1974," *Public Health Reports* 90 (3): 195–204.

Kleck, G. 1981. "Racial Discrimination in Criminal Sentencing: A Critical Evaluation of the Evidence with Additional Evidence on the Death Penalty," *American Sociological Review* 46 (December): 783–805.

LaFree, G., K.A. Drass, and P. O'Day. 1992. "Race and Crime in Postwar America: Determinants of African-American and White Rates, 1957–1988," *Criminology* 30: 157–188.

Lauritsen, J., J. Laub, and R. Sampson. 1992. "Convention and Delinquent Activities: Implications for the Prevention of Violent Victimization Among Adolescents," *Violence and Victims* 7: 91–108.

Leland, J. 1993. "Criminal Records: Gangsta Rap and the Culture of Violence," *Newsweek* (29 November).

Levy, B. 1968. "Cops in the Ghetto: A Problem of the Police System," in Masotti, L.H. and D.R. Bowen, eds. 1968. *Riots and Rebellion: Civil Violence in the Urban Community*. Beverly Hills, CA: Sage.

Lewis, D.O., E. Moy, L.D. Jackson, R. Aaronson, N.S. Restifo, S. Serra, and A. Simos. 1985. "Biopsychological Characteristics of Children Who Later Murder," *American Journal of Psychiatry* 142: 1161–1167.

Loeber, R. and T.J. Dishion. 1984. "Boys Who Fight at Home and School: Conditions Influencing Cross-Setting Consistency," *Journal of Consulting and Clinical Psychology* 52: 759–768.

Loftin, C. and R.H. Hill. 1974. "Regional Subculture and Homicide: An Examination of the Gastil-Hackney Thesis," *American Sociological Review* 39 (October): 714–724.

Lohman, J. 1986. "Law Enforcement and the Police," in Masotti, L.H. and D.R. Bowen, eds. 1968. *Riots and Rebellion: Civil Violence in the Urban Community*. Beverly Hills, CA: Sage.

Long, L.H. 1974. "Poverty Status and Receipt of Welfare Among Migrants and NonMigrants in Large Cities," *American Sociological Review* 39 (February): 46–56.

Long, N. and R. Forehand. 1987. "The Effects of Parental Divorce and Parental Conflict on Children: An Overview," *Developmental and Behavioral Pediatrics* 8: 292–296.

Loring, W. 1955. "Housing Characteristics and Social Disorganization," *Social Problems* 3: 160–168.

Lykken, D.T., B.M. Roth, J.C. Westman, H.G. Schneiderman, E. Ginzberg, W.M. Epstein, W.A. Donohue, R.A. Gordon. 1996. "Liscensing Parents," *Society* 34 (November/December): 29–69.

Manfra, J.A. and R.R. Dykstra. 1985. "Serial Marriage and the Origins of the Black Stepfamily: The Rowanty Evidence," *Journal of American History* 72: 18–44.

Mare, R.D. and C. Winship. 1991. "Socioeconomic Change and the Decline of Marriage for Blacks and Whites," in Jencks, C. and P.E. Peterson. 1991. *The Urban Underclass*. Washington, DC: The Brookings Institution.

Margolin, L. 1990. "Fatal Child Neglect," *Child Welfare* 69: 309–319.

Margolin, L. 1992. "Beyond Maternal Blame: Physical Child Abuse as a Phenomenon of Gender," *Journal of Family Issues* 13 (September): 410–423.

Marsh, C.E. 1993. "Sexual Assault and Domestic Violence in the African American Community," *Western Journal of Black Studies* 17: 149–155.

Martinez, P. and J. Richters. 1994. "The NIMH Community Violence Project: II. Children's Distress Symptoms Associated With Violence Exposure," *Psychiatry* 56: 22–35.

Marullo, S. 1985. "The Migration of Blacks to the North, 1911–1918," *Journal of Black Studies* 15: 291–306.

Massey, J.L. and M.A. Myers. 1989. "Patterns of Repressive Social Control in Post-Reconstruction Georgia, 1882–1935," *Social Forces* 68 (December): 458–488.

McKelvey, B. 1934–35. "A Half Century of Southern Penal Exploitation," *Social Forces* 13: 112–123.

Menacker, J., W. Weldon, and E. Hurwitz. 1990. "Community Influences on School Crime and Violence," *Urban Education* 25: 68–80.

Mercy, J. and L. Saltzman. 1989. "Fatal Violence Among Spoouses in the United States, 1976–1985," *American Journal of Public Health* 79: 595–99.

Meyers, D.J. 1997. "Racial Rioting in the 1960s: An Event History Analysis of Local Conditions," *American Sociological Review* 62 (February): 94–112.

Mitchell, R.E. 1971. "Some Social Implications of High Density Housing," *American Sociological Review* 36: 18–29.

Monkkonen, E.H. 1989. "Diverging Homicide Rates: England and the United States, 1850–1875," in Gurr, T.R., ed. 1989. *Violence in America: The History of Crime*, v. 1. Newbury Park, CA: Sage.

Morgan, P.S., A. McDaniel, A.T. Miller, and S.H. Preston. 1993. "Racial Differences in Household Structure at the Turn of the Century," *American Journal of Sociology* 98: 798–828.

Murphy, R.J. and J.M. Watson. 1970. "The Structure of Discontent," in Cohens, N.E., ed. 1970. *The Los Angeles Riots: A Socio-Psychological Study*. New York: Praeger.

Neely, M.E., Jr. 1979. "Abraham Lincoln and Black Colonization: Benjamin Butler's Spurious Testimony," *Civil War History* 25 (March): 77–83.

O'Carroll, P.W. and J.A. Mercy. 1986. "Patterns and Recent Trends in Black Homicide," in D.F. Hawkins, ed., *Homicide Among Black Americans*. New York: University Press of America.

Oakes, J. 1979. "A Failure of Vision: The Collapse of the Freedmen's Bureau Courts," *Civil War History* 25: 66–76.

Olzak, S. 1990. "The Political Context of Competition: Lynching and Urban Racial Violence, 1882–1914," *Social Forces* 69 (December): 395–421.

Osofsky, J., S. Wewers, D. Hann, and A. Fick. 1994. "Chronic Community Violence: What Is Happening to Our Children?" *Psychiatry* 56: 36–45.

Page, H. 1989. "Childbearing versus Childrearing: Coresidence of Mother and Child in Sub-Saharan Africa" in Lesthaghe, R., ed. 1989. *Reproductive and Social Organization in Sub-Saharan Africa*. Berkeley: University of California Press.

Parent, A.S. Jr. and S.B. Wallace. 1993. "Childhood and Sexual Identity Under Slavery," *Journal of the History of Sexuality* 3: 363–401.

Parker, R.N. 1989. "Poverty, Subculture of Violence, and Type of Homicide," *Social Forces* 67 (June): 983–1007.

Paternoster, R. 1984. "Prosecutorial Discretion in Requesting the Death Penalty: A Case of Victim-Based Racial Discrimination," *Law & Society Review* 18 (3): 437–478.

Phillips, C.D. 1987. "Exploring Relations Among Forms of Social Control: The Lynching and Execution of Blacks in North Carolina, 1889–1918," *Law & Society Review* 21: 361–374.

Phillips, C.D. 1986. "Social Structure and Social Control: Modeling the Discriminatory execution of Blacks in Georgia and North Carolina, 1925–35," *Social Forces* 65 (December): 470.

Pierpont, J. and J. Poertner. 1992. "Active Surveillance of Child Abuse Fatalities," *Child Abuse and Neglect* 16: 3–10.

Plass, P.S. 1993. "African American Homicide: Patterns in Partner, Parent, and Child Victimization, 1985–1987," *Journal of Black Studies* 23: 515–538.

Rabinowitz, H.N. 1976. "The Conflict Between Blacks and the Police in the Urban South, 1865–1900," *The Historian* XXXIX (November): 70–71.

Rabinowitz, H.N. 1976. "From Exclusion to Segregation: Southern Race Relations, 1865–1890," *Journal of American History* (September): 342–45.

Radelet, M. L. and M. Mello. 1986. "Executing Those Who Kill Blacks: An Unusual Case Study," *Mercer Law Review* 37: 911–925.

Radelet, M.L. and G.L. Pierce. 1985. "Race and Prosecutorial Discretion in Homicide Cases," *Law & Society Review* 19: 587–621.

Radelet, M.L. and M. Vandiver. 1986. "Race and Capital Punishment: An Overview of the Issues," *Crime and Social Justice* 25: 94–113.

Raine, W.J. 1970. "The Perception of Police Brutality in South Central Los Angeles," in Cohens, N.E., ed. 1970. *The Los Angeles Riots: A Socio-Psychological Study*. New York: Praeger.

Rainwater, L. 1966. "Fear and the House-as-Haven in the Lower Class," *Journal of the American Institute of Planners* 32: 23–31.

Ransford, H.E. 1968. "Isolation, Powerlessness, and Violence: A Study of Attitudes and Participation in the Watts Riot," *American Journal of Sociology* 73: 581–591.

Reed, J. 1971. "To Live-and-Die in Dixie: A Contribution to the Study of Southern Violence," *Political Science Quarterly* 86 (September): 429–443.

Reed, J.S., G.E. Doss, and J.S. Hurlbert. 1987. "Too Good to be False: An Essay in the Folklore of Social Science," *Social Inquiry* 57 (Winter): 1–11.

Reynolds, D.E. 1964. "The New Orleans Riot of 1866, Reconsidered," *Louisiana History* 5 (Winter): 5–27.

Richters, J. and P. Martinez. 1994. "The NIMH Community Violence Project: I. Children as Victims and Witnesses to Violence," *Psychiatry* 56: 7–21.

Riemer, S. 1945. "Maladjustment to the Family Home," *American Sociological Review* 10: 642–648.

Roberts, S. 1990. "Murder, Mayhem, and Other Joys of Youth," *Journal of NIH Research* 2: 67–72.

Roddy, R. 1921. "Kill Negro By Inches," *Memphis Press*, January 27.

Rogers, W.W. 1976; orig., 1891. "Introduction," to J.C. Powell. *The American Siberia; or Fourteen Years' Experience in a Southern Convict Camp.* Gainesville: University of Florida Press.

Roncek, D. 1981. "Dangerous Places: Crime and Residential Environment," *Social Forces* 60: 74–96.

Roncek, D., R. Bell, and J.M.A. Francik. 1981. "Housing Projects and Crime: Testing a Proximity Hypothesis," *Social Problems* 29: 151–166.

Ruggles, S. 1994. "The Origins of African American Family Structure," *American Sociological Review* 59: 136–151.

Ryan, J.G. 1977. "The Memphis Riot of 1866: Terror in a Black Community During Reconstruction," *Journal of Negro History* 62 (July): 243–257.

Sampson, R. 1987. "Urban Black Violence: The Effect of Male Joblessness and Family Disruption," *American Journal of Sociology* 93 (September): 348–382.

Schubiner, H., R. Scott, and A. Tzelepis. 1993. "Exposure To Violence Among Inner-City Youth," *Journal of Adolescent Health* 14: 214–19.

Schuler, E.A. "The Houston Race Riot, 1917," in Grimshaw, A. 1969. *Racial Violence in the United States.* Chicago: Aldine.

Sears, D.O. 1969. "Black Attitudes Toward the Political System in the Aftermath of the Watts Insurrections," *Midwest Journal of Political Science* 73: 261–284.

Sears, D.O., C. Van Laar, M. Carrillo, and R. Kosterman. 1997. "Is It Really Racism? The Origins of White Americans' Opposition to Race-Targeted Policies," *Public Opinion Quarterly* 61 (Spring): 16–53.

Sellin, T. 1928. "The Negro Criminal: A Statistical Note," *The Annals of the American Academy of Political Science* 140: 52–64.

Schmidt, F.T. and B.R. Wilhelm. 1973. "Early Pro-Slavery Petitions in Virginia," *William and Mary Quarterly* 30 (January): 133–146.

Shakoor, B. and D. Chalmers. 1991. "Co-Victimization of African American Children Who Witness Violence: Effects on Cognitive, Emotional, and

Behavioral Development," *Journal of the National Medical Association* 83: 233–237.

Sheley, J.F., Z. McGee, and J. Wright. 1992. "Gun-Related Violence In and Around Inner-City Schools," *American Journal of Diseases of Childhood* 146: 677–682.

Shihadeh, E.S. and N. Flynn. 1996. "Segregation and Crime: The Effect of Black Social Isolation on Rates of Black Urban Violence," *Social Forces* 74 (June): 1325–1352.

Shin, Y., D. Jedlicka and E.S. Lee. 1977. "Homicide Among Blacks," *Phylon* 38 (December): 398–407.

Sigelman, L. and S.A. Tuch. 1997. "Metastereotypes: Blacks' Perceptions of Whites' Stereotypes of Blacks," *Public Opinion Quarterly* 61 (Spring): 87–103.

Sisk, G.S. 1958. "Crime and Justice in the Alabama Black Belt, 1875–1917," *MidAmerica* 40: 106–107.

Smith, C.H. 1893. "Have American Negroes Too Much Liberty?," *Forum* XVI (October): 176–181.

Spilerman, S. 1970. "The Causes of Racial Disturbances: A Comparison of Alternative Explanations," *American Sociological Review* 35 (August): 627–649.

Staples, R. 1987. "Black Male Genocide: A Final Solution to the Race Problem in America," *The Black Scholar* 18 (May-June), 2–12.

Staples, R. 1990. "Social Inequality and Black Sexual Pathology," *The Black Scholar* (Summer): 29–38.

Staples, R. 1993. "Sexual Harassment: Its History, Definition and Prevalence in the Black Community," *Western Journal of Black Studies* 17 (Fall): 143–149.

Stark, E. 1990. "Rethinking Homicide: Violence, Race, and the Politics of Gender," *International Journal of Health Services* 20: 3–26.

Stark, E. and A. Flitcraft. 1991. "Spouse Abuse," in Rosenberg, M. and J. Mercy, ed. 1991. *Violence in America: A Public Health Approach*. New York: Oxford University Press.

Staub, E. 1986. "A Conception of the Determinants and Development of Altruism and Aggression: Motives, the Self, and the Environment," in Zahn-Waxler, C., E.M. Cummings, and R. Iannotti, eds. 1986. *Altruism and Aggression: Biological and Social Origins*. Cambridge: Cambridge University Press.

Sudarkasa, N. 1981. "Interpreting the African Heritage in Afro-American Family Organization," in McAdoo, H., ed. 1981. *Black Families*. Beverly Hills, CA: Sage.

Sutch, R.L. and R. Ransom. 1972. "Debt Peonage in the Cotton South After the Civil War," *Journal of Economic History* 32 (September): 641–669.

Sutch, R.L. and R. Ransom. 1973. "The Ex-Slave in the Post-Bellum South:

A Study of the Economic Impact of Racism in a Market Environment," *Journal of Economic History* 33 (March): 131–148.

Sydnor, C.S. 1940. "The Southerner and the Laws," *Journal of Southern History* 1 (February).

Szasz, F.M. 1967. "The New York State Slave Revolt of 1841: A Re-Examination," *New York History* XXVIII (July): 215–30.

Taylor, A.E. 1942. "The Origin and Development of the Convict Lease System in Georgia," *Georgia Historical Quarterly* (June).

Taylor, D.L., F.A. Biafora, Jr., and G.J. Warheit. 1994. "Racial Mistrust and Disposition to Deviance Among African American, Haitian, and Other Caribbean Island Adolescent Boys," *Law and Human Behavior* 18: 291–317.

Thornberry, T.P., M.D. Krohn, A.J. Lizotte, and D. Chard-wierschem. 1993. "The Role of Juvenile Gangs in Facilitating Delinquent Behavior," *Journal of Research in Crime and Delinquency* 30 (February): 55–87.

Tolan, P.H. 1987. "Implications of Age of Onset for Delinquency Risk," *Journal of Abnormal Psychology* 16: 47–65.

Tolnay, S.E., E.M. Beck, and J.L. Massey. 1989. " Black Lynchings: The Power Threat Hypothesis Revisited," *Social Forces* 67 (March): 605–622.

Tomlinson, T.M. 1968. "The Development of a Riot Ideology Among Urban Negroes," *American Behavioral Scientist* 11: 27–31.

Turpin, T. 1834. *Christian Advocate and Journal*, 8 (January 31), cited in Raboteau, *Slave Religion*. New York: Oxford University Press.

Tuttle, W.M. Jr. 1969. "Labor Conflict and Racial Violence: The Black Worker in Chicago, 1894–1919," *Labor History* 10 (3): 408–432.

Wasserman, I.M. 1977. "Southern Violence and the Political Process;" W. Pope and C. Ragin, "Mechanical Solidarity, Repressive Justice, and Lynchings in Louisiana," *American Sociological Review* 42 (April): 359–369.

Watts, E.J. 1973. "The Police in Atlanta, 1890–1905," *Journal of Southern History* XXXIX (May).

Whitt, H. and J. Corzine. 1995. "Where is the South? A Preliminary Analysis of the Southern Subculture," in National Institute of Justice, C. Block and R. Block, eds. *Trends, Risks, and Interventions in Lethal Violence: Proceedings of the Third Annual Spring Symposium of the Homicide Research Working Group* (July). Washington, DC: U.S. Department of Justice.

Widom, C.S. 1989. "Child Abuse, Neglect, and Violent Criminal Behavior," *Criminology* 27: 251–271.

Widom, C.S. 1989. "Does Violence Beget Violence? A Critical Examination of the Literature," *Psychological Bulletin* 106: 3–28.

Widom, C.S. 1989. "The Intergenerational Transmission of Violence," in Weiner, N.A. and M.E. Wolfgang, eds. 1989. *Pathways to Criminal Violence*. Newbury Park, CA: Sage.

Wiener, J.M. 1979. "Class Structure and Economic Development in the American South, 1865–1955," *American Historical Review* LXXXIV: 960–992.

Wilbanks, W. 1986. "Criminal Homicide Offenders in the U.S.: Black vs. White," in Hawkins, D.F., ed. *Homicide Among Black Americans*. New York: University Press of America.

Wimpy, W.E. 1919. "Mob Lynching Lynches the Law," *Manufacturer's Record* LXXVI (December).

Wolfgang, M.E. 1974. "Racial Discrimination in the Death Sentence for Rape," in Bowers, W.J., ed. 1974. *Executions in America*. Lexington, MA: D.C. Heath.

Wood, G.S. 1993. "Jefferson at Home." *New York Review of Books* (13 May).

Woodward, C.V. 1974. "History from Slave Sources," *The American Historical Review* LXXIX (April): 470–481.

Work, M.N. 1913. "Negro Criminality in the South," *Annals of the American Academy of Political and Social Science* 49 (September): 76.

Wright, R. 1993; orig., 1940. "How `Bigger' Was Born," in *Native Son* (New York: HarperPerennial Edition): 506–507.

Wright, R.R. Jr. 1908. "Recent Improvement in Housing among Negroes in the North," *Southern Workman*, 37 (November): 602.

Zuravin, S.J. and R.H. Starr, Jr. 1991. "Psychosocial Characteristics of Mothers of Physically Abused and Neglected Children: Do They Differ by Race?" In Hampton, R.L., ed. 1991. *Black Family Violence: Current Research and Theory*. Lexington, MA: Lexington Books.

Unpublished Dissertations and Papers

Alfaro, J.D. "Studying Child Maltreatment Fatalities: A Synthesis of Nine Projects" (unpublished).

Beck, E.M., S.E. Tolnay, and J.L. Massey. 1991. "Lynching in the American South Project" (unpublished, Department of Sociology, University of Georgia, Athens, Georgia).

Clark, D. "Racial Change in Philadelphia," (mimeograph), Philadelphia Housing Association.

Crawford, S.C. 1980. "Quantified Memory: A Study of the WPA and Fisk University Slave Narrative Collections (unpublished Ph.D. dissertation, University of Chicago).

David, J. 1976. "Tragedy in Ragtime: Black Folktales from St. Louis" (Ph.D. dissertation, St. Louis University).

Ferris, W.R. 1969. "Black Folklore from the Mississippi Delta" (Ph.D. dissertation, University of Pennsylvania).

Lynching Goes Underground. 1940. An unpublished report prepared for Senators Wagner and Capper and Representatives Gavagan and Fish.

Mouledous, J.C. 1962. "Sociological Perspectives on a Prison Social System" (M.A. thesis, Louisiana State University).

Raper, A. 1940. "Race and Class Pressures" (unpublished manuscript).

Zimmerman, J. 1947. "Penal Systems and Penal Reform in the South since the Civil War" (Ph.D. dissertation, University of North Carolina).

Films, Music, and Television

CBS Reports. 1986. "The Vanishing Family: Crisis in Black America," B. Moyers, producer.

Holiday, Billie. "Ain't Nobody's Business," Lyrics by B. White, Decca Studio Orchestra with Lester Young (no date). Compiled and remastered by Steve Hoffman from original Decca session tapes, Verve/Polygram, 1989 (C.D. ISMCA).

Holiday, Billie. 1939. "Strange Fruit." Lyrics by L. Allan, E. B. Marks Music Co., Commodore Records.

Menace II Society, Hughes Brothers, New Line Cinema, 1993.

N.W.A. and the Posse. 1989. "A Bitch Iz A Bitch." Hollywood. CA: Priority Records, Ruthless Attack Muzick, ASCAP.

Statutes and Court Cases

Alabama Criminal Codes 4930 (1896), (1903).

Brown v. Board of Education of Topeka, 347 U.S. 483 (1954).

Brown v. Mississippi 297 U.S. 278 (1936).

The Civil Rights Cases 109 U.S. 3 (1883).

Collins v. Mississippi 100 Miss. 435 at 437 (1911).

Frank v. Mangum 237 U.S. 309 (1915).

Furman v. Georgia 408 U.S. 238 (1972).

Georgia v. John S. Williams, Newton Superior Court (1921).

McCleskey v. Kemp 481 U.S. 279 (1987).

Moore v. Dempsey, 261 U.S. 86 (1923).

Plessy v. Ferguson, 163 U.S. 537 (1896).

Powell v. Alabama, 287 U.S. 56 (1932).

The Slaughterhouse Cases, 16 Wallace 36 (1873).

State v. Mann, 13 N.C. (2 Dev.), 263, 267 (1829).

United States v. Cruikshank, 92 U.S. 542 (1876).

United States v. Reese 92 U.S. 214 (1876).

U.S. Statutes 546, *United States Code* 158.

Williams v. Mississippi, 170 U.S. 213 (1898).

Index